CONDUCT UNBECOMING

HOWARD MARGOLIAN

# Conduct Unbecoming:
# The Story of the Murder of
# Canadian Prisoners of War
# in Normandy

UNIVERSITY OF TORONTO PRESS
Toronto Buffalo London

© University of Toronto Press Incorporated 1998
Toronto Buffalo London
Printed in Canada

ISBN 0-8020-4213-9 (cloth)

Printed on acid-free paper

**Canadian Cataloguing in Publication Data**

Margolian, Howard
  Conduct unbecoming : the story of the murder of Canadian prisoners
of war in Normandy

  Includes index.
  ISBN 0-8020-4213-9

  1. World War, 1939–1945 – Atrocities.    2. Prisoners of war – Canada.
  3. Prisoners of war – France – Normandy.    I. Title.

  D804.G4M36 1998      940.54′072      C97-931803-3

University of Toronto Press acknowledges the financial assistance to its publishing
program of the Canada Council for the Arts and the Ontario Arts Council.

Adams, William C.
Anderson, H.E.
Angel, Harold S.
Arsenault, Joseph F.
Arsenault, Joseph R.
Bailey, Harold W.
Barker, Reginald D.
Baskerville, Ernest C.
Beaudoin, Oscar J.
Bebee, Charles W.
Bellefontaine, Oswald J.
Benner, George A.
Beresford, William
Birston, Hilliard J.H.
Bishoff, Emmanuel
Bolt, James E.
Booth, Walter J.
Borne, Cecil M.
Bowes, Arnold D.
Bradley, Ernest W.
Brown, George Andrew
Brown, Lorne
Brown, Walter Leslie
Bullock, Paul
Burnett, Donald J.
Campbell, John R.
Charron, Albert A.
Chartrand, Lawrence
Chartrand, Louis
Cook, Etsel J.
Cranfield, Ernest W.
Cresswell, Sidney J.
Crowe, Ivan L.
Culleton, Stewart
Daniels, Walter
Davidson, Thomas R.
Doucette, Charles
Doherty, Walter M.
Dumont, John D.
Fagnan, Anthony A.
Ferguson, William S.
Findlay, Robert M.
Firman, Roger J.
Fleet, Lambert A.
Fontaine, George
Forbes, J.
Freeman, Lant
Fuller, Austin R.
Gilbank, Ernest N.

Gill, George V.
Gold, David S.
Gosse, Silby
Grant, Thomas J.D.
Guiboche, Lawrence R.
Gurney, Robert J.
Hancock, Arthur R.H.
Hargreaves, Jeffrey D.
Harkness, Alvin J.J.
Harper, Robert J.
Harrison, Francis D.
Henry, Thomas H.
Hill, John W.
Hodge, Frederick E.
Holness, Frederick W.G.
Horton, Charles A.
Ionel, John
Izzard, William L.
Jones, Henry C.
Julian, Anthony
Keeping, Reginald
Kines, Clare D.
Kyle, James F.
Labrecque, Hervé A.
Lawrence, Kenneth S.
Leclaire, Joseph A.M.
Lefort, Elmer J.
Lewis, Gordon J.
Lockhead, Roger
Loucks, William D.C.
Lychowich, John L.
Macdonald, Charles J.
MacDonald Hugh A.
MacIntyre, Joseph F.
MacKinnon, James W.
MacLeod, Angus M.
MacRae, Roderick R.
Marych, Frederick
McGinnis, William J.
McIntosh, James D.
McKeil, Hollis L.
McKinnon, William L.
McLaughlin, Thomas C.
McNaughton, George R.
Meakin, Frank V.
Meakin, George E.
Metcalfe, John
Millar, George E.
Moloney, David T.

Mont, Thomas E.
Moore, Raymond
Morin, Norman J.
Morrison, Wesley K.
Moss, James A.
Muntion, George
Murray, John B.
Mutch, Robert
Nichol, William
O'Leary, Gerard J.
Orford, Douglas S.
Ostir, Frank
Owens, Allan R.
Parisian, Percy
Perry, Clayton G.
Peterson, Alfred M.
Philip, Harold G.
Poho, William
Pollard, George G.
Povol, Ervin
Preston, Lee I.
Reid, James A.
Reynolds, Henry E.
Riggs, Cecil
Rodgers, Henry
Ryckman, Frank
Sawatzky, John
Scott, Robert
Scriven, Gilbert H.
Sigurdson, Kjartan
Silverberg, Frank
Simmons, William E.
Smith, Edward
Smith, Frederick
Smith, Richard G.
Smuck, Harry L.
Slywchuk, Steve
Sutton, Lawrence F.
Taylor, James A.
Thomas, William D.
Thompson, John A.
Tobin, Douglas V.
Vickery, Nelson J.
Webster, James S.
Willett, Gerald L.
Williams, Fred
Williams, James P.
Windsor, Thomas A.L.
*and ten known but to God*

LEST WE FORGET

# Contents

*Map and photographs follow page 50.*

# Preface

It was around four in the afternoon on 7 June 1944 when the shooting stopped. A few scattered, defiant volleys signalled the end of the first major engagement fought by Canadian troops since their landing the previous morning on the Normandy coast of France. For the better part of an hour, until their ammunition was expended, outgunned elements of the North Nova Scotia Highlanders Regiment had valiantly defended the medieval village of Authie against repeated assaults by a much larger German force of SS infantry and tanks. As the attackers mopped up the last pockets of resistance, the fields and orchards south of the beleaguered village revealed the extent and ferocity of the afternoon's fighting. Dead, dying, and wounded soldiers, both Canadian and German, lay intermingled on the littered and pock-marked battlefield. Dotting the landscape were numerous wrecked tanks, their scorched hulls still belching clouds of thick black smoke. Cordite and burning gasoline gave the air an acrid smell, making it difficult to breathe.[1]

As their positions were overrun, the surviving North Novas began to emerge from their trenches, their battle-weary hands held in the air in surrender. One of these bloodied but unbowed warriors was Private Lorne Brown of 7 Platoon, A Company. Exhausted from the long battle, his shattered left wrist beginning to throb, the twenty-two-year-old from Springhill, Nova Scotia, must have pondered the insanity of it all. In the eighteen months since he had signed his enlistment papers, leaving behind the security and comfortable familiarity of family, friends, and steady work in the mines of Dominion Coal, Brown had spent most of his waking hours honing his military skills and intensively rehearsing his part in the coming invasion of Hitler's 'Fortress Europe.'[2] Now, less than thirty hours after the D-Day landings,[3] his war was over. As Brown struggled to his feet, a teenaged SS trooper, holding his rifle menacingly and yelling incoherently, suddenly rushed the dazed North Nova and prodded him with his bayonet until he stumbled backwards and fell. At that moment, the German, behaving as though he were in a drug-induced frenzy, pushed his boot onto the prisoner's neck to hold him down and then plunged his bayonet into the defenceless Canadian's chest and abdomen eight times.[4]

By all but the most degraded standards of soldierly conduct, the killing of Private Brown was a reprehensible act and a clear violation of the rules of war.[5] Moreover, it was no isolated incident. During the first ten days that followed the Normandy landings, 156 Canadian officers, NCOs, and rank-and-file troops, all members of the 3rd Canadian Infantry Division, were deliberately and brutally murdered after capture by elements of the German formation that opposed them, the 12th SS Panzer Division 'Hitler Youth.' Like the bayoneting of Private Brown, some of the killings were on-the-spot acts of spontaneous battlefield violence. The vast majority, however, were cold, calculated, and systematic acts of mass murder, carried out well behind the front lines, a considerable time after the prisoners' capture.

This is the story of the criminal slaughter of Canadian prisoners of war in Normandy and of postwar attempts to prosecute the perpetrators. It does not make for gentle reading. Indeed, most of the killings were so casual in the manner of their execution and yet so ghastly and devastating in their consequences that they beggar the imagination. No one who has read the investigative materials relating to these crimes is apt to forget them – the crushing of several prisoners' skulls with clubs and rifle butts, the machine-gunning of dozens of POWs on a moonlit back road, the murder of the wounded, the indignities done to some of the bodies.

Almost as disturbing as the killings themselves has been the failure of Canada and its wartime allies to bring more than a handful of the perpetrators to justice. In the more than five decades that have elapsed since the end of the Second World War, only two trials involving personnel of the Hitler Youth Division have been held. One, the trial of regimental, and later divisional, commander Kurt Meyer, which was heard before a Canadian military court in December 1945, was hampered and distorted by errors during the investigation, procedural irregularities at trial, and political interference at sentencing. Not surprisingly, then, both the verdict and the subsequent commutations of Meyer's sentence sparked outrage among Canadians at the time and have remained controversial up to the present day. The second set of proceedings, conducted against four lower-ranking suspects by a British military court three years later, resulted in the acquittal of two trigger men and the sentencing to death of two of their superiors. For a variety of well-founded evidentiary reasons, the decision of the British court in that case, like the Meyer verdict, left contemporary observers feeling as though justice had not been served.[6]

*Conduct Unbecoming* has two purposes. First, it is a cautionary tale, a warning of what can happen when soldiers are dehumanized by political indoctrination, the encouragement of ugly prejudices, and the creed of blind obedience. To be sure, the young SS troops who acted so barbarically in Normandy also displayed many admirable qualities – bravery under fire, the ability to improvise, devotion to duty. Yet without the moral courage, spiritual independence, and enlightened patriotism that had characterized the German soldier of the past,[7] their other attributes meant nothing, and they were therefore powerless to resist the criminal doctrines propagated by amoral officers and ruthless political leaders. In the final analysis, the 156 Canadians who were so viciously and callously murdered while in the custody of the Hitler Youth Division were victims of the very evils – tyranny, hatred, and fanaticism – that they had gone overseas to combat and eradicate.

The book's second purpose is to honour oft-forgotten and occasionally scorned heroes. In recent years, Canadian veterans of the Second World War have seen the cause for which they fought and bled debated vigorously, and even attacked in some quarters.[8] However well-intentioned, such historical revisionism cannot help but cause considerable anguish, particularly among the dwindling ranks of the survivors of the Normandy massacres. Beyond its educative function, then, I would hope that this book will provide the Canadian servicemen murdered in Normandy and the family, friends, and comrades who still grieve for them the overdue public acknowledgment, and perhaps with it some measure of symbolic justice, that befits the sacrifice they so selflessly made.

# Acknowledgments

I could not have written this book without the help of a great many people. To begin with, the research would have taken much longer than it did were it not for the assistance of knowledgable and enlightened archivists in Canada and the United States. Nowhere were the qualities of professionalism and service to the public more in evidence than at the National Archives in Ottawa, where I did the bulk of my research. Owing to their efficiency and helpful suggestions, the National Archives staff – in particular Tim Wright of the Personnel Records Unit and James Whalen of the Government Archives Division – made it possible for me to review an enormous amount of primary source material within the space of several months. Indeed, after having carried out research in dozens of archives across Europe and the former Soviet Union, I am confident (and proud) in stating that there is no better place for a historian to work than at the National Archives of Canada.

I also owe a debt of gratitude to Linda Chakmak of the Municipal Archives in Windsor, Ontario, where I reviewed the B.J.S. Macdonald Papers. Despite the fact that I gave her very short notice, Ms Chakmak accommodated my research request and granted me prompt access to this important source. Thanks go as well to the staff at the Department of National Defence's Directorate of History and Heritage, where I reviewed the proceedings against Kurt Meyer. The map of Normandy was prepared with great skill by William R. Constable.

*Conduct Unbecoming* was read in its entirety by J.L. Granatstein and David Bercuson. I cannot thank these two pre-eminent Canadian historians enough for having taken time out of their busy schedules to review and criticize the manuscript. The result is a much improved book. All mistakes, of course, are mine alone.

The people at the University of Toronto Press are also deserving of praise. I am particularly grateful to Gerald Hallowell, who helped to guide a first-time author through the sometimes intimidating process of manuscript review. I must also thank Barbara Tessman, whose skill as an editor has spared readers the excesses of my prose.

My greatest debt is to my wife, Randy. With her characteristic patience and good humour, she endured many nights and weekends of my pecking away at the computer, as well as months of often one-dimensional dinner conversation. For her unwavering love and encouragement, this book is hers.

CONDUCT UNBECOMING

# 1
# The Perpetrators

On the evening of Wednesday, 3 February 1943, families in cities and towns across Nazi Germany were doing what they usually did after a hard day's work: listening to their radios.[1] In the middle of regular programming, a soldier's voice came on and advised the audience to stand by for a special announcement from the High Command of the Armed Forces. As if impelled by a collective reflex, listeners leaned over and turned up the volume on their sets. Seconds ticked by before the agonizing silence was broken by a muffled roll of drums. As the flourish receded, another, more sombre voice read the following message: 'The battle for Stalingrad has ended. True to its oath to fight to the last breath, the Sixth Army, under the exemplary leadership of Field Marshal [Friedrich von] Paulus, has succumbed to the overwhelming strength of the enemy and to unfavourable circumstances.'[2]

The announcement was confirmation of a military disaster. After less than three months of fighting, the three-hundred-thousand-man 6th Army, for a time the strongest force in the German order of battle, had been reduced by enemy fire, hunger, and sub-zero temperatures to ninety-one-thousand exhausted, shivering, and demoralized soldiers. Encircled in the city that bore the name of Germany's most implacable foe, these shattered remnants of a once proud army had been left to their fate, prohibited by Adolf Hitler from trying to break out. Low on ammunition and isolated from one another, units of the 6th Army had continued to defend themselves in the rubble of Stalingrad until 2 February, when Paulus finally surrendered to the Red Army.[3]

In an effort to salvage something from this debacle, the radio announcer signed off by exhorting everyone to keep faith in Germany's eventual victory. To anyone with a son, a husband, or a brother fighting in the east, these clichés must have sounded stale and unconvincing. More appropriately, in view of the enormity of the defeat, state-run radio followed the broadcast by playing a recording of Beethoven's dark Fifth Symphony.[4]

For most Germans, the events at Stalingrad did not come as a surprise. In the weeks leading up to Paulus's surrender, official communiqués had described the fighting in and around the city with phrases like 'drawing the Red Army in' and 'enticing the enemy forward.'[5] These clumsy attempts to conceal the unfolding catastrophe from the German people were to no avail. After years of reading between the lines of Nazi propaganda, all but the dullest person had come to understand such phrases as euphemisms for a critical military situation. Prepared for the worst, the German public took the collapse of the 6th Army with stoical resignation. Indeed, though convinced that the defeat was 'the beginning of the end' for Nazi Germany,[6] Hitler's beleaguered subjects would fight on doggedly for another two years.

One of the ironies of Stalingrad was that Hitler, who fretted about the morale of the German masses to the point of obsession, experienced a much more profound psychological shock from the defeat than did his war-weary people. For several weeks afterward, the supreme Nazi warlord was uncertain, vacillating, and reluctant to make decisions.[7] Faced with the Third Reich's most serious crisis to date, the men of the Führer's inner circle, notably Propaganda Minister Josef Goebbels, stepped into the leadership vacuum. Having weathered Hitler's periods of brooding before,[8] Goebbels took upon himself the task of breathing life into the flagging German war effort. After consulting with other senior officials, the propaganda minister came up with a bold plan to streamline the bureaucracy, drastically cut private consumption, and bring about prodigious increases in the production of arms.[9]

Convincing the Führer of the necessity of such measures would not be easy. During the first four years of the conflict, the German public had been spared many of the hardships of a war economy by government-mandated high wages, price controls, and the continued production of consumer goods.[10] Determined to prevent a repeat of 1918, when the privations of the First World War had caused Germany to descend into chaos and revolution, Hitler had thus far refused to impose austerity on the nation. Accordingly, now, at the hour of gravest peril, neither the political leadership of the Third Reich nor its citizens were prepared to make the necessary sacrifices.

In fact, behind the united façade it presented to the world, Nazi Germany was a simmering pot of social ferment. A good deal of the public's resentment was aimed at the Nazi state, which, during the ten years of Hitler's rule, had mushroomed into a hopeless tangle of overlapping, competing, and redundant departments and agencies. The civil servants who staffed this bloated and inefficient colossus routinely engaged in turf wars with one another, while at the same time warding off the encroachment of interfering Nazi Party officials. Largely shut out of positions of real power, the party hacks, in turn, increasingly ignored the needs of the people and instead channelled their energies into the acquisition of lucrative patronage appointments. The more privileged strata of German society, meanwhile, clung to the illusion that the war could still be won without an appreciable lowering of their living standards.[11]

Fully aware of the fragility of Nazi Germany's social consensus, Hitler had obstinately rejected all previous attempts to introduce the necessary but unpopular regimen of a war economy.[12] It came as no surprise, then, that he initially balked at the radical proposals contained in the Goebbels plan. Undeterred, the propaganda minister attempted to overcome the Führer's opposition with an appeal to the masses. On 18 February 1943, Goebbels delivered a rousing speech to a hand-picked assembly of followers in Berlin. After whipping his audience into a frenzy, the master manipulator culminated his oration by declaring that the nation's very existence was at stake. Survival, Goebbels bellowed, required that the German people put aside their concerns about private comfort and steel themselves to fight a 'total war.'[13] Broadcast on radio throughout the Third Reich, the speech was intended as a warning to all Germans, but particularly to smug bureaucrats, corrupt Nazi Party functionaries, and the upper crust, that their days of high living were about to come to an end.

As might have been expected, reaction to the address was mixed. In at least one segment of the German population, however, Goebbels's call for 'total war' found resonance. Their minds having been warped at an early age by Nazi teachings, German youth, in particular the nine million members of the Hitler Youth, constituted a vast reservoir of supporters whose fanaticism had not yet been fully exploited. By 1943, to be sure, tens of thousands of graduates of the Hitler Youth were serving in the various branches of the German armed forces. Moreover, even youngsters not yet of military age were making a contribution to the war effort. It was the Hitler Youth, for example, and not the regular postal service, who delivered military call-up notices. At harvest time, squads of Hitler Youth were sent to the countryside to assist farmers. During the government's frequent war matériel drives, German households were visited by members of the Hitler Youth, who politely asked whether any scrap metal, iron, paper, or glass could be spared. The Hitler Youth also performed important auxiliary functions with the police, fire departments, and railways. Finally, as the demands of the war began to strain Germany's manpower reserves, thousands of under-age members of the Hitler Youth were pressed into military service as anti-aircraft gunners, searchlight operators, and dispatch riders.[14]

It was within the context of the Nazi regime's reluctant but timely adoption of a 'total war' posture that the Hitler Youth Division was born. No one is certain any longer who first came up with the idea. Most likely, it originated with Artur Axmann, the Reich Youth Leader. A hedonist who threw lavish sex-and-booze parties for the Nazi brass,[15] Axmann was not exactly known for his military acumen. Nevertheless, the man whose job it was to oversee the transformation of ordinary German youngsters into Nazi fanatics deserves much of the credit for the creation of the new division. Within days of Paulus's surrender, Axmann broached the subject in correspondence with Heinrich Himmler, the Reich Leader of the SS and Police. His suggestion was enthusiastically received by Himmler, who resolved to bring it up with the Führer at the next available opportunity.[16]

On 10 February 1943, Himmler presented Axmann's suggestion to Hitler at the 'Wolf's Lair,' the Führer's headquarters near Rastenberg in East Prussia. The idea intrigued Hitler. Indeed, Himmler would later inform Axmann that the Führer had been 'quite pleased.' In the first sign that he was rousing himself from his depression over Stalingrad, Hitler authorized Himmler to commence recruitment immediately. Volunteers for the new division were to be solicited from the 'class of 1926,' that is, from among seventeen-year-olds. Assuming that they met all of the basic requirements, including a minimum height of 5'8" (5'7" in exceptional circumstances) and a Jew-free pedigree going back several generations, the new recruits were to be sent to specially designated Hitler Youth military instruction camps. There they would undergo six weeks of rigorous physical training. This was to be followed by a four-week stint in the Reich Labour Service. Training would culminate with sixteen weeks of intensive military drill conducted under the auspices of the SS.[17]

It may well be asked why the creation of the new division was entrusted to the SS – an infamous organization known primarily for having administered Nazi concentration, forced labour, and extermination camps – and not to the Wehrmacht, the regular German armed forces. There were two reasons. In the first place, the SS had long possessed its own military infrastructure. Designated as the Waffen-SS, or Armed SS, this subsidiary of Himmler's sprawling SS and police empire comprised over half a million men organized into thirty-five combat divisions. Although dependent on the Wehrmacht for logistical support, the Waffen-SS was administratively subordinate to Himmler and under the operational command of the Führer. Their banners emblazoned with names like 'Viking,' 'Reich,' and 'Death's Head,' the elite divisions of the Waffen-SS had already participated in every major German campaign of the war. In the process, they had developed a reputation for tenacity, courage, and unmatched ruthlessness in battle.[18]

The second reason for placing the new division under the jurisdiction of the SS was that Hitler no longer trusted the Wehrmacht. Nine years earlier, after the death of Field Marshal Paul von Hindenburg, the revered Reich President, every officer and soldier in the German army had sworn an oath of 'unconditional obedience' to the Führer.[19] Despite the fact that the army had voluntarily undertaken this pledge in order to prove its unquestioning loyalty to Hitler, a rift soon developed between the army and its new supreme commander. Throughout the latter half of the 1930s, during which Hitler achieved a series of bloodless territorial conquests by resorting to a combination of bluff and belligerence, his military commanders had consistently urged restraint. Even in the face of Hitler's triumphs during the early campaigns of the Second World War, the generals had remained sceptical. Intoxicated by Germany's succession of easy victories, the Führer increasingly contrasted his intuitive military 'genius' with what he regarded as the excessive caution and defeatism of the Wehrmacht leadership.[20] In discussions with his intimates, for example, he denounced General Erich von Manstein, the officer whose bold plan had given Hitler his astounding victory over France in the spring of 1940, as a 'pisspot strategist.'[21] Never was the Führer's disdain for the army more evident than after its defeat at Stalingrad. Stunned upon receiving the news that Paulus had personally surrendered rather than killing himself, Hitler raged against the ingratitude and disloyalty of his generals and vowed that he would never again appoint any of them to the coveted rank of field marshal.[22]

In view of his pathological distrust of the Wehrmacht, the Führer's enthusiasm for the establishment of a new SS division was understandable. Goebbels's initial reaction was not. To Hitler's surprise, the propaganda minister strenuously opposed the idea. It was not the raising of additional SS formations to which he objected; that was in keeping with his own ideas about 'total war.' Rather, Goebbels, ever the propagandist, was concerned that Germany's enemies might view the creation of a Hitler Youth division as an act of desperation. The mass mobilization of under-age recruits, he worried, would be a propaganda bonanza for the Allies. Despite all of his powers of persuasion, on this issue, at least, Goebbels was unable to dissuade the Führer. In yet another indication that his old force of personality was returning, Hitler overruled his propaganda minister.[23]

Actually, Goebbels's concerns were not without foundation. Once word of the new formation had leaked out, Allied press reports began to refer disparagingly to Germany's 'Baby Division.' The articles were accompanied by a variety of satirical cartoons, including a particularly memorable one in which the emblem of the new division was redrawn as a baby's bottle.[24] None of this seems to have fazed Hitler. On the contrary, as the time for its deployment drew nearer, the Führer became the new division's most ardent supporter. During a July 1943 military conference, he confidently (and, as things turned out, accurately) predicted that the Hitler Youth troops would fight 'fanatically.' The enemy, Hitler assured his advisers, would be 'struck with wonder.'[25]

With the Führer's approval secured, the way was cleared to start the process of recruitment. The details were hammered out in a series of talks held between representatives of the Hitler Youth and the Waffen-SS. The key meeting took place in Berlin on 16 February 1943. It was at this gathering that Axmann formally placed thirty thousand Hitler Youth – all members of the 'class of 1926' – at the disposal of the new division. According to arrangements agreed upon at the meeting, the prospective recruits were to present themselves to Waffen-SS induction commissions during the last two weeks of March. At that time, each recruit was to undergo a medical examination. Those given a clean bill of health would be admitted to the designated military instruction camps, where they would begin the six-week preliminary training course. Upon completion of the first phase of their training, the recruits, released from their Labour Service obligations, would be sent on to the new division.[26]

Recruitment got under way as soon as the regional chapters of the Hitler Youth had received Axmann's instructions.[27] After the war, Kurt Meyer, the legendary but tainted SS officer who took over command of the Hitler Youth Division during the Normandy campaign, told Allied interrogators that all of the recruits had been volunteers.[28] While this was true in the vast majority of cases, there is evidence that some young men had been coerced into joining. In a letter written to Himmler just one week into the recruitment drive, Martin Bormann, the Führer's crafty personal secretary, reported that he had received complaints about the recruitment methods of the Waffen-SS from virtually every region in Germany. In the Moselle region, it was alleged, an overzealous induction commission had compelled several teenagers to sign up against their will. Varying degrees of coercion had been used in other parts of the Reich as well. This situation could not continue, Bormann warned. In uncharacteristically blunt terms, the Führer's secretary advised Himmler to put an immediate stop to compulsory recruitment.[29]

The agreement between the Hitler Youth and the Waffen-SS regarding the raising of the new division had stipulated that its ranks were to be filled with volunteers. Significantly, the volunteer provision had been Hitler's idea. Bormann's charges were therefore very serious. Fearful of the Führer's reaction to this breach of one of his decrees, Himmler started an investigation. He found the Waffen-SS to be cooperative but unrepentant. Certainly, the recruiters conceded, individuals who were pressed into service might pose a morale problem later on, but there was no other way to meet enlistment quotas. Young men at or nearing military age, they reminded Himmler, were now at a premium. Indeed, with a massive military expansion contemplated for 1943, the recruiters felt that they were justified in asking whether the manpower needs of the new division could be realized with volunteers alone.[30]

The Reich Leader of the SS and Police was in a quandary. On the one hand, he was bound to carry out Hitler's orders to the letter. This meant that the new division had to be an all-volunteer force. On the other hand, Germany was in the throes of a manpower crisis, and there simply were not enough volunteers to go around. Moreover, since Bormann undoubtedly had informed Hitler of the problem, its resolution had acquired some urgency.

Himmler settled on a three-pronged course of action. First, he authorized the revocation of any enlistments that had been obtained through coercion. Second, he ordered the Waffen-SS to intensify its efforts to promote voluntary enlistment. Recommended tactics included the widespread distribution of recruitment flyers, the holding of public lectures about the Waffen-SS in order to 'enlighten' potential recruits, and the glamorization of life at the front through informal talks given by decorated war veterans.[31] Third, if there were still a manpower shortfall despite these new measures, the Reich Leader of the SS and Police sanctioned the compulsory induction of ethnic Germans from the occupied territories.[32]

Through his sleight-of-hand methods, Himmler was able to ensure that the division would have its full complement of rank-and-file troops by the end of the year. Indeed, as early as June 1943, the first ten thousand recruits, who constituted the nucleus of the newly designated SS Panzer Grenadier Division 'Hitler Youth,' began assembling at the troop-training grounds near the town of Beverloo, Belgium. Shortly after the recruits' arrival, the division was organized into various subunits. These included two motorized infantry regiments, one tank and one artillery regiment, one reconnaissance and one engineer battalion, as well as signals, medical, and other support formations. Most of the subunits were quartered and trained just outside Antwerp. Divisional reserve and replacement personnel were supplied by a training and replacement battalion, which was stationed at Arnhem.[33]

The recruits who filtered into Beverloo during the summer of 1943 were highly motivated, but they knew almost nothing about soldiering. Their preliminary courses at the Hitler Youth's military instruction camps, it turned out, had largely been a farce. As described in the overly generous assessment of the division's historian, the courses had done little more than 'inculcate the basics of military service, harden the youths physically, and help to ease the transition from civilian to military life.'[34]

Notwithstanding their inadequate preparation, the recruits had two things going for them. First, the indoctrination they had undergone as members of the Hitler Youth had thoroughly imbued them with the notion of warfare as something romantic, even beautiful. For the vast majority of the young troops, the idea of fighting and dying for the Fatherland was held in almost mystical reverence. Second, the recruits were superb physical specimens. The Hitler Youth, with its emphasis on toughening the body in the open air and sun, had forged a cohort of tanned, clean-cut, robust young lions, who, despite their tender age, were more than equipped to handle the rigours of military life.[35]

The training methods employed by the SS Panzer Grenadier Division 'Hitler Youth' were conceived with two aims in mind: overcoming the immaturity of the new recruits while exploiting their idealism and youthful enthusiasm. To achieve these potentially contradictory objectives, divisional planners devised a training program that was a shrewd mix of 'live fire' exercises and surrogate parenting. On the training grounds, traditional military drill gave way to familiarization with the soldier's craft under realistic battlefield conditions. Boring pursuits such as parade drill, long marches with heavy packs, and rifle-range practice were generally eschewed in favour of sports competitions, obstacle-course exercises, and the reassembly of dismantled weapons while blindfolded. Great emphasis was placed on learning camouflage techniques, night-fighting tactics, and the science of intercepting enemy communications.[36] Though it could not have been foreseen at the time, such training would return great dividends in the close-quarter, defensive combat that was to characterize much of the fighting in Normandy.

Like its approach to fieldcraft, the Hitler Youth Division's structuring of life in the barracks was highly unorthodox. In place of rigid obedience to the traditional military hierarchy, the division's upper echelons substituted a rather informal relationship between officers and men. Discipline, to be sure, was strict, with the recruits forbidden to smoke, drink, or even date until their eighteenth birthdays. Breaches of military protocol were punished, sometimes with considerable severity. At the same time, platoon leaders and company commanders were encouraged to take an active interest in the welfare and the problems of their young charges. In this vein, it is worth noting that the new division, from its inception, tried to procure better rations for its troops than those that were being allotted to other formations.[37]

In his memoirs, Kurt Meyer characterized the relationship between officers and the rank and file in the Hitler Youth Division as having been much like that between parents and their children.[38] Written more than a decade after the end of the war, the recollections of this SS stalwart in all likelihood were coloured by nostalgia. Still, the impact of the novel personnel policies pursued by Meyer and other of the division's senior officers should not be underestimated. On numerous occasions during the Normandy campaign, young soldiers of the Hitler Youth Division would risk their lives to retrieve the bodies of fallen platoon leaders and company commanders.[39]

If a spirit of self-sacrifice was promoted within the new division by the bonding between officers and men, then what was to become its trademark tenacity in battle was attributable, at least in part, to the intense political indoctrination to which the troops were subjected. In this regard, much preparatory work had been done. Under the Nazi regime, the collective consciousness of German youth was twisted and manipulated, mainly by the teaching of a spurious yet seductive interpretation of German history. Among the topics that were incessantly drummed into the impressionable minds of German youngsters were the supposedly pernicious influence of the Jews, an exaggeration of the danger of a Communist takeover, the theory that Germany had been 'stabbed in the back' by traitors during the First World War, the humiliation visited upon Germany by the Allied powers at the conclusion of that war, and the purported decadence and corruption of the short-lived Weimar Republic. The curriculum was rounded out, of course, by a mythical portrait of Hitler as the saviour sent by Providence to rescue Germany from all of these evils.[40]

In the wake of such sustained and intense brainwashing, political indoctrination within the Hitler Youth Division consisted mainly of refresher courses. To strengthen its fighting spirit, the division's political officers also tried to instil in the troops a blind hatred for Germany's military enemies. Although the Red Army was the usual target of such propaganda, divisional indoctrination sessions increasingly focused on the so-called Anglo-American forces. Typical of such anti-Western diatribes was a December 1943 lecture in which the British were portrayed as being 'wholly without scruples.' To further fan the flames of their hatred for the western Allies, recruits were reminded about the destruction being wrought back home by the Allied bomber offensive.[41] With the drone of American and British planes often audible overhead, this form of propaganda was particularly effective.

Much was accomplished during the new division's first few weeks at Beverloo. Headquarters were established, units were organized, and the first indoctrination sessions were held. Still, there were problems. It was reported that the divisional training grounds were short of most kinds of military equipment, including small arms, ammunition, and heavy guns. What additional equipment could be scrounged from captured stocks, moreover, was usually of dubious quality. This was especially true of the fledgling division's few tanks, troop carriers, and supply trucks, all of which broke down quite often. Even uniforms were in short supply.[42]

Of all the problems that plagued the new division, none was more vexing than the shortage of experienced officers and NCOs. It had been the intention of the division's founders to fill all platoon, company, and battalion commander positions with men who had had combat experience. Less than a month into the recruitment drive, this idea was abandoned as a pipe dream.[43] Himmler later explained the problem as a function of the enormous bloodletting that was taking place on the eastern front. On average, he told an assembly of high-ranking Nazi Party functionaries, 'no company commander [in the east] lasts longer than three or four months.' After that time, 'he is lost through either death or wounding.'[44]

Himmler was not exaggerating. An examination of German casualty lists for 1943 reveals that Waffen-SS officers were being killed or wounded roughly twice as fast as they could be replaced.[45] In view of this grim statistic, it is hardly surprising that the new division experienced considerable difficulties in filling its complement of officer and NCO positions. To cobble together a leadership cadre, four hundred regional leaders and twenty-five hundred rank-and-file members of the Hitler Youth had to be placed at the disposal of the division as officer and NCO candidates. Another six hundred men were transferred out of the Luftwaffe, reclassified as infantrymen, and placed in intensive NCO-training courses.[46]

Though welcomed as a stopgap measure, this pool accounted for only about two-thirds of the new division's officer and NCO requirements. Even more problematic, the officer and NCO candidates from the Hitler Youth and the Luftwaffe were in no way ready to exercise command. Before they could carry out their instructional duties with rank-and-file recruits, they themselves would have to undergo training. This, in turn, could have delayed the start of basic training by months. To avoid such a scenario, it became necessary to cull experienced officers and NCOs from existing formations. The Wehrmacht was approached for assistance, but it would part with only fifty officers, all of whom had previously held leadership positions in the Hitler Youth. Still well short of the minimum number of officers and NCOs required to initiate basic training, Himmler authorized the transfer of five hundred Waffen-SS combat veterans.[47] This decision was to have a profound impact on the further development of the new division.

By any objective military standards, the quality of the transferred Waffen-SS personnel was excellent. Their military worth is borne out by an examination of the files of ninety SS officers who were in command of subunits of the Hitler Youth Division on D-Day.[48] Significantly, the average age of the officers in the sample was just over twenty-nine. This meant that they were young enough to endure the rigours of combat, but mature enough to remain cool in tight situations. Indeed, despite their relative youth, the division's officers were a solid and stable lot. Fifty-three per cent of them were married, and, in keeping with the Nazi regime's policy of increasing the German birth rate, two-thirds of the married officers already had children. Twenty-two per cent spoke at least one other language besides their native German. The second language of 65 per cent of the bilingual officers was either English or French.

More relevant to their ability to lead men in the field, an astounding 94 per cent of the officers in the sample had some combat experience, including 86 per cent who had seen action on the eastern front. A similarly impressive 78 per cent held high German war decorations. Between them, in fact, the military medal holders boasted 72 Iron Crosses Second Class, 48 Iron Crosses First Class, 18 German Crosses in Gold, 14 of the coveted Knight's Cross of the Iron Cross, 4 Knight's Crosses of the Iron Cross with Oak Leaves, and 1 Knight's Cross of the Iron Cross with Oak Leaves and Swords. Remarkably, one of the medal holders, SS Major Willy Müller, who at forty-seven years of age was the oldest man on the new division's active roster, had been awarded his Iron Cross during the First World War![49] In light of these facts and figures, it is not an exaggeration to say that the Canadians who would go up against the Hitler Youth Division would be facing some of the best soldiers that the Germans had to offer.

For all their military virtues, there was a dark side to the new division's cadre of experienced officers. Indeed, the statistical record regarding the officers' involvement in Nazi politics bespeaks a fanaticism that set them apart from all but the most zealous of Hitler's supporters. Of the ninety officers in the Hitler Youth Division sample, just over half held memberships in the Nazi Party, and all but three – each of whom had come over to the division as part of the fifty-man Wehrmacht contingent – were members of the SS. Remarkably, in view of their average age, 41 per cent of those officers who held Nazi Party memberships had joined the party prior to Hitler's rise to power on 30 January 1933, as had 20 per cent of the officers who were members of the SS.

In order to put these numbers into perspective, it ought to be remembered that before Hitler came to power, joining the Nazi Party or its affiliated organizations carried with it certain risks, not the least of which was possible dismissal from one's job.[50] Thus, the figures regarding Nazi Party and SS membership attest both to the officers' intense personal loyalty to Hitler and to their dedication to the twisted cause he espoused. In that regard, the Nazi commitment of some of the officers apparently knew no bounds. According to entries found in their personnel files, a disturbingly high 17 per cent of the officers had been members of one or another of the infamous Death's Head formations, which staffed Nazi concentration camps. Six per cent had either trained or served in concentration camps, Dachau and Mauthausen among them. One officer, a physician, actually did a ten-month tour of duty at Auschwitz, the Third Reich's most efficient and notorious death factory.[51]

In terms of their units of origin, the transferred officers were drawn from many of the existing Waffen-SS divisions. The members of one formation predominated, however. Of the 90 officers in the Hitler Youth Division sample, 62 per cent had previously served in the formidable but controversial 1st SS Panzer Division 'Leibstandarte Adolf Hitler,' or 'Adolf Hitler Bodyguard' Division. The high percentage was not the result of chance. Determined to impart a Nazi spirit and identity to the new division, the Waffen-SS had ordered that as many of its company, battalion, and regimental commands as possible were to be filled with former Leibstandarte personnel.[52] This was done, Himmler later explained, in order to make the Hitler Youth Division a clone of the Leibstandarte.[53]

Why was the Nazi leadership so intent on linking the new division to the Leibstandarte? Mention the name Leibstandarte to former members of the Waffen-SS, and in response you almost certainly will hear nostalgic reminiscences about soldierly virtue, true camaraderie, and a daring attacking style that bordered on the suicidal. Mention the same division to the British, Russian, and American veterans who crossed swords with it, and you will elicit expressions of outrage. Tempting though it may be, these contrasting perceptions cannot be explained away as residual wartime prejudice. Rather, they reflect the Leibstandarte's genuinely schizophrenic personality. On the one hand, the division was a crack military formation, one of the finest that the Germans ever fielded.[54] On the other hand, its shield will forever be tarnished with a litany of crimes rarely equalled in the annals of modern warfare.

Between 1940 and 1945, the Leibstandarte is conservatively estimated to have murdered five thousand prisoners of war. To be sure, most of the victims were Red Army soldiers captured during the division's two-year stint in the hellish cauldron of the Russian front.[55] In view of the savagery of the fighting in the east, it is easy to downplay Leibstandarte criminality there.[56] But there is no rationalizing the Leibstandarte's criminal conduct on the western front. During the Allied rearguard action near Dunkirk, for example, members of one of the Leibstandarte's battalions brutally murdered more than a hundred British prisoners of war just outside the French town of Wormhoudt. Four and a half years later, the Belgian towns of Malmedy and Stavelot became Leibstandarte crime scenes. This time the victims were upwards of 150 U.S. Army troops who were shot after capture by forward elements of the division, which was spearheading Hitler's last-ditch Ardennes offensive.[57]

By transferring several hundred experienced Waffen-SS personnel to the Hitler Youth Division, Himmler placed its teenaged recruits under the tutelage of men who were as bigoted and fanatical in their politics as they were proficient and brave in the performance of their military duties. That was bad enough. By making Leibstandarte veterans the backbone of the new division's officer corps, however, Himmler did something unpardonable; he virtually ensured that the criminal propensities of the one formation would be passed on to the other. With the stroke of a pen, the Reich Leader of the SS and Police placed the Hitler Youth Division in the hands of men who viewed enemy prisoners as objects of hate and who considered their murder to be a powerful and legitimate weapon of war.[58] This was a decision for which more than 150 Canadian POWs would pay dearly in the killing fields of Normandy.

To be fair, it should be noted that not all of the former Leibstandarte officers were implicated in the murder of Canadian prisoners. Nor were all the implicated officers former members of the Leibstandarte. The reputations of old Leibstandarte hands like SS Brigadier General Fritz Witt, who was named commander of the Hitler Youth Division at the end of July 1943, and SS Lieutenant Colonel Max Wünsche, who was put in charge of the new division's armoured regiment around the same time, emerged from the war unsullied by the taint of war crimes. Yet, of the five most senior officers who were implicated, four were Leibstandarte veterans: SS Lieutenant Colonel Karl-Heinz Milius, a competent drill instructor but a man whose fitness to command was doubted by his own superiors; SS Colonel Kurt Meyer, a natural leader of men but a fanatical Nazi who practised a ruthless and remorseless brand of warfare; SS Major Gerhard Bremer, a daredevil on the battlefield and a brawler off it; and SS Lieutenant Colonel Wilhelm Mohnke, a brave soldier but a man beset by unspeakable inner demons, which seem to have been exacerbated by his addiction to morphine. As for SS Major Siegfried Müller, the only senior officer implicated in the Normandy massacres who was not a Leibstandarte veteran, there was little to differentiate him from his Leibstandarte counterparts. Prior to joining the Hitler Youth Division, Müller had done a ten-month stint as the commander of a detachment of concentration camp guards. Even more revealing, he served for about three years with the 3rd SS Panzer Division 'Death's Head.' Like the Leibstandarte, this formation had perpetrated the murder of dozens of British POWs during the fighting near Dunkirk in May 1940.

Such were the men who would lead the Hitler Youth Division into their fateful encounter with Canadian troops in Normandy. They were young, battle-hardened, fanatically devoted to Hitler, and, where the fate of enemy prisoners was concerned, without scruples. Through their Herculean efforts, almost twenty thousand teenaged Hitler Youth recruits were moulded with remarkable speed into a cohesive, motivated, and highly skilled fighting force. So rapid and thorough was the transformation, in fact, that at the end of October 1943 Hitler rewarded the new formation by according it the status of a fully armoured division.[59] To underscore the change, the Führer allocated an additional ninety-three Mark IV tanks, the mainstay of Germany's armoured formations,[60] to the now renamed 12th SS Panzer Division 'Hitler Youth.'[61]

Its basic training completed, its equipment problems at last on the way to being resolved, the division began coordinated unit exercises early in 1944. Of particular importance in this regard was a 6 February exercise conducted by the considerably expanded armoured regiment. Attended by members of the army brass, the exercise was a complete success, with the young tankmen winning high praise for their skill. Indeed, it was largely on the basis of their performance in the February manoeuvres that the division was upgraded to operational readiness. This could not have come at a more opportune time, as a new crisis on the eastern front necessitated the transfer of two western-based SS divisions to the Ukraine at the end of March. Concurrently, the 12th SS was ordered to move from Belgium to the sector in France vacated by one of the redeployed SS formations. By the beginning of April, trains were carrying the division's green but confident troops to an area south of the port of Rouen, between the Seine and the Orne Rivers.[62] Thus, a mere fourteen months after it was conceived, the Hitler Youth Division had been given its first assignment. It was heading for Normandy.

# 2
# The Victims

While the Hitler Youth Division was taking up positions in Normandy, across the English Channel there was feverish activity. In keeping with plans for Operation 'Overlord' – the Allied invasion of Hitler's Fortress Europe – men and equipment were being deployed to staging areas in the south of England. In a dozen Channel ports, an armada of six hundred warships and four thousand smaller craft was being assembled to ferry the invasion force to the Normandy coast. Supporting this massive enterprise, fleets of British and American planes mounted daily bombing raids over German-occupied northern France. In southeastern England, along the coast that fronted the Straits of Dover, a fictitious army group built around legendary American general George Patton issued a steady stream of phoney radio traffic. The purpose of this deception was to divert the Germans' attention from Normandy to the possibility of a landing farther east, at the Pas-de-Calais.

Of the numerous Allied formations that were available for Overlord, one Canadian division had been selected to take part in the initial landing. After months of perfecting the mechanics of seaborne assault, the 3rd Canadian Infantry Division was ready, by the spring of 1944, to practise under realistic battlefield conditions. Accordingly, on 12 April a naval task force approached the southern coast of England. Several miles from shore, dozens of landing craft pulled up alongside equipment- and troop-laden ships. The men of the 3rd Division climbed into the heaving craft, which, once full, resumed their approach. As the craft hit the beaches at Slapton Sands, near Devon, the fully outfitted Canadian troops disembarked and ran towards the causeways that led inland. Offshore, the artillery of the 3rd Division, which had been lashed to the decks of some of the landing craft, fired at coastal targets.[1]

Code-named 'Trousers,' this exercise was the first rehearsal based on the actual plan for the Normandy invasion. It was also the first time that the Canadians were able to practise the landing as a unified formation. Watching the exercise from points inland were several members of the Allied brass, including General Bernard Montgomery, who would command all of the invasion ground forces, and General Miles Dempsey, the commander of the British 2nd Army, to which the 3rd Canadian Division would be subordinated. As they peered through their binoculars, the observers liked what they saw. Many of the most vexing problems, such as the inability to bring sufficient fire support to bear on coastal defences, had been encountered and corrected in earlier exercises. To everyone's relief, Trousers went off virtually without a hitch and was characterized by a high level of professionalism at all levels of command and among all participating units. Just as important, the Canadian troops who landed at Slapton Sands appeared confident, spirited, almost itching for a good brawl. 'Channel fever,' the contemporary name for the loss of nerve that was to afflict a handful of members of the invasion force, was nowhere in evidence on 12 April.[2]

For those men who had been with the 3rd Division since its inception, the success of Trousers was the culmination of nearly four years of hard work. During that time, the division's progress often had to be measured in tiny increments. In the early days, equipment had been in short supply, and what was available more often than not was obsolete. Training in Canada had been rudimentary at best, in part because of the lack of equipment, and in part because of the shortcomings of the division's leadership cadre. Indeed, after the 3rd Division arrived in England in the summer of 1941, the men had to be taught, almost from scratch, such basics as small-unit combat, artillery-infantry coordination, and defensive tactics. In view of these early problems, the selection of the division as one of the Overlord assault formations has to rank as a significant achievement. To put this accomplishment in its true historical perspective, it is necessary to go back to the dark early days of the war.

At exactly 4:45 AM on 1 September 1939, the big guns of the German cruiser Schleswig Holstein began to bombard a Polish fortress on the Westerplatte peninsula, near the port city of Danzig (today Gdansk). Simultaneously, hundreds of German aircraft, including Stuka dive bombers equipped with sirens that made an infernal, disconcerting scream, violated Polish airspace and carried out devastating attacks on aerodromes, railways, and other lines of transportation and communication. Launched without even the decency of a formal declaration of war, this first wave of Nazi Germany's invasion of Poland was followed across the frontier by massed armoured formations and columns of infantrymen clad in the field grey uniforms of the Wehrmacht. Demonstrating a hitherto unheard-of degree of coordination between air, armoured, and infantry forces, the Germans were able to sweep aside their courageous but hopelessly overmatched foes within three weeks. Nowhere was the disproportion between German and Polish forces more in evidence than at a place called Tuchel Heath, where, on 4 September, elements of the renowned Pomorska Cavalry Brigade charged German tanks with lances drawn and sabres flashing, only to be shot out of their saddles en masse.[3]

On the third day of the Nazi onslaught, when Poland was already done for, Britain and France belatedly fulfilled their obligations to their beleaguered ally by declaring war on Nazi Germany. The Canadian government now had a decision to make. Though a dominion of the British Commonwealth, Canada had been in control of its own foreign policy since 1926, and had been a fully self-governing country since 1931. Thus, it was not formally obligated to follow Britain's lead. Of course, in view of the strong ties of loyalty to Britain that English-speaking Canadians still possessed, it seemed inconceivable that Canada would not enter the war.[4]

In the immediate aftermath of the British declaration, Canada's Parliament was recalled from its summer recess. Dispersed across the country, cabinet ministers, MPs, and senators began to make their way back to Ottawa. On 7 September, the House of Commons and the Senate met in joint session. The atmosphere inside the chamber was fraught with tension and anticipation. In a sombre but resolute address, Prime Minister William Lyon Mackenzie King asked the assembled members to approve Canada's immediate entry into the war. Two days of debate followed, after which Parliament gave almost unanimous assent to King's request. The vote was given practical effect on 10 September, when a proclamation was issued declaring that a state of war existed between the German Reich and Canada.[5]

It had taken only a week for Canada to join the battle. It would take much longer to win the war. For the next five and a half years, Canadians would be asked to shed their blood on distant yet familiar battlefields.

Even before the issuance of a formal declaration of war, preparations for the defence of Canadian territory had been undertaken. On 1 September, after news of the invasion of Poland began to trickle in, military units throughout the country were placed on alert and deployed to the most vulnerable points in the districts for which they were responsible. Canals, railway bridges, and airfields received the lion's share of the guard detachments. On the East Coast, fortified gun positions that looked out on the Atlantic Ocean were manned. To strengthen coastal defences, an anti-aircraft unit was moved from Kingston to Halifax. At sea, two of the four destroyers stationed on the Pacific coast were ordered to sail from Vancouver to Halifax. In the skies over Canada, four Royal Canadian Air Force (RCAF) squadrons made their way from the interior to airfields in Montreal and along the Atlantic coast.[6]

Concurrent with the deployment of existing forces, the adjutant general, acting in accordance with the army's contingency plans, ordered all military districts to begin the process of mobilizing additional manpower. As of the fifth day of mobilization, the strength of the active force had more than doubled to almost twenty-three thousand. At least half of these men were diverted into units that were manning coastal and anti-aircraft defences or guarding strategic installations. As of the twentieth day of mobilization, active strength had again more than doubled, and stood at around fifty-six thousand. By the end of September, the number of 'actives' totalled almost sixty-two thousand.[7]

As a tangible demonstration of Canada's resolve to stand with Britain and France in their hour of need, the heightened state of military readiness was of inestimable symbolic value. Furthermore, the enlistment of manpower and such deployments of forces as were carried out may even have been sufficient to meet the requirements of home defence during the war's early days. In practical terms, however, these measures amounted to little more than shadow-boxing.

By any objective military standards, Canada was wholly unprepared to fight a major war. The extent of the problem is revealed by some statistics concerning the country's depleted stocks of military hardware. Of the three branches of the service, the RCAF was probably in the best shape, its inventory consisting of about 100 front-line planes and 130 trainers. Only 30 of these aircraft were considered modern, however. More unsettling was the state of Canada's anti-aircraft defences. On the day that Hitler launched his invasion of Poland, Canadian forces were in possession of exactly four modern anti-aircraft guns. At sea, Canada's navy had only ten fighting vessels, six of which were destroyers. The sum total of the country's armoured strength, meanwhile, was a paltry sixteen light tanks.[8]

The situation with respect to small arms was not much better. Indeed, as makeshift training camps prepared to receive the flood of new recruits, it soon became obvious that even the most basic kinds of military equipment were in short supply. When armoury basements and storage lockers were opened, they were found to contain outdated Lee-Enfield rifles, obsolete Lewis machine guns, and antiquated mortars. Only twenty-three Brens,[9] the light machine gun that would see yeoman service over the next few years, were available across the country. There were no modern uniforms, no combat boots, no field equipment, no overcoats, nor even prepackaged rations.[10] Canada, it appeared, was going into the Second World War with the leftover arms and equipment of the First.

The sorry state of Canada's arsenal could not be rectified immediately, but hope was in sight. With the country going on a war footing, it was reasonable to expect that military stocks would be replenished as soon as industrial production had geared up. A much more serious problem, and one that did not lend itself to easy or quick solutions, was the shortage of qualified officers and NCOs. In 1939, the Permanent Force Army comprised a meagre forty-two hundred men of all ranks. This number did not begin to meet the training requirements of the rapidly expanding pool of recruits. Of course, another five thousand officers were available from the fifty-one-thousand-man non-permanent militia. In view of the militia's reputation as a haven for weekend warriors, however, the instructional capabilities of the officers drawn therefrom were very much in doubt.[11]

Why was Canada so ill-prepared to fight a war in 1939? There were three reasons. First, Canadian public opinion was still haunted by the bloodletting of the First World War. Of the 425,000 Canadians who had served overseas during 1914–18, approximately 60,000 had lost their lives. This was a terrible sacrifice for a nation as sparsely populated as Canada. Consequently, after 1918 there developed within both the political class and the bureaucracy in Ottawa a determination to do whatever was necessary to prevent Canada from becoming entangled in military commitments abroad. The cornerstone of this policy, which during the 1930s was embodied by O.D. Skelton, the senior civil servant at External Affairs and a close adviser to Prime Minister King, was opposition to any attempt on the part of the defence establishment to modernize or expand the armed forces. Even as war clouds began to gather over Europe, the policy of isolationism held sway within the councils of the Canadian government.[12]

The second reason for Canada's lack of military preparedness was the overriding desire to preserve national unity. Beyond its human and material costs, the First World War had disrupted and very nearly destroyed the fragile political consensus between English and French Canada. When Conservative Prime Minister Robert L. Borden's government tried to introduce conscription in June 1917, the move provoked a series of reactions that reverberated for a generation and whose effects are being felt to this day. The governing Tories held together in support of the ill-advised Military Service Bill, but in the process they alienated their nationalist allies in Quebec. The opposition Liberals, on the other hand, split into pro- and anti-conscription factions that all too neatly mirrored the rift between Quebec and the other provinces over the issue. The rift was deepened by the results of the December 1917 federal election, in which the anti-conscription Liberals took all but 3 of Quebec's 65 seats, while the pro-conscription Conservatives and Union Liberals won all but 20 of the 170 seats in the rest of Canada.[13] Profoundly traumatized by the electoral realignment and the political isolation of Quebec, leaders in both major federal parties did their level best during the interwar period not to open the old wounds of conscription. In practical terms, this meant refraining from giving public support to any policy, such as the modernization of Canada's military, that could be construed as preparation for war.[14]

Finally, the sorry state of the Canadian military in 1939 must also be attributed to the impact of the Great Depression. In an effort to deal with the precipitous decline in revenues caused by the economic collapse, the Conservative government of R.B. Bennett slashed expenditures dramatically. The already lean defence budget was not exempted from Bennett's cost cutting. On the contrary, between 1929 and 1933 government expenditures on the armed services fell by roughly one-third.[15] Defence spending reached its nadir in 1933–4, when only about $13 million was allocated to the military, 'just enough,' in the words of one historian, 'to keep the forces alive.'[16] Though the government approved modest increases in the defence budget after King's Liberals trounced the Tories in the 1935 general election, the infusion of new money was in no way adequate to offset nearly two decades of neglect.

The effect of the Canadian government's deliberate inattention to its defences was twofold. On the positive side of the ledger, Canada was able to go to war as a united country. Indeed, thanks to an agreement between Prime Minister King and Dr R.J. Manion, the leader of the opposition Conservatives, conscription was not made an issue in September 1939.[17] On the down side, Canada entered the conflict with a military that was poorly equipped, poorly trained, and poorly led. All of this would change, of course. 'Well before the end of the war,' the historian J.L. Granatstein has concluded, 'the First Canadian Army of two corps, with three infantry and two armoured divisions plus two armoured brigades, was as well led, as well equipped, and at least as effective as any Allied force of comparable size anywhere.'[18] Yet the lack of military preparedness was not without consequences. It took years to get the armed forces up to speed. In the interim, many Canadian soldiers, sailors, and airmen would pay the ultimate price for the questionable strategies, inferior equipment, and ineffectual leadership that were all part of the military's growing pains.

Although the number of Canadians who enlisted in 1939 was sufficient to fill the ranks of two divisions, the shortage of qualified officers and NCOs meant that the growth of the army would have to proceed more slowly than had been hoped. By culling personnel from Canada's three Permanent Force infantry regiments – the Princess Patricia's Canadian Light Infantry, the Royal 22nd Regiment (the 'Van Doos'), and the Royal Canadian Regiment – the army was able to train and deploy to Britain one complete formation, the 1st Canadian Division, by January 1940. A second division was in the works, but it was not expected to be ready until August 1940 at the earliest.[19] This did not unduly perturb Allied military planners. When Germany did not immediately follow up the conquest of Poland with new acts of aggression, the sense of urgency that had informed the initial mobilization of the forces of the dominions seemed to subside. After the Polish campaign, Hitler paused, apparently satiated by his latest territorial acquisitions. There was even talk of a peace conference between Germany and the western powers.[20]

Of course, we now know that Hitler's 'peace offensive' of the autumn of 1939 was a tactical ruse aimed at diverting attention from his preparations for a decisive battle in western Europe.[21] After several months of waging what the British aptly described as 'phoney war,' the supreme Nazi warlord ended the lull on 9 April 1940 by launching Exercise Weser, a combined land, air, and naval attack on Denmark and Norway. The purpose of Weser was to prevent any disruption of Germany's sea link to Sweden's iron ore supplies.[22]

Having secured the raw material essential to his armaments industry, Hitler then unleashed the Wehrmacht on Belgium, Holland, and France. On 10 May, German motorized columns, assisted by coordinated paratroop landings and a merciless aerial bombardment, overran the Low Countries' complex of defence lines and fortresses along the Meuse River. In a matter of hours, the Dutch army had been routed, while the Belgians were forced into a series of withdrawals. The turning point in the Nazi offensive came on 13 May, when three German armoured corps crashed through the supposedly impenetrable Ardennes woods, thereby flanking the French 7th Army and virtually the entire British Expeditionary Force (BEF). After a few more days, it was clear that a military disaster of major proportions was shaping up for the Allies. Only the courage of a combined Anglo-French rearguard and the improvisation of an evacuation from the port of Dunkirk prevented the loss of the BEF. As it was, the 338,000 troops who escaped across the Channel had to leave behind vast quantities of equipment and weapons.[23]

Though heartened by news of the 'miracle' of Dunkirk, the Canadian government faced some tough decisions. With the BEF driven from the continent and the once mighty French army on the verge of collapse, the ability of Britain to continue the war now depended on the military commitment of the dominions. At a minimum, this meant that Canada would have to increase the number of soldiers, sailors, and airmen that it contributed to the war effort. For the second time in a generation, the spectre of conscription loomed on the horizon.

Determined to avoid a repetition of 1917, Prime Minister King handled the delicate question of manpower with his characteristic political savvy. On 21 June 1940, Parliament passed the National Resources Mobilization Act (NRMA). In keeping with Canada's expanded obligations, the act made military service compulsory. Shrewdly, it also stipulated that no Canadian could be compelled to serve overseas. In effect, two classes of soldier were created. The first was the traditional volunteer, who was available for service anywhere.

The second was the compulsorily enlisted NRMA man, who could be mobilized for home defence but who could not be sent abroad unless he chose to 'go active.'[24] A compromise between the contradictory goals of full mobilization and the preservation of national unity, the NRMA system would work well enough until the autumn of 1944, when many home defence conscripts resisted the call-up necessitated by mounting Canadian losses. Some civil disorder erupted, and the stability of the government was threatened by a cabinet crisis. Fortunately, the diminishing number of casualties suffered by Canadian forces during the final six months of the war permitted the anti-conscription agitation to die down of its own accord.[25]

These events were a long way off, of course. Manpower simply was not an issue in the spring of 1940. On the contrary, as the shocking spectacle of France's rapid defeat and the near loss of the BEF played themselves out on the European continent, in Canada a flood of new recruits rushed to the colours. Almost seven thousand enlistments were recorded by Canadian forces during the last days of May. An additional fifty-nine thousand recruits were signed up during June and July. Including officer and nursing-sister appointments, a total of over eighty-five thousand men and women joined the Canadian armed forces during the period May–August 1940.[26] With such an outpouring of patriotic fervour, there would be little difficulty in meeting Canada's expanded military commitments.

The influx of new recruits could not have come at a more opportune time. Following a review of the Allies' deteriorating military situation, on 20 May King's cabinet announced that the army would move up the date of the 2nd Division's deployment to Britain by a couple of months, to June. Since this would leave Canada with inadequate home defence forces, the government also declared its intention to raise a third division. Less than a week later, a fourth division was announced. The 1st and 2nd Divisions would form the nucleus of a Canadian Corps, while the two new formations were to be available for such service as was required in Canada or abroad.[27]

It was within the context of the timely expansion of Canada's military commitment that the 3rd Canadian Infantry Division was born. From British Columbia to Nova Scotia, thousands of newly enlisted recruits streamed into the training camps of their local militia units. There they were organized into companies, assigned to barracks (which more often than not were tents or wooden shacks), and drilled in the basics of soldierly deportment, marching, and the handling of weapons.[28] After several weeks, those units earmarked for integration into the 3rd Division were sent to assembly areas in the Maritimes. Among the formations that were to provide the division's infantry were regiments such as the Royal Winnipeg Rifles and the North Nova Scotia Highlanders. The Winnipegs, the North Novas, and the other militia regiments that supplied manpower to the 3rd Division were by no means elite units, but most had long and venerable combat records.

Recruits to the 3rd Canadian Division were concentrated at a new camp in Debert (near Truro), Nova Scotia, and at the recently refurbished camp in Sussex, New Brunswick.[29] Awaiting them was the core of what was to become the new division's leadership cadre. The officers and NCOs who had been assigned to the 3rd Division faced a daunting task. First, they had to organize disparate units into a combat division. Then they had to train it. After some delay, three brigades were formed in the early autumn of 1940.[30] Designated as the 7th, 8th, and 9th Brigades, each was made up of three infantry battalions, which in turn consisted of four rifle companies each. To the infantry were subsequently added field and anti-tank artillery, engineers, signals, medical, and other support formations.[31]

After the war, Canadian military planners became the target of criticism, some of it justified, over the way that the army's divisions had been organized. The criticism focused on two issues: the ratio of infantry to support units, and the so-called regimental tradition. Compared with the divisional set-up in the British, American, and German armies, the Canadian army allocated a higher percentage of men to support units. Out of a Canadian division's basic complement of 18,376 men, less than half were in the infantry, while a comparable percentage served in support units. Even more problematic, the percentage of men carrying out non-combat support functions such as first aid and cooking was higher than in the typical Allied or enemy division. The somewhat skewed ratio of infantrymen to support personnel meant that Canadian divisions, once they were heavily engaged in battle, tended to experience difficulty in maintaining their front-line units at sufficient fighting strength.[32] This would prove to be a major problem for the 3rd Canadian Division in Normandy.

Postwar criticism of the organization of Canadian divisions was not confined to the infantry–support personnel ratio. There was also concern over the use of the regiment as the basic building block of the army. It was the job of a militia regiment to raise men from a particular area or town, teach them about the regiment's history and traditions, and provide them with basic military training. The theory was that men from the same locality, imbued with pride in their regiment, would fight fiercely for the good of the unit and out of loyalty to one another.[33] Though founded on a number of intangible factors, this theory cannot be dismissed out of hand. Time and time again during the initial phase of the Normandy campaign, desperate situations would be turned around by the breathtaking courage and *esprit de corps* of relatively small units of the 3rd Canadian Division.

From the point of view of morale and fighting spirit, then, the regimental tradition had much to recommend it. It was not without its drawbacks, however. For example, regimental loyalties often won out over merit in the selection of battalion and company commanders. Similarly, the bond that the men had forged with their regiment tended to inhibit the growth of loyalties to the higher formations, like brigades or divisions, to which they were subordinated. Critics of the regimental tradition believe that it produced officers who found it difficult to effectively carry out military operations that had been planned on a brigade or divisional scale.[34] It has even been suggested that this phenomenon may have been at work during the 3rd Canadian Division's early operations in Normandy,[35] some of which, unfortunately, were characterized by poor coordination and control at the battalion, brigade, and divisional levels. Of course, the same criticism has been levelled at the early operations of the Hitler Youth Division, which, unlike its nemesis, was born of a military tradition that encouraged strong divisional ties.[36] Perhaps the problems of the 3rd Canadian Division in Normandy had little to do with the regimental tradition, but instead reflected weaknesses at the upper echelons of command.

From the autumn of 1940 to the end of the war, the 3rd Canadian Infantry Division had five different commanding officers.[37] None could really be described as a top-flight battlefield commander. The first man to lead the division was Major General Ernest W. Sansom, a graduate of the British army staff college at Camberley who had commanded a machine-gun battalion during the First World War. Sansom's stay with the 3rd Canadian was a brief one. After supervising the early organization and training of the division, in the spring of 1941 he was transferred to a more glamorous post, namely, command of the 1st (later the 5th) Canadian Armoured Division. Sansom was replaced by Major General C. Basil Price. A militia officer who at war's outbreak was running a Montreal dairy, Price lasted until the summer of 1942, when he was relieved after a less than stellar performance during a military exercise. Although Price probably was not up to the task of battlefield command, in fairness it should be noted that the exercise that led to his undoing coincided with the death in combat of his son, who was an RCAF officer. In any event, Price was replaced by Major General Rodney F. Keller.[38] A graduate of the Royal Military College in Kingston and a member of the Princess Patricia's Canadian Light Infantry, Keller shepherded the 3rd Division through a critical period in Britain, during which it was transformed from a motley collection of half-trained individuals into a cohesive and skilled fighting force considered worthy of being selected as one of the five D-Day assault formations. Popular with the men but held in low esteem by his fellow officers, the tough-talking, hard-drinking, and womanizing Keller came in for considerable criticism for his handling of the division during the Normandy campaign. Wounded during the fighting on the road to Falaise, he was replaced by Brigadier Dan C. Spry, who was promoted to the rank of Major General and who took over the command of the division on 18 August 1944. Spry led the 3rd Division until 22 March 1945, when he was appointed to command Canadian reinforcement units in England. With the war in Europe just about over, Major General Holly Keefler took his place.

Infantry training for the 3rd Canadian Division got under way in the autumn of 1940. It was expected that the division would be battle-worthy by the summer of 1941.[39] This was wishful thinking. The men who embarked for Britain in July 1941[40] may have looked like soldiers, but they were in no way ready to wage war.[41] In fact, it took two years of intensive training in Britain for the 3rd Division to learn how to fight as a cohesive force. At first, the division was put through the paces of battle drill, the controversial practice of making small units repeat a series of battlefield manoeuvres until they responded to certain situations automatically. Later, the men took part in battalion-, brigade-, and even divisional-scale exercises, during which they learned how to coordinate artillery and armour in either attack or defence.[42]

The training in Britain was rigorous, and progress was often slow. Eventually, all the hard work began to pay dividends. On 3 July 1943, General Andrew G.L. McNaughton, the senior combatant officer of the Canadian Army Overseas, informed General Harry D.G. Crerar, then commander of the 1st Canadian Corps, that the 3rd Canadian Infantry Division had been selected for assault training with a view to taking part in the Overlord operation.[43]

Over the next ten months, the division rehearsed its role in the coming invasion of Hitler's Fortress Europe. Assault training was carried out in four phases. In phase one, the men of the 3rd Division practised embarkation and disembarkation in mocked-up landing craft, learned how to scale natural and man-made coastal obstacles, and were taught how to clear mines. The second phase of Overlord training focused on the mechanics of seaborne assault and consisted of simulated battalion-scale landings supported by artillery fired from landing craft. During the third phase, brigade groups, operating in conjunction with the naval task force, conducted landing exercises that were characterized by ever increasing realism. Division-scale rehearsals, such as the kind that was carried out in the Trousers exercise, marked the fourth and final phase of training for Overlord.[44]

The 3rd Division's assault training continued until the last week of May, when all military camps in the invasion staging areas were sealed. Thereafter, no one could get in or out without a special pass. On 26 May, all officers whose units would be participating in the initial assault were briefed in tightly guarded rooms. Through the use of maps, aerial photographs, and plaster models, the officers were able to familiarize themselves with the terrain of the invasion front. They still did not know the location of their actual objectives. Owing to the need to preserve operational secrecy, all of the props used during the briefing bore code names and fictitious coordinates. It was only after embarkation that the men were told of their actual destination. But this was a mere formality. The die had already been cast. The 3rd Canadian Division was headed for Normandy.[45]

From the perspective of their creation and development as combat formations, it may appear that the 3rd Canadian and the 12th SS Divisions bore more than a passing resemblance to one another. For example, both divisions were formed at a time when the fortunes of their respective military alliances were at a low ebb. Born out of crushing defeats on the battlefield, the inception of both divisions was attended by high expectations. Once organized, both divisions had to confront the problem of a shortage of qualified officers and NCOs. Both had to improvise where training and equipment were concerned. Despite these and other obstacles, both developed into first-rate military formations. Finally, both would experience their baptism of fire in Normandy.

Whatever the superficial similarities, the differences between the two divisions were far more profound. Nowhere was the gulf more apparent than in their respective approaches to recruitment. Recruits to the 12th SS, as we have already seen, had to be near perfect specimens of German manhood – at least 5'8" tall, with no physical defects of any kind. In keeping with Nazi ideology, they had to be of impeccable Germanic stock, without the blemish of a Jewish ancestor on their family tree. Fanatical devotion to Hitler and to the twisted cause he espoused was a further prerequisite for membership in the 12th SS. And, like all SS soldiers, Hitler Youth Division recruits had to learn to love war for its own sake.

By contrast, the 3rd Canadian Division was not an elite formation. Good health and a willingness to fight for one's country were the only qualifications required for membership. To be sure, upon enlistment prospective recruits were probed about their family backgrounds. Unlike the 12th SS, this was not done for purposes of exclusion, but rather to ensure that in the event of his death a soldier of the 3rd Division might be buried according to the rituals of his faith. Once they had entered military service, moreover, the 3rd Canadian's recruits were not subjected to the drumbeat of political indoctrination. Like Cromwell's 'good soldiers,' they were expected to know and to love that for which they were fighting.[46] Finally, no one denied them the right to hate war, so long as they hated tyranny more.

Who were these 'good soldiers,' these citizen warriors? An examination of the personnel records of the Canadian victims of the Normandy massacres provides some revealing answers.[47] At the time of their murder, the average age of the men was twenty-five and a half years old. Only 22 per cent were married, and only 19 per cent of the married men had children. Notwithstanding their relative youth, more of the men had enlisted during the first year of the war than in any subsequent year. Of the 145 victims of the Normandy massacres on whom personnel files were found, 38 per cent had joined up in 1939–40, as compared with 19 per cent in 1941, 21 per cent in 1942, and 22 per cent in 1943.

The victims came from every region, indeed, every province, in Canada. At almost 30 per cent, Ontario residents constituted the largest provincial bloc in the sample. Native Manitobans were a close second, constituting 28 per cent. Twenty-one per cent hailed from Nova Scotia, while just under 10 per cent came from Saskatchewan. There were several men each from Prince Edward Island, New Brunswick, and Quebec. Although the order of battle of the 3rd Canadian Division did not include any units from the two westernmost provinces, three of the victims of the Normandy massacres called Alberta or British Columbia home. Interestingly, fourteen of the men had not been born in Canada. Of these immigrants, eight were from Britain, six from the United States.

In terms of their ethnic or national origin, fully 77 per cent of the men in the sample were of British extraction. This was hardly surprising in a country where in 1939 more than half of the people considered themselves to be British in origin.[48] Yet in keeping with the already significant diversity of Canada's population, persons of ethnic or national background other than British were also represented. For instance, 13 of the 145 men in the sample were of aboriginal descent (Cree and Mi'kmaq). Five were francophones. There were also four Ukrainians, three persons of Scandinavian origin, two Poles, two Rumanians, one Russian, one Dutchman, and one German. One of the victims, a member of the North Nova Scotia Highlanders, was black.

There was similar diversity in the victims' religious affiliation. Roman Catholics, members of the United Church, and Anglicans predominated, constituting 28, 24, and 23 per cent of the sample respectively. Presbyterians made up the next largest group at almost 12 per cent. Of the remaining nineteen men, there were seven Baptists, four Lutherans, two members of the Greek Orthodox Church, two Jews, two Methodists, and one Christian Missionary. Despite his creed's doctrinal opposition to military service, one of the victims was a Mennonite.

It has been suggested that many of the men who joined the Canadian armed forces during the Second World War did so in order to seek relief from unemployment or to escape from dreary, low paying jobs.[49] The extent to which the latter condition influenced enlistment is virtually impossible to measure, but the sample of victims of the Normandy massacres suggests that unemployment was not a significant motivating factor. Of the 145 men in the sample, 76 per cent were holding down full-time jobs at the time of their enlistment. Another 19 per cent were working part-time jobs or were seasonally employed. Only 5 per cent were actually unemployed, and, of this group, more than half were still in school. Of the 137 men who were working full- or part-time when they enlisted, more than 60 per cent, to be sure, were stuck in low-paying, unskilled jobs.[50] On the other hand, 23 per cent were skilled blue-collar workers, while the remainder were engaged in a variety of white-collar pursuits.

Such were the men who would fall victim to the criminality of the SS troops who opposed them in Normandy. They were fathers and sons, husbands and brothers, friends and neighbours. They were clerks and coalminers, farmers and fishermen, storekeepers and salesmen. They were men like the Meakin brothers, twenty-three-year-old George and twenty-one-year-old Frank from Birnie, Manitoba, who the army tragically put in the same ill-fated platoon. They were men like Ervin Povol, an American citizen who ran away to Canada to escape a repressive home life, and who, out of gratitude to his adopted country, bequeathed his meagre estate to a Saskatchewan orphanage. They were men like Francis Harrison of Owen Sound, Ontario, who, despite the army's psychiatric evaluation of him as being 'of insufficient intelligence' to serve, persevered through basic training and became a good soldier. They were men like Anglican minister Walter Brown, the gentle but courageous man of God who insisted on taking his place in one of the D-Day landing craft. Like all of their 3rd Division comrades, the victims of the Normandy massacres had little in common except their unit, their training, and the conviction that their sacrifice, should it be necessary, would be for the greater good. And there was one other thing that bound these men to one another. They were Canadians.

# 3
# Deployment for Battle

In the days that followed the 26 May Overlord briefing, the foot soldiers of the 3rd Canadian Division headed for the ports from where the invasion of Fortress Europe would be launched. The division's support units and the 2nd Canadian Armoured Brigade came into the marshalling areas on the heels of the infantry. For one or two nights, the men slept in auditoriums or warehouses. Then, on 1 June, they were ordered to begin boarding the troop ships that were anchored at Southampton and Stokes Bay. The process of embarkation took three days. By late afternoon on 4 June, the Canadians were crammed into the holds of the vessels, waiting for word that the invasion was on.[1]

Once aboard ship, the officers of the Canadian assault force received the OK to open their sealed packages of maps. It was at this time that they learned the place names of their objectives.[2] According to the Overlord plan, the 3rd Canadian Division was to make its D-Day assault against a four-and-a-half-mile stretch of beach code-named 'Juno,' which was located in the centre of the sector allotted to the British 2nd Army. To the west of Juno, on the Canadian right, the (British) 50th Northumbrian Division was to land on 'Gold' Beach between Le Hamel and La Rivière and carve out a bridgehead that included Bayeux. East of the Canadians, the (British) 3rd Infantry Division was to land on 'Sword' Beach between Lion-sur-Mer and Ouistreham, from where it was to secure a bridgehead over the Orne River and capture Caen.[3]

After a massive air and naval bombardment, the Canadian assault was to proceed on a two-brigade front, through sectors known as 'Mike' (on the right) and 'Nan' (on the left). Mike included the villages of Courseulles-sur-Mer and Graye-sur-Mer, while Nan included Bernières-sur-Mer and the western outskirts of St Aubin-sur-Mer. The eastern part of St Aubin and the village of Langrune-sur-Mer, up to the boundary with the (British) 3rd Division, were to be assaulted by the four-hundred-man No. 48 Royal Marine Commando.

Assuming that the landing craft successfully navigated the tricky sea approach, which was punctuated by a series of rocky ledges that paralleled the shoreline, the men were to cross Juno as quickly as possible and secure the causeways that led inland. In Mike sector, the Canadians would find a fairly wide beach, behind which lay ten-foot-high sand dunes and two exits wide enough for vehicles. In Nan sector, the beach was a combination of sandy stretches and rocky outcrops. Here too there were suitable exits. In a few places, the assault troops would require scaling apparatus to get over the sea wall.[4]

The Overlord plan called for General Keller's troops to seize an area extending some ten miles inland, including the high ground west of Caen that was astride the highway to Bayeux, by the end of D-Day. The day's work was to be carried out in four stages. In stage one, two of the 3rd Division's three infantry brigades were to land on either side of the mouth of the Seulles River, secure the beaches, and break German resistance in the coastal region. Stage two was to involve the crossing of the Seulles and the taking of the high ground on the eastern flank near the villages of Colomby-sur-Thaon, Anisy, and Anguerny. In stage three, the brigade that had come through Mike, assisted by the reserve brigade, was to secure the Caen-Bayeux highway. The fourth and final stage of the assault was to consist of consolidation and reorganization in order to meet the expected German counterattack.[5]

The landing of the 3rd Canadian Division on Juno Beach was to be part of the greatest amphibious assault in history. Planning for this massive enterprise had begun in earnest early in 1943. The blueprint for Overlord was prepared by a combined Anglo-American staff under the direction of British Lieutenant General Sir Frederick E. Morgan. For their invasion target, Morgan's staff selected a fifty-mile strip of beach along the Normandy coast of France bounded by the Orne River in the east and the Cotentin Peninsula in the west. The operation they proposed was a straightforward one. Five Allied infantry divisions, along with some armour, were to be landed at five- to ten-mile intervals along the Normandy coast after American and British paratroop divisions (the latter including a Canadian parachute battalion)[6] had secured the flanks. Once a beachhead had been carved out, the Allies were to undertake military operations aimed at the destruction of Germany's armed forces and the liberation of all territories that were under the Nazi yoke.[7]

Not since 1688 had an invading army attempted to cross the English Channel. In view of the Allies' overwhelming naval and air superiority, the sea passage was expected to meet little opposition. The landings were another matter. Blocking the entry of the Allied assault divisions to the continent were the formidable coastal defences of Hitler's Fortress Europe. Under the energetic direction of the legendary German commander Field Marshal Erwin

Rommel, an elaborate system of mined underwater obstacles, artillery emplacements, pillboxes, wire entanglements, tank traps, land mines, and other hazards had been constructed along the northern coast of France with the express purpose of stopping an invasion at the beaches.[8] Behind these defences were 58 divisions, including 32 coastal, 14 infantry, 10 armoured, and 2 anti-parachute formations.[9] Although of uneven quality, these German forces outnumbered the thirty-nine divisions that were available to the Allies on the eve of Overlord.

Despite the disparity in ground forces, the Allies had reason to be confident. For one thing, only fourteen of the German divisions in the western theatre of operations were stationed at or near the Normandy coast. Owing to the elaborate Allied deception known as Operation 'Fortitude,' the centrepiece of which was an army group of ten to fifteen fictitious divisions organized around American General George Patton, the Germans had concentrated the bulk of their available forces to the northeast of Normandy, in order to defend against an assault on the Pas-de-Calais across the relatively narrow Straits of Dover.[10] Secondly, Allied air forces had established virtually total supremacy in the skies over northern France. This meant that any German counterattack against the invasion force would almost certainly be slowed by cratered roads and bombed bridges, not to mention constant harassment from the air. Finally, the Allies had an overwhelming advantage in shipping and matériel. If they could establish a foothold on the continent, then they would be able to build up their invading army at a faster pace and to a greater weight than the Germans would be able to reinforce their defences.

The launching of Overlord had originally been planned for early May 1944.[11] After a postponement occasioned by developments in the Mediterranean theatre of operations, the invasion was rescheduled for 5–7 June.[12] These dates were selected because they were the next period on the calendar when there would be a convergence of optimal conditions of moonlight, tides, and time of sunrise. Moonlight was required so that the airborne drops that were to precede the landings could be made accurately. The Channel crossing had to be carried out at night so that the strength and direction of the Allied convoys would be concealed from German ships and reconnaissance planes. And the seaborne assaults had to go in at low tide so that Rommel's beach obstacles and mines would be visible to the incoming landing craft.

As the narrow window of opportunity drew nearer, Overlord was tentatively scheduled to go on 5 June. At the meteorological conference held on 4 June, however, American General Dwight D. Eisenhower, the Supreme Commander of the Allied Expeditionary Force (AEF), got the bad news – a major storm was brewing. According to Group Captain J.M. Stagg, the chief meteorological officer at AEF headquarters, the storm was expected to be of sufficient severity to ground all Allied aircraft, impair the naval bombardment of the Germans' coastal defences, and render the Channel crossing perilous. After discussing the matter with his chiefs of staff, Eisenhower decided to postpone the invasion.

The storm predicted by Stagg hit on the evening of 4 June with a fury rare even by North Sea standards. Packing almost hurricane-strength winds and torrential rains, it seemed impossible that the tempest would abate in the next two days. Yet that was exactly what happened. As if to benefit the Allies by divine intervention, the storm began to dissipate on 5 June. The reprieve was confirmed at that morning's meteorological conference. Barely able to contain his excitement, Stagg predicted that a weak ridge of high pressure would settle over the invasion area by the end of the day. This, he assured the surprised assault-force commanders, foreshadowed a period of up to thirty-six hours of relatively calm weather.

Eisenhower was now faced with one of the toughest decisions that a military commander ever had to make. If he gave the go-ahead, the initial assault almost certainly would have the benefit of clear skies, relatively calm seas, and good weather. At the same time, the lull in the storm was expected to be shortlived. Should Stagg's predictions as to the duration of the lull prove to be accurate, then the build-up of forces after the initial landings might have to be interrupted. Unfortunately, any such delay would leave the original assault force vastly outnumbered and highly vulnerable to German counterattacks.

On the other hand, deferring the invasion was also fraught with peril. According to Stagg, there might be only thirty-six hours of good weather. In the event that the storm returned on 7 June, the invasion would have to be put off again. This time the postponement would be measured not in days, but rather in weeks, until optimal conditions of moonlight and tides again prevailed. The consequences of such a delay were incalculable. Among the members of the invasion force, there would be the inevitable drop in morale, not to mention the problem of maintaining operational secrecy. Even if another attempt could be mounted soon, the delay would enable Hitler to further strengthen his Fortress Europe defences. Finally, one had to take into account the potentially adverse reaction of the Russians. Already of the view that the Allies' much heralded 'second front' was long overdue, Josef Stalin, the ruthless and paranoid Soviet dictator, likely would have regarded another postponement as a deliberate betrayal. This may well have led him to explore other strategic options, including, perhaps, a separate peace with the Third Reich, a nightmare scenario that Allied governments were loath to contemplate.[13]

All of these considerations weighed heavily on Eisenhower's mind as he listened to Stagg's report. Despite the Hobson's choice that confronted him, the decision of the supreme commander was not long in coming. At 4:15 AM on 5 June, Eisenhower announced that the invasion would go forward.

Overlord began at exactly 11:31 on the night of 5 June. At that moment, Royal Air Force (RAF) squadrons began bombing the ten massive coastal guns that guarded the sea approach to Normandy.[14] Forty-five minutes later, gliders transporting pathfinders of the British 6th Airborne Division began their descent into German-occupied France, just east of the Orne River, near the town of Ranville. By 1:00 AM, the main force of the 6th Airborne had floated into its drop zone. At about the same time, on the western flank of the invasion front, paratroopers from the American 82nd and 101st Airborne Divisions began landing in the southeastern corner of the Cotentin Peninsula.[15]

The British airborne drops went well. Indeed, within a few hours of touching down, the 6th Airborne was able to secure all of its objectives. These included the demolition of five bridges in the Dives River valley, the purpose of which was to prevent or at least delay the approach of German reinforcements, and the destruction of the coastal battery near Merville. By dawn, the British paratroopers had moved their anti-tank guns into place south of Ranville, where they awaited the anticipated German counterattack.[16]

Things went less smoothly for the Americans. As their planes neared the drop zone, they came under heavy fire from German forces stationed near Carentan and St Mère Église. Forced to take evasive action, the planes dropped the paratroopers in pell-mell fashion. As a result, some landed as far as thirty miles from their targets.[17] Ironically, the wide dispersal of airborne troops seems to have worked to the advantage of the Americans. Captured German records reveal that the scattered airborne drops caused considerable disarray among the defenders of Fortress Europe.[18] While the German High Command was trying to sort things out, the Americans took the opportunity to establish a foothold at the mouth of the Vire River, from where they advanced southward to their first objectives.[19]

Supported by heavy fire from Allied destroyers, the seaborne assaults began just after 6:30 AM on 6 June.[20] On the American right, landing craft containing elements of the 4th U.S. Infantry Division made the ten-mile-long run from the troop ships to 'Utah' Beach. Owing to a navigational error, the craft beached about a mile from their intended landing zone. By chance, this sector was lightly defended. Facing only token opposition, the assault battalions were able to secure Utah and push inland rapidly. By 1:00 PM, spearheads of the 4th Division had linked up with the 101st Airborne.[21]

Forty-five minutes after the landings on Utah, craft containing elements of the 1st and 29th U.S. Divisions hit the beach code-named 'Omaha.' Here the Americans found the going very rough. Instead of a low rise from the beaches inland, the first assault groups discovered that Omaha was dominated by steep bluffs on which the Germans had dug in and from which they were raining down artillery shells and raking the beach with murderous machine-gun fire. What was worse, Allied intelligence had somehow failed to detect that the 352nd Infantry Division, a capable and experienced German formation, had been deployed in the Omaha sector some three months earlier.[22] Thus, the men had to traverse Omaha under withering fire. Those who did so successfully could do little else but huddle for protection under the sea wall. Behind them the beach became increasingly congested with newly landed men and equipment. Things got so bad that it appeared that Omaha might have to be abandoned. Indeed, the assault there was to hang in the balance until late in the afternoon, when platoon-sized detachments, rallied by 29th Division commander Brigadier General Norman D. Cota and 16th Infantry Regiment commander Colonel George A. Taylor, finally breached the sea wall and began the tortuous push inland.[23]

Farther to the east, the three assault divisions of (British) 2nd Army began landing at about 7:30 AM.[24] Neither the British nor the Canadians experienced anything comparable to the carnage of Omaha. Still, it was hard slogging all the way. In the west, at 'Gold' Beach, the (British) 50th Division had to fight through fairly heavy German opposition before it was able to take its coastal objectives. From the villages of Le Hamel and La Rivière, the 'Green Howards' moved on to capture the high ground between the coast and Bayeux. On the eastern flank, the (British) 3rd Infantry Division swept aside the German coastal defenders and, by late afternoon, was advancing on Caen.[25] Heavy resistance prevented the city's capture, however.

At around 7:45 AM, the 3rd Canadian Infantry Division began its assault on Juno Beach. The assault was spearheaded in Mike sector by elements of the 7th Infantry Brigade, followed shortly thereafter by the 8th Brigade in Nan sector. The run-in to the beach was not without its problems. Loading the landing craft took longer than expected, so that the assault started about ten minutes late.[26] The tide further complicated matters. Low tide had occurred between 3:00 and 3:30 AM.[27] Thus, by the time that the Canadian assault was under way, the water level had risen substantially. This wreaked havoc with the landing craft, some of which were damaged when they hit mines attached to underwater obstacles. Though fitted with special flotation devices, many of the duplex-drive tanks that were to support the assault foundered and sank in the choppy seas.[28]

Opposing the Canadians at Juno Beach was the (German) 716th Infantry Division. Though only at about two-thirds strength, the division contrived to give a good account of itself. Positioned across the length of Juno in concrete pillboxes and casemates, forward elements of the 716th met the oncoming Canadians with a hail of artillery, mortar, and machine-gun fire. Strongpoints at Courseulles and St Aubin offered particularly stout resistance. In a few places the defenders simply turned and ran,[29] but on the whole the 716th proved a tough nut to crack. According to British records, it was not until 10:20 AM that Juno had been cleared of resistance.[30] Not surprisingly, then, the majority of the 961 casualties suffered by the Canadians on 6 June were inflicted during the first few hours it took to secure the coastal area.[31]

Despite the problems encountered during the landings and the stiff opposition offered by the 716th Division, the Canadian assault went well. Indeed, once the beach defences had been overcome, the advance proceeded inland at a good pace. Though none of the 3rd Canadian Division's three brigades attained their planned objectives, by day's end they had pushed southward from Juno more than seven miles. Lead elements of 7th Brigade had crossed the Seulles River and were dug in at Pierrepont, only three miles from the Caen-Bayeux highway. The spearheads of the 9th Brigade had advanced even farther and by nightfall were patrolling as far south as the village of Villons-les-Buissons, which was less than four miles from Carpiquet Airfield.[32] This constituted the deepest penetration of any Allied formation on D-Day.[33] Only in the Canadian centre were the results disappointing. Held up by fierce German resistance around the radar station at Tailleville, the 8th Brigade was delayed in its advance. Nonetheless, by evening individual units had penetrated to within sight of the brigade's objective, the high ground between Anguerny and Anisy.[34]

Similar breakthroughs were made all along the invasion front. In the east, the (British) 3rd Division had driven inland several miles and was within striking distance of Caen. In the centre, the (British) 50th Division had also made good progress and was planning to launch an attack on Bayeux at first light. In the west, the 4th U.S. Division had advanced from Utah to La Barquette, within sight of Carentan, its D-Day objective. Even Omaha sector had been stabilized. While the penetration there was much more shallow than elsewhere, by nightfall the Americans had secured the coastal area.[35]

With the enemy's forces having successfully landed all along the Normandy coast, the Germans' only hope for defeating the invasion lay in breaking up the still-tenuous Allied beachhead with an armoured counterattack. Three tank divisions were sufficiently close to the battlefield to be able to get there before the day was out. Nearest to the invasion front was the 21st Panzer Division. Stationed just south of Caen, the recently refitted 21st Panzer constituted a significant striking force, although as many as one-third of its 146 tanks were obsolete models captured during the Battle of France in 1940.[36] Farthest from the Allied beachhead was the 130th Panzer Lehr Division. Concentrated around Chartres, about 120 miles due south of the Normandy coast, this newly formed division boasted a complement of 183 tanks, all of which were modern. Commanded by Major General Fritz Bayerlein, an old friend of Rommel's who had been the Desert Fox's chief of staff during his victorious campaigns in North Africa, the Panzer Lehr was probably the most powerful division in the Wehrmacht's order of battle.[37] Located between these two formations was the 12th SS Panzer Division 'Hitler Youth.'[38]

Had any of the three formations available to the Germans arrived at the beachhead by the early afternoon, the results of D-Day might have been different. As it happened, only the 21st Panzer was able to launch a counterattack on 6 June, and it went into battle too late to seriously disrupt British or Canadian operations.[39] As for the Hitler Youth and Panzer Lehr Divisions, they had been designated as the strategic reserve of the Wehrmacht High Command, which meant that they could not be moved without authorization from the Führer. In the months preceding the invasion, Rommel had pleaded with Hitler to transfer to him operational control of the two armoured divisions (along with two other more remotely deployed formations), but to no avail.[40] What was worse, the Führer, whose perennial nocturnal restlessness had developed into full-fledged insomnia in recent months, took sleeping pills on the night of 5 June and ordered his attendants not to disturb him.[41] Unable to obtain the release of the armour that might have turned the tide against the Allies, the commanders of German forces in Normandy spent the first few hours of the invasion on the phone engaged in argument and mutual recrimination.

Hitler did not rouse himself on D-Day until about 9:00 AM. Had he then acceded to the appeals of his commanders to commit the Hitler Youth and Panzer Lehr Divisions to the battle, the day might still have been won. Fortunately for the Allies, the Führer's insistence that all details of the invasion force's operations be referred to him wasted many more precious hours. Indeed, it was not until an early afternoon military conference atop his Obersalzburg mountain retreat that the supreme Nazi warlord, after silently poring over maps of northern France, at last exclaimed, 'So this is it!'[42] That was the signal to act. At 2:30 PM, General Alfred Jodl, chief of the operations staff of the Wehrmacht High Command, belatedly released the 12th SS and 130th Panzer Lehr Divisions for deployment along the invasion front. Forty minutes later, the two armoured formations received the order to move out. For the Hitler Youth Division, which was concentrated around Evreux, some seventy miles southeast of the beachhead, the orders were to proceed to the area west of the Orne River, engage the enemy, and throw him back into the sea.[43] The assignment of this sector to the 12th SS put it on a collision course with the 3rd Canadian Infantry Division.

The first units of the Hitler Youth Division to appear at the invasion front on D-Day were the three infantry battalions of the 25th Panzer Grenadier Regiment.[44] Riding in a staff car at the head of a reconnaissance detachment was the regiment's thirty-four-year-old commander, SS Colonel Kurt Meyer.[45] At just 5'9", of medium build, and with dark hair and eyes, Meyer hardly looked the part of the Germanic superman supposedly embodied by the SS. Yet there were few officers whose place in German military lore was more assured. An early member of both the Nazi Party and the SS, Meyer had spent the better part of the 1930s in the Leibstandarte, first as a platoon leader and later as a company commander. Awarded the Iron Cross 2nd Class for bravery during the September 1939 Polish campaign, Meyer began to attract the attention of the Nazi brass the following year, when he executed the breathtaking capture of several Dutch towns during the Wehrmacht's romp through western Europe. The Meyer legend continued to grow during the Balkan campaign of the spring of 1941. Trapped by Greek forces at a place called Klissura Pass, the quick-thinking Meyer spurred his troops forward by tossing a hand grenade behind the last man in the line. In recognition of his daring, if unorthodox, style of leadership, Meyer was awarded the coveted Knight's Cross of the Iron Cross. After Nazi Germany's invasion of the Soviet Union on 22 June 1941, he accompanied the Leibstandarte into southern Russia, where he served for two long and harrowing years. It was in Russia, at the head of the Leibstandarte's reconnaissance battalion, where Meyer refined the relentless, close-quarter style of combat that would give the Canadians fits in Normandy. For his heroics on the eastern front, he was awarded the Oak Leaves to his Knight's Cross.

Despite his obvious gifts as a military commander, Meyer had a dark and ruthless side. A true believer in Nazism, he saw war as something more than merely the means by which some military objective could be attained. Combat for Meyer was a rite of purification, and the battlefield a laboratory where Nazi theories of German racial supremacy could be put to the test. According to some of his subordinates, a favourite tactic of Meyer's was to lead a company through enemy lines into a village, where they would allow themselves to be encircled, always, of course, leaving a narrow escape route open. In order to prevent the trap from closing, he and his men would have to shoot their way out. Under cover of the ensuing battle, Meyer's troops, it was said, would raze the village to the ground and annihilate its unfortunate inhabitants.[46]

As Meyer's car sped towards the front, he could not help but contrast the beautiful Normandy countryside with the bleak desolation of the snowswept Russian plains under which so many of his Leibstandarte comrades were buried. Momentarily lost in memories of the eastern front, he snapped out of his daze as the motorized column reached the outskirts of the town of Grainville-sur-Odon, some six and a half miles southwest of Caen. It was now dusk. After stopping to orient himself, Meyer ordered the reconnaissance detachment to split up and fan out to the north (towards Cheux) and northwest (towards Bayeux) in order to gather information regarding Allied dispositions. With a small escort, he resumed the ride to Caen. Passing through Venoix, a suburb of the city, the group came upon a chateau nestled among some tall leafy trees. As this location afforded some measure of cover from Allied air attacks, Meyer selected it as the site of the division's provisional headquarters.[47]

At around 11:00 PM, while awaiting the return of the reconnaissance company, Meyer was visited at Venoix by an officer of the 21st Panzer Division. The man informed him that the commanders of both the 716th Infantry and the 21st Panzer Divisions were holed up in a bunker located at the outskirts of La Folie, less than two miles north of Caen. With still no word from his reconnaissance units, the impatient commander set out for La Folie in the hope of obtaining a clearer picture of the situation. He arrived there around midnight.[48]

As he descended the steps into the underground command post, Meyer was momentarily overcome by its dank and depressing atmosphere. The air smelled of perspiration and a hint of antiseptic. In the flickering light, the visitor saw why: lying haphazardly on the bunker floor were a number of wounded men awaiting attention by overworked doctors and medical orderlies.[49] Stepping gingerly around his stricken comrades, Meyer was ushered to the command centre, where he was introduced to Lieutenant General Wilhelm Richter, who was the commander of the 716th Division, Lieutenant General Edgar Feuchtinger, the commander of the 21st Panzer, and a detachment of liaison officers from the Panzer Lehr. After exchanging the usual formalities, the ramrod-stiff SS officer apologized for the delay in his arrival. He and his men, he explained, had spent half of their eight-hour march to the front in ditches hiding from Allied aircraft.[50] Then Meyer, who was by far the youngest commander in the room, was invited to sit down as the generals prepared to fill him in on the day's operations.

A haggard Richter started the briefing. The 716th Division, he reported, had borne the brunt of the Allied assault in the Bayeux-Caen sector and no longer existed as an effective fighting force. A few strong points were holding out near the coast and inland, but communication links with them had been severed.[51] Feuchtinger followed Richter, and his review of the day's events was just as pessimistic. Though his armoured formations had had some success against British airborne troops, their encounter with the main Allied force, he reported, had been disastrous. The enemy's excellent anti-tank defences, according to the beleaguered general, had inflicted 25 per cent casualties on his division and had left him with only seventy battle-worthy tanks.[52]

It took all of Meyer's self-control to keep from interrupting Feuchtinger's lamentations. As a ten-year veteran of the SS, he had come to expect this kind of defeatism from the hidebound officer corps of the regular army. Still, it made his blood boil.[53] Thus, when Feuchtinger finished reciting his litany of woes, Meyer arrogantly dismissed the British and Canadians as 'little fishes' and boasted that he would throw them back into the sea.[54] Whether this fanatic genuinely believed that the destruction of the Allied bridgehead was possible, or simply intended to shake the battle-weary generals from their stupor, his show of bravado did not correspond to the facts on the ground. Indeed, the desperateness of the situation must have become apparent even to the outwardly confident Meyer, when, at about 1:00 AM, he received word that his reconnaissance units had returned to Venoix. Their report confirmed what Richter and Feuchtinger had told him: there were no organized German defences north of Caen. Buron was being held by stragglers from the decimated 716th Division, Carpiquet Airfield was abandoned, its Luftwaffe defenders having fled without a fight, while Les Buissons was in Allied hands.[55]

His confidence vis-à-vis his younger and more charismatic SS counterpart momentarily bolstered, Feuchtinger now strenuously argued against the launching of a full-scale counterattack until the arrival in strength of the Panzer Lehr and the rest of the Hitler Youth Division.[56] Notwithstanding the evident weakness of the available German forces, Meyer urged an all-out assault on the Allied bridgehead. The exchange between the two commanders became more heated. Glaring at Feuchtinger, Meyer bluntly informed him that, come what may, in a few hours he would move his regiment north to St Germaine-la-Blanche-Herbe in preparation for a counterattack.[57] Then, in what appears to have been a deliberate affront to the more senior officer, he got up to leave. At that moment, the telephone rang. Taking the receiver from Richter's adjutant, Meyer recognized the voice of SS Brigadier General Witt, his divisional commander. Witt informed him that orders had come down from 1st SS Panzer Corps calling on the 12th SS and the 21st Panzer Divisions to attack the Allied beachhead at 4:00 PM (in less than fifteen hours) and attempt to drive through to the sea.[58]

His instincts having been validated by higher authority, the placated Meyer again sat down. Taking charge of the conference, he suggested that his and Feuchtinger's forces carry out a coordinated attack northwards in the direction of Douvres-la-Délivrande. His regiment, Meyer promised, would start to form up along the 21st Panzer's left flank during the morning and would concentrate there for the 4:00 PM attack. If the initial advance were successful, he continued, both his troops and those of the 21st Panzer would attempt to drive to the coast through a three-mile-wide corridor bounded by Cairon in the west and Cambes in the east, thereby splitting the Allied forces and exposing their flanks. Despite his misgivings, the chastened Feuchtinger quietly acquiesced.[59]

Once Feuchtinger's agreement had been secured, Meyer quickly departed the tomb-like bunker and set out for Venoix in order to plan his regiment's part in the upcoming attack. On the way back, he passed through the battered city of Caen. Riding along its deserted, debris-strewn streets, his nostrils filling with the smell of smoke and his way lighted by the fires that had been ignited by American B-17s, Meyer's thoughts turned to home and to the fires that no doubt were raging there.[60] Very soon, he would avenge the aerial bombardment of his beloved Germany.

# 4

# The Battle of Authie

Meyer made it back to his headquarters before 2:00 AM. Although he had been awake for about twenty-three hours,[1] he resisted the urge to sleep, concentrating his attention instead on maps of the Caen-Bayeux sector. Running on adrenalin, he quickly drew up an operational plan. At 3:00 AM, his battalion commanders were summoned to Venoix for a briefing.

After having endured a full day of strafing by Allied fighters and fighter-bombers, against which there had been no effective defence, the officers who gathered at Meyer's headquarters during the early morning hours of 7 June were heartened to learn that they were at last going to have a chance to hit back at the enemy. The audaciousness of their commander's plan further emboldened them. Under cover of darkness,[2] the regiment's three infantry battalions, each of which was to be reinforced by sections of 150mm cannon and 20mm anti-aircraft guns as well as by at least one company (numbering seventeen) of either Mark IV or Mark V Panther tanks, were to begin to deploy across a three-and-a-half-mile front from La Folie in the northeast to Franqueville in the southwest. Additional firepower would be provided by the 3rd Battalion of the divisional artillery regiment, whose three batteries – each of which consisted of three heavy (150mm) field guns and one light (105mm) howitzer – were to take up firing positions from where they could cover the advance of each infantry battalion.

In concert with the 21st Panzer Division, which was holding positions directly to the east, the three battalions would advance northward towards the coast in assaults timed to secure their respective flanks. This meant that the 3rd Battalion, which was deployed at the southwestern end of Meyer's regimental sector, would be the last to swing into action, with a thrust in the direction of the village of Authie. Coverage of the left flank was to be provided by the recon-naissance company, which was to deploy to the west, along the road to Tilly-sur-Seulles. In order to be able to direct the battle personally, Meyer ordered the establishment of an advance command post at the Abbaye d'Ardenne, a massive Gothic ruin well-suited for observation, which was located in the grain-fields just northwest of St Germaine-la-Blanche-Herbe.[3]

After the war, opponents and fellow commanders alike criticized Meyer for his decision, exemplified by his battle plan for 7 June, to throw forces into action piecemeal as they arrived at the front.[4] While in retrospect such tactics were bound to cause German operations to appear improvised and uncoordinated, an objective evaluation of the situation on the ground suggests that Meyer had no real alternative. As of the morning of 7 June, a gap of about ten miles, extending westward from St Germaine to the area just southwest of Fontenay-le-Pesnel, existed between his regiment and the 2nd Battalion of Wilhelm Mohnke's 26th Panzer Grenadier Regiment, the German formation in closest proximity.[5] Harassed by Allied fighter-bombers throughout the journey, forward elements of the Panzer Lehr, moreover, were nowhere near the front, and in fact did not reach their divisional staging area south of Bayeux until the morning of 8 June.[6]

Facing this porous line was a British–Canadian bridgehead almost twenty miles in length – extending from Bayeux in the west to the area of Cambes in the east – and at least five miles in depth. With only the 25th Panzer Grenadier Regiment's reconnaissance company standing in the way,[7] a determined British or Canadian attack through the vulnerable western part of the German front undoubtedly would have succeeded in flanking the 12th SS. Thus, Meyer was faced with the unenviable choice of staying put, thereby risking encirclement, or attacking before his forces had come up to strength. Since the likelihood of the Germans being able to constrict or eliminate the bridgehead diminished proportionately with every hour that the Allies were able to bring ashore fresh troops, armour, and supplies, the decision to attack on 7 June would seem to have been the lesser of two evils.

The vulnerability of the German left flank meant that the successful execution of Meyer's battle plan hinged on the performance of his regiment's 3rd Battalion. If it should falter, then the enemy would have the opportunity to go around the German flank and cut off the 1st and 2nd Battalions, which would already be on the march northward. In that scenario, elements of Meyer's regiment, isolated and out in the open, would have made easy pickings for the Canadian and British forces that were massing in the Caen-Bayeux sector.

From the point of view of leadership in the field, Meyer had reason to be concerned about the 3rd Battalion. As to the depth of its officers' Nazi sympathies, of course, there could be little doubt. Three of the battalion's four company commanders were among the fifty Wehrmacht officers selected for transfer to the 12th SS because they at one time or another had been group or regional leaders in the Hitler Youth.[8] Similarly, SS First Lieutenant Georg-Walter Stahl, the other company commander, had spent his formative years in the Hitler Youth before joining the Nazi Party in 1939.[9]

Meyer's doubts about the 3rd Battalion's officers had nothing to do with their political convictions. Rather, it was the level of their skill as commanders about which he was concerned. None of the four company commanders had front-line experience. With respect to the three officers transferred to the battalion from the Wehrmacht, it is significant that the army's personnel bureau had not kicked up a fuss when compelled to relinquish these men to the 12th SS. The reason for the army's inaction was simple: the officers came from technical support units, not combat formations. Thus, they had never led men in battle.[10] The same was true of SS Lieutenant Stahl. Just twenty-two years old, Stahl would get his first taste of combat in Normandy.[11]

The 3rd Battalion was under the command of thirty-three-year-old SS Lieutenant Colonel Karl-Heinz Milius. On paper, at least, the battalion commander possessed solid political *and* military credentials. Milius had been an early convert to Nazism. A member of the SS since before Hitler's rise to power, he had spent the 1930s serving in various of the Death's Head (i.e., concentration camp) units. Indeed, his early career had been marked by a two-year stint as the leader of a platoon of guards at the infamous Dachau concentration camp. When war broke out in September 1939, Milius was serving at Waffen-SS headquarters, and he remained in that capacity throughout the Polish campaign. By the time of the German invasion of France in May 1940, he was on active duty with the SS 'Verfügungsdivision,' or 'All Purpose Division.' It was as an NCO with this newly created formation that Milius distinguished himself, garnering both the Iron Cross First Class and Second Class for bravery. With the disbanding of the division at the conclusion of the French campaign, he was transferred to an SS military school, where he eventually was named commander. Between 1941 and 1943, Milius was employed as an instructor for SS recruits. Therefore, he did not take part in the fighting on the eastern front. He was transferred to the Hitler Youth Division in mid-October 1943.[12]

Despite possessing an impressive résumé, Milius was not the ideal candidate to lead a battalion. In evaluating his subordinate after the war, Meyer referred to his lack of battlefield experience and the problems this had caused.[13] More germane to the issue of leadership, Milius's SS file contained repeated references to personality flaws that may well have precluded his being an effective commander. For example, an October 1940 efficiency report characterized him as aloof, overconfident, and reluctant to take advice.[14] Perhaps Milius projected himself in this manner in order to compensate for his relative slightness of build. At only 5'7" tall, he measured a full inch below the Hitler Youth Division's minimum height requirements.[15] Whatever its cause, Milius's distant and sometimes obstinate demeanour seems to have prevented him from forming the bond with the ordinary soldier that is so often the trademark of a successful commander.[16] Thus, the officer entrusted with the most crucial assignment in the upcoming attack was a man who had not seen combat in the last four years, who had never led a fighting unit larger than a platoon, and whom superiors generally regarded as sorely lacking in leadership skills. These flaws, coupled with the inevitable brutalizing effects of the two years he had served as the commander of concentration camp guards, did not bode well for Milius's ability to control either his junior officers or his teenaged troops once they had experienced the first shock of combat.

Though neither side was yet aware of the proximity of the other, Meyer's plan of attack was to send Milius's battalion hurtling headlong into forward elements of the 9th Canadian Infantry Brigade. Just north of the villages of Villons-les-Buissons and Anisy, a vanguard of the brigade composed of C Company from the North Nova Scotia Highlanders and light reconnaissance tanks, known as Stuarts,[17] from the Sherbrooke Fusiliers (27th Canadian Armoured Regiment), had dug in during the night of 6–7 June. Positioned behind this vanguard, astride the Anisy–Les Buissons–Caen crossroads, was the 9th Brigade's main advance guard, which consisted of A, B, and D Companies from the North Novas and the Sherman tanks of A, B, and C Squadrons of the Sherbrooke regiment. Deployed towards the rear were the Stormont, Dundas and Glengarry Highlanders.[18] As Milius's 3rd Battalion moved up to its assault starting point just south of Franqueville during the morning of 7 June, it was separated from the spearhead of the 9th Canadian Infantry Brigade by a mere four miles of gently winding country road.

Other than carrying out patrols, Canadian forces had been ordered to undertake 'the utmost preparation' during the night of 6–7 June in order to meet a German counterattack, which was expected at first light. When the anticipated counterattack failed to materialize, the 3rd Canadian Division ordered its three brigades to resume their southward advance. On the Canadian right, forward elements of the 7th Infantry Brigade moved out cautiously at 6:00 AM. Encountering no opposition, at 8:00 AM units of the brigade started to go 'flat out' for their objectives. By morning's end, the Royal Winnipeg Rifles had taken Putot-en-Bessin, the Regina Rifles were in Bretteville l'Orgueilleuse and Norrey-en-Bessin, while the Canadian Scottish Regiment had taken Secqueville-en-Bessin.[19] In the centre of the Canadian line, the 8th Infantry Brigade resumed its drive to take the radar station south of Tailleville, but, despite the determined efforts of the North Shore (New Brunswick) Regiment, progress was negligible.[20]

On the Canadian left, divisional headquarters ordered the 9th Brigade's vanguard to move out as soon as its forces were ready. At 7:40 AM, the Sherbrooke regiment's Stuart tanks began advancing through Villons-les-Buissons southward along the road that passed through Buron, Authie, and Franqueville on the way to Carpiquet Airfield, which was a little over three miles away.[21] Carpiquet was the key to these early Canadian operations, as its capture would have provided the Allies with both a forward base from which to launch air attacks in support of the troops and an inland site for the landing of supplies. Following close behind the tanks were the men of C Company of the North Nova Scotia Highlanders, who were riding in troop carriers, as well as four detachments of anti-tank gunners, two sections of pioneer assault troops, two mortar detachments, and several reconnaissance sections from 11 (machine-gun) Platoon of C Company of the Cameron Highlanders of Ottawa.[22]

The task force was led by Major John Learment, the erstwhile commander of the North Novas' C Company. With Learment in charge of the vanguard, command of C Company fell to Captain Frederick Fraser, known as 'Hank' to the men.[23] One and a half hours after the vanguard had started for its objective, 9th Brigade headquarters ordered the main advance guard to move off as well. This force comprised A, B, and D Companies of the North Novas, which were deployed along with the Sherman tanks of A, B, and C Squadrons of the Sherbrooke Fusiliers.[24]

Initially, the Canadian advance proceeded well against light opposition. At Les Buissons, about half a mile south of the starting point, German infantry and an 88mm gun[25] held things up, but the lead Canadian tanks cleared this pocket of resistance, and the vanguard resumed its advance at 9:30 AM. Despite heavy mortar fire from the St Contest area (probably emanating from surviving elements of the 716th Infantry Division), the Canadian column pressed on and the vanguard took Buron before noon. While D Company of the North Novas was left in Buron to mop up German stragglers, A and B Companies, their men riding the Sherman tanks of A and B Squadrons of the Sherbrooke Fusiliers, bypassed the town to the west and east and started for Authie, which was just half a mile down the road.[26]

The vanguard's forward elements, meanwhile, pushed their way into Authie. The Stuarts had a relatively easy time of it, driving through the village on their way to Franqueville, which they reached around 12:30 PM. The North Novas' C Company, on the other hand, ran into intense fire from three German machine-gun emplacements in the north end of the village. The advance of his infantry stalled, Major Learment requested armoured support, which he received when Shermans commanded by Lieutenants Thomas Windsor and N. Fitzpatrick of the Sherbrooke regiment's A Squadron and Lieutenant

R. MacLean of C Squadron were pulled from their positions to the west and east of Authie. MacLean's troop had difficulty locating the vanguard, but Windsor and Fitzpatrick arrived in good order and proceeded to silence the German machine guns. By 1:00 PM, Learment was able to report that Authie was in Canadian hands.[27]

Although things had gone well on the morning of 7 June, Canadian fortunes would change dramatically in the afternoon. The first indication that something was amiss occurred after the North Novas' C Company had consolidated its hold on Authie. Along with machine-gun crews from 11 Platoon of the Cameron Highlanders, the North Novas had taken up positions just southwest of the village. The rest of Learment's vanguard had stopped in the north.[28] At about 1:30 PM, while Captain Fraser's men rested and ate some rations, heavy German shell and mortar fire began to rain down on the Canadian positions in and around Authie.[29] A number of fatal casualties resulted, including Lieutenant Couper and Privates A.R. Goodall and V.J. Baulne of the Camerons. Several other Camerons were wounded and evacuated into the village.[30]

Since Meyer's attack was not supposed to start for another two and a half hours, and since the 12th SS's artillery had orders to hold its fire, it is possible that the barrage had been unleashed by surviving pockets of the 716th Infantry Division, or by the artillery of the 21st Panzer Division, which was also in range.[31] Whatever the source, the German fire became so intense that Learment radioed for tank and artillery support to counter it. Unfortunately, the forward observer of the 14th Canadian Field Artillery Regiment reported that its 105mm guns, which were being held up by fierce German opposition on the road out of the coastal town of Bernières-sur-Mer, were out of range. An attempt was made to have one of the British cruisers anchored off the Normandy coast take out the German guns, but a communications breakdown deprived the Canadian outpost in Authie of this support as well. Meanwhile, the tanks that Learment had requested, comprising elements of the Sherbrooke regiment's C Squadron, arrived at Authie, only to be decimated almost immediately by the German artillery fire.[32]

Learment's vanguard was now in serious trouble. In front of him, the Stuarts were engaged around Franqueville, almost two miles southwest of the Canadian position. To Learment's right, most of the Sherbrooke regiment's A Squadron, with the exception of the troops of tanks commanded by Lieutenants Windsor and Fitzpatrick, were still well to the north, around Buron. This gap on the vanguard's right was mitigated somewhat by the presence northwest of Authie of the North Novas' A Company. On Learment's left, however, the situation was far more dangerous. After dropping off the infantry at Buron, the Sherbrooke Fusiliers' B Squadron had driven east about a mile to Galmanche, where they observed the movement of German tanks, carriers, 88mm guns, and infantry at a distance of about three thousand yards to the south, around St Germaine. This activity, of course, was the deployment of forward elements of Meyer's regiment to their assault starting positions. The tanks of B Squadron moved south to engage the numerous German targets, but as they did so they were pummelled by mortar and artillery fire and were forced to disperse. Thus, there were no Canadian armoured formations within less than two miles of Learment's left flank. To make matters worse, the North Novas' B Company was still well up the road from Authie, actually closer to Buron than to the forward Canadian positions.[33]

Informed as to how dangerously exposed his left flank had become, Learment sent a message to Lieutenant Colonel Charles Petch, the North Novas' young commander, requesting permission to withdraw C Company to the high ground north of Authie. Petch agreed to the redeployment and further ordered B Company to move up to a position east of Authie, dig in, and thereby close the dangerous gap that had developed on the Canadian left. Pinned down by heavy mortar and artillery fire, B Company unfortunately never got past the southern outskirts of Buron. An additional bit of bad luck occurred when A Company's 7 Platoon, led by Lieutenant L.J. Sutherland, did not get word of the redeployment in time and so was forced to hastily take up a defensive position along the Authie-Cussy road, just east of C Company.[34] As the shelling of Authie became heavier, Captain Fraser reported that German tanks could be seen closing in on his position, which was in an orchard located just to the southwest of the village.[35] It was 2:10 in the afternoon.[36] Within minutes, all hell would break loose.

Several hours earlier, Meyer and his driver had set out for the Abbaye d'Ardenne, the advance command post for the 4:00 PM attack. Arriving by Volkswagen jeep on the abbey grounds around 9:00 AM, the still energetic commander bounded up the narrow, spiral stairway of the chapel, emerging at the top of one of its massive turrets. Gazing northward, he could make out virtually the entire front of his regiment. Deployment of the infantry of his 1st and 3rd Battalions had largely been completed, but in the centre he observed companies of the 2nd Battalion still on the march, heading towards the village of Bitot.[37]

In the hope of lighting a fire under SS Major Hans Scappini,[38] the commander of the 2nd Battalion, Meyer descended his perch atop the chapel and drove a half mile or so to the village of Cussy, where he caught up with the plodding column. Concerned about the failure of his reconnaissance units to glean much information regarding Allied dispositions, he sped to the front of the column and led it northward along a dirt road in the direction of Buron.[39]

Meyer's jeep had gone only a few hundred yards when it came under fire from tanks – undoubtedly those of the Sherbrooke regiment's B Squadron – positioned between Buron and St Contest. His own armour having not yet been deployed, Meyer beat a hasty retreat to Cussy. There he met the commander of the 21st Panzer Division's 104th Panzer Grenadier Regiment, who had established his headquarters in the village. Meyer tried to get an updated situation report from the officer but was told that communications in his sector had been disrupted and that no information as to the disposition of enemy forces would be forthcoming for a while. Increasingly anxious about the presence of Allied armoured formations of indeterminate strength along the front across which his regiment would be attacking, Meyer sped back to the Abbaye d'Ardenne in an effort to gauge his opponent's intentions.[40]

From his vantage point in the chapel turret, Meyer could see the Canadian tanks fanning out to the west and east of Buron. This convinced him that a significant Allied thrust was forming up between Caen in the east and Rots (about one and three-quarter miles west of Authie) in the west. If the German counterattack was to have any hope of success, time was of the essence. Thus, as soon as the tanks of the 12th Panzer Regiment's 2nd Battalion began arriving at his headquarters, Meyer ordered them to their staging areas. In the centre, the 7th Panzer Company was deployed to the southeast of the abbey, from where it could support the advance of the 2nd Battalion. On the German right, the 8th Panzer Company was sent to an area just south of La Folie, from where it was to support the attack of the 1st Battalion. On the crucial left flank, the 5th Panzer Company was deployed to Franqueville and the 6th to the west side of the abbey, from where they would support the attack by three infantry companies of Milius's 3rd Battalion.[41] In some places, German and Canadian forces were now separated by no more than fifteen hundred yards.

At noon, Meyer inspected the forward positions of his three battalions. Satisfied with the progress of their deployment, he drove back to his regimental headquarters. Awaiting him there were SS Brigadier General Witt, his divisional commander, and SS Lieutenant Colonel Wünsche, the commander of the Hitler Youth Division's tank regiment. Meyer provided the visitors with a briefing on the morning's extensive preparations, then listened as Wünsche reported that the 1st Battalion of his regiment was stuck east of Caen, waiting to be refuelled. This meant that the upcoming attack would lack the striking power of fifty to sixty additional tanks. Undaunted, Meyer left the meeting in a positive frame of mind and returned with Wünsche to the Abbaye d'Ardenne.[42] It was nearing 2:00 PM.

On arriving at the abbey, Meyer met SS Captain Hans-Siegfried Siegel, who was about to move out with his 8th Panzer Company.[43] After a brief discussion

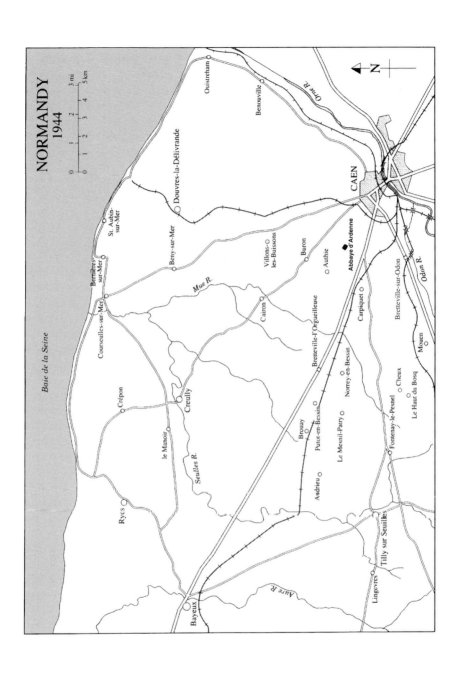

NORMANDY
1944

Baie de la Seine

Ouistreham
Benouville
Orne R.
CAEN
Douvres-la-Délivrande
St. Aubin-sur-Mer
Bernières-sur-Mer
Beny-sur-Mer
Courseulles-sur-Mer
Villons-les-Buissons
Buron
Authie
Abbaye d'Ardenne
Mue R.
Cairon
Bretteville-sur-Odon
Odon R.
Carpiquet
Mouen
Bretteville-l'Orgueilleuse
Norrey-en-Bessin
Cheux
Le Haut du Bosq
Crépon
Creully
Brouay
Putot-en-Bessin
Le Mesnil-Patry
Fontenay-le-Pesnel
le Manoir
Seulles R.
Audrieu
Ryes
Tilly sur Seulles
Lingèvres
Aure R.
Bayeux

Personnel of the North Nova Scotia Highlanders aboard a landing craft during a pre-invasion exercise, circa May 1944

Members of the Royal Winnipeg Rifles awaiting embarkation for the invasion of
Hitler's 'Fortress Europe,' 1 June 1944

Troops of the North Nova Scotia Highlanders and the Highland Light Infantry of Canada going ashore from LCI (Landing Craft Infantry) 299, Bernières-sur-Mer, Normandy, 6 June 1944

Members of the Regina Rifles firing from inside a captured German position, France, July 1944

French military memorial in the ruins of Norrey-en-Bessin, July 1944

Members of the 12th SS Panzer Division 'Hitler Youth' under guard by Canadian troops, 15 June 1944

The Abbaye d'Ardenne

Lieutenant General H.D.G. Crerar,
Canadian Military Headquarters,
London, England, 1940

The entrance to the grounds of the Abbaye d'Ardenne, early 1945. It was through the archway that seven Canadian prisoners were escorted at noon on 8 June 1944.

SS Brigadier General Kurt Meyer, handcuffed to Major Arthur Russell, on arrival at Aurich, Germany, 31 October 1945

SS Brigadier General Kurt Meyer in court, flanked by Major Arthur Russell (left) and Captain Elton D. McPhail, 10 December 1945

with Wünsche, Meyer ordered Siegel to dismount from his Mark IV and take a motorcycle to reconnoitre for Allied armour. It was not long before Siegel spotted the Canadian tanks and determined the axis of their advance. Within minutes, the tank commander returned and made his report.[44]

His heart pounding with excitement, Meyer ascended the chapel tower once more, using his field glasses to scan the front from west to east. When his gaze reached the area between Buron and Authie, he found to his amazement that Siegel's information had been 100 per cent accurate. Rolling down the country road towards Authie was a column of Sherman tanks – probably those of the Sherbrooke Fusiliers' A Squadron – its left flank seemingly unprotected. Meyer strained to find a flank guard. As he continued to scan eastward, he finally saw a lone Sherman pushing through the orchards in St Contest. Only one tank was covering the enemy's advance! Sensing that this was a turning point in German fortunes, Meyer immediately ordered that a telephone line be run from his turret down to Wünsche's command tank on the abbey grounds. As soon as they were connected, he began pinpointing the location of the Canadian armour for Wünsche, who in turn radioed this information to the now fully deployed German tank companies.[45]

The German attack was not scheduled to begin for another two hours. Yet the opportunity presented by the exposed Canadian flank was too good to pass up. On his own initiative, Meyer decided to attack at once. Countermanding his previous operational plan, the mercurial commander reversed his regiment's order of battle. In the new scenario, the three infantry companies of the 3rd Battalion, supported by the 5th and 6th Panzer Companies, would attack first, with their objectives being Authie and Buron. As soon as Authie had been secured, the regiment's 2nd Battalion would start advancing from its positions south of Bitot. After Meyer notified the 21st Panzer Division and his own divisional command of the change in plan, the attack was set to begin. The tanks of the 5th and 6th Panzer Companies moved out, followed closely by the 9th, 10th, and 11th (infantry) Companies of Milius's 3rd Battalion, which were deployed in a V formation.[46] It was now just after 2:00 PM.

At 2:10 PM, elements of the Sherbrooke regiment's B Squadron made contact with German tanks, those of the 6th Panzer Company, to the east of Authie. Shortly thereafter, to the west of the village, A Squadron ran into the 5th Panzer Company.[47] Violent tank battles ensued. Though the Canadians gave a good account of themselves, their losses were high. Indeed, within twenty minutes the Sherbrooke Fusiliers reported to headquarters that they were 'heavily engaged' with enemy armour and needed reinforcements urgently.[48]

To the west of Authie, Lieutenant Fitzpatrick of A Squadron lost two of his three tanks in a matter of minutes. With his remaining Sherman, Fitzpatrick moved up to a position just south of the village, only to discover that his 75mm cannon would not fire, owing to a failure of its breech mechanism. He then tried to fend off the German attack with the Sherman's Browning machine gun, but was forced to evacuate when a shell hit his tank in the turret, killing two of his crewmen and wounding a third.[49] Meanwhile, Lieutenant Windsor's three tanks managed to withdraw in the face of superior German forces, but in the process Windsor's tank was hit. Wounded in the leg, Windsor and the rest of his crew scrambled out of the stricken Sherman and took cover in a ditch southwest of Authie.[50] They remained hidden there until they were discovered by Milius's infantrymen, who took them prisoner.[51]

To the east of Authie, B Squadron, whose Shermans were engaging the 6th Panzer Company, fared somewhat better. After determining the direction of the main German thrust, Lieutenant L.N. Davies reorganized his formation of eleven tanks and confronted the larger German force. A few hundred yards apart, the two sides opened up on one another with murderous fusillades. Initially, Davies's Shermans got the better of the exchange, knocking out several German tanks and actually driving the others back. As they pressed forward, however, the Canadians became bogged down in a tank trap. Their movements inhibited by huge logs and other obstructions, Davies's Shermans were subjected to intense anti-tank and artillery fire. Finally extricating itself after several harrowing minutes, what was left of B Squadron withdrew to Gruchy, some one and three-quarter miles north of Authie.[52] When the five remaining tanks limped into the village, their crews were disheartened to learn that they had been drawn into an elaborate German trap.

Adding to the difficulties of the Sherbrooke Fusiliers this day was the fact that the Germans kept breaking into their radio traffic with false reports and orders. In another example of the bad luck that seemed to dog the Canadians on the afternoon of 7 June, the Fusiliers' adjutant and intelligence officer had been captured during one of the morning's skirmishes, with the result that the enemy gained possession of the regimental radio codes.[53] In the course of the tank battles that developed along the axis of the German thrust, a radio operator from the 12th SS would direct Canadian armour to pre-arranged fields of fire, where they were easy pickings for 75mm anti-tank guns, with which Meyer's regiment was lavishly arrayed.[54] Indeed, the German radio operator was apparently so adept at imitating the voice of Lieutenant Colonel M. Gordon, the commander of the Sherbrooke regiment, that it became a 'trying and exacting business' for Canadian tank commanders to distinguish between the two.[55]

With the shattering of Canadian armoured forces to the west of Authie and the dispersal of those to the east, the way was now cleared for Milius's infantry to advance. Sweeping behind battered but still formidable tank forces, the

10th and 11th Companies of the 3rd Battalion pushed past Authie on both flanks and headed for the next objective, Buron. Bringing up the rear, the 9th Company, supported by nine tanks, prepared to assault Authie.[56]

At this point, all that stood between the Germans and the retreating Canadian forces were two platoons of Captain Fraser's C Company and Lieutenant Sutherland's platoon from A Company. In the process of the withdrawal from Authie, these men had been cut off from the rest of the 9th Brigade's vanguard by the swiftness of the German attack.[57] Their tank support having been decimated by the first German wave, deprived of their anti-tank weapons by the vanguard's withdrawal, the North Novas nonetheless resolved to stand fast and make a fight of it. The thirty-year-old Fraser took command of the situation and improvised the defence of Authie. On his orders, C Company quickly transformed its orchard position into a fortress. Behind the hedge that bordered the orchard, they placed three Browning machine guns that had been stripped from knocked-out Shermans.[58] The one good tank that was left near the village, much of its store of seventy rounds of ammunition intact, its newly mounted seventeen-pound gun ready to do battle, was brought to the Canadian outpost.[59] Aiming their weapons in the direction of Franqueville, Fraser's men awaited the German assault.

Kurt Meyer watched the battle for Authie unfold from his perch atop the Abbaye d'Ardenne. Just able to make out the Canadian position in the orchard, he ordered his artillery to bombard it in advance of the 3rd Battalion's assault. The German barrage ripped holes in Fraser's already thin lines. Gamely, the North Novas held on.[60] After a few minutes, the artillery ceased firing and Milius's infantry and tanks moved up the road towards Authie.

Fraser's men had hunkered down during the furious German barrage. When it was over, they took stock, did what they could for the wounded, and once more aimed their weapons in the direction of Franqueville. Owing to the undulating nature of the countryside, the view from the orchard was obscured. Thus, it was not until the Germans came to within a few hundred yards of their positions that the men of C Company could see the outlines of tanks rumbling towards them.[61] To the rear of and alongside the armour, the khaki camouflage uniforms of SS troops could be discerned.

We do not know what was going through the minds of the North Novas as the nine German tanks and massed infantry bore down on them; relatively few of the men in the orchard survived the ensuing battle, and only a handful of the survivors were interviewed after the war.[62] One can imagine, however, that the spectacle must have been terrifying. By their long barrels and wide, sloping, heavily armoured hulls, the tanks would have been identified as the twenty-five-ton Mark IV, whose 75mm gun could fire a fifteen-pound shell at a muzzle velocity of almost twenty-five hundred feet per second.[63] Pitted against such massive destructive force, the Canadians' lone Sherman and small arms must have seemed pitifully inadequate. The odds weighted overwhelmingly against them, Fraser's men probably were thinking the things that soldiers throughout the ages have thought just before going into a desperate battle – Will I do my job? Will I be killed? How will the family get along without me? Some stole a last look at tattered photographs. Others felt for their pocket Bibles and mouthed a silent prayer. Tense, but determined to hold out, the North Novas waited for the unequal struggle to begin.

As their column came to a rise in the fields south of the village, the Germans realized that they were no longer concealed from observation. The advance came to a halt. Moments later, the gun of the lead German tank whirred into position, then opened fire. The Canadians answered with fire from the Sherman's big gun and the cannibalized Brownings. One after the other, the rest of the German tanks opened up, and a full-scale firefight was under way. Several shells from the Mark IVs overshot the defenders' position and slammed into the southern end of Authie, pulverizing its stone buildings and sending up clouds of white powder. Soon French civilians began to appear at C Company's trenches, motioning towards the village and pleading with the North Novas to help their injured neighbours. Partly in response to their entreaties, and partly because he wanted to know the location of the Cameron Highlanders' carrier, with its powerful Vickers machine gun,[64] Fraser sent Lieutenant Jack M. Veness, the commander of 13 Platoon, Lieutenant R.C. Graves, the commander of 15 Platoon, and a stretcher bearer into the village.[65]

Veness and his small party were led down Authie's main street into a courtyard. At the back was a small shed. When one of his guides opened the door, the lieutenant was confronted with a nightmarish scene. Eight villagers of various ages, including three wrapped in blankets, were lying bleeding and hysterical on the floor. The most serious case was a six-year-old girl who had been wounded in the abdomen. Sadly, there was little that the Canadians could do. After ordering the medic to give the girl a shot of morphine, Veness advised his hosts that they should move everyone, including the injured, into cellars. Then he and his men went back into the street.[66]

On their way towards the north end of the village, Veness's party came upon more than a dozen Canadians who were trying to take shelter in a small gravel pit. Virtually all were wounded, many seriously, some mortally. Veness recognized them as Sherbrooke Fusiliers and Ottawa Camerons. He ordered the stretcher bearer to stay and do what he could for them. Then he and Graves continued down the street.[67]

Near the north end of the village, the two lieutenants finally located the

Camerons' carrier. Lying beside it were Lieutenant Couper and Privates Good-all and Baulne. They had been killed by an airburst from the shell of a German 88. Veness gazed at the dead men. Then he and Graves checked the carrier. To their surprise, it had sustained only minor damage, and its Vickers gun was in working order. Veness got in and started to drive back towards the south end of the village. Graves stayed behind in order to look for stragglers. Meanwhile, the shelling from the German tanks intensified.[68]

To the troops defending Authie, Veness's return with the added firepower of a Vickers gun was a welcome sight. Under cover of the German barrage, elements of the 9th Company of Milius's battalion had infiltrated to within yards of the orchard, and now were pouring small-arms fire into the Canadian outpost.[69] While the Brownings and the lone Sherman continued to duel with the German tanks to the south, the carrier was positioned at the western edge of the orchard, where it began to return the SS infantry's fire.[70]

A battle of epic proportions was shaping up. Sensing that this fight would be decisive, Fraser tried to get a message back to Lieutenant Colonel Petch to send reinforcements. The company's radio having been knocked out by shrapnel, Fraser succeeded in getting through to the Sherbrooke regiment's headquarters on the tank set. From there the message was patched through to 9th Brigade headquarters, which in turn relayed the news of C Company's plight to the North Novas' commander. Via the same circuitous route, Petch radioed back that Fraser should hang on, and assured him that help was on the way.[71]

The promised reinforcements were never sent. As a consequence, two platoons of C Company, along with A Company's 7 Platoon, bore the brunt of the attack by Milius's battalion. In view of the size and ferocity of the German attack, the Canadians' stand along the southern outskirts of Authie was nothing short of remarkable. The Germans threw everything they had into the battle. Artillery and tank fire pounded the orchard, creating an almost unbearable din and sending earth, shrapnel, and slivers of wood flying through the air. After each bombardment, waves of Milius's infantry would hurl themselves at the Canadian positions, only to be turned back with casualties by the murderous fire of the Brownings. When their massed assaults failed, the SS troops tried advancing in smaller groups, under covering fire. Sometimes they sought to confuse and demoralize the Canadians by calling out to them in English. Nothing worked. The North Novas and Camerons coolly opened up on each new assault group with deadly accurate fire, forcing the foe back in disarray.[72]

The embattled Canadian outpost held out for close to an hour. Finally, word came in that there was fighting at the north end of Authie, and that German infantry – members of the 11th Company – were on the verge of breaking through A Company's position. Fraser's men had been flanked, and they were in danger of being surrounded. In what must have been a truly grim scene, the brave captain now ordered Lieutenant Veness to take anyone who could still walk out of the orchard before the ring of German steel closed around them. He would stay behind with the tankmen and the wounded and would try to cover the escape. Led by Veness and the remnants of his platoon, small groups of men, perhaps totalling two dozen, made their way into Authie and the adjacent fields. Meanwhile, Captain Fraser, Lieutenant J.H. Langely, and a handful of men held out in the orchard, fighting to the last round, finally succumbing in hand-to-hand combat. The battle for Authie was over. It was just after 4:00 PM.[73]

While Fraser's men were making their heroic stand at Authie, elsewhere Milius's forces were breaking through. West of the village, the 11th Company, supported by the 5th Panzer Company, surrounded the North Novas' A Company, and, after encountering fierce resistance, overran the Canadian position and took a large number of prisoners. To the east, the 10th Company and the tanks of the 6th Panzer Company swept through the virtually undefended Canadian left flank all the way to Buron, which was now being held by elements of the North Novas' B and D Companies. Dug in, these men were prepared 'to hold on to the last.' Over the next few hours, a vicious see-saw battle ensued in which Buron changed hands several times before a final charge by the remnants of Learment's advance guard drove the Germans out for good. Owing to the high cost of the victory, the Canadians did not feel that they could consolidate their hold on the town. They therefore requested and received permission to withdraw to the high ground at Les Buissons, through which they had passed early in the morning and which was a meagre half mile from their starting positions.[74]

As the battered forces of the 9th Canadian Infantry Brigade licked their wounds during the night of 7–8 June, the men must have been bitterly disappointed by the loss of virtually all the ground they had gained that morning. After all, no soldier wants to pay for the same real estate twice. Still, in view of their exceedingly high losses – the North Nova Scotia Highlanders had suffered 242 casualties, of which 84 were fatal, while the Sherbrooke Fusiliers had lost 63 men, including 26 killed, as well as twenty-five to thirty tanks knocked out of action or destroyed altogether[75] – they at least could console themselves that they had lived to fight another day. For their comrades who had been captured during the battle for Authie, the afternoon and evening hours of 7 June would bring horrors greater than anything they had experienced on the battlefield.

# 5

# The Milius Murders

For the vast majority of the men in Milius's 3rd Battalion, the fighting at Authie was their baptism of fire. Despite their inexperience, the teenaged SS troops had acquitted themselves well against a courageous and stubborn enemy. In the process, they inflicted a significant local reverse on Canadian forces. At the moment when its vanguard had advanced to within sight of its primary objective – Carpiquet Airfield – the 9th Canadian Infantry Brigade was thrown back some three miles. It would take a month to make up the lost ground. Though by nightfall on 7 June the Germans were still more than six miles from the Normandy coast,[1] the success of Milius's attack, in the words of the official Canadian military historian, 'helped to ensure that Caen would remain in German hands and [that] the eastern flank of the Allied bridgehead would be much more constricted than had been planned.'[2]

In light of their bravura performance, one might have expected a certain amount of jubilation, or at least self-satisfaction, from the ranks of the 3rd Battalion. Yet this was not the case. On the contrary, the Canadians taken prisoner by Milius's troops in the aftermath of the battle for Authie recalled that their young captors were in a downright surly mood. As they were being assembled for what should have been the routine process of conveyance to the German rear, the exhausted and dejected prisoners found themselves being subjected to verbal abuse, uncalled-for roughness, and physical threats.[3] Private J.M. MacDonald of the North Nova Scotia Highlanders' A Company described his escorts as 'maniacs'; a few of them, he remembered, were actually frothing at the mouth.[4] Major Learment, the commander of the 9th Brigade's vanguard, expressed a similar view, characterizing his captors as 'wildly excited and erratic,' as if under the influence of drugs.[5] Ominously, in Buron a group of North Novas was lined up against a wall and ringed with machine-pistol-toting SS NCOs. Only the last-second intervention of a German officer prevented the makeshift firing squad from carrying out its intentions.[6]

Their emotions stoked up to the boiling point by tension, adrenalin, and fear, soldiers in battle often fight in a kind of rage. Thus, the contempt and anger displayed by Milius's troops towards their Canadian prisoners were not altogether unusual. Indeed, for the men of the 3rd Battalion, there was reason to be doubly enraged. Success at Authie had not come cheaply – twenty-eight members of the battalion had been killed, seventy had been wounded, and twelve were missing.[7] Moreover, the Hitler Youth Division's aura of invincibility, so carefully cultivated since its inception, had been irreparably shattered. Thoroughly imbued with the elitist traditions of the Waffen-SS, the men who took part in the attack on Authie had been led to believe that they were the finest soldiers in the world; it had been profoundly disconcerting, then, to confront an enemy who could fight them to a standstill, exacting a very high price in the process. In the aftermath of having seen so many of their comrades' lives extinguished with frightening suddenness and numbing finality, it is perhaps not surprising that some of the troops in SS khaki camouflage began to think darkly of revenge.[8]

The orgy of mayhem and murder in which Milius's battalion was to indulge itself on 7 June began just as the fighting around Authie was petering out. The first man to succumb to the berserk state[9] of the SS troops was Private Lorne Brown of the North Nova Scotia Highlanders' 7 Platoon. Along with Lance Corporal W.L. Mackay and another North Nova, Brown was dug in between the Authie-Cussy road and the orchard where Captain Fraser and his men had tried so valiantly to stave off the German attack. At the height of the fighting, Mackay had been hit in the face and the arm, while Brown had sustained a serious wound to the left wrist. The third man had been killed. Although bleeding profusely from the mouth, Mackay had been lucky; the bullet had passed through his cheek and had emerged at the back of his jaw. On the verge of blacking out, the corporal mumbled to Brown that their position was untenable, and motioned for him to withdraw while there was still time.[10] But Brown refused to leave his stricken comrade. This was a decision for which the brave young private would pay with his life.

As the Germans overran them, both wounded North Novas were lying prostrate. To the best of Mackay's recollection, he lost consciousness momentarily from the loss of blood. When he came to, he saw Brown trying to stand up in response to an order from an SS trooper. Watching out of the corner of his left eye, Mackay saw the SS man suddenly force the stunned North Nova to the ground. Holding him down with the heel of his boot, the young trooper bayoneted Brown repeatedly, cursing his victim all the while.[11] Fearing that he might be next, Mackay lay as still as possible in the hope that the German would leave him for dead. His rage apparently spent by the massacre of Private Brown, the SS man moved on. Dazed from his loss of blood and shocked by what he had seen, Mackay stayed down, lapsing in and out of consciousness until rousted from his trench by another SS trooper.[12]

In all likelihood, the murder of Private Brown was one soldier's act of spontaneous battlefield vengeance. The teenaged thug who perpetrated this crime had not been ordered to do so, nor had he been incited by his comrades. Yet despite its seemingly isolated nature, the murder acted like a spark to the smouldering anger of the SS troops. After the killing of Private Brown, the brutality and violence with which Canadian prisoners were rounded up escalated out of control. Already trigger-happy, Milius's men went on a rampage, killing randomly, savagely, maniacally. In the process, they turned an impressive German feat of arms into a day of infamy that would forever sully the reputation of the 12th SS Panzer Division 'Hitler Youth.'

From the behaviour of the survivors of Fraser's stand in the orchard, it is clear that they hoped to continue the battle for Authie within the village itself. According to Constance Raymond Guilbert, who lived on Authie's main street, at about 4:15 PM he saw a number of Canadian soldiers retreating past his house. As they ran, they warned anyone in sight that the Germans were coming, and urged them to return to their homes. Only when the street was clear did the Canadians seek cover.[13]

Within minutes, the first SS troops entered the village. Almost immediately, they were pinned down by small-arms fire from improvised strongholds. Despite the danger, Guilbert went up to a rear window and watched the battle unfold. Down a laneway, he saw a Canadian come out of the garden of the Godet residence with his arms raised. When the soldier got to within a few yards of some German infantrymen, one of them shot him down in cold blood.[14] Elsewhere, the remnants of Fraser's company continued to hold out.

Moments after he had witnessed the murder of the soldier who had tried to surrender, Guilbert turned his attention to the front of his home, where a detachment of SS troops was machine gunning a Canadian stronghold in the church located across the street. Close by the German position, lying on his back, was Private William Nichol of the North Novas. Along with other survivors from the orchard, Nichol had retreated into Authie, where he took up a defensive position in the village's main street. Wounded in the right leg during the ensuing skirmish, Nichol was immobilized, but still very much alive.[15] His gun was out of reach. According to Guilbert, when Nichol attempted to move, the officer in command of the detachment ran over to the defenceless Canadian, picked up his rifle, and in a fury repeatedly struck him about the head with the butt, crushing the left side of his skull. Then he fired a gratuitous round into Nichol's limp body.[16]

After several more minutes of fighting, the guns fell silent and the rest of the Canadians began to emerge from their positions. Soon the last holdouts from Fraser's stand, along with members of the North Novas' A Company, which had been surrounded near Buron, began to trickle into Authie under escort. One of the first to arrive was Lance Corporal Mackay.[17] According to Mackay, who by this time was in a frightful state, something peculiar happened when he and the SS trooper who was guarding him got to the centre of the village. Instead of putting him with the other prisoners, his escort shoved him into a doorway and headed across the street into an alley, apparently signalled by two of his buddies. The three men spoke briefly, after which they seemed to come to a decision. From the alley they headed back to the street, where eight members of the North Novas' C Company – including Corporal Thomas Davidson and Privates John Murray, Anthony Julian, and James Webster[18] – were sitting under guard. Mackay did not like the looks of this. Unfortunately, he was in no shape even to call out to his comrades. When the SS men got to the middle of the street, they ordered the eight prisoners to remove their helmets. Then, without warning or provocation, they lifted their guns, took aim, and shot the unsuspecting Canadians down where they sat.[19]

It was at this point that the descent into purgatory really began. After the cold-blooded killing of the eight unarmed prisoners, one of the shooters pulled the bodies of Davidson and another of the murdered men into the middle of the street. His intention was to have passing traffic run over them.[20] Some villagers tried to move the corpses back to the edge of the street, but were prevented from doing so by the SS troops, who now required new entertainment to satisfy their bloodlust. They would not be disappointed. Within minutes of the shootings, a tank that was moving through Authie on the way to the fighting farther north stopped where Davidson and the other man lay, then repeatedly ran over them.[21] So badly crushed were their bodies that the villager Guilbert, who after some difficulty convinced the Germans to allow him to bury them, recalled that he had to collect the remains with a shovel.[22]

Mackay and the other Canadian prisoners in Authie watched the behaviour of Milius's men with a mixture of horror and outrage. All burned with the desire to strike back at their captors. This was particularly true of C Company's Sergeant Stanley Dudka, who even through the blood and gore recognized the visage of Tom Davidson, with whom he had grown up and worked in the coal mines at Stellarton, Nova Scotia.[23] But revenge would have to wait for another day. The Hitler Youth troops were armed to the teeth, and any physical retaliation, however noble in intent, would have made the situation even worse. So the Canadians could only look on as the Germans descended to new depths of barbarism.

To the growing number of prisoners who were being escorted into Authie, the scene that greeted them was truly apocalyptic. The mutilated bodies of their comrades lay strewn in the street, several homes were on fire, and the SS troops were whooping it up like drunken pirates. In a bizarre and particularly disgusting celebration of their triumph, a few of the more undisciplined louts propped up the corpse of one of the murdered Canadians, placed an old hat on his head, and stuffed a cigarette box into his mouth.[24]

Authie, it will be remembered, was assaulted by the 9th Company of Milius's battalion. The members of that formation, then, bear exclusive responsibility for the initial atrocities that were perpetrated against Canadian prisoners. The 9th Company was not the only unit under Milius's command to engage in mass murder on 7 June, however. On the German left, where after a fierce battle the 11th Company and its armoured support had subdued the North Novas' A Company and 15 Platoon of C Company, a new round of killings took place. As if possessed by the same demons, members of the 11th Company continued the frightening ritual begun by their comrades in the streets of Authie.

The first victim of the berserk state of the 11th Company was Private John Metcalfe of Glace Bay, Nova Scotia.[25] Metcalfe was among a group of fifteen to twenty Canadian prisoners who had been herded into Buron after capture. Lined up on the village's main street, each man in the group was subjected to a cursory, albeit rough, search. When Metcalfe's turn came, the unidentified NCO doing the search felt something in the North Nova's jacket pocket. Unable to retrieve the item, he angrily tugged at the breast pocket with such force that he ripped it open. In the process, he sent the tired Metcalfe sprawling. As the unlucky North Nova tried to right himself, the NCO lifted his machine pistol and fired four shots into him at close range. Hit in the abdomen, Metcalfe went down in a heap. With a sadistic smile on his face, the killer let his victim lie writhing in pain for several minutes before going over and putting him out of his misery with three shots to the head. Then, as if to signal his omnipotence, the NCO emptied his magazine into Metcalfe's body.[26]

It was suggested after the war that Private Metcalfe had been shot because he was carrying a grenade in his pocket.[27] Even if that were true, it would not have justified his killing. After all, Metcalfe was otherwise unarmed, had his hands in the air, and posed no danger to his captors. Furthermore, there is no evidence that at the time of his capture he had anything as lethal as a hand grenade in his possession. On the contrary, two eyewitnesses swore that the item in Metcalfe's pocket was not a grenade, but rather a metal tin containing an emergency ration of chocolate.[28] Perhaps the tin felt like a grenade through the material of Metcalfe's jacket, but it certainly did not look like one, a fact that would have been plainly evident to the SS NCO, had he bothered to check. So Private Metcalfe was murdered over a tin of chocolate.

Another man who was murdered during a search was Lance Corporal Joseph R. Arsenault of the North Novas' A Company.[29] Captured just north of Authie, Arsenault was ordered to put up his hands, whereupon he was hustled into a line-up with several of his comrades from 9 Platoon. While awaiting his turn to be searched, he unclipped two grenades from his jacket and held them up in plain sight. This attracted the attention of an SS officer. The unidentified commander walked over to Arsenault, sized him up, and then spoke to him in French. Not suspecting anything, the private, who was bilingual, responded in kind. Upon hearing French spoken, the officer, for reasons known only to himself, brought up his pistol, aimed, and fired a shot through Arsenault's neck. The body of the murdered North Nova was left on the road where he had fallen.[30]

The round-up of Canadian prisoners in Buron coincided with the start of a massive bombardment of the Caen sector by British warships.[31] Forced by the devastating cannonade to withdraw with casualties, the Hitler Youth troops retaliated by lashing out at their Canadian prisoners. Private Jeffrey Hargreaves fell victim to this German reprisal on the road between Buron and Authie.[32] Wounded in the right leg, Hargreaves was shot dead by an SS trooper when he could not keep up with the column of prisoners, who had been ordered to run double time.[33] Farther down the road, Corporal William McKinnon, Lance Corporal James Taylor, and Private Ralph Richards were felled by machine-pistol fire from one of the escorts.[34] Private Richards was hit once in the chest, and was saved only by the intervention of an unidentified German officer, who permitted two other prisoners to attend to his wound. McKinnon and Taylor, on the other hand, were not so lucky. McKinnon was killed instantly, while Taylor, who had been hit in the abdomen, managed to stagger back into the column and continue on the march, only to die two or three days later in hospital.[35]

As the shelling from the British warships intensified, the incensed Germans seemed bent on picking up the pace of the killing. In a particularly shameful incident, six prisoners from the column that was being marched through Authie were suddenly hustled into the kitchen of a private home, ordered to face the wall, and shot execution style in the back of the head.[36] Another thoroughly dishonourable act was the murder of a soldier who had been wounded by one of the offshore salvos. While bandaging the North Nova's leg, the villager Louis Alaperrine was approached by an SS officer and a trooper. Brushing Alaperrine aside, the officer drew his pistol and shot the injured man twice in the head, killing him instantly.[37]

The North Nova who was being attended by Alaperrine was not the last man to succumb to the Germans' flagrant disregard for Canadian wounded. According to Private Gordon Talbot of the North Novas' C Company, as the column of prisoners of which he was a part was being marched through Authie, they came upon a medic from the 27th Canadian Armoured Regiment. The unidentified man[38] was working on the shoulder of a wounded North Nova. Despite the fact that the medic was wearing a Red Cross armband, which under the rules of warfare entitled him to special treatment as a non-combatant, both he and his patient were gunned down in cold blood by one of the column's NCO escorts.[39]

After witnessing the killing of the medic, Major Leon M. Rhodenizer, the commander of the North Novas' A Company, had had enough. Drawing the attention of his escorts by calling out to them in their native German, which he spoke fluently, Rhodenizer attempted to dissuade them from further killing. The appeals worked. The guards who were responsible for Rhodenizer's column seemed to realize that they had gone too far, and for the duration of the march to the rear they behaved themselves.[40]

Unfortunately, the German troops who were coming up to the line as reinforcements were another matter. As the Canadians turned on to the Authie-Cussy road, they ran into an SS detachment that was advancing to the front. When the two columns converged, the officer in the lead began yelling angrily. Suddenly, without any provocation, he pulled out his pistol and opened fire on the bedraggled prisoners. Soon his men joined in, and the Canadians, at least those who had not been hit, scrambled for cover. Spotting the uninjured Private Douglas Orford, the officer who had started the mêlée walked over and shot him point blank in the stomach. Then he and his troops resumed their march. As the Germans left the scene of their latest atrocity, nine men, including Orford and Private Joseph F. Arsenault (not to be confused with Lance Corporal Joseph R. Arsenault), lay dead or dying on the road.[41]

So endemic was the killing on 7 June that even support personnel of Milius's battalion got into the act. As the column of Canadian prisoners, which numbered more than a hundred, wended its way towards the German rear and an uncertain fate, they were overtaken by a truck bearing Red Cross markings. Although the road was clear, with plenty of room to pass, the vehicle suddenly veered sharply into the column, taking down three prisoners in the process. One of the victims, Sergeant Major R. Adair, survived the encounter, but the other two – Privates Roderick MacRae and Douglas Tobin, both of the North Nova Scotia Highlanders – died of their injuries.[42]

The running down of the Canadians was no accident. According to the numerous eyewitnesses, not only had the collision been avoidable, but as the truck sped away from the scene the men in the cab had jeered and shaken their fists at the prisoners. Even the Germans tacitly admitted their responsibility for this particular incident. Conscious of the impact that the hit-and-run killings might have on public opinion in Allied countries, the 12th SS forced some of the captured Canadian officers to sign papers stating that MacRae and Tobin had died of wounds sustained in battle.[43] Later the division staged an elaborate funeral for the two men, burying them at Bretteville-sur-Odon with full military honours. Among those in attendance was a German army cameraman. The officer filmed the entire proceedings, apparently for propaganda purposes.[44]

If there was one murder that more than any other reflected the twisted state of mind of Milius's troops, it was the killing of Captain Walter Brown.[45] The last of the thirty-seven Canadians known to have been murdered on 7 June by elements of the 3rd Battalion, Captain Brown was the chaplain of the Sherbrooke Fusiliers. Early in the evening, he had requisitioned a jeep in order to visit a wounded officer who was recuperating at the Canadian field hospital in Les Buissons. Accompanying him would be Lieutenant W.F. Grainger, also of the 27th Canadian Armoured Regiment, and Lance Corporal J.H. Greenwood, a mechanic, who would act as their driver.[46] The party did not head out until close to 11:30 PM. Unfamiliar with the terrain, Greenwood missed the turn for Les Buissons and instead continued heading southward, in the direction of Cussy. After a few minutes, it became clear to the Canadians that they were lost.

Disoriented in the enveloping darkness, Greenwood stopped the jeep near the village of Galmanche. While he and Grainger were trying to get their bearings, they were spotted by a German patrol. One of the SS troops called out to them. Thinking that they were being ordered to surrender, Greenwood, Grainger, and Brown started to get out of the jeep. At that moment, the Germans opened fire, killing Greenwood and wounding Grainger. From his position on the ground, Grainger watched as Captain Brown, his hands raised above his head, walked slowly towards the patrol. Then the lieutenant passed out. By the time that he came to, there was no one around, so Grainger assumed that the chaplain had been taken prisoner. By a supreme effort of will, he pulled himself back into the jeep, started it, and drove back to regimental headquarters, where he received medical attention.[47]

As Grainger was unconscious for some time, we do not know precisely when Chaplain Brown was killed. Indeed, his fate was not confirmed until several weeks later, when elements of a British armoured unit stumbled upon his body.[48] From the location of the corpse, which had been left unburied not far from where the three Canadians had run into the German patrol, as well as from the forensic evidence, which indicated that he had been killed by a single bayonet thrust through the heart,[49] it appeared that the chaplain had died in the following manner.

Unarmed, his clerical collar clearly visible, the chaplain walked up to the SS troopers. There were probably between ten and twenty of them. One would have looked at his papers, while another would have searched him. Satisfied that Brown was carrying no weapons, a small detachment would have been given the task of marching him back to battalion headquarters. A few hundred yards down the road, the man in charge of the escort, probably an SS NCO, must have had a change of heart. Instead of continuing on to the rear, he directed the party into the field that abutted the road. It was at this point that he would have ordered one of the troopers to kill Chaplain Brown. Perhaps the teenager designated to carry out this repulsive task was reluctant to do so. Perhaps he even protested. But orders were orders, especially in the SS. At some point, the trooper would have taken up his rifle, as he had done so many times in training, and thrust his bayonet into the chest of the brave padre.

Apart from the NCOs and rank-and-file troops who did the actual killing, those most responsible for the murders perpetrated in and around Authie were the junior officers and commanders of the 3rd Battalion's 9th and 11th Companies. While in at least two instances (the makeshift firing squad in Buron and the wounding of Private Richards), officers actually intervened to limit the mayhem, it was an officer who initiated and provoked the murder of Private Orford and eight of his comrades on the road from Authie to Cussy. On the other occasions, officers either could not or would not do anything to stop the carnage.

In general, there seems to have been a breakdown in the command structure of the 3rd Battalion on the afternoon of 7 June.[50] Thus, when Allied investigators first recommended that SS Lieutenant Colonel Karl-Heinz Milius be included among the officers of the Hitler Youth Division to be indicted for war crimes,[51] they were putting the blame for the Authie murders squarely where it belonged – on the shoulders of the battalion commander. Milius, as we have seen, was not very highly regarded as a leader of men. Before Normandy, he had never commanded a unit larger than a platoon. He personally had not seen combat for more than four years. Under different circumstances, these flaws might not have amounted to much. But when added to the already combustible mix of his troops' inexperience, overconfidence, and desire for vengeance, they proved lethal. Weakness at the top of the chain of command was taken as licence at the bottom. In the absence of a firm hand, what happened in and around Authie during the afternoon hours of 7 June was hardly surprising.

After the war, the Authie killings were listed in a lengthy war crimes' indictment against Kurt Meyer. In support of this charge, Canadian military prosecutors would introduce evidence that, prior to the Normandy invasion, Meyer had encouraged his troops not to take prisoners.[52] Though he was in fact found guilty of this charge, Meyer was acquitted of responsibility for the Authie killings because a link could not be established between them and his earlier incitement to deny quarter.[53] Indeed, owing to the confusion wrought by the ongoing battle, the breakdown in discipline on the German side, and the numerous and scattered crimes scenes, we probably will never know for certain to what extent, if any, Meyer had a hand in the killings perpetrated on 7 June by the 3rd Battalion of his 25th Panzer Grenadier Regiment. But that does not mean that Meyer's hands were clean where the fate of Canadian prisoners was concerned. In the aftermath of the battle for Authie, events would transpire at Meyer's headquarters that made the Milius murders pale in comparison.

# 6

# The Meyer Murders

After the shooting of Private Orford and the eight other men on the Authie-Cussy road, the conveyance of Canadian prisoners proceeded without further incident. From the site where it had been intercepted, the column marched another three-quarters of a mile to Cussy. Still occupied by elements of the 21st Panzer Division, the village, which was located close to the junction of three secondary roads, was well situated as a point of convergence for units escorting prisoners to the rear. An orchard on the southern edge of Cussy was chosen as the site where the prisoners would be assembled. As the Canadians were ushered into the orchard, they were counted by SS First Lieutenant Günther Doldi.[1] The Hitler Youth Division's senior intelligence officer, Doldi was responsible for ensuring that all prisoners were properly logged and interrogated.[2] Assisting Doldi was a section of Feldgendarmerie, or military police, whose duties included the transport of enemy prisoners progressively to the rear, from battalion to regiment and from regiment to division.[3]

Under normal circumstances, the Canadians, as prisoners of the 3rd Battalion of the 25th Panzer Grenadier Regiment, would have been escorted from Cussy to Milius's battalion headquarters. Since the 25th Regiment's HQ at the Abbaye d'Ardenne was closer,[4] it was decided to drop them off there. Early in the evening, when the last Canadian stragglers had been brought in, the prisoners were formed up and marched the half mile that separated the orchard from the abbey. On arrival at the abbey, the Canadians were escorted into its courtyard. There they were thoroughly searched. All paybooks and other papers were taken from them. Upon completion of the search, the prisoners were allowed to put their hands down and walk around. Smoking was permitted as well.[5]

After the horrific events of the late afternoon, the Germans had become remarkably solicitous in their concern for the Canadians. Whether this change of heart was the result of their transfer to the custody of Doldi and the Feldgendarmerie, or rather was due to the appearance on the scene of Kurt Meyer, is unclear. At his trial, Meyer claimed to have chatted with some of the prisoners, and further asserted that it was he who had given the order to allow the Canadians to put their hands down and smoke if they wanted to.[6] In his memoirs, Meyer painted an even more benevolent picture of the treatment that had been accorded to the Canadians, claiming that their wounded were given medical attention at the same time as his own.[7] This claim appears to have been pure fiction, although one of the Canadians who was at the abbey on 7 June did concede that the Germans had allowed them to put their wounded on wagons, so that they would not have to make the trek to the 12th SS's divisional headquarters on foot.[8] Whatever the case, the only untoward incident occurred when Lieutenant Thomas Windsor and his tank crew were escorted onto the abbey grounds. Pulled aside by an NCO of the Feldgendarmerie, Windsor, who was nursing a leg wound, was subjected to a barrage of questions. He replied that he was only obligated to give his name, rank, and military identification number. Angered by what he regarded as the officer's impertinence, the policeman slapped Windsor across the face.[9]

The Canadians' stay at the abbey was a brief one. According to Sergeant Dudka, they were only there about half an hour.[10] While the prisoners were milling about the abbey courtyard, pondering what destiny held in store for them, three or four members of the Feldgendarmerie came over and asked for volunteers. Corporal John Campbell of the North Novas tried to find out what they wanted, but was put off. Their suspicions aroused, none of the Canadians stepped forward. Trying their best to appear casual, the Germans moved about the now deathly silent courtyard, picking ten prisoners at random. Those selected were Corporal Joseph MacIntyre and Privates Ivan Crowe, Charles Doucette, and James Moss of the North Novas, as well as Lieutenant Windsor and Troopers James Bolt, George Gill, Thomas Henry, Roger Lockhead, and Harold Philip of the 27th Canadian Armoured Regiment.[11] Their 'volunteers' in tow, the military policemen departed.

Shortly afterward, at around 8:00 PM, Meyer ordered Doldi to move the Canadians out.[12] It was at this point that a couple of peculiar things happened. Contrary to procedure, the prisoners were not placed under guard by the Feldgendarmerie. Instead, five or six members of Meyer's regiment were detailed for that purpose.[13] Even more unusual, several military policemen were sent ahead to the town of Bretteville-sur-Odon, to prepare a POW holding centre there.[14] The town, which was located more than a mile southwest of the abbey, was a mile due west of Venoix, where the 12th SS had its provisional headquarters.[15] Why the Canadians were dispatched to Bretteville, some distance from where procedure dictated that they ought to have been sent, remains a mystery.

What is clear is that it could not have been done without orders from, or at least the approval of, the regimental commander (i.e., Meyer) or an officer delegated by him.[16]

While the mass of Canadian prisoners were being mustered for the march to Bretteville, a different and darker fate awaited eleven of their comrades. Left behind were the ten prisoners who had been selected by the Feldgendarmerie, along with the seriously wounded Hollis McKeil of B Company, North Nova Scotia Highlanders. At about the time that the column of Canadians was marching off, the ten segregated prisoners were escorted into a chateau, which was adjacent to the ancient abbey.[17] What happened next can only be pieced together from forensic evidence and hearsay witness testimony.[18]

As they entered the chateau, the Canadians probably were ordered to sit down. Soon the Germans' purpose would have become clear: they intended to interrogate the prisoners. Some time after 8:00 PM, a name would have been called out. Prompted to his feet by one of the guards, the first prisoner would have been escorted out to the chateau's garden. It would have been fairly dark out there, with the only light coming from inside the chateau. Tired and hungry, the Canadian would have been confronted by two or three military policemen, each of whom was armed with a machine pistol. To further intimidate the prisoner, one of the Germans might have been tapping his hand with his truncheon. Another would have been leaning on a large cudgel.[19]

The prisoner would have been brought before the policeman best able to speak English. Face to face with his quarry, the designated interrogator would have begun the questioning with something basic, like the location of the prisoner's battalion headquarters. Anxious, but not yet bereft of hope, the prisoner would have revealed only his name, his rank, and his military identification number. The interrogator would have tried again. Where was battalion headquarters? Again the prisoner would have replied with his name, rank, and ID number. It was perhaps at this point that the first blow was struck. Not wanting to give his captors the satisfaction, the prisoner probably would have held his tongue. The interrogator, his voice now hissing with anger, once more would have demanded the location of battalion headquarters. In a tone that signified both defiance and resignation, the prisoner likely would have answered – name, rank, and number.

When it became clear that the Canadian was not going to impart more than the information required under international law, the interrogator would have ordered him killed. From the physical evidence, it may be assumed that this was initially done by crushing blows to the head.[20] With the first interrogation abruptly and brutally ended, the process would have been repeated with the next prisoner. And the next. In all, six Canadians would be put through this horrendous ordeal before the Germans, having grown weary of bludgeoning their victims to death, would dispatch the last four, including Lieutenant Windsor, Privates Doucette and MacIntyre, and Trooper Lockhead, with single gunshot wounds to the head.[21] Then it would have been the turn of Private McKeil. Although experiencing a great deal of difficulty in breathing, McKeil, who probably was still conscious,[22] may well have been interrogated before he was killed. We will never know for sure.

The murders of McKeil and the ten other Canadians in the garden at the Abbaye d'Ardenne constituted one of the charges in the lengthy war crimes indictment filed against Kurt Meyer at the end of the war.[23] The evidence against Meyer on this charge, though circumstantial, was overwhelming. For one thing, as long as the prisoners were being held at the headquarters of the 25th Panzer Grenadier Regiment, which Meyer commanded, he was responsible for their security, interrogation, and timely conveyance to the rear.[24] That being the case, it was hard to see how the various breaches of military protocol that took place on the night of 7 June – including the sending of most of the Canadians on a hike to Bretteville-sur-Odon rather than the 12th SS's divisional headquarters, the improper deployment of the Feldgendarmerie, and the failure to interrogate the ten prisoners until after the remainder had been sent on – could have been planned or carried out without Meyer's orders or approval.[25] Second, Meyer admitted having been present at the abbey throughout the night of 7 June. Third, and most importantly, he admitted having seen the prisoners lining up in front of the chateau just prior to their departure for Bretteville.[26] This placed him at the scene at around the time when the ten Canadians and their Feldgendarmerie escorts would have been entering the chateau.[27] Finally, even if one accepted Meyer's claim that he had no prior knowledge of the 7 June killings, it seems inconceivable, given the proximity of his headquarters to the chateau's garden, that he would not have heard the shots that killed Lieutenant Windsor, Privates Doucette and MacIntyre, and Trooper Lockhead.

Based on the preponderance of the evidence, the military court that tried the case found Meyer guilty of complicity in the murder of the eleven Canadians.[28] Yet despite the compelling nature of the prosecution's case, the unrepentant Meyer persisted in maintaining that he had not known what had transpired on the night of 7 June. As the body count at his headquarters began to rise, however, Meyer would find it more difficult to use ignorance of the facts as a defence. On 8 June, seven additional Canadian prisoners were brought to the abbey, interrogated, and shot. This time, the evidence of Meyer's involvement would be unequivocal. Besides the testimony of forensic experts and the weight of circumstantial evidence, Canadian investigators held a trump card. There had been an eyewitness.

During the night of 7 June, while eleven Canadian prisoners were being massacred just yards away, Meyer pored over maps at a large table that had been set up for him inside the abbey.[29] As midnight approached, a situation report came in from divisional headquarters. It was not good news. Owing to the belated arrival at the front of Wilhelm Mohnke's 26th Panzer Grenadier Regiment, a gap of about four miles still existed between the 12th SS's two main infantry formations. Even more discouraging, the powerful Panzer Lehr Division, without whose armour there was virtually no chance of rolling back the Allies, still had not reached its staging area south of Bayeux.[30]

Anxious about the continued presence of large holes in the German line, Meyer decided that the time had come to swing his regiment to the west for a thrust along the Caen-Bayeux highway.[31] If successful, this attack would close the gap between his regiment and Mohnke's. It would also relieve the pressure on the 15th Reconnaissance Company, which had been spread extremely thin trying to protect the German left flank.

In order to brief his battalion and company commanders on the upcoming operation, Meyer summoned them to a midnight meeting. Unlike the previous morning's session, the mood this time was grim. Entrenched along a line that extended east-northeast from Franqueville,[32] his regiment's three battalions could not be redeployed to the west without weakening the already tenuous German front. Not sanguine about the attack's prospects, the assembled officers gave vent to their criticisms. SS Major Johann Waldmüller, the commander of the 1st Battalion, was particularly vocal in this regard.[33] In response to the sceptics, Meyer assured his commanders that the attack could be carried out without denuding the front. In place of the regimental infantry, he would put together a battlegroup comprised of the available tank companies from Max Wünsche's 12th Panzer Regiment and the motorized infantry of the 15th Reconnaissance Company.[34] Under cover of darkness on the night of 8 June, the battlegroup would advance in a wedge formation along a northwest axis that would take it through the village of Rots and on to its primary objective, Bretteville l'Orgueilleuse, which was in the hands of the Regina Rifles.[35] Their concerns allayed by the convincing arguments of their stalwart commander, Meyer's officers returned to their units.

In preparation for the attack, Meyer ordered elements of the 15th Reconnaissance Company to scout the area between Carpiquet Airfield and Rots.[36] Among the troops who mounted up on the morning of 8 June was SS Private Jan Jesionek. One of the five hundred or so ethnic Germans from occupied eastern Europe who had been pressed into service in the Hitler Youth Division, Jesionek was the driver of an armoured reconnaissance vehicle. In terms of combat experience, the teenager was still wet behind the ears. Though his column had encountered some strafing by Allied planes during the march to the front on D-Day, the upcoming reconnaissance operation would be his introduction to the ground war.[37]

Split into two groups, the 15th Company moved out from the Abbaye d'Ardenne around mid-morning on 8 June.[38] The group of which Jesionek was a part headed for Cussy, from where it was to turn left onto the road that led into Rots. As it approached the junction, the column of vehicles slowed down. Just then, the air reverberated with the sound of an explosion and the lead car skidded off the road. It had struck a land mine, seriously wounding its occupants. While the injured men were being evacuated to the nearest first-aid post, Jesionek was dispatched to headquarters with orders to replace the disabled vehicle. Disappointed, he headed back to the abbey on foot. His combat career was not off to an auspicious start. The beleaguered conscript could not have known it at the time, but his day was only going to get worse.

When Jesionek returned to the Abbaye d'Ardenne, it was with the intention of finding an alternative means of transportation and rejoining the patrol. He eventually was able to requisition a motorcycle, but a quick examination revealed that it was not roadworthy. For the time being, therefore, Jesionek was stranded. During the noon hour, while completing repairs on the bike, he noticed two SS troopers who were escorting seven Canadian prisoners onto the abbey grounds. The prisoners were Privates Walter Doherty, Reg Keeping, Hugh MacDonald, George McNaughton, George Millar, Thomas Mont, and Raymond Moore, all of them North Nova Scotia Highlanders.[39] Involved in the previous day's fighting around Authie and Buron, they had apparently managed to evade capture for several hours.

Jesionek watched as the Canadians were marched into a stall that adjoined the abbey. Once the prisoners had been secured, one of the two escorts approached the conscript and asked where he might find the regimental commander. Eager to please, Jesionek took the trooper to the abbey entrance, where Meyer was standing with several other officers.[40] When the trooper reported that he had brought back seven prisoners, Meyer, who was visibly angered, retorted: 'What should we do with these prisoners; they only eat up our rations?' After this outburst, the volatile commander turned to one of the officers and spoke to him, but did so in such low tones that Jesionek could not make out what he was saying. Then, in a voice loud enough for all to hear, Meyer made the following announcement. 'In the future,' he declared, 'no more prisoners are to be taken!'[41]

We cannot be certain of what Meyer whispered to his unidentified subordinate. Based on the officer's subsequent actions, however, we can hazard a good guess. After Meyer went back inside the abbey, the man to whom he had spoken posted one of the two original escorts at the archway entrance to the garden and stationed an NCO inside, to the right. Then he returned with the other escort to the stall where the seven prisoners were being held.

With the dispersal of the crowd from the front of the abbey, Jesionek started to return to his motorcycle. Realizing that his hands were covered with grease, he tried to wash at the water pump near the garden's entrance. Shooed away by the sentry, he walked over to a wash basin that was located across from the stall. From there he could see the man to whom Meyer had spoken. The officer was standing among the seven Canadian prisoners, conducting interrogations. Jesionek noted with interest that any time a prisoner's answer displeased him, the officer would laugh contemptuously. When one of the Canadians came to tears, he actually sneered. Evidently getting nowhere, the officer abruptly terminated the questioning, confiscated the prisoners' paybooks and papers, and left.

Something evil was afoot. Jesionek could feel it. After a few more minutes, his worst fears would be realized. A name was called out. At this prompt, the prisoner who had been summoned had to walk from the stall up to the passageway that led into the garden. There the guard who had been posted at the entrance directed him inside, to the left. As soon as the prisoner turned, the NCO who was standing inside raised his machine pistol and fired into the back of his victim's head.

This cold-blooded and cruel procedure was repeated for each of the seven Canadians. The whole nasty business took at least ten minutes to complete. Once or twice, when the first shot was not fatal, a cry, then more shots, could be heard. When it was all over, the executioner came out of the garden and nonchalantly reloaded his gun.

The departure of the NCO and the sentry allowed Jesionek and three of his fellow drivers, all ethnic German conscripts, to take a look. The sight that greeted them in the garden was appalling. Lying in a heap, their bodies framed by large and spreading pools of blood, were the seven prisoners. Nearby was a British ration canister that had been dropped into the area by parachute. One of Jesionek's buddies retrieved its contents. In the 12th SS, evidently, a full belly was a more valued commodity than common decency.

From Jesionek's postwar testimony, it is clear that in the interval between their interrogation and their execution, the Canadians realized exactly what was going to happen to them. When his time came, each prisoner shook hands with his comrades, clasping them firmly, letting go only reluctantly, so as to gain a few more precious seconds of life. Each walked to the garden slowly and proudly, holding his head high. There were no pleas for mercy, no attempts to escape. There was only a gritty and dignified resolve, a desire to do their unit and their country proud to the very end. That they did.

The shooting of the seven Canadians at the Abbaye d'Ardenne during the noon hour on 8 June was the culmination of a period of unspeakable terror and criminality. Since late afternoon the previous day, fifty-five Canadian prisoners of war had been done away with in the most cruel and vile manner by elements of the 12th SS Panzer Division 'Hitler Youth.' Many of the murders had been committed after the initial clash of arms between the 12th SS and the 3rd Canadian Infantry Division, and so might be understood, though not condoned, as a product of the unchecked emotions of young and inexperienced troops. No such mitigation can be contemplated for the massacre witnessed by Jesionek, however. In contrast with the Milius murders, the Abbaye d'Ardenne killings were cold, calculated, and systematic. They were the revelation of a terrible secret, something that even the perpetrators may have thought was buried forever under the snowswept plains of Russia. They were Leibstandarte methods rearing their ugly head all over again. And they were only the beginning. Over the next few days, Meyer's fellow commanders, as if by intuition or instinct, would zealously follow his example. In the process, they ensured that the 12th SS would shed the nickname 'Baby Division' for one far more appropriate and enduring. As a result of its crimes, the 12th SS would come to be known and feared, by friend and foe alike, as the 'Murder Division.'[42]

# 7
# The Battle of Putot-en-Bessin

During the first twenty-four hours or so after the Allied landings in Normandy, only Kurt Meyer's 25th Panzer Grenadier Regiment, supported by a battalion of armour, stood as an impediment to the expansion of the British–Canadian bridgehead. Meyer's troops would not have to hold the line alone for long. While the 25th Regiment was attacking Authie and Buron, some five and a half miles to the west elements of the Hitler Youth Division's 12th Reconnaissance Battalion were moving up to the front. Led by fanatical, battle-hardened officers and lavishly equipped with armoured personnel carriers,[1] the arrival of this formidable unit was a welcome sight for the beleaguered German defenders in Normandy. By nightfall on 7 June, the battalion had established strongpoints along a line that extended northward for almost three miles from La Caude Rue (just northwest of the village of Fontenay-le-Pesnel) through Hill 103 and Pavie, up to Audrieu. In the process, it relieved the growing pressure on the German left flank.[2]

The 12th Reconnaissance Battalion was commanded by SS Major Gerhard Bremer. Tall and burly, Bremer was renowned in Waffen-SS circles, both for his pugnacious attitude and his reckless approach to combat. A confirmed Nazi who had joined the SS at nineteen years of age, he began his military career as a member of the 'Germania' Regiment. After rising through Germania's ranks during the 1930s, Bremer was transferred to the Leibstandarte on the eve of the outbreak of the war. First as a platoon leader and later as a company commander, he distinguished himself in the Leibstandarte's victorious campaigns in Poland, France, and the Balkans. Awarded the Iron Cross First Class and Second Class for his bravery in Poland and in western Europe, Bremer became one of the Leibstandarte's earliest recipients of the coveted Knight's Cross of the Iron Cross, garnering the prize for his outstanding leadership during the initial phase of the campaign in Russia. Not surprisingly, in view of his stellar war record and Nazi credentials, he would prove to be a tenacious opponent in Normandy.[3]

Bremer's timely appearance meant that the flanks of the Hitler Youth Division were now secured. Things were still tenuous in the centre, however. Indeed, it was not until early evening on 7 June that the division's 26th Panzer Grenadier Regiment, after a long and inexplicable delay,[4] at last began arriving at the invasion front. From Grainville-sur-Odon, through which Meyer's 25th Regiment had passed the day before, the 26th Regiment plodded northward, thereby closing the dangerous gap in the German line. The regiment's 1st Battalion, which was commanded by SS Major Bernhard Krause, a highly decorated former member of Leibstandarte, advanced from Grainville due north to the village of Cheux, where it set up headquarters. The 2nd Battalion, which was headed by SS Major Bernhard Siebken, one of the Leibstandarte's charter members, moved past Cheux northward all the way to the village of Le Mesnil-Patry. Under the quiet but effective leadership of SS Major Erich Olboeter, yet another highly decorated Leibstandarte veteran, the 3rd Battalion took up positions around Cristot, on the left flank of the regimental front.[5]

While its battalions were deploying to the front, the headquarters company of the 26th Regiment was setting up a command post near a cluster of houses known as Le Haut du Bosq, which was located in a wooded area between Grainville and Cheux.[6] Supervising the activity was SS Lieutenant Colonel Wilhelm Mohnke, the regiment's commanding officer. Like his subordinate Siebken, Mohnke had the dubious distinction of having been one of the original members of the Leibstandarte. An enthusiastic Nazi who had joined the SS early on, Mohnke spent the prewar years as a company commander in the Leibstandarte. Awarded the Iron Cross First and Second Class for the leadership and bravery he demonstrated in the Leibstandarte's baptism of fire in Poland, Mohnke also served with distinction during the following year's campaign in the west, taking over from his wounded battalion commander at a critical juncture in the fighting. Promoted to the rank of SS Major, he was put in charge of the Leibstandarte battlegroup that spearheaded the Germans' spring 1941 campaign in the Balkans. On the first day of the fighting in Yugoslavia, Mohnke sustained massive wounds that necessitated the amputation of his right foot. Though severe enough to keep him off the eastern front, the injury did not end his military career. Through sheer force of will, Mohnke endured months of painful convalescence and rehabilitation, and eventually was able to return to active duty as commander of the Leibstandarte's reserve battalion. He was transferred to the newly formed Hitler Youth Division in September 1943.

Acknowledged as a skilful and courageous soldier, Mohnke nonetheless was a man about whom even fellow officers had nothing good to say. His lack of popularity seems to have stemmed from his dour manner and violent temper. It has been suggested that Mohnke's turbulent personality really only manifested itself after he became addicted to morphine, which had been administered to him on a daily basis during his post-amputation convalescence.[7] Certainly an addiction of this kind might exacerbate an already explosive temper, particularly under battlefield conditions, where access to the narcotic on which he was dependent would be inconsistent at best. Yet there is evidence that Mohnke was prey to ungovernable rages long before his wounding in the Balkans. After going years without garnering a promotion, a frustrated Mohnke finally cracked in August 1939, allowing a drunken argument with one of his NCOs to degenerate into fisticuffs. Only the outbreak of war a few weeks later and the need for experienced officers at the front spared him the embarrassment of a disciplinary hearing and almost certain expulsion from the SS.

Perhaps the clearest indication of Mohnke's instability came less than a year after this incident, during the fighting that attended the evacuation of the BEF from Dunkirk. Under intense pressure following his sudden and unexpected accession to the post of battalion commander, Mohnke lost control, when, on the afternoon of 28 May 1940, a column of British prisoners was marched up to his headquarters near the French town of Wormhoudt. Raving like a madman, he ordered the escorts to turn the prisoners around, herd them into an adjacent field, and shoot them en masse. Over the next few harrowing hours, more than a hundred POWs were sacrificed on the altar of one man's uncontrollable wrath. Four years later, in a scene eerily reminiscent of Wormhoudt, Mohnke would intercept a column of Canadian prisoners in Normandy, with the same devastating consequences.[8]

Facing Bremer's and Mohnke's troops across the front line were forward elements of the (British) 50th Division and the 7th Canadian Infantry Brigade. On the left flank of the 12th SS, between the towns of St Ducy-Marguerite and Brouay, the (British) 69th Infantry and 8th Armoured Brigades were marshalling for an assault through Audrieu southward to the high ground near Villers-Bocage. In the centre, from Putot-en-Bessin in the west to Norrey-en-Bessin in the east, the Royal Winnipeg Rifles and Regina Rifles were completing their deployment. The Winnipegs' A and C Companies, reinforced by men from the Queen's Own Rifles of Canada, were positioned in front of Putot, just north of the Caen-Bayeux railway line. The regiment's B Company, which also included a large contingent of reinforcements, occupied an orchard in the north end of Putot, while D Company was in reserve. In the Regina Rifles' sector, B and C Companies held positions to the east and the north of Norrey, while A Company was in Bretteville l'Orgueilleuse and D Company in La Villeneuve.[9]

Supporting the Winnipegs and the Reginas were the 94th Battery of the 3rd

Canadian Anti-Tank Regiment as well as three machine-gun platoons from the Cameron Highlanders of Ottawa. The anti-tank men were distributed to positions from Putot in the west to Bretteville in the east, while the Camerons' 3, 13, and 4 Platoons were placed to give covering fire to the Winnipegs' A and C Companies and the Reginas' D Company respectively. Acting as right-flank guard and liaison with the British was the Winnipegs' 7 Platoon, which was positioned between Brouay and Putot, just north of the Caen-Bayeux railway line.[10]

In keeping with the Germans' desperate strategy of striking at the Allied bridgehead as soon their forces had arrived at the front, Mohnke ordered his three battalions to launch attacks on Brouay, Putot, and Norrey before dawn. His intention was to wrest control of the Caen-Bayeux railway line back from the Canadians, whose continued hold over this important transportation link would have enabled them to choke off the flow of reinforcements and supplies to the beleaguered German forces farther west.[11] In preparation for the attack, each of Mohnke's battalions undertook patrols during the night of 7–8 June. Reconnaissance in force was carried out in all sectors, particularly around Putot and Norrey, where run-ins with Canadian patrols led to some fairly intense firefights.[12] In one such engagement, a patrol from Siebken's 2nd Battalion came upon a mine-laying party of Winnipegs and Royal Canadian Engineers in a field between Putot and the village of Les Saullets. The Germans opened fire and the Canadians, who had not been given adequate covering support, were forced to withdraw. In the ensuing confusion, sappers John Ionel and George Benner, along with Private Allan Owens of the Winnipegs, were cut off from the rest of the party. Surviving by drinking water from streams and taking shelter in abandoned barns or farmhouses, the three Canadians would wander around no man's land for the next seventy-two hours before finally being caught by Mohnke's grenadiers.[13]

Mohnke's regiment began its attack early on the morning of 8 June. Just after 2:00 AM, the regiment's 1st Battalion, spearheaded by the 3rd Company, began to move out from its positions north of Cheux. The advance guard quickly overran a small covering force of Reginas at St Manvieu and proceeded northward to the 3rd Company's next objective, Norrey-en-Bessin. But as soon as they crossed the Mue River, the attackers were greeted by heavy mortar fire, probably from the Reginas' B Company, and their advance quickly bogged down. The 1st Company had better luck, pushing all the way to La Villeneuve, where it forced the Reginas' D Company to withdraw. The 2nd Company also made a significant penetration, advancing beyond Norrey to where the Caen-Bayeux railway line passed northwest of the town. Owing to the stout resistance offered by the Reginas' C Company, however, this attempt to flank Norrey was repulsed, and the town remained in Canadian hands. All in all, the attack of the 1st Battalion did not achieve the results Mohnke had hoped for, although it was sufficiently worrisome to necessitate the redeployment to the Mue River valley of one squadron of tanks from the front of the 9th Canadian Infantry Brigade.[14]

In contrast with the attack of the 1st Battalion, those of Mohnke's 2nd and 3rd Battalions were pressed with considerable vigour. Not surprisingly, then, they met with a greater measure of success. Between 5:00 and 5:30 AM, advance elements of the 2nd Battalion's 5th Company, supported by armoured personnel carriers and one refitted Mark III tank from the 3rd Battalion,[15] began to move out from their positions north of Les Saullets. As this force approached the rail- way bridge located just to the southeast of Putot, it ran into the Winnipegs' 8 Platoon and 3 Platoon of the Cameron Highlanders. Initially, the battle went well for the Canadians. Entrenched behind the Caen-Bayeux railway line, the Winnipegs and Camerons hosed the field with small-arms fire. Their murderous fusillade, coupled with artillery and anti-tank support, was enough to stop the German advance in its tracks. Indeed, by 6:35 AM, the Winnipegs were able to report that they had beaten off the attack.[16]

Unfortunately, the success at the railway bridge was shortlived. Even as 8 Platoon was turning back the 5th Company, the other Winnipeg positions were being subjected to attacks by the rest of Mohnke's 2nd Battalion. Directly south of and to the west of Putot, C Company and a platoon of A Company bore the brunt of violent frontal assaults by the 6th and 7th Companies. At first, these too were repelled. Like their counterparts at Authie, however, Mohnke's troops were openly disdainful of the heavy Canadian fire and just kept on coming, moving forward recklessly, arrogantly, inexorably. By late morning, they were being supported by a battery of self-propelled artillery, which pummelled the Winnipegs' positions under the weight of a thundering barrage. Still more diffi- culties ensued when the Germans successfully infiltrated a number of small par- ties into Putot itself. From strongholds in private homes and behind ruined buildings, the SS troops sniped at and rained down mortar shells on the Cana- dian positions, inflicting many casualties and wreaking havoc with the Win- nipegs' attempts to get more ammunition to their beleaguered forward units. Things got so bad that even the Winnipegs' headquarters was under siege for part of the day.[17]

Notwithstanding their increasingly desperate situation, the Canadians fought on doggedly. Ignoring breakthroughs on their flanks, small groups of Win- nipegs and Camerons held their ground, pouring fire into the swarming enemy, blunting their advance, and buying time for the help that did not come until it was too late. By 1:30 in the afternoon, the gallant defenders of Putot were com- pletely surrounded. Soon after, communications with them were lost. Isolated from one another, most of their automatic weapons knocked out, the Winnipegs made a desperate attempt to withdraw under cover of smoke. Only a few men got back to battalion headquarters. As for the Camerons, a section from 13 Platoon and several men from 3 Platoon managed to fight their way to safety. The rest of the Canadians were in imminent danger of capture.[18]

Mohnke's 3rd Battalion was the last to go into action on the morning of 8 June. Spearheaded by the 11th Company, the battalion launched its attack at 8:00 AM. As they approached the rail line between Putot and Brouay, the SS troops were met by enfilade fire from the Winnipegs' 7 Platoon. Unable to move forward, the 11th Company sheered off to the left, reaching the outskirts of Brouay by mid-morning. They soon were joined in the deserted village by the 10th Company, which had advanced unopposed in the centre of the battalion sector. The 9th Company, which was acting as the left-flank guard, moved from Cristot in a northwesterly direction toward Audrieu, where it established contact with patrols of Bremer's reconnaissance battalion.[19]

By early afternoon on 8 June, Mohnke's regiment had attained most of its objectives. Brouay, Putot, and La Villeneuve were in German hands, and Norrey, though still holding out, was almost completely cut off. Putot would be retaken by the Canadians later in the day.[20] But the cost of the fighting in and around the village had been high. The Royal Winnipeg Rifles alone lost 256 men killed, wounded, or captured. Within a matter of hours, three companies had been effectively wiped out. Reeling from its defeat, what was left of the regiment's 1st Battalion was withdrawn to Secqueville-en-Bessin early the next morning.[21]

At least 150 of the casualties reported by the Winnipegs on 8 June were in fact prisoners. The Germans captured the bulk of this POW contingent when the 7th Company of Mohnke's 2nd Battalion surrounded the Winnipegs' B Company in its orchard stronghold north of Putot. A few of the prisoners were from the Winnipegs' C Company, but most of the remainder were members of A Company who had tried to regroup a few hundred yards east of the railway bridge at Putot, but who, with few exceptions, found their escape cut off by the 2nd Battalion's 6th Company. Even those who got away before the vice closed around Putot, including a number of men from 9 Platoon, soon fell into the hands of Mohnke's 3rd Battalion. So did a few men from 7 Platoon, who were captured in the fighting at Brouay.[22]

Shortly after their capture, the more than a hundred Canadians who had been taken prisoner at Putot were turned over to the Feldgendarmerie for conveyance to the rear.[23] Their safe arrival at Mohnke's regimental command post in Le Haut du Bosq later that afternoon was confirmed by a member of the headquarters company there.[24] By contrast, the forty remaining prisoners were not sent back right away, but rather were escorted to the farm of Mme Lojelen in Putot. Although they were crammed into a stable, there was no repeat of the abominable thuggery that had been visited upon Canadian prisoners by Milius's battalion the previous day. Indeed, their captors appeared well versed in the international conventions governing the treatment of POWs. After conveying the Canadians to 2nd Battalion headquarters, which was located on the farm of George Moulin in Le Mesnil-Patry, the SS troops dispensed first aid and water to the wounded. Then they placed the prisoners in Moulin's barn.[25] Whatever apprehensions the Canadians may have had, these began to dissipate as they awaited the return of the Feldgendarmerie escort. The Germans would play by the rules. Or so it seemed.

# 8

# The Bremer Murders

While more than three dozen of the Canadians who had been captured in and around Putot were cooling their heels at the Moulin farm, two miles to the west a group of twenty-four Canadian and two British prisoners were being marched in the direction of the village of Pavie, near where Gerhard Bremer's 12th Reconnaissance Battalion had its headquarters. The Canadians included Major Frederick Hodge, the commander of the Royal Winnipeg Rifles' A Company, thirteen members of A Company's 9 Platoon, two of whom – George and Frank Meakin from Birnie, Manitoba – were brothers, eight men from A Company's 7 and 8 Platoons, and two reinforcements from the Queen's Own Rifles.[1] Hodge and the men from 8 and 9 Platoons had broken out of the encirclement of Putot, only to be captured while trying to cross a railway bridge west of the beleaguered village. The men from 7 Platoon and the two British soldiers had been taken prisoner during the fighting at Brouay.[2]

As they marched two abreast down the road to Pavie, the twenty-six prisoners were under escort by troops of the 3rd Battalion of Wilhelm Mohnke's regiment. How and why they ended up in the custody of Bremer's battalion is something of a mystery. The respective headquarters of the 3rd Battalion and Bremer's unit were roughly equidistant from the place where the prisoners had been rounded up. Both headquarters, moreover, were accessible by road. In view of the fact that the prisoners are known to have been held for a while at a junction just east of Pavie,[3] it is possible that the column was heading for 3rd Battalion headquarters at Cristot when it ran into a patrol dispatched by Bremer. It is further possible, although it certainly would have been unusual, that Bremer's men either offered or demanded to take custody of the prisoners and escort them to their own headquarters. Whatever the case, the twenty-four Canadian and two British soldiers never got to Cristot, but rather were marched on to Pavie. This seemingly innocuous turn of events sealed the prisoners' fate.

At the crossroads east of Pavie, the column was ordered to halt. The first thing Bremer's men did was to instruct the prisoners to remove their helmets. Then, while they kept their hands clasped behind their heads, each prisoner was subjected to a thorough, sometimes rough, search. All papers and personal effects were confiscated. Identification documents were taken by the NCO in charge, while photographs, money, and other personal items were tossed willy-nilly to the ground, although the Germans did make a point of pocketing ciga-rettes.[4] At the conclusion of the search, the prisoners, their hands still up, were marched another few hundred yards to the rear of a chateau. It was around 2:00 in the afternoon.

Compared with the horrors of combat, the scene that greeted the prisoners on the grounds of the chateau must have seemed positively idyllic. Nestled among tall, leafy trees and other greenery, the chateau, named Château d'Audrieu, after the neighbouring village, recalled simpler, gentler times. With its lush garden, servants' quarters, and dense adjacent woods, the chateau could have been the estate of eighteenth-century French nobility. So lovely were the surroundings, in fact, that after the war a shrewd entrepreneur bought the site, restored it, and converted the chateau into a luxury hotel and restaurant. The tourists who sit by the pool today cannot imagine the scene of carnage that took place there on the afternoon of 8 June 1944.[5]

While the prisoners were being escorted onto the grounds of the chateau, Bremer and SS Captain Gerd von Reitzenstein, the commander of the head-quarters company, were poring over maps, planning operations. They had arrived at the chateau around noon. A quick tour of the site had convinced them that it was the ideal place to set up battalion headquarters. Located near a cross-roads, the chateau had the advantage of being enveloped by foliage, which could provide at least some cover against sighting by Allied aircraft. Without much ado, Bremer had given the order; this would be the spot. While a trooper went to procure food from the kitchen, the headquarters company established a command post behind the chateau, at the edge of an open grassy space, under a giant, low-hanging sycamore tree.[6]

It was in the shade of the sycamore where Bremer and Reitzenstein came face to face with their quarry. Slated for interrogation, the prisoners were brought to the command post in small batches. The first to be called forward were Major Hodge and Lance Corporal Austin Fuller of the Winnipegs and Pri-vate Frederick Smith of the Queen's Own Rifles. Bremer, who spoke English fluently,[7] did most of the questioning.

According to one eyewitness, the interrogations went on for a good fifteen minutes.[8] We do not know what information, if any, Bremer was able to elicit from the three Canadians. It is hard to imagine that Major Hodge would have revealed more than his name, rank, and military identification number. During a training exercise in February 1942, this brave soldier had been wounded while saving one of his men from the explosion of an errantly thrown grenade.[9] Anyone that cool in the face of danger would not have been easily intimidated, even when confronted by the burly and menacing Bremer. Indeed, Bremer probably had no more success with Fuller and Smith. Just prior to capture, the morale of A Company was reported to have been 'very high.'[10] It seems most unlikely that in the space of less than two hours unit cohesion could have broken down to the point where the men of A Company would have willingly revealed information to their captors.

After getting nowhere with Hodge, Fuller, and Smith, a frustrated and angry Bremer reverted to the method of dealing with enemy prisoners with which he had become familiar as a member of the Leibstandarte – he ordered them killed. At around 2:15 PM, the battalion commander beckoned SS First Lieutenant Willi-Peter Hansmann, SS Technical Sergeant Leopold Stun, and two motorcycle dispatch riders. After a brief conference, Hansmann strode along the path that led from the command post to the edge of the woods, where he stopped and waited. Meanwhile, the Canadians, who still had not been permitted to lower their hands, were instructed to get into single file. Flanked by the two SS troopers, with Stun bringing up the rear, Hodge, Fuller, and Smith were then ordered to move out to where Hansmann was standing.[11]

As the scenario unfolded, it bore all the earmarks of a classic execution. The Canadians must have realized what was in store for them, because without exception the eyewitnesses to their lonely death march were struck by the sad and resigned expressions that darkened their young faces. Nevertheless, there were no desperate attempts to escape, nor any pleas for mercy. On the contrary, Hodge, Fuller, and Smith, in the manner of the North Novas at the Abbaye d'Ardenne, would meet their end with courage and dignity. As they approached the edge of the woods, one of the doomed men did falter momentarily, but he resumed the march when Sergeant Stun, who had carried out this kind of duty before and who was obviously enjoying himself,[12] kicked him from behind. Jolted back to reality, the prisoner moved up directly behind his comrades, whereupon Hansmann directed the entire party onto a path that led to a cluster of shrubs and small trees.

As they got to the patch of undergrowth, Stun ordered the Canadians to halt. Next the NCO had his intended victims turn around, so that they would face away from the firing squad. Then, at his command, the two SS troopers levelled their rifles, aimed, and fired. Stun joined in with his machine pistol. Wounded in the shoulder, Major Hodge fell forward, only to be finished off by several shots to the head. Fuller and Smith, on the other hand, appear to have swivelled around just as the Germans opened up, thereby defiantly confronting their murderers as they were shot.[13]

While the grounds of the chateau were still reverberating with the executioners' salvo, a second batch of prisoners was being escorted to the battalion command post. Apprehensively, Privates David Gold, James McIntosh, and William Thomas of the Royal Winnipeg Rifles gathered around Bremer in the shade of the sycamore tree. A stretcher bearer who was wearing a Red Cross armband, Gold was entitled to special treatment as a non-combatant.[14] Having just ordered the murder of three POWs, Bremer, of course, was not likely to begin observing the niceties of international law. Instead, as he had done with Hodge, Fuller, and Smith, he resorted to direct interrogation. Once more he ran up against a stone wall of stubborn resistance. His patience wearing thin, the seething commander only went through the motions of questioning the prisoners. Indeed, as soon as he spotted Stun and his party returning from the woods, Bremer terminated the interrogation session. After exchanging a few words with his trusted henchman, he turned the prisoners over to him, with the same orders as before. At around 2:30 PM, Gold, McIntosh, and Thomas were seen being escorted across the chateau grounds and into the woods.[15]

Once in the thicket, the prisoners were taken along a different path than the one where the martyred Hodge, Fuller, and Smith lay. They walked until they came to a clearing, whereupon Stun ordered the party to halt. Not wanting a repeat of the defiant display put on by Fuller and Smith, this time the NCO took no chances. First, he ordered the intended victims to lie on their stomachs. Next, apparently to ensure 'clean' kills, he instructed the Canadians to prop up their heads by resting on their elbows. Then each trooper stood directly above his assigned target. On Stun's command, they fired from almost point-blank range. Gold, McIntosh, and Thomas died instantly from massive head wounds.[16] After a short while, the shooters emerged from the woods. Their appetites not the least bit diminished by their detestable and disgusting duty, Stun and his men stopped for food and cider at the chateau kitchen.[17]

For all the entertainment value that he and his staff were deriving from the murderous spectacle, it must have become apparent to Bremer that this was a very inefficient way to dispose of prisoners. To interrogate and then to kill them three at a time could take until evening. The fluid situation at the front simply did not allow for such a protracted procedure. As it happened, shortly after the shooting of Gold, McIntosh, and Thomas, word came in that British tanks were massing on the battalion's left flank.[18] That helped the commander to make up his mind. He had to attend to his defences. The prisoners could wait. On Bremer's orders, the remaining eighteen Canadians and two British, who were sitting around at the rear of the chateau, were brought to an adjacent orchard, where they were kept under heavy guard. To the relief of the prisoners, who must have heard the shots of Stun's execution party, they had been granted a reprieve. It would be only temporary.

Under Bremer's reckless but effective leadership, the 12th Reconnaissance Battalion repulsed a frontal attack on the village of Audrieu by advance elements of a British armoured brigade. Although a second British force, which was deployed further west, succeeded in flanking the village and taking the strategically important Hill 103, by 4:00 PM the reconnaissance troops had once more stabilized the front.[19] Bremer returned to his command post shortly thereafter. Probably not by coincidence, the massacre of prisoners resumed upon his arrival.

Between 4:30 and 5:00 in the afternoon, Leon Leseigneur, a local farmer, and Eugene Buchart, one of his farm hands, were walking along a dirt road past the hen house of the Château d'Audrieu. Gazing to the right, they noticed thirteen unarmed Canadian soldiers standing in the chateau's orchard. All were members of 9 Platoon of the Winnipegs' A Company. They were Mrs Jennie Meakin's boys, George and Frank, both of whom were corporals, as well as Privates William Adams, Emmanuel Bishoff, Lawrence Chartrand, Sidney Cresswell, Anthony Fagnan, Robert Harper, Hervé Labrecque, John Lychowich, Robert Mutch, Henry Rodgers, and Steve Slywchuk. The prisoners were being guarded by a detachment of SS troopers. Buchart noted with interest that there were several officers among the guard.[20]

About forty yards past the hen house, Buchart and his employer headed into the pasture where the Leseigneur farm was situated. Just as they turned off the dirt road, the two men heard heavy bursts of gunfire. Buchart and Leseigneur instantly realized what this meant, but, after four years of brutal German occupation, they knew better than to investigate. Instead, the two men hurried back to the farm and tried to keep a low profile. A few minutes later, an SS officer and two troopers came by in order to appropriate Leseigneur's ladder. Forcing Buchart to carry the ladder for them, the Germans escorted him back towards their headquarters. As he passed the hen house and glanced left at the orchard, his worst fears were confirmed. The prisoners he had seen earlier were gone.[21]

We now know that the volleys heard by Buchart and Leseigneur were the reports of the guns of the guard detachment in the orchard. Though no one outside the orchard witnessed the actual massacre, it is possible to reconstruct the final moments of the thirteen Winnipegs from what Buchart and Leseigneur saw and heard, as well as from the forensic evidence. Confined to the orchard by Bremer, the men of 9 Platoon probably milled about, exchanging small talk, bucking up each other's spirits. At around 4:30 PM, the guard detail was joined by several officers, with Bremer perhaps among them. A palpable tension would have filled the orchard. On orders from the most senior German officer (Bremer or a subordinate), the prisoners were lined up in a row. Facing them was a rough-and-ready firing squad, consisting of SS troopers with rifles, NCOs with machine pistols, and officers with sidearms.[22]

At the command to fire, the executioners opened up with a murderous fusillade. All of the Canadians went down with the first volley, although some clearly were not killed outright. Hearing the moans of Privates Bishoff, Labrecque, and Mutch, whose wounds were not fatal, an officer walked over to where they lay and finished them off with shots to the head. As he moved down the line of stricken men, kicking each of them to see if he showed signs of life, the officer discovered that Lance Corporal Meakin and Private Slywchuk had not been hit at all. Slywchuk had apparently timed his dive perfectly, whereas Frank Meakin had been saved when George, in a last act of brotherly love, had stepped in front of him, taking a burst of machine-pistol fire across the chest. There would be no more reprieves, however. As Meakin lay waiting next to his lifeless brother, he was given the *coup de grâce*. Then the officer emptied his pistol into Slywchuk's head.[23] As the echo of the last shots faded, an eerie silence descended over the orchard.

With the killing of the men from 9 Platoon, the toll of prisoners murdered at Bremer's headquarters had reached nineteen. Shortly afterward, Allied ground and naval artillery began to pound the area around Audrieu in advance of a major British armoured thrust along the western part of (British) 2nd Army's front. Owing to the intensity of the bombardment and the pressure being exerted by the enemy's tanks, Bremer's battalion had to pull back under cover of darkness to positions south of Cristot. They would not return to the chateau until the following evening.[24] But what of the five Canadian and two British POWs unaccounted for? The missing men included Lance Corporal William Poho and Privates Louis Chartrand, Kenneth Lawrence, and Frank Ostir of the Royal Winnipeg Rifles, Private Francis Harrison of the Queen's Own Rifles of Canada, as well as Privates E. Hayton of the Durham Light Infantry and W. Barlow of the 50th Northumbrian Division. Their fate was determined about three weeks later, when British troops found their bodies in the woods adjacent to the chateau, not far from where the first two groups of Canadian prisoners had been murdered.

We do not know when the last seven were killed. But we do know how. On the basis of the post-mortems – which revealed that the bodies had sustained small-calibre bullet wounds to the head, face, and chest at close range and were at the same stage of decomposition as those of the six other men found in the woods – a military court of inquiry concluded that they had probably been killed on 8 June in a manner consistent with the other murders.[25]

In writing about such horrific events, historians tend to suspend moral judgment, leaving the interpretation of their deeper meaning to theologians or philosophers. The cornerstone of the historian's craft, such detachment is necessary if the past is to be reported accurately and in proper context. Yet there comes a point in every narrative when mere reporting is not enough, when understanding is lost in a sea of facts, when human lives are reduced to so many digits. We may well have reached this point in the story of the murder of Canadian prisoners of war in Normandy. At the risk of violating the tenets of scholarship, then, it would seem appropriate to pause in order to make a brief digression into the realm of editorial comment. This is not done in order to raise the emotional stakes, but rather to personalize and universalize in some meaningful way what happened at the Château d'Audrieu and at a dozen other crimes scenes in the countryside of northern France.

Of all the murders of Canadian prisoners perpetrated by the 12th SS Panzer Division 'Hitler Youth,' surely none is more poignant or as haunting as that of Private Francis Harrison. As was noted in an earlier chapter, army psychiatrists had evaluated Harrison as being 'of insufficient intelligence to complete basic training.' Indeed, his impairment was severe enough to prompt the army to consider his discharge.[26] For reasons unknown, Canadian military authorities changed their minds. Harrison stayed on, and, with the men of his company looking out for him, he got through basic and became a good soldier. A member of the contingent of Queen's Own Rifles that on the evening of D-Day was sent to bolster the depleted Winnipegs, Harrison fought at Brouay, where he was taken prisoner. Escorted to a forward German headquarters along with twenty-five other POWs, he shared their tragic fate.

It may be wrong to single out one prisoner because of his impairment. After all, every murder perpetrated by the 12th SS was a Canadian tragedy, every victim a Canadian hero. Still, it is hard to shake the image of what Harrison's final moments must have been like. In reviewing the investigative materials relating to the Audrieu killings, one cannot help but wonder to what extent Harrison had been aware of what was about to happen in the minutes before Bremer's thugs shot him down. Certainly he would have seen Private Fred Smith, a fellow member of the Queen's Own Rifles and as such the only familiar face in the crowd of prisoners, being led away. Then he would have heard the shots and the nervous whispers that followed. Had he understood? And if he had not, did that make his remaining moments any easier? Standing amidst a throng of strangers, how did Harrison get along? Did anyone talk to him, explain things to him, calm his fears?

As no one who was with Private Harrison on 8 June survived to tell his story, these questions afford no definitive answers, only speculation. Nevertheless, a clue may have been provided by the British troops who discovered his body. Among the items found nearby was a letter from home and a photograph of him and his parents back in Owen Sound.[27] The Germans had obviously missed these items during the search they conducted outside Pavie. Whatever else was going through his mind on the afternoon of 8 June, it is at least possible that Harrison spent his last moments reading the letter from home, gazing at the photograph, remembering happier times. We will never know for sure, of course. But it is a thought and a hope in which we may take comfort.

During the initial phase of the Allied investigation into the killings, it was suggested that they had been ordered by SS Captain von Reitzenstein in reprisal for the wounding of Bremer during the Allied bombardment of the Audrieu sector.[28] Certainly it is not the intention here to let Reitzenstein off the hook. After all, witnesses placed him at the scene during the first two sets of shootings. But Bremer was there too, and, as commanding officer, it was he, and not Reitzenstein, who would have had the ultimate authority to order the execution of prisoners. Besides, according to witnesses, the barrage that inflicted Bremer's injuries did not begin to land in the immediate vicinity of the chateau until around 6:30 PM, by which time the shootings would have been completed.[29] Thus, like Kurt Meyer at the Abbaye d'Ardenne, Bremer had no alibi or excuse. He may not have pulled the trigger, but he was responsible. However, as we shall see in a subsequent chapter, Bremer, unlike Meyer, was never brought to account for his crimes.

# 9
# The Mohnke Murders

In contrast with the murder and mayhem perpetrated at the headquarters of Gerhard Bremer's 12th Reconnaissance Battalion, the treatment accorded to Canadian POWs at the HQ of Bernhard Siebken's 2nd Battalion on 8 June was downright civilized. A large group of Canadians, in excess of a hundred, was transferred without incident from the 2nd Battalion to the command post of the 26th Panzer Grenadier Regiment, which was located a few miles to the south, in the tiny hamlet of Le Haut du Bosq. Meanwhile, a smaller group, totalling forty prisoners – Lieutenant William Ferguson, Sergeant James Reid, Corporals George Brown, Roger Firman, Clare Kines, James Kyle, Hector McLean, and Robert Scott, Lance Corporals Stewart Culleton and John Hill, and Privates Walter Booth, Ernest Bradley, Walter Daniels, Arthur Desjarlais, Gordon Ferris, Robert Findlay, Lant Freeman, Lawrence Guiboche, Charles Horton, Henry Jones, Elmer Lefort, Gordon Lewis, John MacDougall, Angus MacLeod, Frederick Marych, Wesley Morrison, Percy Parisian, Alfred Peterson, Frank Ryckman, Kjartan Sigurdson, Edward Smith, and John Thompson, all of the Royal Winnipeg Rifles, Private Richard Smith of the Queen's Own Rifles, Lieutenant Reginald Barker, Sergeant William Beresford, and Gunners Hilliard Birston, Weldon Clark, Thomas Grant, and Alvin Harkness of the 3rd Canadian Anti-Tank Regiment, and Private Donald Burnett of the Cameron Highlanders of Ottawa[1] – was held at 2nd Battalion headquarters pending the return of the Feldgendarmerie escort. During the interval, Siebken's men gave the Canadians water and dispensed first aid to their wounded. In view of the solicitude shown the prisoners, one might have expected their conveyance to the rear to have proceeded uneventfully, in much the same fashion as had that of the earlier group. Unfortunately, although through no fault of Siebken's, this did not prove to be the case. For the forty Canadians being held at the Moulin farm, the change in their circumstances would be sudden, terrifying, and devastating.

The first hint at the turn for the worse in the prisoners' fortunes came a few hours after their capture. Late in the afternoon on 8 June, Siebken received a call from his regimental commander, SS Lieutenant Colonel Wilhelm Mohnke. Reporting that he had taken custody of the large batch of POWs dispatched by Siebken earlier in the day, Mohnke, who was obviously annoyed, told him not to send back so many prisoners.[2] The battalion commander took this to mean that prisoners should not be taken in the first place, and, if they were, that they should be shot immediately after capture. Surprised and repulsed by Mohnke's barbarous and patently illegal order, Siebken quickly regained his composure and replied that he was going to send prisoners to the rear all the same.[3] Later in the evening, he did just that. Upon learning of the return of the Feldgendarmerie escort, Siebken ordered the forty Canadians brought from the barn in which they had been held to the front of the Moulin farmhouse. After looking over the prisoners, whose ranks included at least two stretcher cases,[4] Siebken had them form up in a column under the guard of seven or eight men. The escort consisted both of Feldgendarmerie and regular SS troops. Sometime after 8:00 PM, Dietrich Schnabel, Siebken's special missions officer, sent the prisoners on their way.[5]

The column proceeded southward along a path that led out of 2nd Battalion headquarters, past fields in which crops were already standing.[6] Had the prisoners continued on the footpath, they eventually would have reached the Caen–Fontenay-le-Pesnel road. By crossing this artery and continuing for another quarter mile or so, they then would have come to a secondary road that ran directly into Le Haut du Bosq. A mere one and a half miles more and they would have arrived at Mohnke's headquarters. Despite its proximity, the Canadians never reached their intended destination.

Around 9:00 PM, at a spot just north of the Caen-Fontenay road, the column of prisoners was intercepted by a staff car. As the column halted, an officer resplendent in SS uniform and overcoat got out and strode over to the sergeant in charge of the escort. It was difficult to make out the officer's face in the enveloping darkness, but those who survived the encounter with him will never forget his demeanour. From the outset, the officer was very agitated, and he seemed to become increasingly incensed as the conversation with the NCO went on.[7] Two of the prisoners later recalled that the officer had yelled at the escort leader, while another was of the view that he had actually threatened him.[8] Whatever the case, after a few minutes the martinet abruptly terminated the conversation, angrily pointed in the direction of the Caen-Fontenay road, and issued a torrent of orders to the hapless NCO.[9]

The sudden appearance of the officer and his subsequent violent outburst must have been profoundly disconcerting to the Canadian prisoners. At least a few of them guessed his real intentions. Though he did not understand German, Private Gordon Ferris of the Royal Winnipeg Rifles remembered thinking that the guards were going to kill all of the prisoners after the way that the officer had carried on.[10] This opinion was shared by Corporal Hector McLean, also of the Winnipegs. According to McLean, his worst fears were confirmed by Lieutenant Reg Barker of the 3rd Anti-Tank Regiment, who was one of two officers among the forty Canadian POWs (the other was Lieutenant William Ferguson of the Winnipegs). The American-born Barker, who spoke some German, told McLean that the escorts had in fact been ordered to kill the prisoners, but he promised that he would try to talk them out of it.[11]

Following the officer's orders, the SS guards escorted the Canadians to within sight of the Caen-Fontenay road. As the column approached the road, a large number of vehicles, including tanks and half-tracks, could be seen heading in an easterly direction.[12] Heartened by the sight of all this firepower, a couple of the escorts waved and yelled out 'Panzer! Panzer!'[13] Continuing on its way, the column was marched southward until it got to within a hundred yards of the convoy. Halted at a road junction less than a mile northeast of the village of Fontenay-le-Pesnel, the prisoners were diverted in a westerly direction into a grassy area adjacent to a grainfield. After going another fifty yards or so, they were ordered to sit down, facing east. Ominously, the prisoners were bunched together in several rows, with the stretcher cases placed in the middle. While the Canadians sat and waited in anxious silence, the Germans deployed menacingly around them.[14]

The prisoners' stay in the field must have seemed like an eternity. In fact, only three or four minutes had passed before the last half-track in the convoy peeled off the highway and headed for the spot where the prisoners were sitting.[15] Dressed in khaki camouflage uniforms and armed with machine pistols, several SS troopers jumped out of the vehicle and approached the sergeant in charge. A brief conversation ensued, after which the NCO ordered all but two of his men over to the vehicle. There one of the new arrivals exchanged the escorts' rifles for machine pistols, while another man pulled clips from a haversack and passed them around. Armed to the teeth, the men from the half-track and the original escorts advanced together towards the prisoners. The impromptu execution squad was joined by the two remaining escorts, who had retained their rifles.[16]

As the SS men closed in on them, even the most optimistic of the Canadians now realized what was about to happen. Any lingering hopes were dashed when Lieutenant Barker, who was in the front row and who would surely face the first salvo, calmly advised, 'Whoever is left after they fire the first round, go to the left [i.e., north].'[17] At a distance of about thirty yards, the Germans stopped.

One of them taunted his intended victims, saying in heavily accented English, 'Now you die.'[18] At that moment, the executioners opened fire.

Hit by the initial burst, the men in front were mowed down where they sat. Many were killed instantly. Others were only wounded and lay writhing in agony on the ground. In the middle rows, pandemonium erupted. As bullets thudded into flesh and soil around them, those who had not yet been hit scrambled in desperation. Shouts, curses, and heart-rending screams filled the night air.

Only those prisoners who had been sitting in the back row had any chance of survival. By advancing in a straight line and neglecting to cordon the area, the Germans had left an escape route open. Acting on instinct, several men made a break for it. Gunners Weldon Clark and Thomas Grant of the 3rd Anti-Tank Regiment ran off together. Clark made his getaway into the adjacent grainfield, but Grant was cut down after having run only a few yards. Corporal McLean and Private Ferris of the Winnipegs also ran in tandem. McLean was hit, but both men reached the adjacent field, where they took cover amid the standing crops. Corporals George Brown and Robert Scott and Privates Gordon Lewis and John MacDougall, also of the Winnipegs, followed McLean's and Ferris's example, but all were struck down by the Germans' second salvo. Of these men, only Private MacDougall, who was wounded in the leg, was able to make good his getaway.[19]

The most hair-raising escape of all was that contrived by Private Arthur Desjarlais of the Winnipegs' 15 Platoon. Sitting in the back row, Desjarlais actually froze when the Germans fired their first burst. Failure to hit the dirt when bullets are flying around is usually a prescription for disaster. Yet somehow the upright rifleman was not touched. Suddenly realizing the extent of his predicament, Desjarlais got onto his belly and slowly crawled towards the grainfield. Their attention diverted by the chaotic scene in front of them, the SS thugs never noticed him, and Desjarlais was able to slip away.[20]

Of the forty prisoners who found themselves in the Germans' gun sights on the fateful night of 8 June, only five – Corporal McLean and Privates Ferris, MacDougall, and Desjarlais of the Royal Winnipeg Rifles, along with Gunner Clark of the 3rd Anti-Tank Regiment – lived to tell about it.[21] Unfortunately, all five men were recaptured by other German units almost immediately after their brush with death. Thus, it would be months before they were repatriated from POW captivity and were able to tell their stories. By that time, potential German witnesses had either been killed in battle or were missing, and the evidentiary trail had largely gone cold. Hampered by false leads, Canadian war crimes investigators never were able to establish with certainty even the units involved, much less the individuals.[22] This was a failure of tragic proportions, for if any of the crimes committed by the 12th SS Panzer Division 'Hitler Youth' cries out for justice, it is surely the cold-blooded murder of thirty-five Canadian POWs on a moonlit back road in the countryside of northern France. Indeed, the machine gunning of the thirty-five prisoners near the village of Fontenay-le-Pesnel on the night of 8 June ranks as the single worst battlefield atrocity perpetrated against Canadians in the country's military history. So dastardly was this crime that some have since labelled it the 'Canadian Malmedy,' after the strikingly similar and much more famous (or infamous) massacre of American troops during the Nazis' last-ditch Ardennes offensive.[23]

Ironically, with the passage of time new information has come to light that now renders it possible to identify the instigator, if not the actual perpetrators, of the Fontenay-le-Pesnel massacre. A review of the extant investigative records leads to a seemingly inescapable conclusion: the officer in the staff car who intercepted the column of Canadian prisoners was none other than Wilhelm Mohnke. This conclusion is based on several pieces of persuasive, albeit circumstantial, evidence. For one thing, the description of the officer provided by the survivors, in particular that offered by Corporal McLean, seems to fit Mohnke.[24] Second, there was Mohnke's anger at Siebken for having earlier burdened him with a contingent of more than a hundred POWs, as well as his order, which was overheard by the telephone operator who patched through the call, admonishing his subordinate not to send so many prisoners back in the future. Third, the officer's meddling in the conveyance of the prisoners and his display of anger at the scene were very characteristic of Mohnke. Indeed, they made what transpired along the Caen-Fontenay road seem eerily similar to his interception of a column of British POWs at Wormhoudt almost exactly four years earlier. Fourth, since the order to send the Canadians to the rear came from Siebken, only he or a superior officer had the authority to countermand it. One could argue, of course, that Siebken or someone delegated by him had stopped the column. But that begs the following question: if Siebken had intended to kill the prisoners all along, then why did he send them on a three-mile hike when it would have been much easier to do away with them at his headquarters? Finally, Mohnke's behaviour over the next twelve hours, as attested to by several witnesses, was entirely consistent with someone who had ordered the shooting of prisoners.

After stopping the column of Canadian POWs, Mohnke proceeded to Siebken's headquarters. He seems to have been intent on chewing out the commander of the 2nd Battalion for his failure to follow orders. Already in a state of high agitation, Mohnke required only the slightest push to go over the emotional edge. The catalyst for the explosion that was to take place at Siebken's HQ was the unexpected arrival there of a wounded Wehrmacht officer.

While Mohnke was reprimanding Siebken for having sent a second POW contingent to the rear in contravention of his orders (the forty prisoners whose execution he had just decreed), Count Clary-Aldrigen, a captain and adjutant in the artillery regiment of the Panzer Lehr Division, was brought wounded to the kitchen of the Moulin farmhouse. While he was being patched up in the make-shift first-aid post by the battalion clerk, an SS private named Klöden, Clary recounted a disturbing story. Earlier in the day, during a reconnaissance mission around Hill 102, which was situated just south of Cristot, Clary and a small group of soldiers belonging to the staff of the artillery regiment – including a Colonel Luxenburger, who was regimental commander, a Major Zeissler, who commanded one of the regiment's battalions, and six other men – had been captured by an armoured car patrol of C Squadron of the (British) Inns of Court Regiment. According to Clary, the British, in flagrant violation of international law, had demanded that he and his comrades allow themselves to be used as human shields during the ride back through German lines. When they refused, two British officers, Clary alleged, had beaten Luxenburger unconscious and tied him to the front of one of the armoured cars. As they moved out, the patrol had opened fire on the rest of the Germans, killing everyone but Clary. On the way back to its own lines, the car to which Luxenburger had been tied was hit by anti-tank fire, which resulted in the fatal wounding of the regimental commander. As for Clary, though he had been wounded and left for dead along with the rest of his comrades, he regained consciousness and dragged himself to the village of Le Mesnil-Patry, where he was picked up by Siebken's troops.[25]

The accuracy of Clary's account, in particular his contention that the British had massacred the remaining members of his detachment, would be called into question in the late 1970s with the publication of the definitive history of the Panzer Lehr Division.[26] Still, the conduct of the Inns of Court patrol on the morning of 8 June had been highly questionable, and the Germans had every right to note the incident and lodge a formal protest with the Allies. Yet they elected to forego the diplomatic route in favour of much more direct action, or at least Mohnke did. Upon being informed of the incident, the volatile commander exploded, raging against the enemy and calling on Siebken to deny quarter thereafter and to execute any POWs already in his custody.[27] If the Allies were not taking prisoners, he spluttered, then why should the Germans? Taken aback by the intensity of Mohnke's tirade, Siebken advised against such a course, arguing that it would only lead to an escalating cycle of reprisals. Mohnke was not appeased, but he took his leave without further comment. For the moment, at least, that appeared to be the end of the matter.[28]

Around midnight, Michael Wimplinger, a driver at Siebken's headquarters, left the Moulin farmhouse and briefly went outside. About fifty yards in the distance, he spotted someone lying in a patch of long grass. Believing at first that the figure was a wounded German soldier, Wimplinger went over for a closer look. In the glare of his pocket flashlight, the driver recognized the uniform of the enemy. Noticing that the man's left foot was bleeding, Wimplinger called out to the kitchen for assistance. Medical orderly Heinrich Albers emerged and rushed over.

After setting him on his feet and searching him for weapons, the two SS troopers helped the wounded soldier into the first-aid post. Arming themselves, Albers and Wimplinger then went back out to conduct a more thorough search of the grounds. They quickly found two more enemy soldiers. One was suffering the effects of a mild concussion, while the other had sustained a flesh wound to his left knee. After being searched, these men were also helped into the first-aid post.[29]

We now know that the wounded soldiers found on the grounds of Siebken's headquarters on the night of 8–9 June were Canadians. The man discovered by Wimplinger was Private Harold Angel of the Cameron Highlanders of Ottawa. The other two were Privates Frederick Holness (with the concussion) and Ernest Baskerville (with the knee injury), both of the Royal Winnipeg Rifles.[30] All three had been involved in the fighting at Putot-en-Bessin earlier in the day,[31] and all three, despite their injuries, had somehow evaded capture for several hours after the battle. Tired, hungry, and in need of medical attention, they must have finally given up trying to get back to their own lines. Spotting the Moulin farmhouse, the three men probably decided to risk capture. It was a decision they would come to regret.

Initially, the prisoners were treated in an entirely correct manner. Once inside the Moulin kitchen, they were attended by Dr Schütt, the 2nd Battalion's medical officer. Schütt, who spoke English, conversed freely with the prisoners, learning, for example, that Private Angel lived in Ottawa, was married, and had four children. After bandaging their wounds, the good and decent doctor ordered that beds of straw be prepared for the Canadians. He also saw to it that blankets were provided. Grateful for the humane way in which they were being treated, Privates Angel, Holness, and Baskerville fell into a deep, unbroken sleep.[32]

Schütt's kindness was typical of the treatment accorded to the Canadian prisoners who passed through 2nd Battalion headquarters on 8 June. It did not sit well with Mohnke, however. While Siebken was immersed in preparations for the following day's operations, the regimental commander paid him a return visit, apparently to drive home his point regarding enemy POWs. As it happened, Mohnke's arrival at the battalion command post coincided with the appearance there of Dr Schütt, who had come to Siebken to report the presence of the three wounded Canadians. When Mohnke learned that the 2nd Battalion had taken more prisoners, he ordered that they be shot without delay. Siebken refused. A terrible argument ensued. If Siebken's postwar testimony is to be believed, Mohnke was beside himself with anger. He purportedly berated Siebken for his insubordination, after which he called in Schnabel and ordered him to carry out the execution of the prisoners. When Schnabel took the same position as that of his immediate superior, Mohnke stormed out.[33]

Following Mohnke's departure, the mood at 2nd Battalion headquarters was grim. Resolved to prevent the killing of his prisoners, Siebken realized that he could not protect them on his own. Accordingly, at the first opportunity he put through a call to 12th SS headquarters. The purpose was to find out whether the shooting of prisoners had been authorized by division. Insofar as it circumvented the normal chain of command, this call was an extraordinary breach of military protocol. However, Siebken had been deeply shaken by Mohnke's violent outburst. Besides, if he was going to disobey the direct order of a superior officer, he wanted to be sure that he would have the backing of the upper echelons.[34]

Divisional commander Witt was unavailable when Siebken's call came through, so the battalion commander was instead put on to SS Major Hubert Meyer (no relation to Kurt Meyer), the Hitler Youth Division's chief of staff. Siebken asked Meyer point blank: Had division issued an order to shoot all prisoners? Meyer assured him that it had not. On the contrary, he told Siebken, POWs were the best and often the only source of information as to enemy dispositions. Thus, he advised the taking of as many prisoners as possible.[35]

Before putting down the phone, Meyer asked Siebken why he had posed such an odd question. Siebken replied by recounting the confrontation that had just taken place at his battalion headquarters. Troubled by Mohnke's rather erratic deportment, in particular his issuance of orders directly to Schnabel, which violated the sanctity of the military hierarchy, Meyer immediately rang up the 26th Panzer Grenadier Regiment. With Mohnke still absent, the chief of staff spoke to his adjutant, SS Captain Kaiser. According to Meyer's postwar testimony, he asked what action was being taken with regard to the shooting of POWs in the regiment's sector. When Kaiser responded that he knew nothing about it, Meyer told him the same thing that he had told Siebken: as many prisoners as possible should be taken, and they should be treated in accordance with the provisions of the Geneva Convention.[36]

With divisional command fully apprised of the situation, one might have expected Mohnke to at last let the issue of POWs rest. Yet he was unable to do so. In his twisted state of mind, the killing of the three Canadian prisoners had become a matter of honour. Immediately upon his return to his headquarters, a seething Mohnke telephoned the 2nd Battalion and tried to find out whether his order had been obeyed. Siebken was unavailable, having since gone to the front to check on the deployment of his forward units. Mohnke spoke to his adjutant instead. When the officer informed him that the execution of the three prisoners had not yet been carried out, Mohnke flew into another rage, then abruptly hung up.[37]

If Siebken's beleaguered staff thought that they had seen or heard the last of Mohnke, they were wrong. In a terrifying display of obsessive behaviour, he soon returned to the Moulin farm. Ranting once more about insubordination and disloyalty, Mohnke cornered Siebken's adjutant and demanded to know the battalion commander's whereabouts. When the officer replied that Siebken was still at the front, Mohnke then asked for Schnabel. He too was unavailable. Frustrated, but undeterred, Mohnke left yet again.[38]

Unaware of the controversy that their capture had provoked, Privates Angel, Holness, and Baskerville awoke between 8:00 and 9:00 on the morning of 9 June. They asked for and received permission to go outside to wash up. Upon their return, the three prisoners were questioned briefly by an unidentified SS officer, in the presence of Dr Schütt. After the interrogations, they were allowed to relax. Still weak from their wounds, two of the men elected to return to their straw beds, but the other sat up in an easy chair. Shortly thereafter they were brought a canister of fresh milk, which they gulped down heartily.[39]

While the Canadians were enjoying their unexpected breakfast, Mohnke suddenly reappeared. Siebken was still absent, but Schnabel had returned, and it did not take long for Mohnke to find him. If postwar testimony given on Schnabel's behalf is to be believed, Mohnke drew his pistol, pointed it at the junior officer, and ordered him to carry out the execution of the three prisoners.[40] Clearly, this was the end of the line. There would be no more reprieves for the Canadians.

A shaken Schnabel drove over to the Moulin farmhouse. In the kitchen he found Dr Schütt and the medical orderlies Heinrich Albers, Fritz Bundschuh, and a third man known only as Ischner. According to Wimplinger, who was in the next room, Schnabel informed Dr Schütt that an order had been issued to shoot the prisoners. Schütt muttered his disgust, but his protest went for naught. Not wanting another confrontation with Mohnke, Schnabel motioned for the orderlies to get the Canadians up. Their hands above their heads, Angel, Holness, and Baskerville hobbled out the door.[41]

Schnabel and his underlings escorted the prisoners across the front yard and into an adjacent garden. Owing to their injuries, it was only with considerable difficulty that the three Canadians managed to traverse the yard. Private Baskerville was able to limp unaided, but Private Angel had to be supported by Private Holness. Finally reaching the end of the garden, the procession halted. It was at this point that the Canadians must have realized what was in store for them. In order not to have to look his victims in the eye, Schnabel ordered them to turn around. Next he had Albers, Bundschuh, and Ischner train their machine pistols on their targets. At the order to fire, each shooter let loose with a ten- to twelve-round burst from a distance of less than twenty feet. The three Canadians went down simultaneously. Though none of them betrayed any signs of life, Schnabel drew his pistol, walked over to their bodies, and applied the *coup de grâce* to each.[42] Mohnke's uncontrollable wrath and his pathological obsession with enemy prisoners had claimed three more victims.

After the war, former officers of the 12th SS Division and their partisans suggested that the shooting of the Canadians at 2nd Battalion headquarters on the morning of 9 June had been a legitimate reprisal for the Clary incident.[43] Since the rules governing the resort to military reprisals are quite strict and circumscribed, it is highly debatable whether a reprisal would have been justified in this instance. Beyond the legal issues involved, the circumstances in which the killings were carried out tend to undermine the notion that they had been conceived and ordered in reprisal for what had happened to Clary and his fellow officers. Indeed, it could be argued that the lives of Angel, Holness, and Baskerville were forfeit from the moment that the men were captured in the sector in which Wilhelm Mohnke was in command.

As proof, one need only consider the following facts. Late in the afternoon of 8 June, Mohnke made a call to Siebken in which he ordered him not to send back so many prisoners. The same night, Mohnke intercepted a column of forty Canadian POWs and ordered their execution. Shortly thereafter, he proceeded to Siebken's headquarters and reiterated that he did not want prisoners to be taken. While Mohnke was speaking to Siebken, Count Clary was brought in and recounted his story regarding the dubious conduct of the (British) Inns of Court Regiment. Upon hearing of the Clary incident, Mohnke exploded and once more ordered Siebken to deny quarter to the enemy. All of this went on before Mohnke learned, quite by accident, that Siebken's troops had taken more prisoners. Then, and only then, did he specifically call for their execution. It is therefore reasonable to assume that had Angel, Holness, and Baskerville turned up at Siebken's HQ at any time prior to either Clary's arrival or Mohnke's second visit, their fate, once Mohnke became aware of their capture, would have been sealed. Viewed in the context of what went on at the Moulin farm during the night of 8–9 June, the connection between the first-aid post killings and the Clary incident would seem to have been very tenuous indeed.

Notwithstanding its questionable legal and factual basis, the Clary incident undoubtedly would have been raised had Mohnke ever been tried for the first-aid post killings. Whether a military court would have entertained such a defence is a matter of speculation. More certain is that the reprisal defence would not have been available to Mohnke in the case of the next and last incident of POW killings in which he was known to have been involved. On this occasion, there were no extenuating circumstances, nor was there any doubt as to the identity of the instigator.

On 11 June, at around 4:30 PM, two SS troopers in khaki camouflage uniforms were escorting three prisoners down a country road near the hamlet of Le Haut du Bosq. Sappers John Ionel and George Benner of the 6th Company of the Royal Canadian Engineers and Private Allan Owens of B Company of the Royal Winnipeg Rifles were dirty, exhausted, and without helmets or equipment. There was good reason for the prisoners' bedraggled appearance. For the past seventy-two hours, since the ambush that had resulted in their separation from the mine-laying party of which they had been a part, the Canadians had been wandering around no man's land, trying to find their way back to their own lines. In order to avoid capture, they had been forced to move by night and hide by day, taking shelter in ditches, thickets, and abandoned barns. The men survived on their emergency rations, and, when these ran out, by drinking water from streams.

As they came to an old farmhouse, which was fronted by a high stone wall, the prisoners were directed to the other side of the road, through an open gateway. Marched across a small patch of pasture, they were taken down a laneway that led into an orchard. This was where the 26th Panzer Grenadier Regiment had set up its headquarters.[44] Inside the orchard there was the bustle of military activity. Dispatch riders could be observed coming and going, officers were seen conferring, and a number of SS troopers were standing alongside what appeared to be freshly dug slit trenches. The firing of heavy guns could be heard in the distance.[45] Despite the outwardly confident demeanour of the Germans at the headquarters, there was a palpable tension in the air.

After waiting momentarily, the two escorts and their prisoners were called over to an open car near which several members of the Feldgendarmerie were sitting. The troopers handed the Canadians over to the sergeant in charge. The NCO and another of the military policemen then brought the prisoners to the front of the regimental command post, which at the time was housed in an army truck. After another minute or two, Mohnke, his adjutant Kaiser, and a third man, possibly SS Technical Sergeant Runge, who spoke English, emerged from the makeshift HQ. While the officers looked the Canadians over, the Feldgendarmerie sergeant searched them, appropriating all of their identification papers and personal possessions. While this was going on, Mohnke, as he invariably was when confronted by enemy prisoners, seemed to be very angry.[46]

Upon completion of the search, the Germans began questioning the prisoners. The interrogations lasted for a good fifteen minutes. Neither of the two SS troopers who witnessed the proceedings were close enough to hear what was said.[47] But it was clear to them that Mohnke was unhappy with the answers he was getting. Part way through the questioning, the regimental commander, who must have struck the prisoners as deranged, began shouting and gesturing wildly. This went on for the duration of the session.[48]

At the conclusion of the interrogations, the military policemen directed the prisoners from the front of the command post to a spot some thirty yards away. There they ripped off the Canadians' identity tags and threw them into nearby bushes.[49] Whether Ionel, Benner, or Owens understood the significance of this action is by no means certain. Yet it was fraught with sinister implications. Had the Germans planned to convey the three men on to division, the retention of the tags, which contained their names, ranks, and military identification numbers, would have been essential for a host of administrative reasons. That the tags were instead disposed of in so cavalier a fashion is compelling evidence that no such prisoner transfer was ever intended.

Within minutes of the stripping away of the prisoners' last vestiges of personal identity, the Germans' real purpose became frighteningly apparent. In full view of Mohnke and Kaiser, the two military policemen marched the Canadians northward into a meadow. After they had gone about three hundred yards, they were ordered to halt near a bomb crater, one of many made by Allied planes over the past few days. As soon as the prisoners had come abreast of one another, the sergeant of the Feldgendarmerie fired his machine pistol into their backs in a long, continuous burst. Hit by numerous rounds, Ionel, Benner, and Owens fell face first and lay motionless at the edge of the crater. Gratuitously, one or both of the military policemen pumped additional shots into the fallen Canadians. Then the impromptu firing squad returned to the front of the regimental command post, where Mohnke and Kaiser were still standing, looking out at the macabre execution site.[50]

Though other POW murders would be perpetrated in the sector of the 26th Panzer Grenadier Regiment, the shooting of Owens, Ionel, and Benner on the afternoon of 11 June were the last killings of Canadian prisoners in which Wilhelm Mohnke was known to have been involved. Taken together with the first-aid post shootings and the massacre along the Caen-Fontenay road, the toll of POWs murdered by forces under Mohnke's command was at least forty-one. In terms of sheer numbers, then, Mohnke was responsible for more murders than any other senior officer in the 12th SS Panzer Division 'Hitler Youth.'

During the first five days of battle after the Allied landings in Normandy, he personally ordered, instigated, or abetted more atrocities than fellow officers Gerhard Bremer, Kurt Meyer, or even Karl-Heinz Milius. Yet like Bremer and Milius, Mohnke would never be called to account for his crimes. The reasons for this glaring failure of Canadian justice, as we shall see, is a story in and of itself.

# 10

# The Murders at Bretteville and Norrey

Taken together, the shootings of Canadian prisoners of war by troops under the command of Mohnke, Bremer, Meyer, and Milius accounted for 120 of the 156 POW murders known to have been committed by the Hitler Youth Division during the first ten days of fighting in Normandy. The other thirty-six Canadians who died while in the custody of the 12th SS were killed in a number of smaller-scale incidents. Some of these incidents continued the pattern, initiated by Meyer at the Abbaye d'Ardenne, of cold-blooded and systematic shootings carried out well behind the lines. The remainder were a reversion to the more or less spontaneous battlefield atrocities that Milius's men had perpetrated in and around Authie on the afternoon of 7 June. In some cases, the subunits involved in the latter incidents were identified, and warrants issued for the apprehension of their commanding officers. In the others, the responsible subunits could not be determined.

The first of the smaller-scale incidents took place on the night of 8 June during an attack on the town of Bretteville l'Orgueilleuse by a battlegroup drawn from Kurt Meyer's 25th Panzer Grenadier Regiment and Max Wünsche's 12th Panzer Regiment. It will be remembered that Meyer had planned the attack the previous night in order to close what was then a gaping four-mile hole in the German line. To be sure, things had stabilized since the arrival in Normandy of Mohnke's regiment. Indeed, by evening on 8 June, the 12th SS had established itself across an eleven-mile-long front, from Cristot in the west to Epron in the east. In the German centre, however, where the Regina Rifles were grimly hanging on to Bretteville and Norrey-en-Bessin, there remained an irritating and potentially dangerous salient. Thus, twenty-four hours after the fact, the rationale for Meyer's plan of attack was still valid.[1]

Accordingly, at around 6:30 PM on 8 June, Meyer's formidable battlegroup – which consisted of two companies of Panthers, one company of motorized infantry, and a battery of self-propelled artillery – began to assemble at its staging area in Franqueville. While the vehicles were being fuelled up, the company commanders attended a final briefing. Then, at 9:00 PM, the signal was given and the battlegroup began to rumble down the country road that linked Franqueville with the village of Rots, which was located less than three miles to the west. Riding in a two-seat motorcycle at the head of his regiment's reconnaissance company, Meyer led its armoured cars out. Behind them came the tanks. These were deployed in a wedge formation, with the 4th Panzer Company on the right and the 1st Panzer Company on the left.[2]

Initially, the German advance proceeded unhindered. Following Meyer's plan to the letter, the battlegroup bypassed Rots, which was to be assaulted from La Villeneuve by the 1st Company of Mohnke's regiment, and entered Le Bourg instead. Finding the tiny hamlet deserted, the motorized infantry and tanks formed up in single file in order to cross the nearby Mue River bridge. This was done successfully, whereupon the battlegroup resumed its westerly advance along the Caen-Bayeux highway.[3]

After crossing the Mue, Meyer ordered a few of his tanks to proceed ahead of the battlegroup.[4] Just before 10:00 PM, this armoured vanguard was spotted by a Regina Rifles patrol.[5] In response to the threat that appeared to be developing on the left flank of the 7th Canadian Infantry Brigade, a section of the carrier platoon of the Reginas' support company was sent out to meet it. The section deployed a few hundred yards in front of Bretteville, just south of the Caen-Bayeux highway. It soon was joined by a machine-gun section of 4 Platoon of the Ottawa Camerons' A Company, which took up positions directly to the north, on the other side of the road.[6] The task of these forward units was to intercept the German column and delay its advance for as long as possible.

As the vanguard of Meyer's battlegroup descended a gentle slope in the road before the outskirts of Bretteville, it came into the sights of the Reginas' and Camerons' anti-tank and machine-gun emplacements. The Canadians opened up from both sides of the highway. One of the first Germans to fall in the hail of fire was SS Captain Horst von Büttner. The commander of the 15th Reconnaissance Company, Büttner was perched in the turret of the lead Panther when it was hit by an anti-tank shell, killing him instantly.

In the face of the murderous crossfire, German casualties began to mount quickly. Indeed, had luck been on the side of the Canadians, they might have done in no less than their nemesis himself. Early on in the skirmish, several machine-gun bullets hit Meyer's motorcycle, fatally wounding his driver, piercing the gas tank, and igniting the fuel. The daredevil commander suddenly found himself engulfed in fire. He was fortunate that some of his men were close by. Wrestled to the ground and rolled so as to smother the flames, Meyer escaped with only minor burns.[7]

The forward detachments of Reginas and Camerons fought bravely, but they could not stem the inexorable tide of tanks and infantry. After holding out for about half an hour, they were overrun, with only a few men managing to work their way back to Norrey, where they rejoined the rest of the Reginas' B Company. Meanwhile, the SS battlegroup blasted its way into Bretteville.[8] This was the start of a bitter struggle for the town. The fighting would go on for hours. Though pummelled throughout the night by Meyer's ubiquitous Panthers, detachments of the Reginas' headquarters company held their ground, using PIAT (Projector Infantry Anti-Tank) guns and small arms to inflict heavy losses on the Germans before finally driving them out in the morning.[9] Thanks to the Reginas' heroic stand in the face of the enemy's armour, Bretteville would remain in Canadian hands.

Despite being on the receiving end of a sound thrashing, elements of Meyer's battlegroup continued to probe the Canadian positions in and around Bretteville well into the afternoon of 9 June.[10] Thus, it was not until the following day that members of the Reginas' carrier platoon were able to return to the outpost they had manned before being overrun. When the survivors of the initial skirmish reached their original defence line, they were confronted by a scene of utter devastation. Dead soldiers, both Canadian and German, lay on the Caen-Bayeux highway and strewn in the adjacent fields. Twisted, charred steel was all that was left of the Reginas' carrier. Down the road, several wrecked Panthers dotted the landscape.

As they pondered the carnage in reverential silence, Sergeant Edward Smith and Private James Boyer found their attention drawn to something odd. In a clearing about a hundred yards south of the highway, they spotted four of their comrades – later identified as Lance Corporal David Moloney and Privates Cecil Borne, Norman Morin, and John Sawatzky – who appeared to be lying shoulder to shoulder, with their personal belongings piled up in front of them. The Reginas went for a closer look. As they approached the bodies, they saw that each man had sustained numerous bullet wounds to the head. To Private Boyer, it appeared that they had been shot in the side of the face from very close range while kneeling on the ground. Sergeant Smith, on the other hand, who noticed expended machine-pistol shell casings lying right on top of some of the bodies, thought that his platoon mates must have been shot while lying down. 'The whole scene,' Smith remembered, 'looked to me as if the men had been made to lie down and had been shot deliberately.'[11]

Whatever the precise circumstances, one thing was clear: Smith and Boyer had stumbled onto the site of yet another German atrocity. The piling up of their personal belongings, the positioning of their bodies, and the nature of their wounds, all indicated that the Canadians had been captured, searched, and then shot down in cold blood. Shocked and angered by their grisly discovery, the two Reginas began to check the other corpses. A short distance from where the murdered Moloney, Borne, Morin, and Sawatzky lay, they found the bodies of Privates Charles Bebee and Robert Gurney. These men also appeared to have been machine gunned in the face from almost point-blank range.[12]

As they moved up the skirmish line towards the highway, Smith and Boyer spotted the body of Private Nelson Vickery. Like his unfortunate comrades, Vickery had been killed by bursts of machine-pistol fire to the face and chest, in circumstances highly suggestive of an execution. Lying a few yards away, right at the edge of the highway, where on the night of 9 June Boyer had seen him operating his Bren gun, was Corporal Ervin Povol. Apparently Povol had been found wounded by a German officer, who then dispatched him with a single pistol shot through the forehead. Finally, as they crossed the highway, Smith and Boyer came upon four Camerons whose bodies also bore the telltale signs of having been shot after capture. Later on, while retracing his escape route through the adjacent grainfield, Boyer would find the body of Regina Rifleman H.E. Anderson. A cursory examination revealed that Anderson had also received a machine-pistol burst in the face from very close range.[13]

In total, Smith and Boyer found the bodies of thirteen Canadians who, by all appearances, had been murdered after capture in a cruel and savage manner. For reasons that remain obscure, neither witness came forward with what he had seen until after the war. By then, Canadian investigators were unable to establish which subunit of the 12th SS had perpetrated this heinous crime. Despite the passage of time, the investigators' failure to do so is puzzling, since the circumstantial evidence, including the location of the bodies and the timing of the murders, all pointed in the direction of Kurt Meyer's battlegroup. Even more perplexing is the fact that neither Meyer, who was in custody for more than a year before he was tried for the Abbaye d'Ardenne killings, nor SS Private Jan Jesionek, the ethnic German conscript who testified against Meyer and who had himself taken part in the battle,[14] was ever questioned regarding the murder of POWs at Bretteville.

Part of the problem seems to have been that Canadian investigators initially confused this crime with another atrocity purportedly involving victims from the Regina Rifles.[15] But the real stumbling block may have been the inconvenient timing of Smith's and Boyer's revelations. By the time that the two Reginas were deposed (late November and early December 1945 respectively), Meyer was already set to go on trial. Though the official correspondence is silent as to how Canadian authorities reacted to this latest allegation, one suspects that the connection between the killings at Bretteville and the attack on the town by Meyer's battlegroup was never made, or, if it was, that it was dismissed as an unwelcome complication to the upcoming prosecution.

The massacre of thirteen Reginas and Camerons on the night of 8 June was not the only instance of POW murder associated with the attack on Bretteville. The following afternoon, two more Canadians would be subjected to the inimitable brand of treatment that the 12th SS all too frequently meted out to enemy prisoners. Like the previous incident, this one took place along the front lines, in the immediate aftermath of a battle. It too bore all the earmarks of a killing carried out in response to volatile combat emotions. There was a difference between the two incidents, however. This time, there would be an eyewitness.

By morning on 9 June, Meyer's battlegroup was in considerable disarray.[16] Meanwhile, the salient in the German front, far from having been eliminated, had not even been reduced to any appreciable degree. With Meyer having his burns treated at Rots, responsibility for the continuation of operations fell to SS Lieutenant Colonel Max Wünsche. According to his postwar testimony, the commander of the Hitler Youth Division's tank regiment immediately revised Meyer's battle plan.[17] Forgoing a renewed attack on Bretteville, Wünsche decided instead to mount an attempt to drive the Canadians out of Norrey-en-Bessin.

Norrey, which was about a mile south of Bretteville, certainly was a thorn in the Germans' side. As long as it remained in Canadian hands, cooperation between the left wing of Meyer's regiment and the right wing of Mohnke's, which was essential if the salient in the front of the 12th SS was to be eliminated, would prove to be difficult, if not impossible.[18] Accordingly, Wünsche's orders called for an all-out armoured thrust on the village. In the revised plan, the 1st Panzer Company was to bypass Norrey to the south, then wheel around and attack from the southwest. At the same time, the 3rd Panzer Company, which had just arrived at the front, was to deploy at La Villeneuve, roll south through the nearby railroad underpass, and then turn and attack from the southeast. While the tanks were hitting Norrey from both flanks, the 1st Battalion of Mohnke's regiment was to furnish support by assaulting the village from the south.[19]

The attack on Norrey began at noon.[20] Despite being heavily outnumbered, the Reginas' gallant B Company withstood the onslaught. During two hours of heavy fighting, Norrey's defenders, assisted on their left by a squadron of tanks from the Sherbrooke Fusiliers (27th Canadian Armoured Regiment) and on their right by elements of the 1st Hussars (6th Canadian Armoured Regiment), knocked out as many as twenty enemy tanks.[21] By mid-afternoon, the Germans were in headlong retreat. Wünsche's battegroup had been routed. The significance of what happened at Norrey was not lost on the architect of the ill-fated attack. 'I could have screamed with rage and grief,' Wünsche would later recall, as he watched his shattered forces limp back into Rots.[22]

Several hours before the start of the German attack, Sergeant Thomas Wood of the Reginas' 2 Platoon, B Company, had sent two of his men on outpost duty. The men, Privates L.W. Lee and Ernest Gilbank, had taken up a position about a half mile east of Norrey, some three hundred yards to the north of the Caen-Bayeux railway line.[23] Shortly after noon, Sergeant Wood spotted the spearhead of the 3rd Panzer Company approaching his platoon's position from over the crest of a ridge. When he radioed this information back to B Company head-quarters, he was ordered to hold his fire so as not to give his position away.[24] This proved to be a sound tactic, for by holding its fire, 2 Platoon allowed the unsuspecting German formation to complete the lateral manoeuvre called for in Wünsche's plan, thereby exposing its right flank to the Reginas' anti-tank guns. Unfortunately, it also meant that Lee and Gilbank were cut off from their unit.

As soon as the German armour came within range, the Reginas' let loose with a withering cannonade from their PIATs. In a matter of minutes, three of the spearhead's five Panthers were ablaze, while the remaining two broke off the attack, firing wildly as they withdrew.[25] From his vantage point on the out-skirts of Norrey, Wood could see the survivors bailing out and running across the railway line. It was at this point that one of the dismounted tank crews must have stumbled upon the Canadian outpost, because Lee and Gilbank were seen standing with their hands held above their heads. After picking up the Reginas' weapons, the Germans began marching their prisoners back towards the rail-road tracks.[26]

Immediately after capture, Lee and Gilbank were escorted to a spot about five hundred yards south of the railway line. There they were met by an officer who was described as having several decorations on his tunic. The officer, who spoke English, began questioning the prisoners. Over the course of the interro-gation, he became very angry. Suddenly, in Mohnke-esque fashion, he pulled out his pistol and fired three shots into Gilbank's stomach. As the Regina lay dying, the officer shot him in the head.[27]

His rage apparently not yet spent, the officer turned his pistol on Lee. No more than a few feet away, the Regina stood transfixed, powerless to do any-thing. The German fired, and Lee went down with a bullet wound in the groin. At that moment, artillery shells began to land in the area. The officer squeezed off a few more rounds at the prone figure on the ground, but, miraculously, all of them missed. Meanwhile, the barrage intensified and the Germans scattered for cover. Not taking any chances, Lee lay where he had fallen until well after dark. Then, convinced that it was safe to do so, he began crawling along the railway line. After a remarkable thirty-six-hour odyssey, which he made without food or water and during which he managed to evade an enemy patrol, an exhausted Lee dragged himself to another Regina Rifles outpost, where he told of his harrowing encounter with the unknown German officer.[28]

As was the case with the incident near Bretteville, the perpetrator of the murder of one Canadian prisoner and the wounding of another just outside Norrey was never positively identified. Initially, an Allied court of inquiry implicated Mohnke in the shootings.[29] There were good reasons for believing that Mohnke had been the triggerman. In its essentials – the officer's interception of POWs being escorted to the rear, his loss of temper during their interrogation, and the shooting down of unarmed and defenceless prisoners – what happened near the Caen-Bayeux railway line in the early afternoon of 9 June bore Mohnke's signature. However, upon further investigation it was learned that Mohnke's regiment had failed to support the attack on Norrey. Since it was therefore reasonable to assume that the regimental commander had been nowhere near the scene when the murder of Gilbank was committed, the investigative focus necessarily shifted elsewhere.

No new leads were developed in the case of Gilbank's murder until Canadian war crimes investigators questioned Max Wünsche, the author of the ill-fated attack on Norrey. Wünsche informed them that the 1st and 3rd Panzer Companies had taken part in the attack.[30] It was later established that SS Captain Anton Berlin had been the commander of the 1st Panzer Company at the time, while SS First Lieutenant Rudolf von Ribbentrop, the son of Hitler's foreign minister, had been commander of the 3rd.[31] Inexplicably, neither man was brought in for interrogation after the war. To be sure, it is not at all clear whether it would have done much good to question Berlin about the incident, as his 1st company had attacked Norrey from the southwest, and therefore could not possibly have come into contact with the outpost manned by Lee and Gilbank. Ribbentrop appeared to be a more promising suspect, since undoubtedly it had been members of one of his company's tank crews who had captured the two Reginas. Yet this officer had a seemingly ironclad alibi. Having been wounded in the left arm by an Allied fighter plane a few days before the start of the invasion, he had relinquished command of his company to a Wehrmacht captain by the name of Lüdemann. Though he had bolted his military hospital and rejoined the tank regiment just in time for the attack on Norrey, with his arm still in a sling Ribbentrop had been relegated to headquarters duty.[32] Thus, the killer of Gilbank, like the perpetrators of the Bretteville massacre, would never be identified, much less called to account for his crimes. Nor would the Norrey incident be the last to go into the 'unsolved' file.

# 11
# The Murders at Le Mesnil-Patry

After the battles of Bretteville l'Orgueilleuse and Norrey-en-Bessin on 8–9 June, things quieted down for a while along the front of the 12th SS Panzer Division 'Hitler Youth.' This was true not only in terms of the cessation of offensive military operations, but also as it concerned the fate of Canadian prisoners. Indeed, it was not until more than two days later that the spectre of POW murder once more reared its ugly head. At around 5:00 in the afternoon on 11 June, SS Lieutenant Colonel Wilhelm Mohnke, adhering to the barbaric code of warfare that had guided his conduct since his arrival in Normandy, ordered and then watched the execution of three Canadian prisoners at his Le Haut du Bosq headquarters. Vile and criminal though it was, the shooting in cold blood of Private Owens of the Royal Winnipeg Rifles and Sappers Ionel and Benner of the Royal Canadian Engineers was only the start of what would develop into an evening of murder and mayhem. Over the next several hours, the men of SS Major Bernhard Siebken's 2nd Panzer Grenadier Battalion and SS Major Siegfried Müller's 12th Engineering Battalion would indulge in a rampage frighteningly similar to that perpetrated by Milius's troopers on 7 June. By the time that it was over, thirteen more Canadian prisoners would lie dead, the victims of random and senseless battlefield atrocities.

The catalyst for this next round of POW murders was a large-scale Canadian tank attack in the vicinity of the village of Le Mesnil-Patry. Conceived within the framework of a British plan to capture Caen by flanking and then encircling the city, the Canadian operation was intended to cover the advance of the left-flank guard of one of the British pincers.[1] To fulfil their relatively modest mission, the Canadians were supposed to occupy Le Mesnil-Patry, proceed south from there to clear the Mue River valley, which was constantly being infiltrated by detachments of Siebken's battalion, then take and hold the high ground between Le Haut du Bosq and Grainville-sur-Odon.[2] The operation, which was expected to last about two days, would be carried out by elements of the 2nd Canadian Armoured Brigade, supported by infantry from the Queen's Own Rifles of Canada.

Launched at 2:20 PM on 11 June,[3] the attack on Le Mesnil-Patry was a complete and costly failure. Early on, things appeared to be going well. Led by the Shermans of the 1st Hussars' B Squadron, on which the men of D Company of the Queen's Own were riding, and the tanks of C Squadron, which acted as right-flank guard, the Canadian task force moved out from Bray, then proceeded briskly in a southerly direction past Bretteville, over the Caen-Bayeux railway line, and through Norrey-en-Bessin. It was clear sailing until the vanguard entered the grainfields that dominated the terrain immediately to the south and southwest of Norrey. At that moment, the unsuspecting Canadians were spotted by the 1st Company of Müller's battalion, which immediately opened up with deadly accurate machine-gun and mortar fire. After a minute or so of confusion, the vanguard determined the source of the barrage and headed for it. A hotly-contested battle ensued in which the Canadian tanks milled about the enemy's trenches, firing their machine guns in all directions while the SS engineers and troopers defended themselves with grenade launchers and magnetic charges. After close to an hour of intense, close-quarter fighting, the tenacious Germans began to pull back.[4] Their withdrawal afforded B and C Squadrons the opportunity to resume their advance.

Though a considerable number of Canadian infantrymen had been killed or wounded in the first assault,[5] the operation seemed to be back on track. However, as B Squadron got to the northern outskirts of Le Mesnil-Patry, the battle took a dramatic turn for the worse. At 4:15 PM, the armoured vanguard suddenly came under heavy tank fire from southeast of the village. Lieutenant Colonel R.K. Colwell, the commander of the vanguard, apprised 2nd Brigade headquarters of the situation, but was informed that the tanks opposing him were in fact 'friendly' (i.e., British). Ordered to hold his fire, Colwell passed the word on to his squadron commanders, even going so far as to instruct them to have their formations fly recognition flags.[6] This proved to be a tragic blunder. It was not friendly fire that the Canadian tanks were encountering,[7] but rather a counterattack by the 2nd Battalion of the 12th SS's armoured regiment. Alerted by the din of the battle south of Norrey, SS Major Karl-Heinz Prinz, the commander of the regiment's 2nd Battalion, had ordered his companies into action at precisely the right moment, before the Canadians could break into Le Mesnil-Patry.[8]

Prinz's attack on the exposed left flank of the Canadian vanguard was devastating. Heavily outgunned by the Germans' Panthers,[9] Colwell's Shermans were literally shot to pieces. In the space of less than two hours, the 1st Hussars lost thirty-four tanks, which represented fully one-third of the regiment's losses for the entire European campaign. Almost half of C Squadron was destroyed, while B Squadron was virtually annihilated.[10] Canadian personnel losses were even more staggering. The 1st Hussars suffered 80 casualties, of which 59 were fatal, while D Company of the Queen's Own Rifles lost 96 of its 135 men, including 55 who were killed.[11] Though the 12th SS's manpower losses were also heavy, its armoured formations had not been seriously damaged.[12] More importantly, the strategic high ground between Le Haut du Bosq and Grainville-sur-Odon remained firmly in the Germans' grasp.

In recounting and assessing the debacle at Le Mesnil-Patry, contemporaries and historians alike have tended to focus on the failures of command, the tactical errors, and the carnage that resulted.[13] This is as it should be. After all, mistakes unquestionably were made on the Canadian side – numerous, shocking, and, in some cases, scandalous mistakes.[14] But we do a disservice to the men who were sacrificed during the afternoon and evening hours of 11 June if we reflect only on their lack of operational success. Beyond the fact that it failed, the untold story of the attack on Le Mesnil-Patry was the brutal and patently criminal means that the Germans employed in defeating it. The Canadian tank crews and infantrymen who fought at Le Mesnil-Patry were twice betrayed: once, to be sure, by a flawed battle plan, but also a second time, by the enemy to which they surrendered. Like Milius's troops four days earlier, the men of Siebken's and Müller's battalions would turn an impressive German feat of arms into a day of infamy that further solidified the 12th SS's dubious reputation as the Murder Division.

Most of the Le Mesnil-Patry killings were committed under the cover of combat. Typical of the kind of random battlefield atrocities that were perpetrated on 11 June was what happened to the tank crew of Sergeants William Simmons and E.S Payne and Troopers R.C. McClean and Lee Preston of C Squadron. After his Sherman was disabled and an unidentified trooper killed, Simmons gathered the dazed survivors and attempted to lead them back to Canadian lines. The crew had gone only a few yards when they spotted a Panther coming at them from across an adjacent field. It appeared to be training its machine gun on them. In an act of supreme selflessness, Simmons told his men to scatter, while he himself ran towards the German tank.[15] The courageous sergeant was never seen alive again, but his body was later found in a ditch on the grounds of the headquarters of Siebken's 2nd Battalion. The location and condition of the body suggested that Simmons had been taken prisoner and marched to the nearest HQ, where he was executed in cold blood.[16]

The rest of Simmons's crew had somewhat better luck. Despite taking cover in a ditch, they were quickly discovered by troops of the 7th Company of Siebken's battalion. While marching the three tankmen to the village of Les Saullets, which was just a stone's throw to the east of Le Mesnil-Patry, their escort opened fire on them. Hit in the back, Trooper Preston died instantly, while Sergeant Payne, though only grazed on the ear, and Trooper McClean, who had not been touched, both went down and feigned death. For some reason, the shooters did not bother to check on their victims. Payne and McClean undoubtedly owed their survival to this carelessness or indifference on the part of their would-be killers. After hiding out in the vicinity of Les Saullets for several days, the two tankmen took advantage of a German withdrawal to make their way back to Canadian lines.[17]

While Simmons and his men were having their deadly encounter with Siebken's infantry, the tank crew of Captain Harry Smuck and Troopers Arthur Hancock, William Loucks, and Frank Silverberg fell victim to a similar incident, with even more devastating consequences. As Smuck's Sherman approached an orchard located just north of Les Saullets, it took a direct hit from a Panther and burst into flames. Somehow, all but one of the crew managed to scramble to safety. Smuck and Hancock emerged from the hatch unscathed, but Silverberg's clothes were on fire, while Loucks had serious burns about his neck and head, as well as on his hands. Dazed, the crew stayed close to their wrecked tank, where they soon were joined by Troopers Dodds and Timpey, whose tank had also been hit and put out of action.[18]

Before the Canadians had a chance to get their bearings, SS infantrymen, almost certainly from Siebken's battalion, began to emerge from the nearby orchard. At this point, it became every man for himself. Hancock went in a southerly direction, while Smuck, Dodds, and Timpey headed east along the country road that led back towards Norrey-en-Bessin. Despite their injuries, Silverberg and Loucks also managed to escape, with Silverberg half supporting, half dragging his comrade. When Smuck, Dodds, and Timpey came upon another disabled tank, Timpey decided to keep on running, while Smuck and Dodds elected to hide underneath. The Germans were soon swarming all over the place and were certain to discover the two tankmen. Determined to avoid capture, Smuck and Dodds made a desperate break for it, splitting up in the process.[19]

Though the Canadians had scattered in a timely fashion, all but Dodds and Timpey would be rounded up. Except for the two fortunate tankmen, all would meet the same horrible fate. Smuck and Hancock were captured along with two other Hussars – Troopers Albert Charron and Joseph Leclaire – by members of the 7th Company of Siebken's battalion. Sent back to battalion headquarters with an escort commanded by a trooper known only as Mischke, the four prisoners never reached their destination. Somewhere along the way, Mischke forced the men into a field and presided over their execution. Their bodies were later found in a common grave not far from the route between the respective headquarters of the 7th Company and Siebken's 2nd Battalion.[20]

The remainder of Smuck's crew fared no better. Hampered by their injuries, Silverberg and Loucks did not get very far before they too were captured. It is not known for certain to which unit they surrendered, but the circumstances suggest that it may have been one of the companies of the 12th SS's engineering battalion.[21] Regardless of their subunit affiliation, the Germans clearly were 12th SS, as they comported themselves in the usual way of members of that division when confronted by enemy prisoners. According to the eyewitness account of Trooper Robert Munro, who was hiding in an adjacent grainfield, he saw six or seven SS soldiers surround the still-dazed Silverberg and Loucks and escort them over to an officer. Without any pretence at questioning the prisoners, the unidentified commander ordered them to lie down. Shots were then fired. Though Munro did not see the triggermen, Loucks's body was found in the same place, in a condition highly suggestive of execution after capture.[22] Silverberg's body was not discovered until later some distance from where Loucks lay. Perhaps he had only been wounded by his would-be executioners, and had been able to drag himself away.

No tank crew that surrendered to the 12th SS during the evening of 11 June was immune from the division's trademark wrath towards enemy POWs. Corporal Cybulsky and Troopers John Dumont, Leslie Soroke, and Lawrence Sutton of B Squadron learned this hard lesson after their Sherman was put out of action between Norrey and Le Mesnil-Patry. Following several desultory attempts to get back to their own lines, the tankmen were rounded up by a platoon of SS troops. The Canadians' captors descended on them like madmen, clubbing them with rifle butts and beating them with their fists. After a couple of harrowing minutes, the officer in charge restored a measure of discipline to his unit, but the prisoners' ordeal was only beginning.

Ominously, the platoon leader made no effort to conduct interrogations. Instead, after conferring with a few of his men, he opted to send the Canadians down a nearby road under escort by an NCO. The nature of the orders he imparted to his subordinate would become clear momentarily. After he and his prisoners had gone about a hundred yards, the NCO suddenly called out in English, 'Run, run!' Simultaneously, he opened up on the Canadians with his machine pistol.

Shot in the head, Trooper Sutton died instantly. Dumont was also felled by the first burst. Critically wounded, he would lie moaning for more than five hours before he mercifully expired. Soroke and Cybulsky managed to escape.

As the first two men in the prisoner column, they had an extra split second to react to the NCO's order. While rounds flew past them, the surviving Hussars dashed off, then dove for cover through a hedge. For reasons known only to himself, the executioner did not follow them. Cybulsky took the opportunity to make a clean getaway, but Soroke, who was in a state of shock, did not budge from his hiding place for the next two days. When he finally emerged, the still-shaken tankman was picked up almost immediately by a German patrol. Soroke cursed his bad luck, but at least he could be thankful that his new captors were a different breed from the thugs he had encountered previously. Unlike so many of his martyred comrades, Soroke's second bout of captivity in German hands would be routine and uneventful.[23]

The last criminal violation known to have been committed against Canadian POWs on 11 June occurred at the first-aid post on the grounds of the headquarters of Siebken's 2nd Battalion. The circumstances of this atrocity were and remain obscure, but it is possible that they were similar to those surrounding the shooting two days earlier of Privates Angel, Holness, and Baskerville. During the tank battle that developed just outside of Le Mesnil-Patry, Troopers Arnold Bowes, Gilbert Scriven, and K.O. Pedlar of the 1st Hussars, along with Sergeant Major J. Forbes of the Queen's Own Rifles, were captured and brought to Siebken's HQ. Pedlar and Forbes, both of whom were wounded, were treated at the battalion's first-aid post, probably by the sympathetic Dr Shütt. Pedlar died of his injuries, but Forbes, though not in good shape, was still alive during the night of 11 June. At some point thereafter, Bowes, Scriven, and Forbes were shot to death at close range, and their bodies buried near those of Angel, Holness, and Baskerville.[24]

None of the perpetrators of the six incidents of POW murder that took place in and around Le Mesnil-Patry on 11 June were ever apprehended, much less put on trial. Canadian investigators had their suspicions, but, as was the case with the Milius murders, they were hampered by the absence of German eyewitnesses and the numerous and scattered crime scenes. In at least two of the incidents – the Dumont-Sutton and Loucks-Silverberg murders – it was not possible to ascertain the German units that were involved. In two other incidents, specifically the gunning down of Preston and the execution of Smuck, Hancock, Charron, and Leclaire, the victims were known to have been in the custody of the 7th Company of Bernhard Siebken's battalion just prior to their deaths. Yet despite the fact that (Wehrmacht) Second Lieutenant August Henne, the company commander, was questioned on several occasions by Allied and Canadian war crimes investigators, no charges ever resulted. The same was true of the Simmons murder and the executions at the first-aid post. Though these latter killings had taken place on the grounds of Bernhard Siebken's battalion headquarters, there was too much conflicting evidence, including testimony that placed the volatile Wilhelm Mohnke on the scene, to bring charges against the battalion commander.[25] Thus, like the Bretteville massacre and the murder of Ernest Gilbank at Norrey, the killing of Canadian prisoners of war at Le Mesnil-Patry would go into the 'unsolved' file.

# 12

# An End to the Killing?

The costly affair at Le Mesnil-Patry marked the end of the first phase of operations in the Canadian sector of Normandy. For the better part of the next three weeks, the attention of Allied military planners shifted elsewhere.[1] This did not mean that the 3rd Canadian and 12th SS Divisions disengaged from one another. But it did signal a change in the nature of their encounter. After five days of unremitting attacks and counterattacks, the two battered and weary antagonists settled into a prolonged lull punctuated by feints, patrols, and artillery duels.[2] It was not until the first week of July that full-scale hostilities once more erupted between the two formations.

Concurrent with the cessation of offensive operations along the Canadian front, the number of POW murders decreased dramatically. It has been suggested that the decline in German atrocities at this time was attributable to the perpetrators' realization that the battle was going badly for them. To continue to shoot down unarmed prisoners, so the argument goes, would only have invited retaliation in the short term and prosecution later on.[3] Though plausible, this explanation is not supported by the facts. For one thing, in the week following the Le Mesnil-Patry operation, nine additional Canadians are known to have been killed after capture by subunits of the 12th SS. Furthermore, there is evidence that the division continued to murder prisoners long after its military situation had become desperate. Indeed, two additional massacres, which together claimed at least twenty-two victims, were carried out by elements of the 12th SS in late June and early July 1944. Long forgotten, these latter atrocities give lie to the notion that the perpetrators of previous crimes were beginning to have second thoughts.

After a five-day hiatus, the murder of POWs started up again on 17 June. The opportunity for the resumption of the killing was afforded by a Canadian reconnaissance mission gone awry. Late on the night of 16 June, the Stormont, Dundas and Glengarry Highlanders Regiment sent out a patrol. The detachment consisted of sixteen men from the regiment's D Company and seven sappers from the 18th Field Company, Royal Canadian Engineers. Their mission was a familiar but dangerous one – locate and destroy the guns on disabled but still serviceable German tanks. On this night, the men were to carry out their task along the mile-long stretch of road that led from Vieux Cairon southward into Gruchy. The operation was expected to be of three hours' duration. In charge would be Lieutenant Fred Williams, a fine officer who was very popular with the men.[4]

At 11:30 PM on the 16th, Williams led his detachment out from the Glens' headquarters. Things began to go wrong almost immediately. Indeed, less than a hundred yards into the mission, the lieutenant made a fateful blunder. Contrary to instructions, he failed to bear to the right, which would have taken him and his men onto the Vieux Cairon–Gruchy road, but instead went straight, following the main road that led into Buron. Unbeknownst to Williams, the Germans had turned the Vieux Cairon–Buron axis into a field of fire. The defensive perimeter consisted of several rows of trip-wired signal lights and a minefield. Positioned just beyond the minefield were three machine-gun emplacements, which were manned by crews from the 3rd Battalion of the 25th Panzer Grenadier Regiment.[5] Oblivious to the danger, the Canadians were about to walk into a trap.

By moving slowly and deliberately, the detachment actually managed to avoid the first two rows of trip wires. At around 1:15 AM, however, one of the sappers accidentally triggered a mine. Suddenly, all hell broke loose. From less than a hundred yards down the road, the Germans' machine guns opened up on the surprised Canadians. Nearly half of the men were hit by the first salvo. After experiencing a momentary loss of composure, the rest attempted to fight back. Soon the angry snicker of rifle fire and the explosion of grenades could be heard. But the patrol's battle was a forlorn one. Unable to manoeuvre in the face of the Germans' concentrated fire, the Canadians had no choice but to withdraw. At 2:20 AM, Williams's men began to trickle back to headquarters.[6]

It was not long before the Glens' HQ began to buzz with news of the misfortune that had befallen the patrol. Ten of the twenty-three men were reported to have been wounded in the firefight north of Buron, and four of the wounded men had not returned. Among the missing were Lieutenant Williams, Lance Corporal George Pollard, who was a section leader in D Company, one of Pollard's men, and a sapper. At least three members of the patrol saw Williams go down after he had been hit by the initial burst of machine-gun fire. His condition was not known, but two of the witnesses to his wounding heard the lieutenant say to Corporal John Labonte, 'Take over Johnny, and let them have it!'

Pollard, who had been marching right behind Williams, was also hit by the first burst.[7] Like the lieutenant, his fate was unknown.

Though he had sustained leg and arm wounds, the missing sapper reappeared at the Glens' headquarters later in the morning. Unfortunately, there was no sign of Williams, Pollard, or the third man. In an attempt to locate the missing men, the regiment sent out a search party under the command of Lieutenant Howard Knight. The would-be rescuers spent several hours scouring the countryside, but their efforts were to no avail. Despondent at the apparent loss of their popular comrades, Knight and his men finally trudged back to headquarters at around noon.[8]

Officially, Williams and Pollard were listed as missing in action. Subsequently, their status was updated to presumed killed in action.[9] Three weeks after they went missing, however, disturbing evidence was found suggesting that the two men had fallen victim to yet another atrocity perpetrated by the 12th SS. Just before midnight on 8 July, the Regina Rifles captured the Abbaye d'Ardenne. As they secured the grounds of the ancient abbey, the victorious Reginas spotted the body of a Canadian officer lying unburied about fifty yards from what had formerly been Kurt Meyer's command post. From the identity disc, the body was determined to be that of Lieutenant Williams. An autopsy revealed that he had been shot in the head execution style. No trace of Pollard was found.[10]

It was only after the war that the Glens learned the true fate of their missing comrades. The details of what had happened to Williams and Pollard came out at Meyer's trial. According to the testimony of three former members of the defendant's regiment, on 17 June two wounded Canadian soldiers had been captured, treated at the dressing station of the 3rd Battalion at Cussy, and then evacuated to the first-aid post at the Abbaye d'Ardenne. One of the prisoners was shot soon after his arrival at the abbey, between 4:00 and 6:00 AM. The second POW apparently was held for the better part of the day before he too was shot. On the basis of what was admittedly hearsay evidence, it was determined that the Canadians had been executed because they would not impart the desired information during questioning.[11]

None of the German witnesses who came forward actually saw the 17 June shootings. Still, there can be little doubt as to the identity of the victims. According to SS Second Lieutenant Kurt Bergmann, the 3rd Battalion's adjutant, his formation took only three prisoners between 10 June and 9 July. Two of the three had been captured in mid-June. Both wounded, the two men, Bergmann recalled, had been brought in at around 3:00 AM, treated at the battalion aid station, and then escorted to regimental headquarters.[12] In view of the timing and circumstances of their capture, it was reasonable to conclude that the wounded prisoners to whom Bergmann referred had been the missing Williams and Pollard.

While the names of the victims of the 17 June shootings at the Abbaye d'Ardenne were never really in question, the identity of the perpetrators was another matter. The problem facing Canadian war crimes investigators in this case was uncertainty as to who had been in charge at the abbey at the time when Williams and Pollard were brought in. Up to 16 June, it would have been Kurt Meyer, then the commander of the 25th Panzer Grenadier Regiment. According to testimony given at Meyer's trial, however, the period 16–18 June was one during which the 12th SS Division made several key personnel changes. Necessitated by the death of SS Brigadier General Witt, the changes included the promotion of Meyer to the post of divisional commander, replacing Witt, and the promotion of SS Lieutenant Colonel Karl-Heinz Milius to the post of commander of the 25th Panzer Grenadier Regiment, replacing Meyer. Undertaken concurrent with the capture of Williams and Pollard, these personnel changes made it virtually impossible to ascertain who had been in command of the 25th Regiment during the crucial early morning hours of 17 June.[13]

Like the Abbaye d'Ardenne killings, the second set of POW murders perpetrated on 17 June also took place at a headquarters. At around 6:00 PM on the 17th, seven Canadian prisoners – Trooper Clayton Perry of the 1st Hussars and Sergeant Thomas McLaughlin, Corporal Etsel Cook, and Privates John Campbell, Gerald Willett, Ernest Cranfield, and Paul Bullock of the Queen's Own Rifles of Canada – were delivered to the supply train of the 12th SS's engineering battalion, which was billeted in the village of Mouen.[14] The Canadians, who had been wandering around no man's land since the ill-fated attack on Le Mesnil-Patry, appeared dirty and exhausted.[15] Upon arrival at the HQ, the prisoners were interrogated by an officer. Some four hours later, they were taken under heavy guard to the outskirts of Mouen. On the command of the escort leader, probably an SS NCO, a small execution party shot the Canadians down in cold blood. The killings must have taken some time to complete, as only Cook, Cranfield, Perry, and Willett had wounds consistent with shooting by firing squad, while Bullock, Campbell, and McLaughlin appeared to have been shot one at a time, at point-blank range. The next day, French civilians were ordered to dig a large grave in which SS troopers buried the seven bodies.[16]

Despite the fact that the shooting of the seven Canadian prisoners had taken place at a headquarters within the area of operations of the 12th SS's engineering battalion, no one from that unit was ever charged with the crime. The problem for Canadian investigators was that the various German witnesses who were questioned about the killings all tended to implicate someone higher in the chain of command. For example, SS Second Lieutenant Wilhelm Stremme, a platoon leader in the engineering battalion's 4th Company, pointed the finger at his company commander, SS First Lieutenant Herbert Bischoff.[17] SS First Lieutenant Paul Kuret, the commander of the battalion's 2nd Company and himself a prime suspect,[18] muddied the waters by implicating SS Major Siegfried Müller, the battalion commander. According to Kuret, several days before the incident Müller had directed his company commanders to deny quarter to the enemy.[19] When added to Stremme's contention that Müller used to interrogate prisoners on his own, this allegation put the blame squarely where it seemed to belong – on the shoulders of the battalion commander. Inexplicably, Kuret's evidence was not followed up. Neither Müller nor the other officers who might have been at Mouen on 17 June were ever brought in for questioning.[20]

The executions of Trooper Perry and Sergeant McLaughlin and his men were the last officially recorded POW murders attributed to the 12th SS. They were not the last atrocities perpetrated by the division, however. Between 26 June and 8 July, two additional mass killings of Canadian prisoners took place along the front of the 12th SS. No bodies were found, so neither investigation went very far. Still, there seemed little doubt that the killings had taken place. In one case, an SS trooper recounted what seemed to be reliable hearsay evidence regarding the shooting of Canadian POWs. In the other case, the crime was confirmed by an eyewitness.

The first set of killings 'unofficially' attributed to the 12th SS were perpetrated during a renewed Allied drive to envelop and capture the city of Caen. Code-named 'Epsom,' the operation began on the morning of 26 June with a massive artillery barrage. Led by the (Scottish) 15th Division, (British) 8th Corps attacked German positions through a three-and-a-half-mile-wide corridor bounded by Fontenay-le-Pesnel in the west and St Manvieu in the east. Facing 8th Corps were the remnants of the 12th SS's western front – Müller's engineering battalion and two badly depleted battalions of Wilhelm Mohnke's 26th Panzer Grenadier Regiment. Though it started on a hopeful note, the British attack soon bogged down. Thirty-six hours into Epsom, the advance of 8th Corps had stalled well short of its objectives. Over the next three days, the two sides fought to a grim stalemate. Despite being decimated in the battle, which was contested with a savagery not seen in Normandy since the first few days of operations, the 12th SS succeeded in stabilizing the German front until the arrival of reinforcements.[21]

Still understrength from its earlier exertions, the 3rd Canadian Infantry Division was held in reserve during Epsom. Indeed, its role was confined to pre-operation reconnaissance and the lending of artillery support at the start of the offensive.[22] It is therefore not entirely clear how seven Canadian soldiers fell into the hands of the 12th SS on 26 June. Yet the only witness to their fate swore that the men he had observed in German captivity that day wore the 'Canada' badge on their sleeves. According to Private Bogdan Ziolek, a Polish conscript who at the time was serving in a Wehrmacht anti-aircraft unit, he was riding in the cab of a truck that was headed for the front when it came to an orchard in which twelve to fifteen SS troopers, evidently members of Mohnke's regiment,[23] stood guarding seven Canadian POWs. As the truck slowed, Ziolek saw some of the SS men lift their machine pistols and mow down the Canadians.[24] Despite the fact that the reluctant conscript was able to pinpoint the location of the alleged shooting, no bodies could be found, nor was anyone able to provide corroborating testimony. As a result, Canadian war crimes investigators were forced to close their investigation of the incident.[25]

The second set of POW killings 'unofficially' attributed to the 12th SS were perpetrated during the final Allied drive to take Caen. Code-named 'Charnwood,' the operation was planned as a frontal assault on the city by (British) 1st Corps, comprising the (British) 3rd Infantry Division, the 59th Staffordshire Division, and the now refitted 3rd Canadian Infantry Division. Opposing the (British) 3rd Division on the eastern flank was the inexperienced and ill-equipped 16th Luftwaffe Field Division, which had relieved the battered 21st Panzer only a few days earlier. In the west, where the 3rd Canadian Division was to attack, the way was blocked by elements of the 25th Panzer Grenadier Regiment, the formation that had wreaked such havoc on the the the Canadians on 7 June.[26]

Charnwood, which got under way in the early morning hours of 8 July, was preceded by a massive RAF bombardment of the northern outskirts of Caen. Though intended to disrupt German communication and supply lines, the air strikes in fact did little more than depress the morale of the city's defenders. Nonetheless, on 1st Corps' eastern flank the (British) 3rd Division quickly overran the outclassed 16th Luftwaffe Division. In the west, the 25th Panzer Grenadier Regiment fought with greater tenacity, but by evening on 8 July the SS troops were surrounded in the ruins of Authie and Buron. Fittingly, in view of what had happened a month earlier, the capture of Authie was left to the North Nova Scotia Highlanders. While the North Novas were settling an old score, the Regina Rifles were capturing the Abbaye d'Ardenne. Driven from the grounds of his perennial command post, Kurt Meyer withdrew with his shattered forces to the south bank of the Orne River.[27] Thus, thirty-three days after the Allies had first landed on French soil, the road into Caen was at last open.

The POW killings associated with Operation Charnwood were alleged to have taken place on the morning of 8 July. During an interrogation conducted by American military intelligence officers, Hermann Woersdörfer, who was a former machine gunner with the 2nd Battalion of the 25th Panzer Grenadier

Regiment, admitted that his company (the 5th) had murdered fifteen to twenty Canadian prisoners in the Cambes-Anisy sector. It is not clear what the Canadians were doing in the area. After all, Cambes had been in British hands since 9 June, and in fact was the start line for the assault of the 59th Staffordshire Division.[28] Nonetheless, Woersdörfer was adamant that the victims had been Canadians. On the way back to battalion headquarters, he claimed, the prisoners' escort ran into a column of enemy tanks. To avoid being encircled, the SS troopers shot the Canadians down where they stood and then broke out.[29]

Despite Woersdörfer's apparent sincerity, the bodies of the victims could not be located.[30] Nor did any corroborating witnesses come forward. Thus, this incident, like the one described by Private Ziolek, would go into the 'unsolved' file.

If the unconfirmed killings near Caen and Cambes are added to the tally of confirmed ones, then the number of POW murders for which the 12th SS Panzer Division 'Hitler Youth' was responsible totalled at least 178. Yet even without the 26 June and 8 July atrocities, the 12th SS's toll of prisoner murders was staggering. The extent of the brutality and lawlessness with which this one German formation conducted its operations is revealed by some comparative statistics. Up to and including the Le Mesnil-Patry killings on 11 June, the number of Canadian prisoners known to have been murdered by the 12th SS was 147. During the same six-day period, the 3rd Canadian Infantry Division and the 2nd Canadian Armoured Brigade suffered a total of 1,017 fatal casualties.[31] This means that one out of every seven Canadians killed in Normandy between 6 and 11 June did not die in combat, but rather at the hands of their captors. If the ratio of POW murders to battle fatalities is calculated from 7 June, when the 3rd Canadian and 12th SS Divisions actually began to engage one another, then the result is even more chilling. Of the 677 fatal casualties[32] suffered by the 3rd Canadian Division during the period 7–11 June, one in five were men who had been murdered after capture.

The fighting in Normandy has long been acknowledged as some of the most bloody and vicious of the entire war. But the full measure of its brutality has not been exposed until now. It should be clear from the preceding chapters that there really were two wars going on in Normandy. One was the struggle to take and hold ground. This war was fought by both sides with all of the conventional military means at their disposal. The other war was a secret, more sinister one, fought by one side in Hitler's name and with the criminal methods all too often associated with the twisted cause he espoused. Waged by Nazi fanatics against defenceless POWs in moonlit grainfields, behind hedgerows, at headquarters, and in dozens of other places hidden from view, this 'dirty war' had no justification on the grounds of military necessity. Nor was it conducted in legitimate reprisal for crimes committed by the enemy. On the contrary, the murder of Canadian prisoners in Normandy can only be understood as the inevitable by-product of the noxious atmosphere of hate that had been fostered within the 12th SS by men who ought to have known better – its most senior officers.

Despite the fact that its objectives were pursued with equal fanaticism, the 12th SS's covert war against POWs proved to be no more successful than its military campaign against the Allied invasion force. As far as can be determined, the prisoner massacres had no appreciable effect on the outcome, except, perhaps, that they strengthened the fighting spirit of Canadian troops by infusing them with the desire for revenge. Sometimes, regrettably, this vengeance was paid out in kind.[33] On 8 July 1944, for example, the war diary of the 7th Canadian Infantry Brigade laconically recorded that 'a few old scores' had been settled with prisoners from the 12th SS.[34] In keeping with all that was good and decent in the Canadian military tradition, such incidents of retaliation were few and far between. Indeed, as the bodies of its murdered soldiers began to turn up in the summer of 1944, the Canadian army discouraged private acts of revenge in favour of a more meaningful and lasting reckoning.[35] The story of this well-intentioned but ultimately flawed quest for justice for the victims of the Normandy massacres is the subject to which this book now turns.

# 13
## Indictment

On the evening of 8 June 1944, a ferocious Allied naval and artillery bombardment drove Gerhard Bremer's reconnaissance battalion from its headquarters at the Château d'Audrieu.[1] The following afternoon, elements of the (British) Dorsets Regiment occupied the chateau. Like the Canadian prisoners who had preceded them, the Dorsets could not help but marvel at the beauty of the surroundings. Thinking the place deserted, they were pleasantly surprised when Monique Level, the daughter of the chateau's proprietor, emerged from the main house. Refined in manner and fluent in English, Mlle Level offered food and cider to the new arrivals.[2] After having endured the rough Channel crossing, the bitterly contested landings, and two days of almost incessant close-quarter fighting, the battleweary British troops must have thought that they had entered Shangri-La. Their good feelings would be shortlived.

While the Dorsets were setting up a command post, Level spoke to Major Lloyd Sneath, the regiment's second-in-command. In vivid detail, she recounted for him the previous day's nightmarish events. The major learned that at approximately 2:00 PM on 8 June, more than two dozen POWs had been escorted onto the grounds of the chateau, interrogated in small groups by the German commander (i.e., Bremer), then ushered into the adjacent woods and shot. Shocked and angered by what he had just heard, Sneath demanded to be shown the execution sites. Level complied, taking him to the orchard near the main house. There he observed thirteen bodies, clad in Canadian battledress, lying more or less side by side, as if they had been standing that way when they were gunned down. As he got closer, Sneath recoiled in horror: he recognized some of the faces.[3]

In one of the sad coincidences associated with this story, it turned out that Major Sneath had served for a time as an NCO with the Royal Winnipeg Rifles before being sent 'Canloan' to Britain. During his stint with the Winnipegs, he had come to know many of the men who now lay murdered before him. Unable to bear the sight of his fallen former comrades any longer, Sneath left the orchard and returned to the main house, where he delegated to subordinates responsibility for the preservation of the crime scene and the identification of the bodies. Over the remainder of the afternoon, a small team of Dorsets carried out this difficult but necessary task.[4] They included Captain J. Neil, a medical officer attached to the regiment. Though the fluid battlefield situation did not afford him sufficient time to perform autopsies, Neil did subject the bodies to close visual examination. His findings, which were submitted in a report that eventually ended up on General Montgomery's desk, tended to confirm Level's story. According to Captain Neil, the thirteen Winnipegs had been killed in a manner that ruled out death in combat, and many had sustained head wounds consistent with the application of the *coup de grâce*.[5]

The discovery of thirteen murdered Canadian POWs at the Château d'Audrieu gave the Allies their first inkling of the dirty war that was being waged along the front of the 12th SS Panzer Division 'Hitler Youth.' In the weeks that followed, the lush and picturesque Normandy countryside yielded further grisly evidence of the depths of barbarism to which the 12th SS had descended. Though the Dorsets were forced to withdraw from the chateau on the night of 9 June, two weeks later other British forces liberated it for good. At that time, a more thorough search of the grounds led to the discovery of the bodies of an additional thirteen soldiers – eleven Canadian and two British – whose condition and wounds strongly suggested that they had been shot after capture. During the first week of July, near the village of Galmanche, British troops also came across the body of Captain Brown, the Sherbrooke Fusiliers' chaplain who had been bayoneted to death by his captors late on the night of 7 June. Concurrent with the discovery of the padre, members of a British field artillery regiment happened to stumble upon two shallow graves on the outskirts of Le Mesnil-Patry. When exhumed, the bodies were determined to be those of Privates Angel, Holness, and Baskerville, who had been taken prisoner at the headquarters of Bernhard Siebken's battalion on the night of 8 June and murdered there the next morning, and those of Sergeant Major Forbes and Troopers Bowes and Scriven, who had been captured on the afternoon of 11 June and executed sometime that night.[6]

Two weeks later, Canadian forces made yet another grim discovery. Acting on information provided by the inhabitants of Mouen, they found a grave just outside the village in which were buried the bodies of Trooper Clayton Perry, Sergeant Tommy McLaughlin, and five of McLaughlin's men, all of whom had been shot after capture on the night of 17 June by members of the 12th SS's engineering battalion. Finally, at the end of July, Canadian troops discovered a mass grave that contained the bodies of the almost three dozen men who had been murdered by Milius's battalion in and around Authie and Buron on the afternoon of 7 June.[7]

Every army expects to be confronted with legal issues arising out of their operations, and every army has mechanisms and procedures for dealing with them. The purview of a Judge Advocate General or equivalent agency, such issues can vary widely, but typically they involve violations of military law. Well before they landed on the continent of Europe, each of the Allied armies had a judicial infrastructure capable of investigating and punishing crimes committed by its own troops.[8] But none had the wherewithal to deal with crimes perpetrated by the enemy.[9] As reports began to come in regarding the discovery of the bodies of the murdered Canadians, the Allies realized that the prosecution of such crimes would require the convening of special courts martial. After all, the denial of quarter was a flagrant violation of laws and customs of war that had long been accepted as binding by the civilized nations of the world. For the international conventions governing the conduct of war to have any meaning, the wanton killing of prisoners would have to be stopped, and such POW murders as had already been committed would have to be punished.

As the victims of the Château d'Audrieu killings had been members of Canadian and British formations, 21st Army Group, to which they were subordinated, was given the job of looking into the incident. At 21st Army Group's headquarters, General Montgomery promptly ordered an investigation. Though Monty had vented his disgust when first informed of the murders, his personal anger does not seem to have generated any investigative momentum down the chain of command. On the contrary, (British) 2nd Army, to which Montgomery entrusted the case, sloughed it off on to 30th Corps, which in turn directed one of its subordinate formations, the 50th Northumbrian Division, to conduct the appropriate inquiries. Locked in mortal combat with the Germans, the 50th Division understandably accorded the matter the lowest possible priority.[10]

By their shameless buck passing, the British made it clear that they were not interested in investigating alleged war crimes while the fighting in Normandy was still going on. Disappointed at their ally's inaction, the Canadian army nonetheless refrained from making waves. While conceding that 'the interests of 30 Corps and 50 Div are not evident,' Lieutenant General Crerar, the commander of the 1st Canadian Army, initially did nothing more than apprise 2nd Army of the situation. However, when 2nd Army proved unable or unwilling to jump-start the investigation, the Canadians stepped up the pressure. During a conference held at Canadian Military Headquarters (CMHQ) in London on 4 July, it was decided to inform 21st Army Group that the whole matter 'had been badly handled by Second Army' and to press for the convening of a court of inquiry 'at the earliest possible moment.'[11]

The Canadian protests fell on deaf ears at 21st Army Group. Fortunately, word of the Château d'Audrieu incident had also reached General Eisenhower and his staff at Supreme Headquarters of the Allied Expeditionary Force (SHAEF). His ire aroused by what he rightly regarded as the cowardly murder of defenceless prisoners, Eisenhower immediately authorized the establishment of a court of inquiry.[12] Its mandate was to determine the facts of the case and report its findings to SHAEF. U.S. Army Major General R.W. Barker, who at the time was assistant chief of staff of SHAEF's G-1 Division, was put in charge of the investigation. In keeping with Eisenhower's policy of balancing Allied interests, two British and two Canadian officers were also assigned to the court. The Canadian representatives were Brigadier W.H.S. Macklin, then the commander of the 13th Canadian Infantry Brigade and later deputy chief of staff at CMHQ, and Lieutenant Colonel J.W. McClain, the assistant adjutant general.[13]

The SHAEF court of inquiry started its investigation of the Château d'Audrieu incident on 8 July. With all known civilian witnesses residing in the vicinity of the crime scene, it did not take long for the court to complete its work. Indeed, an interim report was ready by 15 July. The court's final report was issued ten days later. Its conclusions were damning. The court found that during the course of the afternoon of 8 June at least nineteen, and probably twenty-six, Canadian and British POWs had been executed by members of the 12th SS's reconnaissance battalion on the grounds of the Château d'Audrieu. The court went on to allege that SS Major Bremer, the battalion commander, as well as SS Captain Gerd von Reitzenstein, SS First Lieutenant Willi-Peter Hansmann, and SS Technical Sergeant Leopold Stun, all had been present at the chateau on 8 June, and that Hansmann and Stun had actually participated in the killings. Since its findings constituted a prima facie case against the four suspects, the court recommended the issuing of warrants for their apprehension.[14]

Even while SHAEF was looking into the Château d'Audrieu killings, the bodies of the victims of additional incidents of POW murder were turning up. With each new discovery came new questions. Which German formation, investigators asked, had been responsible for the sector in which the crime had been committed? Which German formation had been stationed in the immediate area? And which German formation had actually carried out the killings?

The answer to these questions invariably was the same – the 12th SS Panzer Division 'Hitler Youth.' Indeed, by the end of July, a clear pattern was emerging. So many shootings of Canadian POWs had been perpetrated by different subunits of the 12th SS that it did not seem possible they had been isolated acts.

On the contrary, they gave every indication of having been the fulfilment of a divisional policy of terror and murder aimed specifically at enemy prisoners of war.

Convinced that the crimes that were being uncovered were just the tip of an iceberg, Allied legal officers recommended the establishment of a permanent body to investigate war crimes. Eisenhower concurred. On 20 August, the supreme commander issued an order constituting a standing court of inquiry at SHAEF.[15] This was to mark a turning point in the investigation of the Hitler Youth Division.

Like its predecessor, the standing court was placed under the direction of Major General Barker.[16] In keeping with the precedent established during the Château d'Audrieu investigation, each ally was again granted a seat on the court. But the similarities between the two courts ended there. Unlike the first SHAEF inquiry, which was case specific, the jurisdiction of the new court was far reaching. Though Nazi atrocities against partisans and civilians were off limits, the standing court was invested with the authority to look into *all* allegations of war crimes perpetrated against *any* Allied military personnel.[17]

Upon receipt of such an allegation, the court was charged with doing whatever was necessary to determine the facts of the case and to identify the perpetrators. This included the taking of testimony under oath from all potential military and civilian witnesses, the preservation of all physical evidence, and the securing of all relevant documentation. For these purposes, the court was authorized to travel anywhere in northwestern Europe and to call on any Allied forces for assistance. When an investigation was completed, the court was required to record and publish its findings in a final report. Where warranted, the report was to contain recommendations for further action.[18]

Commensurate with its broad mandate, the standing court at SHAEF was a massive organization. Though comprised of only three presiding officers (as compared with the five who directed the Château d'Audrieu inquiry), the court had access to almost unlimited resources. An impressive staff of intelligence and provost officers, whose availability was essential if more than one investigation was to be carried out at a time, was permanently assigned to the court. To assist in its day-to-day operations, the court was supplied with a veritable army of support staff, including interpreters, stenographers, and clerks. Additionally, a pathologist was detailed to the court to provide expert forensic analysis. Finally, a fleet of vehicles and a large pool of drivers were put on standby so that investigators could be whisked to a crime scene at a moment's notice.[19]

Although he had been personally selected by Eisenhower, Major General Barker's duties at SHAEF prevented him from assuming the presidency of the standing court. Fortunately, his replacement, U.S. Army Colonel Paul E. Tombaugh, was an eminently qualified lawyer. So were the other two members of the court. The British army's representative was Lieutenant Colonel J.H. Boraston. A distinguished London barrister, Boraston was perhaps best-known for having served during the First World War as adjutant to the controversial general Sir Douglas Haig.[20] Representing the Canadian army was Lieutenant Colonel Bruce J.S. Macdonald, a Windsor lawyer and militia officer. Sacked as commander of the Essex Scottish Regiment in the wake of the disastrous Verrières Ridge operation, Macdonald would find his true calling as a military prosecutor.[21]

As it happened, Macdonald was not the only Canadian to sit on the court. Lieutenant Colonel John Page, who had served as secretary to the Château d'Audrieu inquiry, was retained on loan from CMHQ as a court alternate. A capable staff officer who had helped to establish Canada's wartime intelligence service, Page would prove invaluable as the court's caseload mounted.[22]

During the seven months that it was in session, the standing court of inquiry at SHAEF investigated twenty-five cases of crimes perpetrated against members of the various Allied armed forces. Five of the cases involved Canadian victims. Of these, two concerned crimes committed against members of the RCAF. The remaining three cases dealt with the 12th SS's atrocities against members of the 3rd Canadian Infantry Division.[23]

The first case on the standing court's agenda was the Authie incident. Completed a month after the court first convened, the inquiry determined that on the afternoon of 7 June at least twenty-seven, and probably thirty-three, Canadian prisoners of war had been murdered after capture near the villages of Authie and Buron by elements of the 3rd Battalion of the 12th SS's 25th Panzer Grenadier Regiment. Though there was no direct evidence of his participation, the court found that SS Lieutenant Colonel Karl-Heinz Milius, the commander of the 3rd Battalion, had been implicated by virtue of the chain-of-command theory, on the grounds that in his capacity as commander he bore vicarious responsibility for any criminal violations committed by his subordinates. The second case involved the Château d'Audrieu murders. Here the standing court essentially echoed the findings of its predecessor. The third case dealt with the Mouen incident. On the basis of its inquiry, the court concluded that the execution of seven Canadian POWs on the night of 17 June had been the work of elements of the 12th SS's engineering battalion. The court also found that SS Major Siegfried Müller, the battalion commander, had been implicated in the murders. Once more the basis for this conclusion was the chain-of-command theory, although there were also indications that Müller had interrogated the prisoners prior to their execution.[24]

The investigative work done on the Authie, Château d'Audrieu, and Mouen cases provided the background material for a comprehensive report on the 12th SS's dirty war against POWs in Normandy. Presented to SHAEF by the standing court on 19 April 1945, the report was considered to be of such evidentiary significance that it was submitted as a prosecution exhibit at the Nuremberg trials seven months later.[25] Bearing in mind that at the time many of the court's inquiries were far from finished, the report was remarkably accurate and thorough. It remains to this day a powerful document, written as much to deter future evildoers as to indict contemporary ones. As the members of the standing court declared in their introduction to the report, 'The conduct of the 12th SS Panzer Division "Hitler Youth" presented a consistent pattern of brutality and ruthlessness. This characteristic was so marked as to make it appear desirable to assemble in a single document the results of those investigations which involved the "Hitler Youth" Division, with a view to facilitating subsequent action and to making the shameful character of this unit a matter of record.'[26]

The standing court estimated that as many as 109 Allied POWs, all but six of them Canadians, had been murdered by various subunits of the 12th SS in more than a dozen incidents. The court arrived at its estimate by adding up the number of victims from confirmed atrocities. At least twenty-seven, and probably thirty-three, Canadian prisoners of war were believed to have been murdered in the aftermath of the fighting in and around Authie and Buron on 7 June. At least forty-four, and probably forty-six, Canadian and British POWs were believed to have been murdered in the aftermath of the fighting at Putot-en-Bessin on 8 June. And approximately thirty Canadian, British, and American POWs were believed to have been murdered over the next two weeks in a number of separate incidents.[27]

The reader undoubtedly will have noted the discrepancy between SHAEF's estimate of 103 Canadian victims and the figure of 156 posited in this book. The discrepancy is easily explained. For one thing, the evidence available to the court at the time that it issued its comprehensive report suggested that only twenty POWs had been machine gunned to death on the Caen-Fontenay road,[28] not the thirty-five who were later confirmed to have been killed. Second, the court had not yet become aware of the Abbaye d'Ardenne murders, which had claimed another eighteen victims. Third, as we have already seen, the killing after capture of thirteen Canadians at Bretteville l'Orgueilleuse on the night of 8 June was not reported to war crimes investigators until several months after the end of hostilities. Fourth, because of the failure to turn up the body of Lance Corporal Pollard, who along with Lieutenant Williams had been executed on the grounds of the Abbaye d'Ardenne on 17 June, SHAEF did not consider his murder to have been confirmed. Lastly, owing to an administrative error, the execution of Privates Angel, Holness, and Baskerville on 9 June and that of Sergeant Major Forbes and Troopers Bowes and Scriven on 11 June were not included in the standing court's tally.[29] When these additional fifty-three victims are added to the SHAEF estimate, the total number of Canadian prisoners who were murdered while in the custody of the 12th SS Division reaches 156.

In fulfilment of its mandate, the standing court did not merely record the litany of atrocities perpetrated by the 12th SS; it also made recommendations for how SHAEF should deal with them. Citing the 'prevalence' of criminal behaviour throughout the division as evidence that its senior officers had either abetted or openly approved a policy of executing prisoners, the court recommended that Kurt Meyer, Wilhelm Mohnke, Gerhard Bremer, Karl-Heinz Milius, and Siegfried Müller be brought to trial on charges of having denied quarter to the enemy and of having failed to prevent violations against prisoners by the men under their command. It also recommended that Bremer, Müller, Gerd von Reitzenstein, and several lower-ranking officers and NCOs be charged with murder, either as perpetrators or as accessories before or after the fact. Finally, with an eye towards future prosecutions, the court further recommended that no member of the 12th SS currently being held in POW captivity be released until he had been 'thoroughly interrogated' by investigators regarding either his knowledge of or participation in any of the division's confirmed atrocities.[30]

The standing court's report constituted a searing indictment of the conduct of the 12th SS Division in general and that of its senior officers in particular. Indeed, the crimes described therein were so heinous that they cried out for justice. Yet there seemed little hope that lawful retribution would be exacted any time soon. Of all the division's senior officers, only one, Kurt Meyer, was in the custody of the Allies as a POW, and almost nothing was known about his role in the killing of prisoners. As a consequence, at the time he could have been tried only on the basis of the chain-of-command theory. Unfortunately, even such a limited prosecution did not seem to offer much prospect of success. As Lieutenant Colonel Macdonald conceded in a report to General Barker, the evidence amassed thus far against Meyer 'was insufficient to ensure a conviction.'[31]

All of this would change. Within days of Macdonald's pessimistic appraisal, evidence came to light that breathed new life into the Meyer investigation. On 30 March 1945, SS Private Jan Jesionek, the ethnic German conscript who had witnessed the execution of seven Canadian prisoners at the Abbaye d'Ardenne almost a year earlier, deserted and crossed over American lines. It did not take long for him to start singing to Allied war-crimes investigators. In the process of unburdening himself, Jesionek unequivocally implicated Meyer in the killings at the abbey.[32] Just when it looked as though a prosecution might be in the offing, however, the quest for justice was dealt a seemingly mortal blow.

At around the time that Jesionek was contemplating his desertion, SHAEF announced that its standing court would be shutting down. The reason was the U.S. Army's decision to prosecute its own cases. Rooted in the growing political pressure for Washington to take some kind of action on the Malmedy killings, the American pullout caused a domino effect at SHAEF. Realizing that the closure of the standing court left their own cases in limbo, the British announced that 21st Army Group would take over the investigations and recalled Lieutenant Colonel Boraston for that purpose. The writing was now on the wall. As of 1 April 1945, there no longer would be legal machinery at SHAEF for dealing with crimes perpetrated against Allied military personnel.[33] Henceforth, if there was to be any justice for the 156 Canadian victims of the Normandy massacres, the initiative would have to come from CMHQ in London and the Canadian government in Ottawa.

# 14
# The Twisted Road to Justice

The closure of the standing court at SHAEF left Canadian policy makers with three choices. One possibility was to allow the war crimes issue to lapse altogether. The war in Europe was winding down, after all. Rather than engaging in what the enemy undoubtedly would dismiss as 'victor's justice,' perhaps it would be better simply to forgive and forget. Another possibility was to go the American route and launch a full-scale war crimes prosecution effort. This would necessitate commitments that might be beyond the capacity of Ottawa's already strained resources. Between these two extremes lay a third option – that of sounding out the British as to whether they would be willing to take on war crimes cases in which all or a majority of the victims had been Canadians.

By the spring of 1945, the Canadian public had been well informed as to the brutality, if not the scale, of the Normandy massacres.[1] Accordingly, any attempt to sweep the war crimes issue under the rug at this time would have been politically untenable, not to mention morally indefensible. This is not to say that the idea did not receive at least passing consideration. There was a body of opinion within the Canadian government that was strongly opposed to the prosecution of war criminals on both legal and political grounds.[2] But its advocates were relatively few in number, and they had long since lost any influence. Indeed, as early as October 1942, after learning that the Germans were unlawfully shackling Canadian POWs,[3] Ottawa had pledged to support the establishment of a postwar international war crimes commission.[4] This was followed up within a year by the striking of a blue-ribbon panel whose purpose was to advise the government on the war crimes issue. Among the panel's recommendations was that Canada reserve the right to set up its own war crimes investigative apparatus.[5]

Notwithstanding what the panel had recommended, neither the bureaucrats in Ottawa nor the military authorities at CMHQ regarded the establishment of an independent Canadian war crimes unit as either necessary or desirable. Vincent Massey, the Canadian high commissioner in London, was the leading civilian proponent of this view. In a memorandum written to CMHQ shortly after the closure of SHAEF's standing court, Massey expressed confidence that the war crimes advisory panel would itself be sufficient to take up the slack.[6] The logic behind the high commissioner's reasoning is not easy to discern. Comprised of only five members and a secretary, the panel was based in Ottawa, an ocean away from where the atrocities had taken place.[7] It had no in-house counsel, no investigators, and only a limited budget. That such a body could be conceived of as an alternative to the SHAEF court was at best wishful thinking, at worst wilful indifference.

Massey's reluctance to support the establishment of an independent Canadian war crimes unit, while certainly cause for concern, was to some extent understandable. Among the duties he fulfilled as high commissioner, Massey served as liaison between the government in Ottawa and the Canadian military in London. The support of CMHQ was integral to his effectiveness in this role. Established shortly after the outbreak of the war, CMHQ was responsible for carrying out all military-administrative tasks not directly connected to operations in the field. Though nominally the highest-ranking Canadian representative in London, Massey, as a civilian, was largely at the mercy of the experts at CMHQ, upon whom he had to rely for advice on matters of military policy.[8]

If Massey can be excused for his failure to grasp the significance of the closure of the SHAEF court, the same cannot be said of CMHQ. Indeed, it is difficult to fathom the organization's position in this regard. After all, Canadian military authorities had seen first-hand the cavalier manner in which (British) 2nd Army had handled the Château d'Audrieu investigation. They had even complained about it to 21st Army Group. Yet when faced once more with the prospect of British involvement in Canadian war crimes cases, CMHQ seemed prepared to let bygones be bygones. In a letter to Major General Eedson L.M. Burns, who was the ranking Canadian officer with 21st Army Group, Major General E.G. Weeks, the head of administration at CMHQ, suggested that 'it might be preferable to have a joint British–Canadian method of investigation rather than independent Canadian investigating teams.'[9] Inexplicably, Burns concurred, characterizing a joint British–Canadian approach as 'more economical' and 'fully satisfactory.'[10]

In light of CMHQ's attitude, the closure of SHAEF's standing court probably would have spelled the death knell for the investigation of the Normandy massacres had it not been for the personal intervention of Lieutenant Colonel Macdonald. With the winding up of the SHAEF court's business, Macdonald had been reassigned. Exercising its characteristic illogic, CMHQ had not loaned him out to the newly formed war crimes unit at 21st Army Group, where his talents might have been employed most effectively, but instead had ordered his transfer to the military government section of 1st Canadian Corps. In dread of the dull bureaucratic routine that his new post would surely entail, Macdonald decided to make one more pitch for the establishment of an independent Canadian war crimes unit. With his transfer not scheduled to take effect until 16 April, he used his hiatus to prepare and file with both SHAEF and CMHQ copies of a progress report on the 12th SS investigations. In it he urged an acceleration of evidence gathering and the assignment of additional legal counsel for that purpose.[11]

Macdonald's crusade for an independent Canadian war crimes unit was a lonely and frustrating one. Typical of the inertia and opposition he encountered were the opinions he heard voiced during a meeting held at Canada House on 24 April 1945. Remarkably, in light of the Château d'Audrieu experience, the officers and bureaucrats in attendance were virtually unanimous in their view that the Canadian cases could be adequately handled by the British. To be sure, they conceded, this option had caused problems in the past. Provided that Canadian representatives were attached to the British investigative unit, however, they were confident that Canada's interests would be protected.[12]

The Canada House meeting convinced Macdonald that all of SHAEF's painstaking work was going down the drain. Worried, but not yet ready to concede defeat, he intensified his lobbying efforts. In a lengthy memorandum, Macdonald reminded CMHQ that the investigation of the 12th SS cases was far from completed. He further warned that the process being contemplated at 21st Army Group 'does not cover the needs of Canadian representation in cases to be investigated in the UK, *nor for the completion of cases reported by the SHAEF Courts* [italics added].'[13] Emphasizing the pitfalls inherent in any joint British-Canadian approach, Macdonald urged that serious consideration be given to the convening of a Canadian court with the authority to investigate war crimes 'independently of 21st Army Group.'[14]

Not content merely to establish a paper trail, Macdonald also sought for his cause the support of influential allies. Front-line commanders figured prominently in this strategy. Setting his sights high, Macdonald tried to speak with General Crerar. The commander of 1st Army was unavailable, but Macdonald was able to schedule a meeting with members of his staff. Evidently, he was very persuasive. Speaking on behalf of their boss, two senior staff officers informed Macdonald that the army high command was 'pleased' to hear that action was at last going to be taken against the German perpetrators of battlefield atrocities. As a matter of course, they pledged 'whatever assistance or cooperation might be required.'[15]

Macdonald's tenacity soon paid off. The effect of his meeting with Crerar's staff seems to have been particularly salutary. In mid-May, Massey and the reluctant authorities at CMHQ relented. Unable to ignore the strong feelings that existed within the fighting forces on this issue, they recommended to the government that Canada set up its own apparatus for the investigation of war crimes.[16] Ottawa concurred, and on 4 June 1945 the No. 1 Canadian War Crimes Investigation Unit (CWCIU) was born. In keeping with Macdonald's suggestion, the new unit was subordinated to the Adjutant General's branch of CMHQ.[17] Headquartered in Suite 602, 2 Cockspur Street in London, CWCIU would become the nerve centre of the quest for justice for the victims of the Normandy massacres.

In terms of both its mandate and its organization, CWCIU was patterned after the SHAEF standing court. By order of Brigadier Beverly Matthews, the deputy adjutant general, the unit was authorized to investigate and file reports on any and all war crimes alleged to have been committed against members of the Canadian armed forces. For this purpose, it was assigned a permanent cadre of twenty-two military prosecutors, investigators, interpreters, and clerks. The cadre was divided into three teams. One was based in London and was responsible for managing the caseload. A second team was deployed to Bad Salzuflen in western Germany and was charged with conducting all investigative work in the field. Finally, a three-man contingent was detailed to 21st Army Group in order to liaise with the British war crimes unit.[18]

Lieutenant Colonel Macdonald was among several military prosecutors assigned to CWCIU. Though not formally put in charge of the unit until September, he was, by virtue of his SHAEF experience, de facto commander from the moment of its inception. His deputy was Major (later Lieutenant Colonel) Clarence Campbell, who is better known for his long postwar tenure as president of the National Hockey League.[19]

The creation of an independent Canadian war crimes unit was a personal victory for Macdonald and a testament to his dedication to the memory of the murdered POWs. It also was an essential first step in a process that many hoped would lead to a meaningful reckoning with the perpetrators. But the mere existence of CWCIU did not ensure that a spate of prosecutions would be forthcoming. The road to justice was littered with procedural and logistical hurdles. Until these had been cleared, CWCIU would have to confine itself to evidence gathering.

Of all the problems that stood in the way of prosecution, the procedural ones required the most immediate resolution. CWCIU had been created by administrative fiat. Thus, while the unit could investigate alleged war crimes and recommend further action, there was as yet no legal basis for it (or any other agency) to undertake prosecutions. By virtue of Canada's constitutional ties with Britain, some thought was given to invoking that country's war crimes regulations. In Britain, the regulations whereby the armed forces were authorized to prosecute suspected war criminals had recently been promulgated by the king in his capacity as commander-in-chief. Issued under a so-called royal warrant, the British regulations had the full force of law, even though they had not been brought into effect by statute, order-in-council, or other parliamentary means. For all practical purposes, the royal warrant permitted the prosecution of war criminals at the 'will and pleasure' of the Crown.[20]

Though it had the advantage of convenience, the suggestion that the British royal warrant could be relied upon as a means of legitimizing Canadian prosecutions was rejected by the war crimes advisory panel. The panel offered three reasons for its opinion. First, the royal warrant regulations were at variance with Canadian legal traditions. Whereas British common law allowed for the prosecution and punishment of offences not codified, in Canada a doctrine had developed whereby only those offences explicitly written in law at the time of their commission were subject to legal sanctions. Second, in Canada there was some doubt as to whether the governor general had the same royal prerogatives as those that the king had exercised in issuing the British regulations.[21] There certainly were no Canadian precedents in this regard.[22] Third, even by the standards of field general courts martial, the speed with which an accused could be brought to trial and the ease with which hearsay evidence could be admitted under the British regulations were unseemly, to say the least.[23]

In retrospect, the interests of justice probably would have been better served had Canada's war crimes regulations been brought into effect in the usual parliamentary manner. However, it was and remained Macdonald's position, one in which he was supported by both the cabinet and the bureaucracy, that such a course would have all but precluded the launching of prosecutions.[24] With the war in Europe ended, demobilization of Canadian forces was only a matter of time. Once disengagement was under way, potential Canadian witnesses would be dispersed and much harder to track down.[25] More importantly, there was no guarantee as to how long potential German witnesses would remain in POW captivity.[26] Time was clearly on the side of the perpetrators, and it had to be countered in a tangible way.

In this connection, it should be noted that by the time CWCIU came into existence, Parliament had already adjourned for its summer recess. This left the government with only one other means of legitimizing the regulations: it could refer them to the Supreme Court. But there was no guarantee that the high court would work any faster than Parliament. After careful consideration of the alternatives, the war crimes advisory panel made a difficult and controversial recommendation – Canada would act on the British precedent. In the panel's view, cabinet had the authority to pass war crimes regulations by an order-in-council, which in turn could be approved by the governor general in his capacity as commander in chief of the Canadian armed forces.[27]

By asserting that the governor general had the same right to issue war crimes regulations as did the Crown, the panel skirted the delicate political question of whether either Parliament or the Supreme Court ought to be consulted. There remained, however, the matter of finding the legislative vehicle whereby the regulations could be brought into effect. Traditionally, the governor general had only approved regulations not previously considered by parliament by reference to some pre-existing statute or order-in-council. Since the British royal warrant had already been deemed inappropriate for this purpose, another means would have to be found. The panel settled on the War Measures Act.[28]

Invoked in 1939 so as to enable the government to direct Canada's war effort more efficiently and effectively, the War Measures Act did have certain advantages. The most important of these was that it authorized Ottawa to govern by order-in-council, thereby enabling it to forgo parliamentary discussion and debate. Accordingly, the act would enable the government to eliminate precisely what it felt it could not afford with respect to the pending war crimes regulations – time-consuming discussion and debate. Still, resort to the act posed certain legal problems. For one thing, section 4 stipulated that the maximum penalty for violations under its provisions was five years' imprisonment. This hardly seemed sufficient punishment in view of the gravity of the crimes that had been committed by the 12th SS Panzer Division 'Hitler Youth.'[29] Secondly, there was the crucial matter of the jurisdiction of the courts that were to be convened under the new regulations. The War Measures Act had been intended to apply to people living in Canada, not to foreigners. Nonetheless, the government was contemplating its use against persons who were citizens of, and whose alleged crimes had been perpetrated in, foreign jurisidictions.

Notwithstanding the fact that the penal and jurisdictional issues had yet to be addressed,[30] in early July 1945 a subcommittee of the war crimes advisory panel began drafting regulations based on the War Measures Act. The work was slow going. Indeed, one month into the process, there was virtually no progress to report. In an effort to light a fire under the plodding bureaucrats, a frustrated Lieutenant Colonel Macdonald once more took the initiative. He prepared his own draft regulations, submitted them to the war crimes advisory panel for comment and criticism, and then arranged meetings with representatives of the consulting government departments.[31]

By mid-August, the process at last began to yield results. At that time, a third version of Macdonald's draft regulations was presented to the Department of

Justice, whose approval was a prerequisite for their submission to cabinet. On 18 August, the minister of justice and the prime minister gave the regulations their endorsement. Ratification was now just a formality. At its 29 August meeting, the full cabinet chimed in with its support, and an order-in-council was prepared. The regulations were published on 10 September and announced in the House of Commons three days later.[32]

Enacted as PC 5831, the war crimes regulations provided Canadian prosecutors with powerful weapons – too powerful, some would later contend – in their legal battle with the perpetrators of the Normandy massacres. The provisions that dealt with the admission of evidence, membership in a criminal organization, and command responsibility stand out in this regard. As to what would constitute evidence in any future war crimes proceedings, it must be conceded that the regulations invested Canadian military courts with much greater discretion than that typically exercised by their civilian counterparts. According to subsection 10(1), a court that was trying a case under the regulations was permitted to admit 'any oral statement or any document *appearing on the face of it to be authentic*, provided [that] the statement or document appears to the court to be of assistance in proving or disproving the charge [italics added].' The list of admissible materials included (1) depositions by deceased or simply unavailable witnesses, (2) any pre-trial statements made by the accused or other witnesses, regardless of whether or not they had been preceded by a caution against self-incrimination, (3) all or portions of reports of military courts of inquiry (such as the comprehensive report prepared by the standing court at SHAEF), (4) originals or copies of documents purportedly issued by Allied or enemy forces or governments, and (5) any personal documents, including diaries and letters, that appeared to contain information relevant to the charges.[33] In effect, the regulations gave the prosecution carte blanche in the presentation of its case.

Though they provided for a degree of access to hearsay evidence that would have been inconceivable in civilian courts, in this regard, at least, the Canadian war crimes regulations were consistent with the evidentiary standards applied by field general courts martial. The same cannot be said of other sections of the regulations. One particularly troubling innovation was the subsection that made it an offence merely to have been a member of a military unit known to have been involved in the commission of a war crime. To be sure, it is a long-established principle of criminal law that anyone who by action or inaction wilfully assists another in the commission of a crime, or who by word or by deed abets another in the commission of a crime, or who counsels or enlists another in the commission of a crime, is a party to and guilty of the crime. But there is a world of difference between adherence to this traditional concept of an accessory and acceptance of the novel and rather distasteful notion of guilt by association. Yet the latter was precisely what the regulations asked Canadian military courts to do. According to subsection 10(3), any and all members of a military unit that had been implicated in the commission of a war crime could be presumed responsible for that crime, irrespective of their individual conduct. In such a case, the court was permitted to try any or all members of the offending unit jointly. Conversely, the court was within its authority to reject applications by any of the defendants to be tried separately.[34]

Another disquieting departure from long-established norms of military justice involved those sections of the regulations that dealt with command responsibility. The idea that an officer could be held responsible for the actions of his men was nothing new, of course. On the contrary, it was explicitly recognized in the codes of conduct of both the Allied and the German armed forces.[35] Once again, however, the Canadian war crimes regulations far exceeded the conventions of military law. Subsection 10(4), for example, stipulated that where there was evidence of more than one war crime having been committed by a unit, the commander of that unit was automatically assumed to be responsible. Subsection 10(5) went even further, stipulating that a unit commander could be presumed responsible for a lone, random war crime, provided that it had been committed by his troops in the presence of an officer or NCO.[36]

It is clear that in their rush to get prosecutions under way, Macdonald and the war crimes advisory panel drafted regulations that were quite at variance with both Anglo-Saxon legal traditions and the Canadian sense of fair play. By precluding challenges to the authenticity of prosecution documents, they deprived the defendant of the right to make full answer and defence. By permitting the introduction of the depositions of deceased witnesses, they deprived the defendant of the right to cross-examine his accusers. By allowing entry of all statements made by the accused, whether or not these had been preceded by the customary caution against self incrimination, they indirectly compelled him to give evidence against his will. Finally, by invoking the notion of guilt by association, they provided the prosecution with a rather unsavoury means of pressuring the members of an offending unit to testify against one another.[37]

To be fair, it should be noted that some checks and balances had been built into the Canadian war crimes regulations. Before a case could go to trial, the charges had to be reviewed by the Judge Advocate General. Any court that tried a case under the regulations had to consist of not less than two and not more than six officers of equal rank to the accused. The president of the court was required to have legal training, and, if such a person was unavailable, then a judge advocate or military lawyer had to be appointed to assist the court. If a trial resulted in a guilty verdict, the defendant had the right to submit a petition against the court's finding. Apart from the accused's right to appeal, the sentence was subject to automatic review by the commander of Canadian forces in Germany, who had the power to either mitigate or remit any punishment imposed by the court.[38]

Notwithstanding these safeguards, it cannot be denied that Canada's war crimes regulations were weighted heavily in favour of the prosecution. But before one condemns the officials who drafted the regulations as incompetent, or worse, one must understand the constraints under which they were operating. Justice delayed invariably is justice denied. Perhaps nowhere was that maxim more true than in the case of the Normandy massacres, where demobilization of Canadian troops and repatriation of German POWs quite literally would have scattered the evidence to the winds. As for the procedural advantages that the regulations accorded to the prosecution, it may well be that Macdonald and the advisory panel were simply being realistic. After all, the experience of war crimes prosecutions since the end of the Second World War has shown just how difficult it can be to assign individual responsibility for atrocities perpetrated under cover of shot and shell.

Did Canada's war crimes regulations lean too far in the prosecution's favour, serving little purpose, as one critic has alleged, other than to sanction what amounted to judicial vengeance?[39] Probably. Does this mean that a defendant tried under the regulations could not possibly have received a fair hearing? That question can only be answered by examining the record of postwar Canadian war crimes proceedings. As it happened, of all the suspected perpetrators and instigators of the Normandy massacres, only one, Kurt Meyer, was ever brought to trial under the 1945 war crimes regulations. It is to his historic and controversial case that this book now turns.

# 15

# The Case against Kurt Meyer

Kurt Meyer's fall from grace began within weeks of the last POW murders. As we have seen, by nightfall on 8 July 1944, Canadian forces had driven Meyer's division back across the Orne River. Though badly mauled, the remnants of his once mighty formation held out along the opposite river bank throughout 9 and 10 July. In the process, they denied Allied armour passage into the flat, tank-friendly country south of Caen. Relief came on 11 July. In a redeployment fraught with irony, the depleted Hitler Youth Division handed over the Caen sector to its spiritual and institutional forerunner, the always dangerous and now completely refurbished Leibstandarte.[1]

The 12th SS's respite would be a brief one. After just a week in reserve near Falaise, the division was reinserted into the front line. Over the next month or so, Meyer's battle-weary troops became locked in a depressingly futile cycle of defence, counterattack, and withdrawal.[2] The spell of defeat was broken only once. For a few days in mid-August, the division fought a brilliant delaying action along the northern flank of the Falaise-Argentan pocket. By virtue of its exertions, tens of thousands of German troops were able to avoid encirclement and capture. Seemingly doomed to destruction inside the shrinking pocket, the 12th SS's rearguard, including Meyer and part of his divisional staff, managed to break out on 20 August.[3]

Following its narrow escape from Falaise, the division began an orderly but inexorable retreat eastward through France and Belgium. It was at the Maas River in Belgium where Kurt Meyer, now an SS Brigadier General,[4] came to the end of the road. According to his own account, on 6 September, at around 2:00 in the afternoon, a headquarters detachment of the 12th SS was on the move when it was ambushed by an American armoured column. Two of the division's staff cars were shot to pieces in the ensuing battle. The remainder, including the car in which Meyer was riding, beat a hasty retreat into a nearby village.

With the Americans in hot pursuit, Meyer and his driver elected to hide in the first structure they spotted. This proved to be a fateful blunder. In a matter of hours, the fugitive SS men were betrayed by the farmer in whose barn they had taken refuge. Held under the watchful eyes of several well-armed Belgian partisans, Meyer was turned over to American forces the next morning.[5]

In the course of his transfer to American custody, one of Meyer's new captors tried to rob him of his medals. When he resisted, the guard lashed out, inflicting a vicious beating with the butt end of his rifle. The once imposing commander emerged from the encounter physically battered. In addition to numerous bruises and lacerations, the attack left Meyer with a slightly fractured skull. More importantly, he had been humiliated to the core.[6] There was no excuse for this kind of behaviour, of course. Still, it was perhaps fitting that the scourge of Canadian prisoners had at last received a taste of his own medicine.

Meyer's injuries were serious enough to warrant a lengthy sojourn in a Belgian hospital. Indeed, almost a month would pass before he had recovered sufficiently to be discharged. Not until the beginning of October was Hitler's shaky but indomitable servant returned to the custody of the American military police. Shortly thereafter, he was interned in an American POW camp at Compiègne, near Paris.[7]

Clad in the uniform of a Wehrmacht officer, Meyer had thus far managed to hide his SS affiliation from his captors. The ruse would not work for long. The Compiègne camp was teeming with informers. On 8 November 1944, the reputation of Hitler's youngest general finally caught up with him. Tipped off by a stool-pigeon, the camp commandant ordered Meyer to remove his shirt and raise his arms in the air. As soon as he complied, the game was over. On the inside of Meyer's left arm, for all to see, was his SS blood group tattoo.[8]

Upon the discovery of his true identity, Meyer was immediately segregated from the rest of the prisoner population. The next morning, he was taken by train to Paris. From there he was flown to London, where Allied intelligence officers eagerly awaited his arrival. Following a lengthy processing procedure, Meyer was confined to the London District Cage (LDC), a special detention centre reserved for the most fanatical and contemptible of Hitler's acolytes.[9]

Internment in the London Cage meant doing hard time. Somewhere in the bowels of this Alcatraz for Nazis, Meyer first locked horns with Allied war crimes investigators. The LDC men were renowned for their ability to get enemy prisoners to talk. Each of the Cage's dozen or so interrogators spoke flawless German, and each was an expert on the inner workings of the German armed forces. Their chief was Lieutenant Colonel Alexander P. Scotland, a legendary former spy and soldier of fortune. One of the ablest minds ever recruited by British intelligence, Scotland was a meticulous and relentless investigator.[10]

By resorting to well-established techniques – solitary confinement, protracted interrogations, the 'good cop–bad cop' routine – as well as to some less savoury practices, Scotland and his LDC bloodhounds had broken the will of many a Nazi fanatic. Yet they were completely unsuccessful with Meyer. The man who one interrogator would refer to as 'the personification of National Socialism' seemed immune to London Cage methods. Far from being intimidated or worn down, Meyer steadfastly held to his story that he knew nothing of the killing of prisoners. To be sure, there were times when he came close to cracking. When a question struck too close to home, for example, he would lose his composure, then fix an icy stare on his adversary. But on the whole Meyer was able to beat the system.[11] Thus, for one of the rare times in his illustrious career, Scotland had to admit defeat. After a few more desultory attempts to break Meyer's spirit, the LDC chief threw in the towel and had him transferred to the lower-profile prisoner of war camp at Enfield, north of London.[12]

Enfield was the first in a series of POW camps that Meyer would call home for the next few months. Apart from being shunted from one place to another, the only breaks in the dreary regimen of his captivity were the visits of Canadian war crimes investigators. In that regard, Meyer's first encounter with the man who would become his nemesis took place towards the end of March 1945. Early on the morning of 25 March, without any advance notice, Enfield's most notorious inmate was rousted out of bed, escorted to the local train station, and whisked back to the London Cage for questioning. Over the next three days, he was grilled by members of the soon to be disbanded SHAEF standing court, including, of course, Lieutenant Colonel Macdonald. Having successfully stonewalled the LDC's crack team of interrogators, the arrogant suspect had no trouble against the determined but conspicuously overmatched Canadian prosecutor. So deflated was Macdonald after their initial skirmish, in fact, that he felt compelled to advise SHAEF that the case against Meyer was still quite weak.[13]

Apart from Meyer's unwavering determination to resist his captors, the main problem facing Macdonald was that he had almost nothing to go on. At the time of the March interrogation, the entire case against Meyer rested on questionable evidence that had been proffered by an unreliable witness. In testimony given before the SHAEF standing court, former SS Private Friedrich Torbanisch had woven Meyer into a compelling but not entirely credible tale involving clandestine meetings, secret orders, and oaths of silence.

By his own admission an unwilling conscript, Torbanisch had murdered an officer and then deserted from the 12th SS's reconnaissance company on 4 April 1944. One evening just prior to his desertion, Torbanisch told the SHAEF court, he and the other members of his company had been summoned to a special roll call. As soon as all were present and accounted for, the company sergeant major, an NCO named Hagetorn, read out a list of secret regimental orders. Most were unremarkable. The exceptions were the ones that dealt with the treatment of captured Allied soldiers. Those orders, Torbanisch alleged, were anything but routine; they expressly forbade the taking of prisoners. If prisoners were taken in any event, the orders stipulated that they were to be executed immediately after questioning.[14]

The issuance of such orders, if it could be confirmed, would have constituted a gross violation of the rules of war. Torbanisch alleged that his superiors were well aware of their criminal nature. As proof, he offered additional testimony about a strange ritual to which he and the rest of his company were subjected that fateful April night. Prior to dismissing the men, Hagetorn, according to Torbanisch, had each of them sign a piece of paper. At the top of the document was a solemn declaration that bound the signatories, under penalty of death, never to reveal or discuss the orders.[15]

Torbanisch's testimony, if true, placed Meyer at the head of a conspiracy whose express purpose had been the murder of Allied prisoners of war. Before Meyer could be charged as the ringleader, however, several issues had to be resolved. Not the least of these was determining whether Torbanisch, an admitted murderer and deserter, could be believed. Even assuming that he had been truthful, there still were serious doubts as to the probative value of his testimony. First of all, the former SS trooper had not directly linked Meyer to the issuance of the alleged orders. Second, he had fixed the time of their issuance as the first week of April 1944, a full two months before any POW murders had been committed. Third, much of what he had told the SHAEF court was hearsay. Under ordinary trial circumstances, only Hagetorn could testify as to the content of the alleged orders, and he was dead, having been killed in action within days of the Normandy landings.[16]

Uncertain as to whether Torbanisch's evidence would be admissible (this was prior to the passage of the Canadian war crimes regulations), Macdonald was reluctant to try Meyer on what amounted to the chain-of-command theory. The suspect's recent virtuoso performance under interrogation had done nothing to dissuade him from that view. On the contrary, the London Cage fiasco convinced Macdonald that if Meyer was ever to be brought to trial, it would have to be done on the basis of direct evidence. Hopeful that such evidence could be found somewhere in the Allies' teeming POW camps, he pressed SHAEF and CMHQ for an acceleration in the questioning of captured members of the 12th SS.[17] While awaiting a decision on his recommendation, help dropped into Macdonald's lap from an entirely unexpected source.

At around the time that the Canadian prosecutor was sparring with Meyer in London, SS Private Jan Jesionek, who had witnessed the Abbaye d'Ardenne murders, was preparing to follow his former commander into POW captivity. Seriously wounded during his company's attack on Bretteville l'Orgueilleuse, Jesionek had spent the better part of three months in hospital. Upon his release, he had been transferred to a reconnaissance unit at Paderborn, a city located about 150 miles north of Frankfurt am Main.[18]

By the end of March 1945, Jesionek could see the writing on the wall. On the eastern front, the Red Army had broken through German defences in East Prussia, while in the west the Allies had captured the Rhineland and much of Westphalia. For all intents and purposes, the war was over. As American troops got to within striking distance of Paderborn,[19] Jesionek made his decision. At the next opportunity, he would desert from his unit, make his way through German lines, and surrender to the advancing American forces.

As a dispatch rider, Jesionek was frequently called upon to deliver messages to the front. Thus, it was not unusual for him to be away from his unit for several hours at a time. On 30 March 1945, the anxious conscript received a routine dispatch order. Realizing that this was his chance, he resolved to make the most of it. After hopping onto his motorcycle, Jesionek headed south along the main road out of Paderborn. The would-be deserter had gone no more than a few miles when he ran into an American patrol. Thanking his lucky stars, he gave himself up and was escorted back through enemy lines.[20]

At the headquarters of the unit that had captured him, Jesionek was subjected to a run-of-the-mill interrogation. Apparently, he did not have much to say at that time. Things changed after his transfer to a POW enclosure in Belgium. Questioned there by a Polish liaison officer, he recounted for the first time the events surrounding the Abbaye d'Ardenne murders.[21]

Under informal arrangements worked out between the western Allies and the Polish government-in-exile, Jesionek's story ought to have been reported to SHAEF.[22] As far as can be determined, no such report was ever made. With the Polish army still fighting in Italy, perhaps Jesionek's interrogator was more interested in him as a soldier than as a potential witness. Whatever the reason, no one took notice when the former SS trooper was sent to a POW camp outside the medieval French city of Chartres, not far from a Polish filtration camp at Chalons.[23] Ostensibly a collection point for displaced Poles, the Chalons camp was being used primarily as a recruiting centre for the Polish army. Unbeknownst to Canadian war crimes investigators, the only man who was prepared to finger Kurt Meyer was on the verge of slipping away.

Every once in a while, a prosecutor who is trying to crack a tough case gets a lucky break. In building the case against Meyer, Macdonald actually had two. The first occurred within minutes of Jesionek's arrival at the Chartres camp. Of all the personnel who were on duty that 22 April 1945, the man with whom

Jesionek first came into contact was Technical Sergeant Sigmund Stern of the American military police. A refugee from the Third Reich, Stern was both fluent in German and an avowed anti-Nazi. Accordingly, when the forlorn POW standing before him indicated that he wished to make a statement about an SS war crime, Stern readily obliged. In his unpolished but passable German, Jesionek recounted everything he had seen that terrible noon hour almost one year ago – the arrival at the abbey of the seven Canadian prisoners, Meyer's angry reaction, the interrogations, the death march each prisoner was forced to make, the sights and sounds of the executions, and the scene of carnage in the abbey garden. Upon completing his statement, Jesionek read over the transcript, satisfied himself that it was accurate, and signed it. Stern then translated the document into English, made copies, and handed the original to his superior officer.[24]

Jesionek's stay at the Chartres camp was a brief one. Within a matter of days, he was on the move again, this time to the filtration camp at Chalons. Like every new arrival there, he was subjected to a series of security checks. The first order of business was determining his nationality. Once his Polish origins had been verified, camp authorities would have questioned Jesionek regarding his wartime activities. It is not known how he responded to these queries. Whatever he told his hosts, they must have been satisfied, because they soon approved him for induction into the Polish army. There was now one more hurdle to overcome – the army physical. Notwithstanding his previous battle wounds, the former SS trooper was given a clean bill of health. Declared fit for military service, Jesionek, along with approximately five hundred other reclaimed Poles, was sent to Marseilles. From there he and his new comrades were to embark for Italy.[25]

While Jesionek was waiting to ship out, his statement was making a tortuously slow climb up the U.S. Army chain of command. Mired in bureaucratic inertia, it would have been weeks before SHAEF learned of the important new evidence against Meyer. By then it would have been too late. Jesionek would have disappeared into the great maelstrom of postwar European migration and resettlement, probably forever.[26]

It was at this point that fate once more smiled on Lieutenant Colonel Macdonald. Sent to the Chartres camp on unrelated matters, he happened to bump into Sergeant Stern. When Stern learned Macdonald's identity, he showed him a copy of Jesionek's translated statement. The prosecutor was thunderstruck. This was the direct evidence for which he had been hoping! His joy quickly turned to despair, however, when he learned that Jesionek had been transferred to Chalons almost a month earlier.[27]

In a frantic effort to locate the man who could put Kurt Meyer away, Macdonald went to U.S. Army headquarters in Chartres, where he sought the assistance of the local commander. After much toing and froing, he managed to convince his sceptical ally to make a few calls. Eventually, Jesionek was traced to Marseilles. Orders were issued to hold him there, and Macdonald drove down the next day. His bewildered passenger in tow, the relieved prosecutor then headed back to Paris.[28]

Upon their return to the French capital, Macdonald had Jesionek placed under round-the-clock guard in an old army barracks. The prosecutor's first formal interview with his potential star witness was held on 28 May 1945. Though Jesionek's story was essentially the same as the one he had told Sergeant Stern, it was lengthier and more detailed, the result, no doubt, of Macdonald's probing questions. One of the new details elicited from the former SS trooper had to do with a speech Meyer purportedly had given on the subject of POWs. About a week before the Normandy landings, Jesionek alleged, his reconnaissance company had been addressed by Meyer. In the course of his speech, the regimental commander had exhorted the troops to make use of the coming invasion to retaliate against the Allies for their bombing of German cities. While Jesionek could not remember the precise language Meyer had used, he and his comrades had been left with the distinct impression that such retaliation ought to be directed against enemy prisoners. That impression was reinforced a short time later, when Meyer's words were echoed by the company commander.[29]

Jesionek's interview lasted several hours. By the time that it was over, Macdonald felt that he had a much better sense as to the extent of Meyer's criminal responsibility. All in all, things seemed to have gone well. Then, just as he was being led away, Jesionek dropped a bombshell. During his deposition at Chartres, he suddenly recalled, something had happened that had disturbed him greatly. According to the now agitated witness, he and Sergeant Stern had been interrupted by another American soldier. The man had glanced at his identification papers, and, realizing that he was a former SS man, had said, 'You ... from the SS, you all are going to be hung up [sic].'[30]

From his experience with Torbanisch, Macdonald was well aware that Jesionek would have trouble establishing his credibility on the witness stand. Military courts tended to look askance at deserters, even deserters from the SS. Jesionek's revelation about the American soldier's remark would only exacerbate the problem. The reason was simple. If a court decided to interpret the American's words as a threat, an interpretation for which Meyer's counsel was sure to argue, then Jesionek's statement might be regarded as having been obtained through coercion, or at least under duress. In that scenario, the court would be inclined to throw out his evidence.

To compensate for the damage caused by the soldier's unfortunate comment,

Macdonald felt that he would have to test Jesionek's truthfulness and reliability to the limit. In that regard, the Canadian prosecutor pursued a two-pronged strategy. First, he and his new CWCIU team subjected their star witness to exhaustive questioning under simulated trial conditions. Then they took him to the crime scene, where he was made to re-enact the events of 8 June 1944 in the minutest detail possible. Jesionek passed both tests with flying colours. So unshakeable was the former SS trooper, in fact, that within a couple of weeks Macdonald had done a complete about-face in his evaluation of the Meyer case. He was now confident that he could win it.[31]

On the basis of Jesionek's statement and the work of the SHAEF standing court, Macdonald drafted a preliminary indictment against Meyer and submitted it to the war crimes advisory panel back in Ottawa. The draft indictment was breathtaking in its scope. Assuming that no new evidence came in, Meyer was to be charged with either murder or incitement to murder in connection with ten of the criminal incidents in which the 12th SS had been implicated. Two of the incidents stemmed from the period immediately following the Normandy landings, during which the accused had commanded the division's 25th Panzer Grenadier Regiment. They included the series of murders committed in and around the villages of Authie and Buron on 7 June, as well as the two sets of executions carried out at the Abbaye d'Ardenne on 7 and 8 June. The remaining eight incidents derived from Meyer's subsequent tenure as divisional commander. These included the various killings perpetrated in the vicinity of Le Mesnil-Patry, the shooting of seven prisoners just outside Mouen on the night of 17 June, and the last known Abbaye d'Ardenne executions (i.e., Lieutenant Williams and Lance Corporal Pollard).[32]

Though different both in form and in substance from the final indictment, the draft charges are nonetheless interesting for what they reveal about the prosecution's theory of the case. As late as the end of March, Macdonald had been reluctant to try Meyer solely on the basis of the chain-of-command theory. The discovery of Jesionek appeared to solve that problem. Indeed, with his star witness in hand, one might have expected Macdonald to downplay the allegations of incitement and base his case instead on the evidence of Meyer's direct involvement in the Abbaye d'Ardenne murders. Yet that did not happen. Macdonald's draft indictment makes it clear that he intended to hold Meyer accountable not only for what had happened at the abbey, but for *all* of the POW murders that had been perpetrated in the sectors in which he had exercised command. With the exception of the abbey killings, of course, Meyer had not been physically present at the crime scenes. Thus, his responsibility for the other POW murders was at best vicarious. To try Meyer on the basis of vicarious responsibility, it seemed, was to turn his case into precisely the kind of chain-of-command prosecution that Macdonald had just weeks earlier been so deter-mined to avoid.[33]

Why did Macdonald fall back on the chain-of-command theory? Unfortu-nately, neither the archives nor the chief prosecutor's personal recollections provide much in the way of an answer. One can only speculate, therefore, as to what might have prompted him to change his mind. Perhaps he was hedging his bets in the event that Jesionek did not hold up well under cross-examination. Or perhaps he simply despaired of the apprehension of other high-ranking perpe-trators and thus tried to make Meyer the scapegoat for the criminal conduct of an entire division. Whatever the reason, the reversion to the chain-of-command theory was not sound trial strategy. To convict Meyer of responsibility for kill-ings at which he had not even been present would be a daunting task. Not only would Macdonald have to prove that Meyer had incited his troops to deny quar-ter, but he would also have to demonstrate a nexus between the incitement and the POW murders that followed. By taking on this additional burden of proof, Macdonald unnecessarily complicated what Jesionek had made a straightfor-ward and winnable case.

Notwithstanding the flaws in the prosecution's theory, Macdonald's draft charges were endorsed by the war crimes advisory panel. The panel, in turn, recommended to Prime Minister King that the Meyer case be approved for trial. King promptly gave his assent. Henceforth, the case would be on the judicial fast track.[34]

With the prime minister's approval secured, the investigation into Meyer's activities in Normandy shifted into high gear. On 24 June 1945, Macdonald set off on a whirlwind trip to POW camps across Canada and the United States.[35] Over the next five weeks, the chief prosecutor and his CWCIU team would interview a total of ninety-nine German witnesses. They would also take the depositions of fifteen Canadian witnesses, all of whom were repatriated servicemen.[36]

The statements given by the Canadian witnesses proved to be of only limited value. Few of the survivors of the Normandy massacres had been in a position to get a good look at the perpetrators, and those who had gave varied and some-times wildly contradictory descriptions. But at least they provided vivid proof of the raft of crimes that had been committed. The German witnesses, on the other hand, were less than forthcoming. Still bound by the oath of loyalty that they had taken upon entry into the SS, most felt no great compulsion to unbur-den themselves. The few who did talk tended to obfuscate, passing responsibil-ity upwards, downwards, or sideways. Met with either stony silence or deft evasion, Macdonald was frustrated at every turn.[37] Even years later, it was clear that the arrogance and intransigence of the former SS men still rankled. In his

1954 book on the Meyer case, for example, Macdonald lamented the fact that at one POW enclosure near Gravenhurst, Ontario, he had found 'hundreds of bronzed, well-fed and fine looking physical specimens of the "master race" swimming, boating and living the life of Riley.'[38]

The lone exception to the stream of unrepentant zealots and liars was former SS Private Alfred Helzel, who was interviewed by Macdonald in Hull, Quebec, on 3 July. Like Torbanisch and Jesionek, Helzel had been a member of the Hitler Youth Division's 15th Reconnaissance Company. During his nine-month tour of duty, he told Macdonald, he had come to know Meyer by virtue of the commander's frequent visits to the company.[39] When questioned about the secret POW orders mentioned by Torbanisch, Helzel confirmed that such orders had in fact been issued, although he quibbled a little about their wording. As for Jesionek's allegation – namely, that Meyer had addressed the reconnaissance company on the question of POWs just one week prior to the invasion – Helzel basically corroborated the testimony of the prosecution's star witness. Though he could not remember the precise language that the regimental commander had used, he was certain that it had been something to the effect that 'my unit takes no prisoners.'[40]

With potential witnesses scattered across a continent, the interviews were not completed until the end of July. Apart from Helzel's corroboration of Jesionek's testimony, Macdonald's trip proved to be a time-consuming and expensive failure. Little new evidence was unearthed, and much of what was turned out to be either hearsay or peripheral. The case against Meyer, though strong enough to take to court, was not yet strong enough to guarantee a conviction. That was about to change.

At the end of August 1945, cabinet approved the new war crimes regulations.[41] Their impact on the Meyer investigation was immediate and profound. This was particularly true of subsections 10(3), 10(4), and 10(5). Subsection 10(3), it will be remembered, made it a criminal offence just to have been a member of a unit that had committed a war crime. In so doing, it gave the prosecution a powerful means of compelling the members of an offending unit to testify against one another. Subsections 10(4) and 10(5), on the other hand, held a unit commander criminally liable for war crimes perpetrated by his troops. Accordingly, they made it possible to convict him almost solely on the basis of his position atop the offending unit's chain of command.

Armed with new and far-reaching prosecutorial powers, Macdonald found that the German witnesses were suddenly much more willing to talk. Concerned lest they be tainted with guilt by association, a number of Meyer's former subordinates began to tell what they knew about the Normandy massacres. In an unseemly if understandable attempt to save their own skins, most tried to pass the blame up the chain of command. One of the first to come forward was former SS Private Hermann Sue, who had been present at the Abbaye d'Ardenne on 17 June when a Canadian prisoner (either Lieutenant Williams or Lance Corporal Pollard) was shot. In interviews conducted on 12 and 18 September, Sue claimed that when he asked a guard about the shooting, he was told that such occurrences were fairly commonplace at Meyer's headquarters. More damaging still were the statements given by former SS Second Lieutenant Kurt Bergmann, who had served as adjutant to the 3rd Battalion of Meyer's regiment, and former SS First Lieutenant Bernhard Meitzel, a special missions officer who had been attached to divisional headquarters. Questioned about Sue's evidence, neither witness could or would confirm his story about the 17 June incident. However, both stated that Meyer had not been appointed to the post of divisional commander until the afternoon of 17 June, which meant that he would still have been in command at the abbey when the prisoner to whom Sue referred was shot. Also adding to Meyer's woes was yet another member of the 25th Panzer Grenadier Regiment, former SS Private Horst Heyer. He did so by providing further corroboration of the statements of Jesionek and Helzel. Before the 12th SS's transfer to Normandy, Heyer alleged, Meyer had declared in an address to the troops that 'my unit takes no prisoners.'[42]

Perhaps the most dramatic change of heart among the German witnesses was that experienced by former SS Corporal Ewald Wetzel. A member of the Feldgendarmerie detachment that had been assigned to Meyer's regimental headquarters, it was suspected that Wetzel had important evidence about the Abbaye d'Ardenne murders. But the man was a hard case. As late as 31 August 1945, this intractable Nazi was still doing his best to stymie Canadian investigators. Within days of the enactment of the war crimes regulations, Wetzel underwent a startling transformation. Faced with the threat of charges under subsection 10(3), the burly former military policeman began to talk. In interviews conducted on 8 and 11 September, Wetzel told Macdonald that he was prepared to testify in open court as to German procedures for the handling of prisoners. From the moment of their capture until their transfer to the custody of the Feldgendarmerie, Wetzel claimed, POWs were the exclusive responsibility of the forward area commander.[43] This was a vitally important piece of information. If true, it tended to preclude the likely defence argument that the Abbaye d'Ardenne killings, while criminal and tragic, could have taken place without Meyer's authorization.

The example of SS Corporal Wetzel demonstrates that the impact of the new war crimes regulations cannot be overestimated. Indeed, it is not an exaggeration to say that the bulk of the evidence on which the prosecution would rely at trial was collected in the two months between the enactment of the regulations and Meyer's formal indictment. So rapid was the accumulation of evidence during this period that even the heretofore serene suspect began to sit up and take notice. Inexplicably and inexcusably without full-time legal counsel,[44] Meyer was being represented on an ad hoc basis by Wehrmacht Lieutenant Colonel von der Heydte, a fellow prisoner and former law professor.[45] The two men followed developments in the case with growing trepidation. With more and more of his former subordinates talking, the noose around the suspect's neck was becoming uncomfortably tight. Against the advice of both von der Heydte and Canadian prosecutor Clarence Campbell, Meyer decided that he had better do some damage control. Accordingly, on 26 October he requested a meeting with Lieutenant Colonel Macdonald.[46]

At the time of Meyer's request, Macdonald was on his way back from Ottawa, where he had just received approval for the final version of his draft indictment. The chief prosecutor was thoroughly drained from the long trip, and it did not seem likely that the meeting for which Meyer was hoping would happen any time soon. But Macdonald's curiosity won out over his exhaustion. After being briefed by Campbell, he scheduled a meeting for the following afternoon.[47]

At 2:00 PM on 28 October, Macdonald, Campbell, and an interpreter paid a visit to Meyer at the London Cage. Without much ado, the beleaguered suspect announced that he wished to make a statement. He again was cautioned about giving evidence without the benefit of counsel, but to no avail. After having given the matter some thought, Meyer admitted, he realized that he had not been entirely candid. Evidence had been omitted during his last interrogation, evidence that he wished to bring forth now.[48]

With his accusers listening in rapt attention, Meyer took them through what he now claimed to know about the Abbaye d'Ardenne murders. On 10 or 11 June 1944, he recalled, two officers reported to him that the bodies of eighteen or nineteen Canadian soldiers had been discovered lying unburied in the abbey garden. Incredulous, he ordered his adjutant, a young lieutenant named Hans Schümann, to investigate and report back to him. The officer confirmed the presence of the bodies, prompting Meyer to have a look for himself. After viewing the murdered Canadians, all of whom seemed to have died from massive head wounds, he ordered them buried where they lay. Then, according to Meyer, he reprimanded and relieved Schümann for having allowed the killings to take place on his watch. Finally, he reported the matter to his predecessor as divisional commander, SS Brigadier General Witt, who testily ordered him to ascertain the identity of the perpetrators.[49]

After Meyer completed his statement, the prosecutors had only one question. Why he had not come forward with this information sooner? Solemnly, but not very convincingly, the suspect answered that he had been too ashamed to admit that German soldiers could have done such a thing.[50]

On the face of it, Meyer's statement seemed plausible enough. However, it soon became apparent that his explanations were not intended to enlighten, but rather to mislead. Concerned that Meyer's last-minute 'confession' might buy him sympathy with the court, Macdonald scrambled for rebuttal evidence. It did not take him long to find it. Just days before the trial was scheduled to begin, he located a French civilian witness who would blow Meyer's story out of the water.

At the time of the Normandy landings, fourteen-year-old Daniel Lachèvre and his family were living on the grounds of the Abbaye d'Ardenne. They continued to be able to move freely about the place until 16 June, when Meyer's troops finally evicted them. At around 8:00 PM on 8 June, Lachèvre told Macdonald, he and his friends had gone to the abbey garden to play on the parallel bars and swings that were set up there. They stayed for about forty-five minutes, then left, returning again and again over the next two days. At no time during their recreation, according to Lachèvre, had they seen any dead bodies.[51]

For all intents and purposes, Lachèvre's statement destroyed Meyer's alibi. If, as the teenager claimed, there were no bodies in the abbey garden as of 8:00 PM on 8 June, nor any time thereafter, then they had to have been buried beforehand. This meant that Meyer's story about his discovery of the bodies had been patently untrue. Indeed, on the basis of Jesionek's account, it was evident that Meyer could not possibly have seen eighteen or nineteen bodies all at one time, since by the noon hour on 8 June only those of the seven Canadians who had just been shot still lay unburied in the garden. The prisoners who had been murdered the previous night had already been interred. All Meyer had done with his feeble attempt to curry favour with the prosecution was to cast even more suspicion on himself. His gambit had clearly backfired.

Meyer's 28 October statement marked the end of the investigative phase of his case. Henceforth, there was little left to do but proceed with the legal formalities. On the morning of 31 October, he was awakened in his London Cage cell and ordered to dress. Accompanied by Macdonald, Campbell, and four other CWCIU personnel, as well as by an armed escort, the former SS hero was driven to an airfield just outside of the city. The overcast sky and drizzle matched Meyer's dampened spirits. Boarding a military transport, the eight men sat wordlessly as the plane's engines revved up for the cross-Channel flight. About an hour later, they landed at Jever airfield, just a few miles west of the North Sea port of Wilhelmshaven. From there it was about a twenty-mile drive to the small town of Aurich, where a deserted naval barracks had been converted into a courtroom.[52]

Upon arrival at Aurich, Meyer was formally arraigned by Lieutenant Colonel R.P. Clarke, the commander of the Royal Winnipeg Rifles. Their encounter was a moment of high drama. Both accuser and accused were suddenly transformed, Clarke symbolizing Canada's righteous indignation over the slaughter of its brave sons, Meyer embodying the evil that had led to the slaughter. Through an interpreter, the Canadian officer began to read both the indictment against the defendant and the order convening the court martial that would try him.[53]

Though pared down considerably from Macdonald's initial draft,[54] the indictment was still very ambitious. The first count charged Meyer with having incited his troops to deny quarter to the enemy. The second held him responsible for the murder of twenty-three Canadian prisoners near the villages of Authie and Buron on 7 June 1944 (i.e., the Milius murders). The third charged him with having directly ordered the murder of seven Canadian prisoners at the Abbaye d'Ardenne on 8 June (i.e., the Jesionek allegation). As an alternative to the third count, the fourth held him responsible for the 8 June murders by virtue of his position as regimental commander. The fifth count held him responsible for the murder of eleven Canadian prisoners at the abbey on 7 June, also by virtue of his position as regimental commander. Finally, a sixth count, which was dropped at trial, held Meyer responsible for the murder of seven Canadian POWs near the village of Mouen on 17 June (i.e., the engineering battalion murders).[55]

After listening resignedly to the charges against him, Meyer was taken to his cell, which was located in a building that had once housed a naval academy.[56] It was there where he marked time while awaiting his day in court. After five seemingly interminable weeks, the waiting was over. On 4 December 1945, Major General Chris Vokes, the commander of all Canadian occupation forces in Germany, ordered the convening of a court martial six days hence. Proceedings in the case of Canada v. Kurt Meyer were to commence at precisely 10:30 AM on 10 December at the converted naval barracks in Aurich.[57] The day of reckoning was fast approaching. Perhaps with it would come justice for the victims of the Normandy massacres.

# 16

# Reckoning: The Trial of Kurt Meyer

By mid-morning on Monday, 10 December, Aurich's makeshift courtroom was packed. Most of those in attendance were members of the armed forces of Canada or its allies. Also on hand was a large contingent of Canadian and British reporters. The few seats that remained had been allotted to German civilians. Hand-picked to observe the trial of one of their own, they sat uncomfortably in the first row, as if on display.[1]

In front of the courtroom, facing the bench, were two tables. The one on the left had been reserved for the prosecution, the one on the right for the defence. Seated at the prosecution table were Lieutenant Colonels Macdonald and Campbell. Clad in standard-issue uniform, Campbell seemed to disappear into the crowd. With his trademark Balmoral cap, moustache, and wire-rimmed glasses, the chief prosecutor, on the other hand, was quite conspicuous. Both men looked grim.

At the defence table, immediately to Macdonald's right, sat Lieutenant Colonel Maurice W. Andrew. To Andrew's right was his assistant, Captain Frank Plourde. A small-town Ontario lawyer and commander of the Perth Regiment, Andrew was older than either of his adversaries. Perhaps for that reason, his face radiated serenity and confidence.

At exactly 10:30 AM, the spectators rose in unison as the members of the court began to file in. First to take his place on the bench was Brigadier J.A. Roberts. Following Roberts in sequence were Brigadier H.A. Sparling, Lieutenant Colonel W.B. Bredin, Major General Harry W. Foster, who would act as court president, Brigadier Ian S. Johnston, and Brigadier H.P. Bell-Irving. Waiting in the wings were the alternates, Brigadiers Pat Bogert and T.G. Gibson.

With the exception of Bredin, the court members and alternates were all line officers. Each had held senior commands during the war, and each had been decorated.[2] Only two had formal legal training. One was Bredin, who had been appointed judge advocate pursuant to subsection 7(7) of the war crimes regulations.[3] The other was Johnston, who had a civil law practice in Toronto.[4]

The composition of the court was no accident. While the war crimes regulations mandated the appointment of court members who were of 'equal or superior rank relative to the accused,' they did not require them to have been line officers.[5] But the commander of Canadian forces in Germany would not have it any other way. Determined that Meyer's actions be judged from 'a combat soldier's' perspective, Major General Vokes had deliberately selected officers who had had battlefield experience.[6] This made sense from the military justice point of view. It was also good public relations. Whatever doubts Meyer and his supporters might have regarding the fairness of the proceedings, they would never be able to claim that he had been denied a trial by his peers.

There was a pause while the court president asked Macdonald and Andrew if they were ready. Both prosecutor and defence counsel indicated that they were. With that, General Foster ordered the bailiff to produce the defendant.

A hush came over the courtroom as Meyer was escorted up to the bench. How the mighty have fallen, many spectators must have thought, as they watched the unfolding drama. Flanked by Major Arthur Russell and Captain Elton McPhail, both of them Royal Winnipeg Rifles, Meyer presented a truly forlorn figure. Bareheaded and clad in a grey uniform devoid of insignia or decorations, he looked nothing like the triumphant Nazi warrior who had once provided the grist for Goebbels's propaganda mill. Nor, for that matter, did he resemble the cold-blooded killer he was now accused of having been.[7]

Meyer maintained a stoical bearing throughout the reading of the indictment. Beneath his impassive demeanour, however, lurked considerable anxiety. This became apparent after he responded to the charges with the expected 'Nicht Schuldig' (i.e., not guilty). As if unsure of what to do next, Meyer bowed awkwardly to the bench. This gesture of servility seemed out of place in a Canadian court. Motioned by General Foster, the defendant returned to his seat.[8]

With the preliminaries out of the way, it was time for the prosecution to make its opening statement. Macdonald got to his feet. The case against Meyer was unusual, the chief prosecutor began, in that the majority of the crimes for which he was being held responsible had been committed by subordinates in his absence. How could the defendant be responsible when he had not even been present at the crime scenes? Macdonald answered the rhetorical question. Meyer was responsible if the men under his command had acted on the basis of 'a known course of conduct and [an] expressed attitude of mind' on his part. He was also responsible if he had failed to exercise 'that measure of disciplinary control over his officers and men which it is the duty of officers commanding troops to exercise.' The prosecution, according to Macdonald, was prepared to prove Meyer's guilt on both levels.[9]

After competently introducing his case, Macdonald proceeded to stumble badly, making errors and drifting into legal irrelevancies. As a consequence, he was interrupted several times by Lieutenant Colonel Bredin.[10] It was only towards the end of his address that he again found his stride. In a flash of inspiration, the chief prosecutor closed with the following powerful words:

We are not trying a private soldier who acted in a single case, or even in several cases, either as a result of his own ignorance or excess of zeal, or in response to an order from his superior, or in conformity with what he thought to be the wish and policy of that superior. We are trying here today a man who, we shall contend, is supremely responsible, both directly and indirectly, for the killing, by those under his command, of the 41 Canadian prisoners referred to on the first charge sheet. We shall seek to establish that he was the motivating force behind the cold blooded, deliberate and calculated murder of these prisoners. Many of them were killed far behind the front line, where there was no conceivable justification or excuse – other than possibly the brutal punishment of a helpless prisoner who refused to answer improper questions asked of him. If he is not directly responsible, then we do contend that the prisoners lost their lives as a result of a wilful or criminal negligence and failure of the accused to perform his duties as commander of the troops concerned.[11]

Upon concluding his address, Macdonald returned to his seat, but only long enough to pick up some papers. Soon he was up again, ready to call his first witness. Unlike the procedure in civilian courts, the military justice system did not permit counsel for the defence to make an opening statement until the prosecution had completed the presentation of its case. Thus, Lieutenant Colonel Andrew was helpless to do anything but sit and watch as the chief prosecutor's blistering attack on his client sank into the collective mind of the court.

Macdonald's first witness was Major John J. Stonborough. A German-speaking intelligence officer with the CWCIU, Stonborough was called to the stand to give evidence about the fighting in Normandy. He was particularly effective when he testified as to the deployment of German formations. Referring to documents and maps, Stonborough was able to show that units of the 12th SS Division had been assigned to sectors in which POW murders had taken place in large numbers.[12] The prosecution was off to a good start, but the momentum would soon shift.

Stonborough had barely stepped down when things started to unravel. Macdonald's next scheduled witness was Friedrich Torbanisch. The former member of the 15th Reconnaissance Company was to testify about the secret POW orders that allegedly had been issued to Meyer's regiment. There was only one problem: Torbanisch had failed to show up.

Deeply embarrassed, Macdonald apologized profusely for Torbanisch's absence, claiming that he could not be located. Notwithstanding the fact that the missing man was a prosecution witness, for whom he was responsible, Macdonald requested that Torbanisch's previous testimony before the SHAEF standing court be read into the record. Then, in a move that reflected his desperation, the chief prosecutor asked that a facsimile of the alleged secret orders also be entered as evidence. The original version was no longer extant, he explained. Torbanisch had dictated the orders from memory prior to his disappearance, and copies of the document were available.[13]

Bound by the overly generous evidentiary provisions of the war crimes regulations, the court had no choice but to admit both the statement and the document.[14] To be sure, the two items constituted tangible evidence that Meyer's regiment had followed a policy of denying quarter to the enemy. Still, the court members could not have been impressed by the manner in which Macdonald was conducting his case. Torbanisch's no-show was bad enough. But to ask that his previous statement and a hearsay document be admitted in his place was worse. Notwithstanding Macdonald's genuine dismay at what had just transpired, his request bore all the earmarks of a sleazy legal manoeuvre, of an attempt to get a key witness's testimony in through the back door, without his being subjected to cross-examination.[15] The prosecution was now definitely on the defensive.

If the Torbanisch incident did not cast him in the best light, then Macdonald's standing with the court was diminished even further by his third witness. Alfred Helzel was supposed to corroborate Torbanisch's testimony about the alleged secret orders, as well as give evidence of Meyer's incitement to deny quarter. Some five months earlier, during his first interview, the former member of the 15th Reconnaissance Company had appeared forthright, relaxed, and confident. Yet within minutes of taking the witness stand, he became 'evasive, ill at ease, and slumped down in his chair.'[16]

At the start of what was to be a long and tortuous examination-in-chief, Helzel merely tried to avoid committing himself. It did not take long, however, before he was repudiating virtually everything he had said earlier.[17] Macdonald did not know what to do. Paralysed, he looked around the courtroom in dismay. By chance, his eyes happened to meet Meyer's. Instantly, he realized what had gone wrong. As he was to remember many years later,

Meyer, who was sitting diagonally across the room from the witness, had fixed him with a glare, the equal of which I had never seen, and which fairly shot sparks across the room. The unfortunate witness, like the proverbial bird caught in the hypnotic stare of the serpent, was panic stricken. His powerful physique meant nothing and his previous assurance evaporated like dew drops in the fierce heat of the sun. It was an amazing demonstration of the tremendous disciplinary hold that this SS officer still had on a former soldier, and of the fear inspired by his presence.[18]

Meyer's blatant attempt at intimidation finally roused Macdonald from his lethargy. In the blink of an eye, the chief prosecutor regained a good measure of his professional savvy. Resorting to a well-worn but effective courtroom tactic, he positioned himself between Helzel and Meyer, thereby shielding his witness from the defendant's incapacitating glare. Then he invoked subsection 10(1)g of the war crimes regulations, which permitted the introduction of a witness's previous statements and which enabled him to treat Helzel as hostile.[19] Both moves had the desired effect. Spared the torment of having to look his former commander in the eye, Helzel gradually regained his composure. By the time that he stepped down, in fact, he had adopted much of his previous testimony and corroborated Torbanisch's statement.[20]

As a result of his quick thinking, Macdonald had averted a disaster. Had Helzel's collapse been total, the only evidence as to the first count of the indictment would have been Torbanisch's questionable and uncorroborated SHAEF testimony, which the court did not appear inclined to give much weight. Clearly, the prosecution had dodged a bullet. Yet Macdonald was far from happy about the way things were going. In particular, he was worried that what had happened to Helzel might repeat itself with his other German witnesses. In such a scenario, Meyer's acquittal was not beyond the realm of possibility. Needing time to regroup, the beleaguered prosecutor was relieved when he heard the court president call for an adjournment.[21]

The next day started out on a more promising note. Horst Heyer, Macdonald's first witness, bolstered the shaky evidence of Torbanisch and Helzel. A former member of the 1st Battalion of Meyer's regiment, Heyer confirmed the defendant's exhortation not to take prisoners. He also testified that the troops had understood the exhortation to be regimental policy. During the march to the front on D-Day, Heyer alleged, his company commander had told the men not to bother about prisoners. Several days later, the witness further alleged, a comrade informed him that he had personally taken part in the shooting of Allied prisoners. More than anything else that had been said up to then, this was compelling evidence that Meyer's regiment had followed a policy of denying quarter to the enemy.[22] The prosecution's case was back on track.

Having completed the presentation of evidence on the first count of the indictment, Macdonald turned to count two, the Authie and Buron killings. To set the stage, he reconstructed the great battle that had erupted between

Meyer's regiment and forward elements of the 9th Canadian Infantry Brigade on the afternoon of 7 June 1944. Depositions and documents from both sides of the line were read into evidence. Canadian operations were pieced together from the statement of Lieutenant Colonel Petch, who at the time was commanding the North Nova Scotia Highlanders, as well as from the North Novas' war diary. Insight into German operations was gleaned mainly from Meyer's postwar interrogations.[23] By the end of this segment, the court had a good idea as to the disposition of opposing forces just prior to the commission of the atrocities.

Macdonald's next witness was Constance Raymond Guilbert. A stonemason and long-time resident of Authie, Guilbert had personally witnessed several of the murders on the afternoon of 7 June. Once on the stand, he described in fulsome detail the killing of Private Nichol, the shooting of an unidentified soldier who was attempting to surrender, the crushing of the bodies of Corporal Davidson and another man by a German tank, and the generally brutal and maniacal behaviour of the SS troops. He also provided one of the trial's few lighter moments.

Concerned that the court might question the credibility of the witness, who currently was serving a three-year sentence for looting and black-marketeering, Macdonald resolved to get his criminal record out into the open. Although this is normally a good trial tactic, in Guilbert's case it caused some difficulties. In answer to Macdonald's question about his conviction, Guilbert claimed that it had all been a terrible mistake, that he had stumbled upon an unattended cache of two thousand bottles of wine, and, being quite thirsty, had brought them home to drink. Macdonald scolded him for asking the court to believe that he had finished the entire two thousand bottles himself. Guilbert's response was precious. 'I made a distribution,' the witness admitted, 'because there were a lot of my friends who were also thirsty.'[24] Muffled laughter could be heard from the spectators.

After Guilbert was excused, Macdonald spent the remainder of 11 December and all of the 12th recapitulating the grim litany of atrocities that had been perpetrated at Authie and Buron. Some of the accounts came in the form of depositions taken from local residents.[25] But the bulk of the evidence was entered through the testimony of the men against whom the rage of the SS troops had been directed. One after another, former members of A and C Companies of the North Nova Scotia Highlanders came forward to recount the horrors of that fateful 7 June.[26] The picture they presented was one of utter chaos and sheer terror. Yet, for all of its power, the survivors' evidence did little more than confirm that terrible crimes had been committed. As to who bore command responsibility, Macdonald had failed to establish any connection between the various crimes and the defendant's earlier incitement to deny quarter. In the mind of the court, Meyer had been fairly remote from the killing.[27]

Corporal John R.B. Campbell of the North Novas' A Company was the last witness on 12 December. Like the eight men who preceded him, the NCO had witnessed several of the murders perpetrated by Meyer's regiment at Authie and Buron, but Macdonald actually had another reason for calling him. As a member of the large prisoner column that had been escorted from Cussy to the Abbaye d'Ardenne on the evening of 7 June, Campbell had been in the abbey courtyard when the Feldgendarmerie came in and sought ten 'volunteers,' all of whom were subsequently murdered.[28] Accordingly, his testimony served as a useful bridge between the conclusion of the presentation of evidence on the second count of the indictment and the start of the prosecution's case on the third.

The most important witness of the entire trial took the stand the next morning. As the only man who claimed to have been present when Meyer gave a direct order to shoot Canadian prisoners, Jan Jesionek was indispensable. If the court believed him, then it would have no choice but to convict. If Jesionek was not convincing, then all that would be left of the prosecution's case was the chain-of-command theory. Not surprisingly, there was considerable tension in the courtroom when the former SS trooper was called to the stand.

Jesionek almost did not get the chance to tell his story. In an attempt to spruce up the image of his star witness, Macdonald had him enter the courtroom wearing an Allied uniform. This was a blunder of galactic proportions. True, Jesionek was a national of a country (Poland) that had been allied with Canada. True, his father had served time in prison for having refused to use the Nazi salute. True, he had not joined the SS voluntarily. And true, he had deserted. Nonetheless, Jesionek had worn the SS uniform and had fought and been wounded in it. For the members of the court, all but one of whom had commanded units at the front, the appearance of the enemy in the uniform of one of their own was almost more than they were prepared to bear. After months of bloody fighting, they had had their fill of the SS, and thus did not appreciate such a clumsy and inappropriate attempt to curry favour with the court.

The frowns emanating from the bench alerted Macdonald to his error. Without skipping a beat, he diverged from his prepared examination and launched into damage control. Once Jesionek had identified himself, the chief prosecutor asked him why he was wearing an Allied uniform. The witness explained that it had been given to him by the Red Cross while he was in POW captivity in Britain, and that he had been wearing it ever since. This seemed to pacify the court.[29] Having dodged another bullet, Macdonald permitted himself a quiet sigh of relief.

After guiding Jesionek through tedious but essential background testimony –

his youth, his compulsory enlistment in the 12th SS, his training, his assignment to the defendant's regiment, the secret orders to which Torbanisch had referred, Meyer's alleged incitement to deny quarter, and the march to the front on D-Day – Macdonald got to the heart of the prosecution's case. With regard to 8 June 1944, he asked the witness, 'Did you see anything that morning which was of interest to you?' Taking his cue, Jesionek proceeded to recount how seven Canadian prisoners had been brought to regimental headquarters and how he had directed them and their escorts to the front of the ancient abbey. He then recounted how the arrival of the prisoners had provoked the defendant's wrath, whereupon he had said: 'What should we do with these prisoners; they only eat up our rations?' Jesionek admitted that he had been unable to hear Meyer's subsequent conversation with his subordinates, but asserted that the regimental commander's next declaration had been loud and clear. 'In future,' the defendant had bellowed, 'no more prisoners are to be taken!' From this point onward, the witness concluded, events followed in rapid succession leading up to the execution of the seven Canadians.[30]

Jesionek's testimony was devastating. Though he had not heard Meyer give the order to shoot the prisoners, a reasonable inference could now be made that the executions would not have proceeded without it. The defence recognized that their client had been severely wounded. Accordingly, Andrew tried his best to discredit Jesionek during cross-examination, raising doubts about his comprehension of German, the inconsistencies in his pre-trial statements, and his motivation for testifying.[31] But the damage had already been done. In the mind of the court, Jesionek's recall had been superb, his testimony persuasive.[32]

The presentation of prosecution evidence continued for another two and a half days after Jesionek stepped down. During that time, Macdonald called or had read into evidence the testimony of an additional twenty witnesses.[33] A few, like former SS First Lieutenant Bernhard Meitzel, former SS Second Lieutenant Kurt Bergmann, former SS Private Hermann Sue, and former SS Corporal Ewald Wetzel, were important in that they helped to establish Meyer's vicarious responsibility for the killings that had taken place at the Abbaye d'Ardenne on 17 June.[34] The rest simply added to the mountain of circumstantial evidence against Meyer. Certainly none were able to steal Jesionek's thunder. Macdonald was reaching the point of diminishing returns. Thus, on 18 December, at 11:55 AM, he rested his case. After six and a half days of unremittingly hostile testimony, it finally would be the turn of the defence.

Proceedings resumed at 2:00 PM on 18 December. In an unusual and risky move, Andrew elected to forgo his opening address in favour of calling his first witness, who was none other than the accused himself.[35] During much of defence counsel's examination-in-chief, which lasted until noon of the following day, Meyer indulged in lengthy expositions on the fighting in Normandy.[36] The former commander seemed to revel in those parts of his testimony, as if by recounting the details of battles won and lost he was somehow transported back to headier, happier times. Of course, when it came to addressing the charges specified in the indictment, the defendant was considerably more circum-spect.[37] Still, he did quite well, impressing the court with his eloquence and apparent candour.[38]

At 2:00 in the afternoon on 19 December, Macdonald rose to cross-examine Meyer. This was the classic courtroom confrontation for which everyone had been waiting. The chief prosecutor started benignly enough, taking the former commander through his previous interrogations, showing him copies of the transcripts, asking him to identify his signature. Once Meyer had done so, the gloves came off. Macdonald waded into the hapless defendant, sparing no opportunity to attack and even ridicule his story. After a while, the cross-exam-ination took on the appearance of a personal vendetta.[39] The court's admoni-tions gave Meyer the chance to catch his breath, but soon Macdonald was back at it again, hammering away at every real or perceived discrepancy. Things got so bad that General Foster actually had to warn Macdonald to rein in his sar-casm and cease his editorializing.[40]

The confrontation reached its climax when Meyer tried to suggest that some of the Canadians who had been found in the Abbaye d'Ardenne's garden had died of wounds sustained in battle. This provoked a particularly bitter exchange, which in turn caused Meyer to lose his composure and glare icily at Macdonald, just as he had done with his interrogators at the London Cage.[41] At this point, the chief prosecutor would later remember,

I began to experience the hypnotic sensations that must have overcome the first witness, Alfred Helzel. Whether Meyer had privately practised and perfected the 'out-staring and glaring technique' said to be part of the training of Prussian officers, I do not know; but I do know that under his amazingly fierce and frightening glare I began to feel a little giddy. My limited experience in such matters would, I am afraid, have led only to solutions obvi-ously unsuited to the occasion. I was no match for him in a glaring competition but some-thing had to be done, and right away, if I was to continue my cross-examination.[42]

Macdonald's answer was to challenge the defendant. When Meyer asked to have part of his testimony read back to him, the angry prosecutor suggested that he was stalling to gain time. As the Meyer glare reached maximum intensity, Macdonald admonished: 'And glaring at me isn't going to answer anything either. You are not going to intimidate me by your glares, I can assure you.'[43] Confronted with those fighting words, the defendant underwent the most astonishing transformation. Meyer, according to Macdonald, 'looked around the courtroom in a sheepish manner, and the glare dropped from his face as if a magic wand had suddenly been passed over it. From that time on, I experienced no further difficulties with the witness. But I had been given a convincing glimpse into a technique of command over others that I would not have previously believed possible.'[44]

Notwithstanding his excessive zeal and histrionics, the chief prosecutor did score some points. He made Meyer's forgetfulness on key matters appear contrived, as though he were trying to evade responsibility for the criminal actions of his men. He also tripped up the defendant on his story regarding the discovery of eighteen or nineteen murdered Canadians at the Abbaye d'Ardenne. Finally, he got him to admit that the bodies had been buried in unmarked graves so as to prevent their discovery.[45] When Meyer finally stepped down, his credibility had been all but shattered.

Three more witnesses were called to testify on Meyer's behalf. By this time, a certain resignation had overtaken the defence team, and Andrew just went through the motions. On 23 December, which, ironically enough, was Meyer's birthday, Macdonald began the rebuttal phase of the case. Of his three rebuttal witnesses, the most important by far was Daniel Lachèvre. As was noted in the previous chapter, Lachèvre testified that he had had complete access to the abbey garden between the evenings of 8 and 10 June, and that at no time during this period had he seen any bodies.[46] The impact of this evidence was not lost on the court. As Macdonald would later recall, Lachèvre's testimony 'was one of the decisive turning points in the trial. It disproved completely, if it ever had been believed, Meyer's last minute explanation of the discovery of the bodies by him on or about June 11th.'[47]

The rebuttal phase of the trial lasted until the morning of 25 December. It was followed by a two-day adjournment for Christmas. Court was back in session on the morning of 27 December, at which time both counsel delivered their closing addresses. Mercifully, the summations were short and to the point. Then, at precisely 1:30 PM, General Foster adjourned proceedings so that the court could consider its verdict.[48] After two and a half weeks, dozens of witnesses, and hundreds of pages of trial testimony, the decision as to Meyer's fate was at last where it belonged, in the hands of his former battlefield adversaries.

It took the court almost three hours to reach its verdict. No record of the deliberations exists. However, Bredin's instructions to the court members, General Foster's recollections, and Macdonald's analysis of the verdict did survive. Taken together, these documents give some insight into the manner in which Meyer's guilt or innocence was decided on each of the five charges.

The verdict on count one (incitement) of the indictment was the easiest at which to arrive. As Bredin aptly summarized the issue, the members of the court had only to consider whether the words allegedly uttered by Meyer to his troops on the eve of the invasion amounted to an incitement to deny quarter. Despite the problems with the testimony of both Torbanisch and Helzel, the court's verdict on this charge was unanimous – guilty. Count two (Authie and Buron) provoked more debate, in large measure because the extent of Meyer's liability for the criminal conduct of troops who were both geographically and administratively remote from him could not easily be resolved. In the end, the court split three–two in favour of acquittal, having apparently heeded the defence's contention that the atrocities had been committed 'in a forward area in the heat of battle ... when conditions were still confused.' Count three (the Jesionek allegation) also prompted a split decision in favour of acquittal, with the issue coming down to whether, as Bredin put it, 'some words were uttered or some clear indication was given by the accused that the prisoners be put to death.' In casting the deciding vote, General Foster did not consider the whispered conversation between Meyer and a subordinate officer as definitive proof of the defendant's guilt. Although having acquitted Meyer of direct responsibility for the Abbaye d'Ardenne killings, the court had no trouble in finding him guilty of vicarious responsibility on counts four and five. Here the determining factors were the lower standard of proof and the implausibility of Meyer's claim that he only learned of the shootings two days after they had been carried out.[49] As General Foster said of Meyer years later, 'It was inconceivable how he, sitting in his headquarters, could have heard a succession of regularly spaced pistol shots less than 150 feet away and not sent someone off to investigate. I would have, as would any commanding officer, particularly so close to the front. Meyer didn't. He didn't because he *knew* what was going on – even if he hadn't given the order.'[50]

At 4:15 in the afternoon on 27 December, court reconvened. In front of a packed courtroom and the assembled press corps, General Foster read out the verdict. The defendant's reaction suggested that it had been somewhat unexpected.[51] Before sentence was passed, Meyer had the right to have character witnesses called on his behalf. The next morning, Captain Plourde, substituting for the dejected Andrew, called four witnesses, including Meyer's wife. Then it was the defendant's turn to address the court. After summarizing his accomplishments and those of the 12th SS Panzer Division 'Hitler Youth,' Meyer lamented that he had, 'during these proceedings, been given insight into things which, in the aggregate, were unknown to me up until now. I wish to state to the Court that these deeds were not committed by the young soldier. I am convinced of it, that in the division there were elements who, due to the year-long battles, due to five years of war, had in a certain respect become brutalized.'[52]

There can be little doubt that the 'brutalized' elements to whom Meyer referred were former Leibstandarte officers and NCOs, who, like him, had been transferred to the 12th SS in order to train and toughen the new division. For the first time since his capture, Meyer appeared to have grasped the true nature of what had happened at the Abbaye d'Ardenne and at a dozen other crime scenes in the countryside of northern France. It was only unfortunate that he did not see fit to lump himself in with those of his deceased or fugitive colleagues who he was now ready to condemn. But perhaps that was too much to expect.

At 11:20 AM, Meyer concluded his address. With that, the members of the court adjourned to deliberate his fate. They returned twenty-five minutes later and took their seats. The defendant searched the bench for a clue as to their decision but was met with stone-faced expressions. The wait was only momentary. Speaking directly to the accused, General Foster announced the following: 'Brigadeführer Kurt Meyer, the Court has found you guilty of the First, Fourth and Fifth Charges on the First Charge Sheet. The sentence of this Court is that you suffer death by being shot. The findings of guilt and the sentence are subject to confirmation. These proceedings are now closed.'[53]

The trial may have been over, but the legal manoeuvring was just beginning. As was his right under section 12 of the war crimes regulations, Meyer immediately filed an appeal. In keeping with his mandate under the regulations, Major General Vokes promptly reviewed the defendant's submission. Though personally unconvinced as to Meyer's guilt, Vokes rejected the appeal. Accordingly, sentence was scheduled to be carried out on 7 January 1946. As the day of reckoning approached, the execution was delayed so that British and American war crimes investigators could question the condemned man.[54] After that, nothing, it seemed, could save Meyer from his appointment with a Canadian firing squad. But something did.

On 5 January 1946, Vokes issued an order postponing Meyer's execution. Concerned because Field Marshal Montgomery, to whom he was subordinate, had broached the subject of British involvement in the review of Meyer's appeal, Vokes wired CMHQ and asked that the matter be referred to the Canadian government. Ottawa responded by sending John Read, who was special legal counsel with External Affairs and a member of the war crimes advisory panel, to London for a conference. It was at this conference, held in High Commissioner Vincent Massey's office on 9 January, that the decision was made to commute Meyer's sentence to life imprisonment. The new sentence was formally approved on 13 January.[55] The same day, a stunned but eternally grateful Meyer was notified of his reprieve.[56]

Needless to say, when word of the commutation got out, the media brayed for blood. 'Meyer's Commutation a Betrayal' screamed one headline. 'Our Brave

Canadian Dead Are Turning in Their Graves,' cried another. Concurrent with the press campaign, hundreds of angry telegrams, letters, and petitions poured into Ottawa from Canadian Legion posts, civic groups, and individuals across the country.[57] Eventually, the opposition Tories got into the act, demanding that Prime Minister King and his government come clean about how and why Meyer's sentence was commuted.[58]

At the root of the furore over the commutation was the suspicion that justice in the Meyer case had been sacrificed to some craven political or diplomatic interest. Though by no means conclusive, there is evidence of this. For example, when Vokes initially granted Meyer a stay of execution, one of the justifications he used was British concern about the implications for Germany's future relations with the West were the sentence to be carried out. Significantly, that issue was raised again at the 9 January conference.[59] Admittedly, the extant documentation shows no direct link between the decision to commute and the exigencies of foreign policy. Given the heavy press coverage accorded to the Meyer case, however, such a link was not out of the question. Indeed, the idea that the commutation was in some way willed by Ottawa in furtherance of its postwar foreign policy objectives is given credence by Vokes's admissions – both in private correspondence and to the press – that the decision to commute had been made on the advice of the aforementioned John Read.[60] It is further suggested by the inordinate lengths to which the government went to have Read issue a denial.[61]

If the government did interfere in the adjudication of the Meyer case, then the following question must be asked: Was it wrong for doing so? The answer is not as clear-cut as one might think. On the face of it, there would seem to be little room for debate. After all, judicial independence is one of the tenets of the Canadian system of justice. As such, it forms the basis of the public's trust in the system. By extension, any breach of judicial independence, such as appears to have happened in the decision to commute Meyer's sentence, would have constituted a grave violation of the trust of the Canadian people.

As a matter of general principle, then, government interference in the judicial process is wrong. However, as regards what was right and wrong in the specific case of Kurt Meyer, the principle became somewhat muddled. To be sure, Meyer had been tried, convicted, and sentenced by a Canadian military court. But he had also been tried according to rules of the game that heavily favoured the prosecution. Under such circumstances, it was legitimate to ask whether the defendant had obtained a fair trial. And if the answer were no, would not the government be warranted in intervening to prevent a miscarriage of justice?

The issue really comes down to the question of whether Meyer had a fair hearing. Despite the flawed evidentiary provisions of the war crimes regulations, it is the contention here that he did, in the end. A recapitulation of the facts will serve to illustrate the point.

It is clear that much of the prosecution's evidence against Meyer would not have been admitted in an ordinary civilian court. We have seen how most German witnesses were extremely reluctant to talk, and how they only consented to be interviewed when faced with the threat of prosecution under subsection 10(3) of the war crimes regulations. We have also seen how subsection 10(1) made admissible the most blatantly hearsay witness testimony and documents. Assuming that all of the evidence obtained under subsections 10(1) and 10(3) was thrown out, Macdonald would have been left with four witnesses – Helzel, Jesionek, Lachèvre, and, of course, Meyer himself. Helzel's near collapse on the stand negated the probative value of his testimony, thereby leaving the prosecution with only three viable witnesses. Of these, Meyer did not say much to implicate himself, but his story about the discovery of the bodies did open his credibility to impeachment by Lachèvre. Finally, Jesionek put Meyer at the scene and in command of the troops who murdered seven Canadian POWs. Taken together, the testimony of the three remaining witnesses likely would have been enough to convict Meyer as an accessory to murder in any courtroom.

As for the revised sentence, this too was probably fair. Jesionek, it will be remembered, did not actually hear Meyer give the order to shoot the seven Canadians. Of course, a reasonable inference to that effect could be drawn from the attendant circumstances. Still, this meant that the evidence against Meyer on the most serious of the charges was circumstantial, not direct. With a man's life hanging on a conversation that the only eyewitness had not heard, it was right of Vokes (or Read) to commute the sentence of the Aurich court.

Kurt Meyer was the first man tried under Canada's war crimes regulations. Though in need of some reform, the system of military justice established by the regulations had worked. A clearly guilty man had been convicted, and his punishment, after review, had been a just one. Thus, the Meyer trial augured well for the future prosecution of war criminals, in particular the other perpetrators of the Normandy massacres. Or so it seemed.

# 17

# The Ones Who Got Away

In recommending the laying of charges against Kurt Meyer, the war crimes advisory panel had observed that 'it is unlikely that there will be any other case as well documented and as readily approved as this one.'[1] Given the hearsay quality of much of the evidence adduced at trial, one might well quarrel with the description of the Meyer case as having been 'well documented.' Yet there certainly is no denying the prophetic character of the panel's observation. Though prima facie cases existed against a number of Meyer's fellow officers, only one of them – SS Major Bernhard Siebken, the commander of the 2nd Battalion of the 26th Panzer Grenadier Regiment – would ever be brought to trial. And Siebken was tried before a British military court. Beset by controversies over command responsibility, mistaken identity, and reprisals, the Siebken proceedings would leave both contemporary and present-day commentators feeling as though justice had not been served.

There were two reasons for Canada's sorry record in prosecuting the perpetrators of the Normandy massacres. The first was the premature dismantling of the country's war crimes investigation infrastructure. Even before the start of the Meyer trial, pressure had been building to either drastically scale back CWCIU or eliminate it altogether. Not surprisingly, the pressure came from CMHQ, whose support for Canada's war crimes prosecution effort, it will be remembered, had been reluctant and half-hearted. As early as November 1945, in fact, Brigadier W.H.S. Macklin, the deputy chief of staff at CMHQ, wrote to Lieutenant Colonel Macdonald asking for an estimate as to when CWCIU would be wrapping up its work. The chief prosecutor was taken aback by this strange request. In the midst of preparations for the upcoming Meyer trial, he gave what seemed to be the only appropriate response. Citing the eighty-one cases that CWCIU still had under investigation, Macdonald replied that he was in no position to provide a definitive time line for the termination of the unit's operations.[2]

For reasons that remain obscure, Macklin was determined to shut CWCIU down. Thus, he could hardly be expected to permit Macdonald's non-committal answer to go unchallenged. Soliciting the aid of High Commissioner Massey, Macklin suggested that Macdonald be given a target date of 1 May 1946 for the dissolution of CWCIU and the completion of all Canadian war crimes investigations and trials. It was not that he was unsympathetic to the cause of justice, the chief of staff explained. 'I am as anxious as anybody else to hang a few of the German perpetrators of outrages against Canadian troops,' he assured Massey. It was simply a matter of the costs outweighing the benefits. The fact was, Macklin grumbled, that 'after a year and a half of investigating, including 6 months by this large and expensive unit [i.e., CWCIU], we have so far succeeded in bringing one single German to trial, and we are not at all sure that we are going to be able to hang him.'[3]

Considered from the perspective of present-day war crimes cases, which as a rule take years to investigate, Macklin's arguments are hard to fathom. It is rare that there is an eyewitness to a murder, and rarer still when such a person comes forward. As a consequence, virtually all murder cases are put together and tried on the basis of circumstantial evidence. This tends to make their preparation rather complicated and time consuming. The problem is compounded in war crimes cases, where the ebb and flow of battle often disturbs or destroys evidence. Accordingly, the notion that CWCIU could wrap up eighty-one investigations in a period of about four months was completely unrealistic, not to mention patently unfair.

Notwithstanding the absurdity of Macklin's suggestion, Massey went along. Always pliable in the hands of CMHQ, the high commissioner agreed that CWCIU had outlived its usefulness, and he promised to draft a message to that effect to his superiors. In mid-December, both National Defence Headquarters and External Affairs in Ottawa received telegrams advocating the disbandment of CWCIU and the termination of all Canadian war crimes investigations by 1 May 1946.[4] Macklin's telegram in particular is instructive for the skilful manner in which it sought to manipulate government policy via bureaucratic channels. In his correspondence with Massey, Macklin had shown his true colours, stating that his desire to shut down CWCIU stemmed from what he regarded as the slow pace of investigation and the lack of results obtained thus far. Of course, whether or not to proceed on the basis of past results was a matter for the government to decide, not the bureaucracy. Had Macklin used this approach with his superiors back in Ottawa, they undoubtedly would have rejected it as an unwarranted intrusion into the realm of policy making.

Surprisingly well-versed in the art of bureaucratic prevarication for a military man, the chief of staff did not launch a frontal assault on the government's war crimes prosecution policy. Instead, he emphasized the administrative difficulties in keeping CWCIU open. Many of the men and officers in the unit were eligible for repatriation, he pointed out, and were eager to get home. 'While we are naturally anxious to bring as many war criminals as possible to trial and conviction,' Macklin advised, 'we feel we must set a date for the termination of these activities.'[5]

The reference to repatriation was a red herring. To be sure, at the time that Macklin was making his case for the closure of CWCIU, the Canadian government was being subjected to growing pressure for an early pullout from Europe. Indeed, when previously announced repatriation target dates were not met, some unrest occurred within Canadian occupation forces in Germany. But there is no evidence that the members of CWCIU had been bitten by the repatriation bug. On the contrary, at least half of the unit had expressed the desire to stay in order to finish the job. Moreover, in the face of the concurrent establishment of a ten-man Canadian unit to assist in the prosecution of suspected Japanese war criminals, the argument that a few more officers could not be spared to finish the European investigations simply did not hold water.[6]

Supported as it was by Massey, Macklin's recommendation was given serious consideration by the government in Ottawa. Generally speaking, it met with a favourable response, although some concern was expressed regarding the political implications of a complete shutdown of the war crimes prosecution effort. Lest Canadian interests be 'jeopardized' by the setting of an arbitrary date for CWCIU's closure, the war crimes advisory panel called for a review of the unit's eighty-one active investigations. The purpose was to determine whether or not the 1 May target date was realistic. This seemed to satisfy Massey, but Macklin, in a remarkable display of impatience and impertinence, testily resubmitted his recommendations. His second telegram met with a stern rebuke from National Defence Headquarters, which reminded him that the prosecution of war criminals was, after all, a 'matter of governmental policy.'[7]

Ottawa's call for a review of all pending war crimes cases afforded CWCIU a respite. If it could be demonstrated that its inventory contained a sufficient number of promising investigations, then the unit might still be saved. The ball, as it were, was back in Macdonald's court. It is therefore ironic that the man who had fought so hard to establish an independent Canadian war crimes unit would be a key factor in its demise.

Prior to the trial of Kurt Meyer, Macdonald had been convinced that prima facie cases existed against Karl-Heinz Milius, Gerhard Bremer, Wilhelm Mohnke, and Siegfried Müller. After the commutation of Meyer's sentence, his optimism seemed to evaporate. Indeed, in a report submitted to the adjutant general in mid-January 1946, just days after the commutation, the discouraged prosecutor painted a bleak picture of the future of the Canadian war crimes program. Vokes's decision, in his view, could not help but have a deleterious impact on future trials. The evidentiary standard for determining a commander's accountability had been raised so high, he contended, that it was now a 'virtual impossibility' to obtain convictions and satisfactory sentences. In light of this development, Macdonald lamented, there was no choice but to close 'a great many' of the cases in CWCIU's inventory.[8]

Coming from the man who had almost single-handedly created Canada's war crimes prosecution program, such negativism was downright shocking. It was as though Macdonald was saying that if the death penalty could not be sought on every case then there was no point in trying suspected war criminals. This was a rather skewed view of the nature of crime and punishment. After all, the threat of tough sentences does not by itself ensure adherence to international norms of conduct. Rather, the best deterrent to those who would contemplate the commission of war crimes is justice that is swift, sure, and, most of all, fair. This was precisely what had happened in the Meyer case. Contrary to Macdonald's opinion, the commutation did not foreshadow an elevated burden of proof for future war crimes cases, but merely signified the desire not to execute a man on the basis of circumstantial evidence. Had Jesionek actually heard Meyer give the order to shoot the Canadian prisoners at the Abbaye d'Ardenne, there is little doubt that the death sentence of the military court in Aurich would have been upheld.

Macdonald's pessimism regarding the prospects for future trials sealed the fate of CWCIU. Though during its respite Canadian military courts tried three more cases, each of which involved crimes perpetrated against downed Canadian airmen and each of which resulted in convictions,[9] by early April 1946 National Defence Headquarters had formally endorsed Macklin's and Macdonald's recommendations. The death of CWCIU was made official at cabinet's 6 May meeting. Henceforth, there was nothing more for the unit's dedicated personnel to do but play out the string. On 31 May 1946, CWCIU's passing was marked without fanfare. 'All files and equipment having been turned in and accounted for,' its last diary entry laconically noted, 'the Unit ceased to function.'[10]

The closure of CWCIU did not mean the end of Canadian involvement in the prosecution of suspected war criminals. The British had indicated that they were prepared to carry on the unit's work, but they requested the assistance of some or all of its personnel. Eleven of CWCIU's original twenty-two-man cadre volunteered to stay on. Together they constituted the Canadian Field Investigative Section of the British war crimes unit.[11]

The decision to maintain a scaled-back war crimes unit was justified on the grounds that it would be sufficient to protect Canadian interests. In actuality, the price of Canada's continued involvement in the prosecution of war criminals was the relinquishing of any say over which cases went to trial.[12] The extent to which this transfer of jurisdiction worked against Canadian interests is demonstrated by some comparative statistics on the rate of prosecution in Canadian and British cases. Between 1945, when they launched their own war crimes prosecution initiative, and 1948, when they shut it down, the British brought to trial 1,085 of 5,900, or roughly 18 per cent, of their active cases.[13] During the same period, by contrast, only 7 of 171 Canadian cases, or a dismal 4 per cent, were brought to trial.[14] This should not have come as a surprise. As early as the summer of 1944, CMHQ had experienced first-hand the low priority with which the British armed forces treated war crimes cases involving Canadian victims. More recently, the British had reiterated their priorities, letting it be known that, where the prosecution of war criminals was concerned, they preferred that Canadians 'wash [their] own dirty linen.'[15] In retrospect, this was advice that ought to have been heeded.

The transfer of Canadian cases to British control would have deleterious consequences for future prosecutions. Perhaps no case foreshadowed the problems that were to be encountered more than that of Wilhelm Mohnke. Mohnke had been a wanted man since the summer of 1944. On 28 June 1944, a Polish-German conscript from his regiment was taken prisoner by a British unit and shipped back across the Channel to Lingfield POW camp. After two weeks in captivity, former SS Private Withold Stangenberg told camp authorities that he had information about a German war crime. His request to make a statement was obliged, and on 10 July his story was recorded by an Allied intelligence officer.[16]

According to Stangenberg, who had served as a mechanic with the headquarters company of Mohnke's regiment, on the afternoon of 11 June 1944 three prisoners were brought to the regimental command post. Within a matter of minutes, Mohnke, his adjutant, and an interpreter appeared on the scene. Through the interpreter, the visibly angry regimental commander proceeded to question the three POWs. The interrogation was conducted with extreme brutality, with Mohnke repeatedly shouting and gesturing in a violent manner. After about fifteen minutes, the prisoners were searched and stripped of all personal possessions, including their identity discs. Then they were marched about three hundred yards across a meadow to the edge of a bomb crater, where they were shot. Throughout the entire execution, Stangenberg alleged, Mohnke had stood near his command post watching and making no effort to intervene.[17]

The incident to which Stangenberg was referring, of course, was the shooting at Mohnke's headquarters of sappers John Ionel and George Benner of the

Royal Canadian Engineers and Private Allan Owens of the Royal Winnipeg Rifles. SHAEF was immediately informed of the incident, and its standing court launched an investigation. Over the course of its inquiry, the court located a second eyewitness, SS Private Heinz Schmidt, who was able to corroborate much of Stangenberg's story. On the basis of the evidence of Stangenberg and Schmidt, Mohnke was included among the suspects named in SHAEF's comprehensive April 1945 report.[18]

Stangenberg was interviewed by CWCIU on 28 June 1945. Macdonald was sufficiently impressed by this first encounter to repeat what he had recently done with former SS Private Jesionek – a re-enactment of the killings. The prosecutor was not disappointed. Accompanied to Normandy by a Canadian intelligence officer, Stangenberg easily located the crime scene and pointed out with remarkable clarity and precision the positioning of both perpetrators and victims on the fateful afternoon of 11 June 1944. The former conscript's recall was so good, in fact, that he was able to identify the now filled-in bomb crater where the Canadians had been shot and in which their bodies were buried. Owing to the bodies' advanced state of decomposition, the cause of death could not be proven conclusively, but Stangenberg's story was given further credence by the bullet holes found in the back of Ionel's shirt.[19]

On the basis of Stangenberg's evidence, CWCIU assigned the Mohnke case the highest investigative priority. In the weeks that followed, a number of witnesses were interviewed, Heinz Schmidt among them. While he had not actually witnessed the shootings, Schmidt corroborated Stangenberg's evidence in all other respects.[20] In the process, he rendered the case against Mohnke stronger than that against Kurt Meyer. Indeed, had Mohnke been in Canadian hands, there is little doubt that he, and not Meyer, would have been the first man tried under Canada's new war crimes regulations.[21] Unfortunately, Mohnke was unavailable, having been captured by elements of the Red Army in Berlin on 2 May 1945 while leading a band of Hitler's last-ditch followers out of the Führer's bunker.[22] Thus, while the Meyer case was being prepared for trial, CWCIU had to content itself with the issuance of international warrants for Mohnke's arrest.[23]

Canadian war crimes investigators learned fairly early on that Mohnke had been captured by the Red Army. To their credit, they persisted for almost a year in trying to persuade the Soviets to hand him over,[24] but their efforts were in vain. Despite the fact that Mohnke had not served with the Leibstandarte during its stint on the eastern front, and therefore had no war crimes charges for which to answer in the USSR, the Soviets would neither confirm nor deny that they were holding him. He became, in effect, a pawn in the Cold War between East and West. In fact, the more that the Canadians pressed for information as to his whereabouts, the more Mohnke's value increased in the Soviets' eyes. With the threat of extradition and prosecution hanging over his head, Mohnke was only too willing to tell Moscow anything that it wanted to hear, including stories about Hitler's Alpine redoubt, alleged plans for a Fourth Reich, and the escape of high-ranking Nazis to South America. The Soviets, in turn, then leaked this information through their intelligence sources in order to discredit the West.[25]

In all likelihood, the Soviets would not have parted with Mohnke regardless of what might have been offered in return. Still, whatever hope there may have been was lost because of British ineptitude or indifference. Upon receiving incontrovertible proof that Mohnke was in Soviet hands, Canadian authorities initiated secret contacts aimed at winning his release into their custody. The Soviets were to be offered a deal – in exchange for Mohnke, against whom no charges were pending in the USSR, they would hand over Meyer, against whom there were.[26] Then, on the eve of the negotiations, the Canadians got the bad news: owing to an administrative error, the British had sent Stangenberg to Germany for repatriation to his native Poland. Macdonald was livid. In a 27 February 1946 letter to the British Adjutant General's office, he railed against the irresponsible release of Stangenberg, pointing out that his loss would not only be 'embarrassing' from the diplomatic point of view, but also 'probably fatal to any chance of obtaining a conviction against Mohnke.' If there was the slightest possibility of holding Stangenberg in Germany before he was repatriated and thereby 'lost for use at any war crimes trials,' the prosecutor pleaded with British authorities to do so.[27]

Macdonald's entreaties were to no avail. The very next day, Major Anthony Terry of the London Cage informed him that Stangenberg's whereabouts were unknown.[28] As Macdonald predicted, the loss of Stangenberg had an immediately chilling effect on diplomatic efforts to effect Mohnke's release. With CWCIU's star witness gone, External Affairs was no longer willing to truck with the Soviets regarding an exchange of high profile prisoners.[29] This left Macdonald no choice but to put the Mohnke case on ice. Three decades would elapse before it would begin to thaw.

The loss of Stangenberg was symptomatic of the low priority that the British accorded to war crimes cases in which the victims were Canadians. Though not to be condoned, such an attitude was certainly understandable from the point of view of British self-interest. More difficult to fathom was the attitude of the Canadian government. If the earlier British handling of the Château d'Audrieu investigation was not a wake-up call, then surely the Stangenberg fiasco ought to have been. Yet it seems not to have disturbed the slumbering tranquility of official Ottawa. Indeed, the decision to close CWCIU was made *two months later*, in the full knowledge of the fatal blow that the British had dealt to the

Mohnke case. The closure of CWCIU effectively sealed the fate of the remaining 12th SS investigations. Henceforth, little heed would be taken of Canadian interests in the prosecution of the suspected perpetrators of battlefield atrocities.

The harm done by the closure of CWCIU went well beyond the loss of prosecutorial discretion over Canadian war crimes cases. In addition, the government's surrender of jurisdiction caused the remnant Canadian Field Investigative Section considerable technical difficulties. This was particularly true where access to previously collected evidence was concerned. After CWCIU was disbanded, its raw investigative files were handed over to the British. The remainder of the unit's records, including exhibits, administrative correspondence, and personnel files, were packed up and shipped back to Ottawa.[30]

Comprising a full year's work, CWCIU's records were quite voluminous. Accordingly, when they arrived at National Defence Headquarters, the first question that arose was one of storage. The task was left to the Directorate of Administration. Suddenly finding himself inundated with boxes of war crimes materials, the officer in charge of the directorate wrote to the Judge Advocate General and pointedly asked: 'What is our purpose in the preservation and filing of all these documents?' Unsure himself as to the answer, the judge advocate acted in time-honoured bureaucratic fashion: he tried to pass the records off to other government departments. First External Affairs was approached. Then it was the turn of the Department of Justice. In the end, the judge advocate had to admit defeat; no one wanted the records. So they ended up back with the Directorate of Administration. In an effort to ease its burden, the judge advocate authorized the directorate to retain only those boxes containing 'rulings and decisions of a judicial character.'[31] Everything else could go. This was a decision that would come back to haunt Canadian military authorities.

In October 1947, former SS Captain Gerd von Reitzenstein of the Hitler Youth Division's reconnaissance battalion was apprehended in France. Along with former SS Major Gerhard Bremer, the battalion's commanding officer, Reitzenstein was wanted in connection with the murder of twenty-four Canadian and two British POWs at the Château d'Audrieu on 8 June 1944. With the intention of prosecuting the apprehended fugitive, the British judge advocate contacted the War Office in London and asked that it make arrangements to obtain from Canada any and all investigative materials on the Château d'Audrieu killings. Shortly thereafter, National Defence Headquarters in Ottawa received the War Office request via the British High Commission.[32]

The request for Canadian records was eminently reasonable and justified. Yet it unleashed a frightful panic at National Defence Headquarters. Within hours of its receipt, employees of the Directorate of Administration discovered that a crucial box of evidence from the Château d'Audrieu investigation was missing.

The box apparently had contained bullets taken from the bodies of the murdered Canadians and several live rounds of German ammunition, as well as finger-prints, photographs, and depositions made by the attending pathologist – in short, all of the forensic evidence. An initial search of headquarters' files yielded copies of the pathologist's depositions, but nothing more.[33]

Thus began months of frantic but ultimately futile searching for the lost items. In an episode reminiscent of the Somalia fiasco, National Defence Head-quarters personnel were required to sift through their filing and storage cabinets for clues as to the whereabouts of the missing evidence box. Indeed, anyone remotely connected with the original investigation was contacted in the vain hope that they might remember what had been done with it.[34] Out of despera-tion, National Defence Headquarters even got in touch with former Lieutenant Colonel Macdonald, who was now in private law practice in Windsor. Some-what amused, the former prosecutor checked his own files and contacted several of the officers who had served under him at CWCIU, but to no avail.[35] The rummaging in Ottawa was equally unsuccessful.[36] Crucial evidence in a major war crimes case had been lost, probably forever.

Notwithstanding the negligence of Canadian military authorities, the news was not all bad. 'Despite [the] lack of exhibits,' the British judge advocate reported in February 1948, satisfactory progress was at last being made in bringing Reitzenstein to trial.[37] Unfortunately, the optimism would be short-lived. At its 12 April 1948 meeting, the Overseas Reconstruction Committee of the British cabinet decided that no further trials of war criminals would be started in the British zone of occupation after 31 August. Owing to delays caused by the search for the missing physical evidence, the case against Reitzenstein was not ready in time, and the British were forced to release him from custody.[38] Once again, justice became a casualty to bureaucratic incompe-tence and indifference.

In the aftermath of the closure of the British war crimes investigation unit, only one more 12th SS case was tried. On 21 October 1948, proceedings were opened against Bernhard Siebken, Dietrich Schnabel, Heinrich Albers, and Fritz Bundschuh before a British military court in Hamburg. The four defen-dants, all former members of the 2nd Battalion of the 12th SS's 26th Panzer Grenadier Regiment, were charged with the murder of the Canadian prisoners Harold Angel, Frederick Holness, and Ernest Baskerville at the battalion's headquarters on the morning of 9 June 1944. The trial lasted almost three weeks, during which substantial evidence was adduced proving the complicity of each of the defendants in the killings. On 9 November 1948, the court announced its verdict: Albers and Bundschuh, the trigger men, were acquitted on the grounds that they had followed superior orders, while Siebken, the battalion commander, and Schnabel, his special missions officer, were found guilty of having issued and carried out the execution order. It seemed to be a just decision. Yet, owing to the fact that numerous witnesses had come forward to testify that Wilhelm Mohnke had been the real instigator of the murders, many observers harboured doubts as to the fairness of the verdict.[39] Whatever the real truth, the controversy surrounding the Siebken trial marked an ignominious close to the search for justice for the victims of the Normandy massacres.

Between the summer of 1944 and the summer of 1948, Canadian war crimes investigators expended countless man-hours building criminal cases against the perpetrators of the Normandy massacres. By any standards of measurement, the results of their efforts were singularly unsatisfactory. Only two trials were held, and only one of these before a Canadian military court. Of the originally fugitive suspects, one (Reitzenstein) avoided having to answer for his crimes because of the negligence of Canadian military authorities. Another (Mohnke) was permitted to slip away because of the incompetence or indifference of British officials. The remainder, including the high ranking Karl-Heinz Milius, Gerhard Bremer, and Siegfried Müller, were simply forgotten or permitted to return to their homes with no questions asked. This is perhaps the deeper tragedy of what had happened in Normandy. The 156 Canadians who died at the hands of the 12th SS Panzer Division 'Hitler Youth' were twice victimized, first by a criminal and abhorrent philosophy of warfare, and then again by a lazy and uncaring military bureaucracy. For everything that the men of the 3rd Canadian Infantry Division did for their country, and for everything that they sacrificed, they deserved better.

# Epilogue

On 8 May 1945, the 12th SS Panzer Division 'Hitler Youth' surrendered to the American 7th Army near the Enns River in Austria. Though the division's ten thousand survivors went into immediate POW captivity, within three years all had been released into the anonymity of private life in postwar Germany.[1] Their number included most of the major perpetrators of the Normandy massacres. Karl-Heinz Milius, whose teenaged thugs had wreaked such murderous havoc at Authie and Buron on the afternoon of 7 June 1944, settled down to a quiet existence with his wife and child in the western German city of Dortmund. Siegfried Müller, whose SS engineers were responsible for the murder of about a dozen Canadians taken prisoner at Le Mesnil-Patry on 11 June and at Mouen on 17 June, also made his way back to western Germany, only to drop out of sight some years later. Reprieved when the clock ran out on the British war crimes prosecution program, Gerd von Reitzenstein returned none the worse for wear to his native Berlin. Since the early 1950s, his whereabouts, like Müller's, have been unknown. Gerhard Bremer, Reitzenstein's co-conspirator in the Château d'Audrieu killings, was the only one of his colleagues not to return to his homeland. Finding both the weather and the political climate in Franco's Spain more congenial, Bremer took up permanent residence there in the late 1940s.

Two of the major perpetrators of the Normandy massacres did pay for their crimes, although by the standards of military justice they got off relatively easy. After his sentence was commuted to life imprisonment, Kurt Meyer was ordered committed to the federal penitentiary in Dorchester, New Brunswick.[2] Separated from his family and highly critical of the conditions of his internment,[3] Meyer nonetheless adapted fairly well to prison life. Initially assigned the menial but arduous task of cleaning up the infirmary, he eventually garnered a plumb job cataloguing books in the library. In addition to being relatively easy, the library work was also not without more tangible rewards.

During the five years that he spent in Dorchester Pen, Meyer collected $53.86 in remuneration.[4]

His constitution weakened by the hardships of war, the former SS general began to suffer a variety of afflictions during his incarceration in Canada. In this regard, he was more fortunate than his German brethren, whose war-torn country was able to dispense only the most rudimentary level of health care. In 1950, for example, Meyer was hospitalized and successfully treated for a serious kidney condition. The same year, a prewar leg injury was corrected with special orthopaedic footwear. Meyer even received regular dental and eye examinations. [5]

While making arrangements for his transfer to Dorchester, the Canadian government appeared to be committed to keeping Meyer in prison for the rest of his life.[6] Times changed, however. The war began to recede from public memory, and the new threat of Soviet expansionism superseded fears of a Nazi revival. Sensing this shift in the geopolitical atmosphere, supporters of Meyer, both in Canada and back in his native Germany, became increasingly brazen about pressuring Ottawa for his early release.[7] In 1951, the pro-Meyer agitation, which by now was being buttressed by the German government in Bonn, paid off.[8] After much hand-wringing,[9] on 18 October 1951 Ottawa authorized Meyer's return to Werl, Germany, in the British zone of occupation, where he was to be interned in an ordinary civilian prison.[10]

In an interesting sidelight, Meyer almost did not make it home. Lost in dense fog, the plane bringing him back to Germany had to make an emergency landing and managed to stop just yards from a deep ravine. A subsequent inspection of the aircraft's undercarriage revealed that four of the five tires had blown out.[11] For not the first time in his life, Meyer had cheated the Grim Reaper. It was as though the gods of war were still watching over him.

Despite the fact that Meyer's transfer to Werl had not been accompanied by any mitigation of sentence, powerful forces soon began to work in an effort to effect a pardon. Using the leverage afforded by Germany's strategic geographic location, the government in Bonn made clemency for war criminals one of the preconditions for its participation in the defence of central Europe against the Soviet threat.[12] In the face of Bonn's trump card, the rate of pardons in both the American and the British zones of occupation began to rise dramatically during the early 1950s.[13] Concerned lest Canada be seen to be lagging behind on this issue, the Canadian ambassador to Germany, Thomas C. Davis, lobbied hard for Meyer's release.[14] It was only a matter of time before Canada fell into line with its wartime allies.[15] What once would have been unthinkable happened less than three years after Meyer's return to Germany. In the early morning hours of 7 September 1954, Canada's former public enemy number one was ushered out a back exit of Werl Prison into a waiting vehicle.[16] Ten years to the day after he was first taken prisoner by Belgian partisans, Meyer was a free man.

Immediately upon his release, the former SS commander was driven to his wife and children in the town of Niederkrüchten, about thirty-five miles north-west of Cologne. There he was given a hero's welcome. Speeches were made, a torchlight procession was organized in his honour, and a red convertible was lent to him by a Düsseldorf auto firm.[17] In light of Meyer's status as a pardoned war criminal, such festiveness seemed inappropriate, even tawdry.

One of the ironies of Meyer's release from prison was that it actually saved the life of a Canadian soldier. Some months earlier, George M——, a private in the Princess Patricia's Light Infantry – which was part of Canada's NATO contingent in Germany – had been tried, convicted, and sentenced to death by a Canadian military court for the murder of a fifty-six-year-old local woman. The private had appealed his sentence up the chain of command, but to no avail. In July, his case was brought before the cabinet of Prime Minister Louis St Laurent. Though there were a number of points, most notably the 'useful effect' it would have on public opinion in Germany, that favoured proceeding with the execution, in the end cabinet decided to commute the sentence to life imprisonment. The main reason, as stated in the minutes of the cabinet meeting, was that the execution of a Canadian soldier 'might cause an unfavourable reaction in Canada since this sentence would be carried out at approximately the same time as the well known German war criminal, Kurt Meyer, was being released.'[18]

After returning home, Meyer began writing his memoirs. Published in 1956, *Grenadiere* was a stirring if somewhat nostalgic account of a memorable and controversial military career. Predictably, Meyer used the book as a platform from which to once more proclaim his innocence of any wrongdoing in Normandy. Popular with ex-soldiers and military buffs alike, *Grenadiere*'s first run sold a very respectable six thousand copies.

Though certainly welcome, the proceeds from the sale of the book did not go very far. To support his family, Meyer went to work for the Andreas Brewery in Hagen, West Germany. His job was to supervise the company's twenty-seven sales drivers. By all accounts, he approached his responsibilities with the same gusto and determination that he had demonstrated in combat. In another of the ironies associated with this story, one of Meyer's best customers was Canada's NATO mess at Soest, Germany.[19] Life was good for this aging but unrepentant Nazi. However, the years of stress and privation eventually caught up with him: he suffered a mild stroke in the summer of 1961, and had two more serious episodes that autumn. On the evening of 23 December 1961, his fifty-first birthday, Kurt Meyer's heart stopped for good.

Meyer's funeral in Hagen was attended by more than five thousand mourners, making it the biggest event by far in the town's history. The former commander was eulogized as a great soldier by numerous old comrades, including Hubert Meyer of the Hitler Youth Division. Tributes sent by various West German politicians, including those of Chancellor Konrad Adenauer, were read out at the memorial service.[20] Needless to say, what had happened at the Abbaye d'Ardenne on 7–8 June 1944 was not listed among Meyer's accomplishments.

For Wilhelm Mohnke, the other major perpetrator of the Normandy massacres, justice was meted out in a more indirect and less discernible fashion. A prisoner of the Cold War, Mohnke spent a decade in Soviet captivity, doing most of his time in the small, overcrowded 'generals camp' at Voikovo, about two hundred miles east of Moscow. Though certainly trying, the conditions at Voikovo were not nearly as appalling as those that confronted his lower-ranking former comrades, most of whom were consigned to Stalin's gulag.[21] Moreover, by refusing to turn him over to the West, the Soviets inadvertently may have saved Mohnke's life. After all, the former SS commander was wanted for various war crimes by no less than three governments – the Canadian, the British, and the American. Had he been extradited to any of those countries in the late 1940s, there is a good chance that he would have stood trial and been executed for his crimes.

Not repatriated to West Germany until October 1955, Mohnke, like Meyer, returned to a very different world. No longer the subject of an Allied manhunt, the former martinet of the 12th SS was able to spend the next two decades in quiet but affluent obscurity, running a successful truck and trailer dealership just outside of Hamburg. Indeed, it was not until the early 1970s that questions about Mohnke's wartime activities again began to haunt the corridors of power in the capitals of the former wartime allies.

In the course of his work as chaplain to the Dunkirk Veterans' Association, Reverend Leslie R. Aitken met a number of British soldiers who had survived the Wormhoudt massacre of May 1940. Their stories were so compelling that he decided to write a book about the incident. During the initial phase of his research, Aitken learned that Wilhelm Mohnke had been the primary suspect in this early Leibstandarte atrocity. He also discovered that Mohnke had been dogged by additional allegations of war crimes – specifically, incidents stemming from the invasion of Normandy in June 1944 – for which he had been wanted by the Canadian government.[22]

Confounded by the numerous unsubstantiated and contradictory rumours regarding Mohnke's whereabouts, Aitken quickly realized that he needed help. Accordingly, in 1975 he wrote for information to Ludwigsburg, Germany, which is home to an agency established for the specific purpose of investigating Nazi war crimes. This agency, known officially as the Central Office of the

Judicial Authorities for the Investigation of National Socialist Crimes, responded to Aitken's query by informing him that Mohnke was alive and residing near the north German city of Lübeck. Encouraged by this news, Aitken wrote back, telling the Germans that there had been a Canadian arrest warrant out for Mohnke after the war, and sending them copies of the relevant pages from the 1954 book by former CWCIU chief prosecutor Bruce Macdonald.[23] Perhaps Mohnke would have to answer for his crimes after all.

In accordance with German legal procedures, the Central Office in Ludwigsburg started an investigative file on Mohnke and passed it on to the Public Prosecutor's Office in Lübeck. It was at this point that Aitken's efforts began to bog down. Apparently unimpressed by the evidence against Mohnke, the Lübeck prosecutor wrote to Aitken in early March 1976, informing him that the investigation would have to be stayed because, as he put it, 'the existing means of proof are not sufficient' to warrant going on. In contrast with the usual thoroughness of German judicial authorities, the prosecutor had arrived at this decision after conducting the most perfunctory investigation. Only a few members of the 12th SS, none of whom had served under Mohnke, as well as Mohnke himself, were questioned. Not surprisingly, no evidence was garnered from these sources. To be fair, the prosecutor did not shut the door entirely. If additional witnesses could be found, he instructed Aitken, then the case might be reopened.[24]

At a dead end with the Germans, on 5 March 1976 Aitken wrote to the commissioner of the RCMP and reported what he had learned about Mohnke. Stating that 'it could be that I am in possession of facts which are not known to the Canadian authorities,' the padre concluded by expressing the hope that the RCMP 'will find the subject of my letter to be of interest.'[25] They did. Aitken's letter was forwarded to the Department of National Defence, which in turn passed it on to the Judge Advocate General's office. Suddenly confronted with a case that was now three decades old, the judge advocate enlisted the aid of the department's Directorate of History. National Defence historians were assigned the task of checking out Aitken's story.[26]

It took less than a month for the Directorate of History to reconstruct Canada's postwar investigation of Wilhelm Mohnke. The results seemed promising. Documentation was located that implicated Mohnke directly or indirectly in three separate incidents of POW murder in Normandy: the killings along the Caen-Fontenay road, the first-aid post killings, and the execution of three prisoners at Mohnke's Le Haut du Bosq headquarters. With respect to the latter incident, Defence Department historians discovered that the key witness against Mohnke, former SS Private Stangenberg, had been repatriated to Poland after the war. With a bit of luck and 'the cooperation of the present Polish and German authorities,' the chief historical research officer concluded, it might still be possible to bring Mohnke to trial.[27]

Despite the optimistic tone of the Directorate of History's report, in the end Canadian authorities did little more on the Mohnke case than establish a paper trail. Indeed, the Department of National Defence received the news of the new leads with a curious mixture of annoyance and resignation. While admitting that 'we would be remiss if we did not notify the appropriate German authorities of documents in our possession,' the judge advocate clearly thought that this would be a waste of time, opining that 'there may exist many reasons why Canada may not wish to be directly involved in the prosecution of alleged war criminals.' He did not elaborate what those reasons might be. Thus, while the new evidence eventually was passed on to the Public Prosecutor's Office in Lübeck, it was done without enthusiasm, nor with any intention of following up on the progress of the German investigation.[28] The Mohnke case was once more on the back burner.

Reverend Aitken's well-intentioned if naive foray into war crimes politics was probably the last best chance to prosecute Wilhelm Mohnke. Withold Stangenberg, the man who in 1946 was prepared to finger Mohnke for the Le Haut du Bosq killings, was still alive at the time and residing in the northern Polish town of Tczew (he died in August 1982). Moreover, Poland's communist government, which, notwithstanding its suppression of basic liberties, never wavered in trying to bring Nazi war criminals to trial, almost certainly could have been prevailed upon to permit Stangenberg to testify against Mohnke. More recently, the Department of Justice's war crimes investigation unit has tried to get the Lübeck Public Prosecutor's Office to re-open the case, but without success. Indeed, unless new evidence is unearthed, which at this stage seems highly unlikely, Mohnke will live out his remaining years in peace and relative comfort, with the generous pension he draws from the German government to act as balm for his pangs of conscience, if he has them.

One cannot help but feel disillusionment at the ease with which most of the perpetrators of the Normandy massacres managed to evade justice. It is one of the sad realities of the postwar era, however, that the vast majority of suspected Nazi war criminals will die peacefully in their beds. Still, the story of the murder of Canadian prisoners of war in Normandy is not without redemption. To be sure, such redemption cannot be found in sterile documents or in self-serving witness accounts. Nor can it be found in considerations of a legal or political nature. Rather, it must be sought where it resides, in the hearts of men, and in their character.

What was the character of the men whose story this book has endeavoured to tell? Nazi propagandists portrayed SS formations like the Hitler Youth Division as knightly, chivalrous orders, as exclusive brotherhoods of idealists who fought to make the world a better place. Conversely, they profaned Germany's enemies as motley collections of uncultured, vulgar gangsters, prone to all kinds of excesses, not worthy of treatment as equals, much less as comrades-in-arms. As Propaganda Minister Josef Goebbels confided to his diary after a particularly heavy aerial bombardment of Berlin, 'it drives one mad to think that any old Canadian boor, who probably can't even find Europe on the globe, flies to Europe from his super-rich country which his people don't know how to exploit, and here bombards a continent with a crowded population.'[29]

The irony no doubt would have been lost on him, but the imagined 'boor' to whom the propaganda minister was referring bore more than a passing resemblance to the worst of the 12th SS's murdering thugs. By contrast, it was the victims of the Normandy massacres who seemed to embody the knightly virtues that were part of the SS's flawed and fraudulent self-image. Who, after all, can fail to find nobility in Private Lorne Brown of the North Nova Scotia Highlanders, who stayed with wounded Lance Corporal W.L. Mackay and paid for it with his life? Or in Sergeant William Simmons of the 1st Hussars, who drew the fire of a German tank away from his fleeing comrades? Or in Frank Silverberg, also of the 1st Hussars, who, though hurt himself, was last seen aiding the more seriously injured William Loucks of his tank crew in a gallant if futile effort to avoid capture? Or in the seven North Novas, who, in the moments before their executions at the Abbaye d'Ardenne, took the time to shake hands and bid each other farewell? Or, finally, in George Meakin, who took a burst of machine-pistol fire from an SS executioner in a last-ditch attempt to protect his younger brother?

By their acts of selflessness, the victims of the Normandy massacres told us something about their character, about what was in their hearts. By their acts of decency, in the shadow of their own deaths, they preserved for all time that which their killers had tried to erase with cowardly murders and unmarked graves – their essential humanity. More than any war crimes trial, more than any monument, this is the real legacy of the 156 Canadians who were so brutally and callously done to death on the killing fields of Normandy. It is a bequest of which we can and should be perpetually proud.

# Notes

**Preface**

1 For gripping accounts of the battle for Authie, see Will R. Bird, *The Two Jacks: The*

*Amazing Adventures of Major Jack M. Veness and Major Jack L. Fairweather* (Toronto, [1955?]), 10–17; Will R. Bird, *No Retreating Footsteps: The Story of the North Nova Scotia Highlanders* (Kentville, NS, n.d.), 89–93; and Reginald H. Roy, *1944: The Canadians in Normandy* (Ottawa, 1984), 28–30.

2 This synopsis of Brown's life in Springhill and his military career was gleaned from documentation contained in PRU, file 03-97828 (Lorne Brown).

3 The North Nova Scotia Highlanders landed on the Normandy coast at 11:40 AM on 6 June. See the war diary (North Nova Scotia Highlanders), entry for 6 June 1944, NA, RG 24, vol. 15122, file June 1944.

4 The killing of Private Brown is described in *Report of the Supreme Headquarters Allied Expeditionary Force Court of Inquiry re Shooting of Allied Prisoners of War by the German Armed Forces in the Vicinity of Le Mesnil-Patry, Les Saullets and Authie, Calvados, Normandy, 7–11 June 1944*, pp. 15–16, DHist, vol. 90/168.

5 According to Article 23(c) of the 29 July 1899 annex to the Hague Convention regarding the laws and customs of war on land, it was prohibited 'to kill or wound an enemy who, having laid down arms, or having no longer means of defence, has surrendered at discretion.' Quoted in Leon Friedman, ed., *The Law of War: A Documentary History* (New York, 1972), 1:229.

6 The case against Bernhard Siebken and Dietrich Schnabel, the commander and special missions officer, respectively, of the 2nd Battalion of Wilhelm Mohnke's 26th Panzer Grenadier Regiment, was revisited recently by British authors Ian Sayer and Douglas Botting in their book *Hitler's Last General: The Case against Wilhelm Mohnke* (London and New York, 1989), 194–236. In my view, they have made a compelling argument that Mohnke was the real instigator of several killings of Canadian prisoners of war, totalling at least forty-one victims, that were carried out in his sector during the first few days after the invasion of Normandy.

7 For those readers who recall the events of the first half of this century, the notion that the German military tradition had its positive aspects may seem a bit far-fetched. To be sure the army of Hitler, and before him the armies of Kaiser Wilhelm II and Bismarck, did not comport themselves in anything like an enlightened manner. Yet within the authoritarian, jingoistic, and aggressive German military establishment, there were always traces of another, more progressive tradition. At various, albeit all too brief, periods in German history, this alternative actually held sway. After the defeat of Prussia by Napoleon in 1807, for example, progressive elements within the Prussian army undertook significant reforms that made possible the liberation of German territories from French domination. In 1848, Prussian liberals, supported in the streets by citizen-soldiers, attempted to reform the army as part of its larger project of democratic constitutional change. In 1918, members of soldiers' and sailors' councils chased out the kaiser and once more tried to reform the army along democratic lines. Though all of these efforts were crushed by the forces of reaction

and totalitarianism, the ideals that had informed them animated the founders of the new West German army in the mid-1950s. For a balanced account of the protracted struggle within the German army between the forces of reform and reaction, see Gordon A. Craig, *The Politics of the Prussian Army, 1640–1945* (Oxford and London, 1955). For the links between progressive military traditions and the post–Second World War German army, see Gordon A. Craig, *The Germans* (New York, 1982), 242–9.

8 The debates over various aspects of Canada's participation in the Second World War, long the preserve of academic historians, became very public in 1992 when the Senate conducted hearings into the CBC's three-part documentary entitled *The Valour and the Horror*, which had aired at the beginning of the year. One-sided and error-filled, particularly in its treatment of the Allied bombing campaign against Germany and the Normandy invasion, the program was roundly criticized by veterans' groups and was described by the Senate committee that looked into it as 'not really a documentary at all but [rather] a personal interpretation.' See *The Valour and the Horror*, Report of the Standing Senate Committee on Social Affairs, Science and Technology (January 1993), 41. Regarding the issue that is of obvious relevance to this book, the show's producers were taken to task for seeming to equate the rare incidence of the killing of German POWs by Canadian troops in Normandy with the systematic slaughter of Canadian prisoners by the Hitler Youth Division. See ibid., 33–4.

## 1: The Perpetrators

1 Detlev Peukert, *Inside Nazi Germany: Conformity, Opposition, and Racism in Everyday Life*, trans. Richard Deveson (London, 1989), 78

2 Quoted in Earl F. Ziemke and Magna E. Bauer, *Moscow to Stalingrad: Decision in the East* (Washington, 1987), 504

3 Joachim C. Fest, *Hitler*, trans. Richard and Clara Winston (New York, 1975), 665

4 Craig W.H. Luther, *Blood and Honor: The History of the 12th SS Panzer Division 'Hitler Youth,' 1943–1945* (San José, CA, 1987), 11

5 Ruth Andreas-Friedrich, *Berlin Underground, 1938–1945*, trans. Barrows Mussey (New York, 1989), 85–6, entry for 29 January 1943

6 This assessment of German public opinion was filed by German security forces the day after the announcement of the surrender of the 6th Army. See report no. 356, 4 February 1943, *Meldungen aus dem Reich, 1938–1945: Die geheimen Lageberichte des Sicherheitsdienstes der SS*, ed. Heinz Boberach (Herrsching, 1984), 12:4751.

7 Fest, *Hitler*, 675

8 Experience had taught him, the propaganda minister later confided to his diary, that 'the duty of the Führer's closest friends in time of need consists in gathering about

him and forming a solid phalanx around his person.' See the entry for 2 March 1943, *The Goebbels Diaries*, ed. and trans. Louis Lochner (New York, 1948), 266.

9  Albert Speer, *Inside the Third Reich*, trans. Richard and Clara Winston (New York, 1982), 256–8

10  Alan S. Milward, *War, Economy, and Society, 1939–1945* (Berkeley and Los Angeles, 1977), 75, 237–8

11  Martin Broszat, *The Hitler State: The Foundation and Development of the Internal Structure of the Third Reich*, trans. John W. Hiden (London and New York, 1981), 262–3, 285–6, 347–8, and Dietrich Orlow, *The History of the Nazi Party, 1933–1945* (Pittsburgh, 1973), 24–5

12  Marlis G. Steinert, *Hitler's War and the Germans: Public Mood and Attitude during the Second World War*, trans. Thomas E.J. de Witt (Athens, OH, 1977), 92–4

13  Andreas-Friedrich, *Berlin Underground*, 90, entry for 19 February 1943

14  H.W. Koch, *The Hitler Youth: Origins and Development, 1922–1945* (New York, 1975), 233, 239–41, and Luther, *Blood and Honor*, 21

15  Michael H. Kater, *The Nazi Party: A Social Profile of Members and Leaders, 1919–1945* (Cambridge, MA, 1983), 225

16  Himmler credited Axmann with the idea in his memorandum to SS Generals Jüttner and Berger, [February] 1943, NARA, RG 242, T-611, roll 2, no frame number, and in his speech, 6 October 1943, BA-Aussenstelle, NS 19, file 4010, p. 43. For a different interpretation of the genesis of the division, see SS Major General Gottlob Berger to Dr Rudolf Brandt, 3 July 1943, NARA, RG 242, T-175, roll 108, frames 2631226–7.

17  Himmler to Axmann, 13 February 1943; note to file by Berger, 9 February 1943; and memorandum from Berger to Himmler, 18 February 1943, NA, RG 24, vol. 20531, file 981SSPzD12.(D 1), folder 1

18  Bernd Wegner, *Hitlers Politische Soldaten: Die Waffen-SS, 1933–1945* (Paderborn, 1982), 114–15; Robert A. Gelwick, 'Personnel Policies and Procedures of the Waffen-SS' (PhD diss., University of Nebraska, 1971), 52–3; and Karl D. Bracher, *The German Dictatorship: The Origins, Structure, and Effects of National Socialism*, trans. Jean Steinberg (New York and Toronto, 1970), 415

19  Gordon A. Craig, *The Politics of the Prussian Army, 1640–1945* (Oxford and London, 1955), 479

20  For an example of Hitler's contempt for the officer corps, see the entry for 9 March 1943, *The Goebbels Diaries*, 288–9.

21  Quoted in Fest, *Hitler*, 669

22  Alan Bullock, *Hitler: A Study in Tyranny*, rev. ed. (London, 1965), 690–1

23  Koch, *Hitler Youth*, 244

24  Kurt Meyer, *Grenadiere* (Munich, 1957), 204

25  Excerpt from the conference, 26 July 1943, *Hitlers Lagebesprechungen: Die*

*Protokollfragmente seiner militärischen Konferenzen, 1942–1945*, ed. Helmuth Heiber (Stuttgart, 1962), 334

26  Memorandum from Berger to Himmler, 18 February 1943, NA, RG 24, vol. 20531, file 981SSPzD12.(D 1), folder 1

27  These were contained in the circular issued by Axmann, 17 February 1943, NARA, RG 242, T-611, roll 2, no frame number.

28  Record of the evidence of SS Brigadier General Kurt Meyer, undated, *Supplementary Report of the SHAEF Court of Inquiry re Shooting of Allied Prisoners of War by 12 SS Panzer Division (Hitler-Jugend) in Normandy, France, 7–21 June 1944*, exhibit no. 8, p. 18, NA, RG 24, vol. 10427, file 205S1.023 (D 9)

29  Bormann to Himmler, 24 February 1943, NARA, RG 242, T-175, roll 70, frames 2586828-31

30  On the recruitment controversy, see the note to file by Berger, 9 February 1943; memorandum from Berger to Himmler, 18 February 1943; and Himmler to Axmann, 13 February 1943, NA, RG 24, vol. 20531, file 981SSPzD12.(D 1), folder 1. See also Himmler to Reich Labour Service Leader Hierl, 20 March 1943, and Hierl to Himmler, 9 March 1943, NARA, RG 242, T-175, roll 70, frames 2586799 and 2586820-1.

31  Himmler to Bormann, 13 March 1943; Hierl to Himmler, 9 March 1943; and Himmler to Hierl, 20 March 1943, NARA, RG 242, T-175, roll 70, frames 2586813, 2586821, and 2586799

32  Ultimately, the Hitler Youth Division ended up with a contingent of about five hundred such foreign troops. See Luther, *Blood and Honor*, 93n. 21. For the experiences of a conscript from Poland, see the testimony of SS Private Jan Jesionek, Proceedings against Kurt Meyer, 10–28 December 1945 (hereafter cited as Meyer Trial), 290–1, DHist, vol. 159.95023.

33  Record of the evidence of SS Brigadier General Kurt Meyer, undated, SHAEF Report, *12 SS*, exhibit no. 8, p. 17; Hubert Meyer, *Kriegsgeschichte der 12.SS-Panzerdivision 'Hitlerjugend'* (Osnabrück, 1982), 1:20; and memorandum issued by the Waffen-SS High Command, 24 June 1943, NA, RG 24, vol. 20531, file 981SSPzD12.(D 1), folder 2

34  Luther, *Blood and Honor*, 33

35  Koch, *Hitler Youth*, 119, 148–50, and 162–4

36  John A. English, *The Canadian Army and the Normandy Campaign: A Study of Failure in High Command* (New York and London, 1991), 212, and Luther, *Blood and Honor*, 64–5

37  Testimony of SS Brigadier General Kurt Meyer, Meyer Trial, 552–3; Meyer, *Grenadiere*, 208; order no. 20 issued by the 12th SS Panzer Regiment, 7 March 1944, NARA, RG 242, T-354, roll 155, frame 3798702; special order issued by the commander of the 12th SS Panzer Division 'Hitler Youth,' 12 April 1944, ibid., roll 154,

frames 3797992–3; and Chief of the SS Economic and Administrative Main Office Pohl to Himmler, 25 June 1943, ibid., T-175, roll 70, frames 2586532–3

38  Meyer, *Grenadiere*, 207

39  Luther, *Blood and Honor*, 62

40  Koch, *Hitler Youth*, 119–22

41  War game situation, 30 November 1943, NARA, RG 242, T-354, roll 154, frame 3797414, and memorandum by the 12th SS Panzer Division, 22 November 1943, ibid., roll 156, frames 3800397–8

42  Speech by Himmler, 6 October 1943, BA-Aussenstelle, NS 19, file 4010, p. 40. See also Meyer, *Kriegsgeschichte*, 17; Luther, *Blood and Honor*, 60; and Meyer, *Grenadiere*, 205.

43  Note to file by Berger, 9 February 1943, and memorandum from Jüttner to the SS Main Office, 10 March 1943, NA, RG 24, vol. 20531, file 981SSPzD12.(D 1), folder 1

44  The quotes are from the speech by Himmler, 6 October 1943, BA-Aussenstelle, NS 19, file 4010, p. 46.

45  Bernd Wegner, *The Waffen SS: Organization, Ideology and Function*, trans. Ronald Webster (Oxford, 1990), 318

46  Draft Führer decree, undated, NA, RG 24, vol. 20531, file 981SSPzD12.(D 1), folder 1, and record of the evidence of Meyer, undated, SHAEF Report, *12 SS*, exhibit no. 8, pp. 7, 17

47  Memorandum from Berger to Himmler, 18 February 1943, NA, RG 24, vol. 10427, file 205S1.023 (D 9); Koch, *Hitler Youth*, 244; and Wegner, *Waffen SS*, 319

48  Thousands of SS officer files fell into the hands of the Allies after the collapse of Nazi Germany in 1945. These files constitute a part of the massive collection of Nazi documentation housed at the Document Centre in Berlin. For almost fifty years, the Document Centre, located in what was formerly the American zone of postwar occupation, was under American administration. With the recent termination of the Four-Power occupation of Berlin, control of the centre was handed over to the German archival administration. As part of the transfer agreement, the Americans were able to make microfilm copies of the Document Centre's holdings. These microfilms, which include all of the SS personnel files, are available to researchers under record group RG 242 BDC A 3433 (SS Officer Dossiers) at the U.S. National Archives, Maryland Branch. That is where I reviewed them during the summer of 1995. Of the 90 officers in my sample, 10 were platoon leaders, 5 commanded artillery batteries, 41 were company commanders, 15 were battalion commanders, and 5 led regiments. The sample also includes the divisional commander, 8 officers assigned to one or another headquarters, and 5 adjutants.

49  See the file of Willy Müller, NARA, RG 242 BDC A 3433, SS Officer Dossier, roll 337A, frames 3–4.

50 This was particularly true if one were employed in the public sector. See Kater, *Nazi Party*, 61, 69–70.

51 The officer was SS Captain Dr Oskar Dienstbach, who attended to the medical needs of Auschwitz camp guards between May 1941 and March 1942. See the file of Dr Oskar Dienstbach, NARA, RG 242 BDC A 3433, SS Officer Dossier, roll 150, frames 236–57.

52 Memorandum by the High Command of the Waffen-SS, 24 June 1943, NA, RG 24, vol. 20531, file 981SSPzD12.(D 1), folder 2

53 Speech by Himmler, 6 October 1943, BA-Aussenstelle, NS 19, file 4010, p. 43. As evidence of the lengths to which the Nazi leadership was prepared to go to foster the relationship between the two divisions, former Leibstandarte officers and NCOs were permitted to wear their old insignia on their new uniforms. See the supplementary orders issued by the 12th SS Panzer Division, 16 November 1943, NARA, RG 242, T-354, roll 154, frame 3797631.

54 Its battle honours include participation in Nazi Germany's victorious wars of aggression against Poland, Holland, France, Yugoslavia, and Greece, the invasion of the former Soviet Union, and, during the final phase of the war, the battles of Normandy and the 'Falaise gap,' the Ardennes offensive, and the defence of the Reich's eastern frontier. Samuel W. Mitcham, *Hitler's Legions: The German Army Order of Battle in World War II* (London, 1985), 440–1.

55 James J. Weingartner, *Hitler's Guard: The Story of the Leibstandarte SS Adolf Hitler, 1933–1945* (Carbondale and Edwardsville, IL, 1974), 129, 146

56 For an example of this kind of questionable rationalization, see Tony Foster, *Meeting of Generals* (Toronto and New York, 1986), 221.

57 The Wormhoudt murders are described in graphic and chilling detail in Ian Sayer and Douglas Botting, *Hitler's Last General: The Case against Wilhelm Mohnke* (London and New York, 1989), 60–85. On the Malmedy massacres, see John S.D. Eisenhower, *The Bitter Woods* (New York, 1969), 292–3.

58 Sayer and Botting, *Hitler's Last General,* 155

59 Memorandum by the High Command of the Waffen-SS, 30 October 1943, NA, RG 24, vol. 20531, file 981SSPzD12.(D 1), folder 3

60 Up to 1942, the Mark IV was the best tank in the German inventory. With 80mm of front armour, it could withstand a hit from the Sherman tank's standard 75mm gun at a distance of a hundred yards. The fifteen-pound shells delivered from its own 75mm gun could penetrate 84mm of armour at a distance of up to a thousand yards, thereby rendering the standard Sherman very vulnerable to it in an exchange of fire. Lighter than the Sherman, in part because of its thinner side armour (30mm, as opposed to the Sherman's 51mm), the Mark IV had a maximum speed of twenty-five miles per hour, about the same as the Sherman. From 1942 on, the Germans concentrated on producing more-powerful tanks, although they continued to introduce improvements

to the durable Mark IV. The newer armour included the Mark V 'Panther' and the Mark VI 'Tiger.' With its 88mm gun, the Tiger was a massive and fearsome vehicle. Fortunately for the Allies, the Germans had relatively few available for service in the West at the time of the Normandy campaign. Almost as deadly, however, was the Panther, which by D-Day had already begun to supplant the Mark IV as the mainstay of German armoured formations. A forty-five-ton tank mounted with a 75mm gun that could propel its shells at a muzzle velocity of over three thousand feet per second, enabling it to penetrate 100 mm of armour at up to two thousand yards, this monster could nonetheless attain speeds of thirty-five miles per hour. In armament, the Panther measured up well even against the Sherman's modified seventeen-pound gun, while in armour it was vastly superior. On the Sherman, see Major L.F. Ellis, *Victory in the West*, vol. 1, *The Battle of Normandy* (London, 1962), 547–9.

61  Führer directive, 3 November 1943, *Hitlers Weisungen für die Kriegführung, 1939–1945: Dokumente des Oberkommandos der Wehrmacht*, ed. Walter Hubatsch (Frankfurt am Main, 1962), 234

62  Luther, *Blood and Honor*, 76–8; 'The preparation of the western front for the Anglo-American invasion (1 April–6 June 1944),' *Kriegstagebuch des Oberkommandos der Wehrmacht (Wehrmachtsführungsstab)*, ed. Percy Ernst Schramm, vol. IV/7 (Munich, 1982), 300; Mitcham, *Hitler's Legions*, 450, 452; Will-say of SS Private Friedrich Torbanisch, undated, 'Draft Abstract of Evidence, Case of Brigadier General Kurt Meyer,' p. 2, NA, RG 24, vol. 12839, file 67/Kurt Meyer Case/1 (392/51); and diagram by the 12th SS Engineering Battalion, undated, NARA, RG 242, T-354, roll 155, frame 3798863

## 2: The Victims

1  Colonel C.P. Stacey, *The Victory Campaign: The Operations in North-West Europe, 1944–1945* (Ottawa, 1966), 3:34, 36

2  Ibid., 34, 38

3  William Carr, *Arms, Autarky, and Aggression: A Study in German Foreign Policy, 1933–1939* (London, 1972), 124; Colonel C.P. Stacey, *Six Years of War: The Army in Canada, Britain, and the Pacific* (Ottawa, 1957), 1:42; Gordon A. Craig, *Germany, 1866–1945* (New York and Oxford, 1978), 715; and William L. Shirer, *Twentieth Century Journey: A Memoir of a Life and the Times*, vol. 2, *The Nightmare Years, 1930–1940* (Boston and Toronto, 1984), 457

4  David J. Bercuson, *Maple Leaf against the Axis: Canada's Second World War* (Toronto, 1995), 5

5  Stacey, *Six Years*, 42, 48

6  Ibid., 41–2

7  Ibid., 42–3, 53

8  C.P. Stacey, *Arms, Men, and Governments: The War Policies of Canada, 1939–1945* (Ottawa, 1970), 4, 103, 106–7

9  The Bren gun was a .303-inch air-cooled light machine gun that took a thirty-round magazine. The Bren had an effective range of a thousand yards, and could fire either single shots or short bursts. Its maximum rate of fire was five hundred rounds per minute. Weighing twenty-three pounds, it most often was fired from its bipod, although a strong man could fire it from the hip. See Major L.F. Ellis, *Victory in the West*, vol. 1, *The Battle of Normandy* (London, 1962), 541; John A. English, *The Canadian Army and the Normandy Campaign: A Study of Failure in High Command* (New York and London, 1991), 233n. 17; and Major General Chris Vokes, *My Story* (Ottawa, 1985), 58.

10  Bercuson, *Maple Leaf*, 17

11  Ibid., 7, 19; Stacey, *Arms, Men, and Governments*, 4, 107; and J.L. Granatstein, *The Generals: The Canadian Army's Senior Commanders in the Second World War* (Toronto, 1993), xii

12  Stacey, *Arms, Men, and Governments*, 1, 71

13  Edgar McInnis, *Canada: A Political and Social History*, 3rd ed. (Toronto, 1969), 488–9

14  Bercuson, *Maple Leaf*, 4

15  Stacey, *Arms, Men, and Governments*, 1

16  Bercuson, *Maple Leaf*, 7

17  Stacey, *Arms, Men, and Governments*, 397–8

18  Granatstein, *The Generals*, xiii

19  Bercuson, *Maple Leaf*, 16–17, and Stacey, *Six Years*, 72–6

20  Alan Bullock, *Hitler: A Study in Tyranny*, rev. ed. (London, 1965), 556–7

21  Joachim C. Fest, *Hitler*, trans. Richard and Clara Winston (New York, 1975), 625–6

22  Craig, *Germany*, 717–8

23  Bullock, *Hitler*, 584–6

24  Stacey, *Arms, Men, and Governments*, 398–9, and Bercuson, *Maple Leaf*, 29

25  J.L. Granatstein and J.M. Hitsman, *Broken Promises: A History of Conscription in Canada* (Toronto, 1985), 232–4

26  Stacey, *Six Years*, 80

27  Ibid., 77–9

28  Bercuson, *Maple Leaf*, 17

29  Stacey, *Six Years*, 80

30  Training Instruction No. 1, undated, appendix 'D' to the war diary (Headquarters of the 3rd Canadian Infantry Division), file January 1941, NA, reel T-7617, frame 415

31  Summary, undated, appendix 1 to ibid., frame 465

32  Stacey, *Victory Campaign*, 284, 631

33  Bercuson, *Maple Leaf*, 7–8

34 Ibid., 8
35 Stacey, *Victory Campaign*, 275. For a somewhat more positive view of the officers produced by the regimental system, see English, *Canadian Army*, 136, 153.
36 See the criticisms of the 12th SS's early operations that are levelled in Stacey, *Victory Campaign*, 137.
37 The information for this paragraph was gleaned from Granatstein, *The Generals*, 30–1, 44–5, 48, 166–7, 285n. 16, 329n. 95, and Stacey, *Victory Campaign*, 224, 531n. 17.
38 Keller's appointment was recorded in the war diary (Headquarters of the 3rd Canadian Division), entry for 10 September 1942, NA, reel T-7618, frame 89.
39 Memorandum by Lieutenant Colonel C. Foulkes, 23 October 1940, war diary (Headquarters of the 3rd Canadian Infantry Division), file 14 September–27 October 1940, NA, reel T-7617, frames 373–6
40 The 3rd Division embarked from Halifax during 18–21 July 1941. On 28 July, the first ships carrying the division arrived at Gourock, Scotland. Three days later, a divisional headquarters was set up at Aldershot, England. See the war diary (Headquarters of the 3rd Canadian Division), entries for July 1944, ibid., frames 766–7.
41 David J. Bercuson's characterization of the battle-readiness of the 1st Canadian Division on the eve of its departure for England seems apropos for the 3rd. See Bercuson, *Maple Leaf*, 17–18
42 Ibid., 64
43 Stacey, *Victory Campaign*, 34
44 Ibid., 35–7
45 Ibid., 38
46 See Brigadier W.H.S. Macklin's 'Report on the Mobilization of the 13th Infantry Brigade on an Active Basis,' in Stacey, *War Policies*, appendix S, 596
47 Of the 156 Canadian troops known to have been murdered in Normandy by elements of the 12th SS Panzer Division 'Hitler Youth,' 10 were never positively identified. Of the 146 victims who could be identified, Canadian army personnel files were found on 145 of them. Part of the massive collection of files on former Canadian military personnel administered by the Personnel Records Unit of the National Archives of Canada, the 145 dossiers were retrieved by submitting the name and service identification number of each deceased soldier. The files were reviewed during the spring of 1995 at the National Archives in Ottawa.
48 Bercuson, *Maple Leaf*, 2–3
49 Ibid., 17
50 Undoubtedly, there is a correlation between the high number of the men who were engaged in unskilled work and their relatively low level of education. Of the 145 victims of the Normandy massacres, 19 per cent had not completed elementary school. Only 8 of the men had completed secondary school. Another 8 had received

some kind of vocational training. One had finished college, while 2 had attended university. The largest groups, at 32 and 23 per cent, had completed grades 7 and 8, respectively.

## 3: Deployment for Battle

1 Colonel C.P. Stacey, *The Victory Campaign: The Operations in North-West Europe, 1944–1945* (Ottawa, 1966), 3:38
2 War diary (Headquarters of the 7th Canadian Infantry Brigade), entry for 5 June 1944, NA, reel T-12014, frame 1546
3 Stacey, *Victory Campaign*, 76
4 Ibid., 76–7
5 Ibid., 76–7, 80
6 The D-Day exploits of the 1st Canadian Parachute Battalion are recounted in Brian Nolan, *Airborne: The Heroic Story of the 1st Canadian Parachute Battalion in the Second World War* (Toronto, 1995), 76–104.
7 Forrest C. Pogue, *The Supreme Command*, United States Army in World War II Series, the European Theatre of Operations (Washington, 1954), 102–3, 122
8 For a brief description of the defences, see 'The preparation of the western front for the Anglo-American invasion (1 April–6 June 1944),' *Kriegstagebuch des Oberkommandos der Wehrmacht (Wehrmachtsführungsstab)*, ed. Percy Ernst Schramm, vol. IV/7, 304–5. For the rationale behind trying to stop the invasion on the beaches, see Major General Dr Hans Speidel, 'The Battle in Normandy 1944: Generalfeldmarschall Rommel, His Generalship, His Ideas, and His End' (1948), and SS Brigadier General Fritz Krämer, 'I SS Panzer Corps in the West in 1944,' Part I (August/September 1948), NARA, RG 338, Foreign Military Studies, ETHINT, C Series, fiche 0017, p. 37, and fiche 0023, pp. 6–7.
9 Stacey, *Victory Campaign*, 63
10 On the various Allied deceptions, see Anthony Cave Brown, *Bodyguard of Lies* (Toronto, 1975), 426, 541, and 603. On the extent to which the Germans were duped by Fortitude, see *Kriegstagebuch des OKW*, vol. IV/7, 297–8.
11 The next six paragraphs are based on Dwight D. Eisenhower, *Crusade in Europe* (New York, 1948), 239, 249–50.
12 Pogue, *Supreme Command*, 106, 115–17, 167
13 A separate peace was not beyond the realm of possibility. During the Allied conference held at Teheran in November 1943, Stalin warned British prime minister Winston Churchill that if there was no Allied invasion of northern France by May 1944, 'it would be very difficult for the Russians to carry on.' Record of the conversations between Churchill and Stalin, quoted in Martin Gilbert, *Winston S. Churchill*, vol. 7, *Road to Victory, 1941–1945* (Boston, 1986), 584

14 Stacey, *Victory Campaign*, 121

15 Chester Wilmot, *The Struggle for Europe* (London, 1952), 238, and war diary (High Command of the German 7th Army), entry for 6 June 1944 (0130 hrs), p. 1, NA, RG 24, vol. 20427, file 981.008 (D 8)

16 Wilmot, *Struggle*, 239–42

17 'The western front from the landing of the Anglo-Americans (6 June) to the parachute drop near Arnhem (17 September) and the setting up of a new line of resistance (6 June–17 September 1944),' *Kriegstagebuch des OKW*, vol. IV/7, 311; Wilmot, *Struggle*, 244; and war diary (High Command of the German 7th Army), entry for 6 June 1944 (0130 hrs), p. 1, NA, RG 24, vol. 20427, file 981.008 (D 8).

18 For example, see the messages received regarding operations along the invasion front (High Command of the German 7th Army), 6 June 1944 (0300 hrs), NARA, RG 242, T-312, roll 1568, frame 939.

19 *Kriegstagebuch des OKW*, vol. IV/7, 311

20 'Radar detections made on the night of the invasion, 5–6 June 1944, [Luftwaffe High Command]' undated, NA, reel T-2420, frames 5130–1

21 Wilmot, *Struggle*, 251–2

22 Carlo d'Este, *Decision in Normandy: The Unwritten Story of Montgomery and the Allied Campaign* (London, 1983), 113–14

23 Wilmot, *Struggle*, 261

24 Craig W.H. Luther, *Blood and Honor: The History of the 12th SS Panzer Division 'Hitler Youth,' 1943–1945* (San José, CA, 1987), 107

25 War diary (Headquarters of the 3rd Canadian Infantry Division), entry for 6 June 1944, NA, RG 24, vol. 13766, file June 1944

26 War diary (Headquarters of the 7th Canadian Infantry Brigade), entry for 6 June 1944, NA, reel T-12014, frame 1546

27 The timing of low tide is recorded in *Kriegstagebuch des OKW*, vol. IV/7, 311.

28 Stacey, *Victory Campaign*, 103–6, 110

29 This is known to have happened at Graye-sur-Mer, where Russian, Armenian, and Georgian conscripts of the 716th Division's 441st Eastern Battalion were stationed. See Stacey, *Victory Campaign*, 66–70.

30 Message from the British 2nd Army recorded in the log of 21st Army Group, 6 June 1944, NA, reel T-2427, appendix Q, sheet 3

31 This figure includes 340 killed, 574 wounded, and 47 taken prisoner. See Stacey, *Victory Campaign*, 112.

32 War diary (Headquarters of the 7th Canadian Infantry Brigade), entry for 6 June 1944, and war diary (Headquarters of the 9th Canadian Infantry Brigade), entry for 6 June 1944, NA, reel T-12014, frame 1547, and RG 24, vol. 14152, file June 1944

33 Tony Foster, *Meeting of Generals* (Toronto and New York, 1986), 304

34  War diary (Headquarters of the 8th Canadian Infantry Brigade), entry for 6 June 1944 (1730 hrs), NA, reel T-12158, frame 776

35  Mary H. Williams, *Chronology, 1941–1945*, United States Army in World War II Series, Special Studies (Washington, 1960), 203

36  By D-Day, the inventory of the 21st Panzer Division's 100th Panzer Regiment consisted primarily of Mark IV tanks, the mainstay of Germany's armoured formations. Its sizeable complement of captured French tanks included Somuas and Hotchkisses – fine models in their day, but frightfully outmoded even after upgrading. See the interrogation of Major General Edgar Feuchtinger, undated, p. 2, NA, RG 24, CMHQ, vol. 10474, file 212C1.3009 (D 60); Major General Edgar Feuchtinger, 'History of the 21st Panzer Division from the time of its formation until the beginning of the invasion' (18 February 1947), NARA, RG 338, B-441, fiche 0422, p. 5; Order of Battle of the 21st Panzer Division, undated, in the war diary (Headquarters of the 3rd Canadian Infantry Division), appendix 1, between pp. 45 and 46, NA, RG 24, vol. 13766, folder 17, file June 1944; and Samuel W. Mitcham, *Hitler's Legions: The German Army Order of Battle in World War II* (London, 1985), 377.

37  On the Panzer Lehr, see the secret report by SHAEF (G-2), 7 July 1944, p. 1, NA, RG 24, vol. 10717, file 215C1.98 (D 399); Luther, *Blood and Honor*, 117; and Mitcham, *Hitler's Legions*, 386.

38  Secret report by SHAEF (G-2), 8 July 1944, p. 1, NA, RG 24, vol. 10717, file 215C1.98 (D 399)

39  Part of the reason for the delay was that the 21st Panzer was at was first deployed against the paratroopers of the British 6th Airborne Division during the early morning hours. See the war diary (High Command of the German 7th Army), entries for 6 June 1944 (0520 and 0645 hrs), pp. 4, 6, ibid., vol. 20427, file 981.008 (D 8). Only later, between 10:00 and 10:30 AM, did the division receive word that its original orders had been scrapped and that it was to cross the Orne River and move against the beachhead. See messages received regarding operations along the invasion front (High Command of the German 7th Army), NARA, RG 242, T-312, reel 1568, frames 943, 945, and the interrogation of Feuchtinger, p. 6, NA, RG 24, vol. 10474, file 212C1.3009 (D 60). As a result, its attack did not begin until 4:30 in the afternoon, by which time the British and Canadian anti-tank forces had been fully deployed. See Stacey, *Victory Campaign*, 124.

40  *Kriegstagebuch des OKW*, vol. IV/7, 300, 302

41  Brown, *Bodyguard*, 643

42  Joachim C. Fest, *Hitler*, trans. Richard and Clara Winston (New York, 1975), 705

43  War diary (High Command of the German 7th Army), entry for 6 June 1944, NARA, RG 242, T-312, reel 1569, frame 6

44  War diary (1st Battalion of the 25th SS Panzer Grenadier Regiment), entry for 6 June 1944, ibid., T-354, roll 156, frame 3799968. Actually, elements of the division's

reconnaissance battalion had put in a brief appearance at the front on the morning
of 6 June. Their report can be found in Hubert Meyer, *Kriegsgeschichte der
12.SS-Panzerdivision 'Hitlerjugend'* (Osnabrück, 1982), 1:57–61.

45  The information in the next two paragraphs was gleaned from the following sources:
Meyer's SS personnel file, NARA, RG 242 BDC A 3433, SS Officer Dossier, roll
313A, frames 1335–1417; Classification Officer R.G. Rowcliffe's report on prisoner
number 2265 (Kurt Meyer), Dorchester Penitentiary, 19 October 1951, NA, RG 73,
acc. 85/86/162, vol. 9, file 2265, part 4; 'Petition of Kurt Meyer and Memorandum
by Counsel Re Trial, Conviction and Sentence,' 12 December 1950, NA, RG 2, vol.
209, file W-41, part 1; and Kurt Meyer, *Grenadiere* (Munich, 1957).

46  One such episode was related to Macdonald by a Wehrmacht Lieutenant Colonel
Müller Rienzburg, who claimed that Meyer had recounted the story to him. See the
document entitled 'Life History of Oberführer Kurt Meyer,' 24 March 1945, MA,
Macdonald Papers, War Crimes box 5, file I-3/1.

47  Testimony of SS Brigadier General Kurt Meyer, Meyer Trial, 562, 563–5, DHist,
vol. 159.95023 (D 7)

48  Ibid., 563, and Meyer, *Grenadiere*, 210–11

49  Meyer, *Grenadiere*, 211

50  See Major General Wilhelm Richter, 'The Battle of the 716th Infantry Division in
Normandy (6 June to 23 June 1944),' NARA, RG 338, B-621, microfiche 0596, p.
25. See also the testimony of Meyer, Meyer Trial, 563. Allied air attacks on the
advancing column are reported in the war diary (1st Battalion of the 25th Panzer
Grenadier Regiment), entry for 7 June 1944 (1740 hours), NARA, RG 242, T-354,
roll 156, frame 3799968.

51  See Richter, 'The Battle of the 716th Infantry Division,' p. 25. See also the testimony
of Meyer, Meyer Trial, 563.

52  See Feuchtinger, 'History of the 21st Panzer Division,' pp. 24–6; interrogation of
Feuchtinger, p. 6, NA, RG 24, vol. 10474, file 212C1.3009 (D 60); and the testimony
of Meyer, Meyer Trial, 563.

53  In his autobiography, Meyer spoke disparagingly of the 'pessimistic mood' that per-
meated Richter's bunker. He also criticized Feuchtinger for having split his forces
when a concentrated attack might have put the British and Canadians in a 'critical
situation.' See Meyer, *Grenadiere*, 213–14. This ignores the fact that Feuchtinger,
correctly anticipating the High Command's orders, had sent a portion of his force
against the British airborne bridgehead east of the Orne River.

54  Interrogation of Feuchtinger, p. 6, and interrogation of SS Brigadier General Kurt
Meyer, p. 3, NA, RG 24, vol. 10474, file 212C1.3009 (D 60)

55  Testimony of Meyer, Meyer Trial, 563, and Meyer, *Grenadiere*, 213–14

56  Interrogation of Meyer, p. 3, NA, RG 24, vol. 10474, file 212C1.3009 (D 60)

57  Testimony of Meyer, Meyer Trial, 564

58 On this episode, see Meyer, *Grenadiere*, 213–14; the messages received regarding operations along the invasion front (High Command of the German 7th Army), entry for 6 June 1944 (2345 hrs), NARA, RG 242, T-312, roll 1568, frame 952; and the interrogation of Meyer, pp. 2–4, NA, RG 24, vol. 10474, file 212C1.3009 (D 60).

59 Interrogation of Feuchtinger, pp. 6–7, and interrogation of Meyer, p. 3 NA, RG 24, vol. 10474, file 212C1.3009 (D 60)

60 Meyer, *Grenadiere*, 214

**4: The Battle of Authie**

1 The Hitler Youth Division had been placed on full alert at 3:00 AM on 6 June. See the war diary (1st Battalion of the 25th Panzer Grenadier Regiment), entry for 6 June 1944, NARA, RG 242, T-354, roll 156, frame 3799967. According to Meyer, he first learned of the Allied landings at 2:00 AM from the radar station situated on the coast, with which he had special liaison arrangements. See the interrogation of SS Brigadier General Kurt Meyer, p. 3, NA, RG 24, vol. 10474, file 212C1.3009 (D 60).

2 Meyer's plan was put into action at 3:45 AM, when the first deployments got under- way. See the war diary (1st Battalion of the 25th Panzer Grenadier Regiment), entry for 7 June 1944 (0345 hrs), NARA, RG 242, T-354, roll 156, frames 3799969, 3799973.

3 Interrogation of Meyer, p. 3, NA, RG 24, vol. 10474, file 212C1.3009 (D 60), and testimony of SS Brigadier General Kurt Meyer, Meyer Trial, 565–6, DHist, vol. 159.95023 (D 7)

4 In a postwar statement, General Feuchtinger of the 21st Panzer steadfastly held to the arguments he had offered in General Richter's bunker on the night of 6–7 June – namely, that a counterattack in the Bayeux-Caen sector by his division had no pros- pect of success unless supported by the full weight of the 12th SS and the Panzer Lehr. See Major General Edgar Feuchtinger, 'History of the 21st Panzer Division from the time of its formation until the beginning of the invasion' (18 February 1947), NARA, RG 338, B-441, fiche 0422, pp. 24–5. Brigadier Harry Foster, the commander of the 7th Canadian Infantry Brigade in Normandy, characterized the ini- tial German counterattacks as rather hasty and ineffective improvisation. Foster's remarks, which are cited in Colonel C.P. Stacey, *The Victory Campaign: The Opera- tions in North-West Europe, 1944–1945* (Ottawa, 1966), 3:137, essentially echo Allied intelligence appraisals of the early German operations in Normandy. See intel- ligence summary no. 139 by 21 Army Group, 29 June 1944, NA, RG 24, vol. 10548, file 215A21.023 (D 7), summaries dated 23 June–1 July 1944, p. 256.

5 According to Allied intelligence, the 2nd Battalion of Mohnke's regiment did not arrive in the vicinity of Fontenay-le-Pesnel until the night of 7 June. See the secret report by SHAEF (G-2), 8 July 1944, p. 1, NA, RG 24, vol. 10717, file 215C1.98

(D 399). That same night, Mohnke established his regimental headquarters farther to the southeast, in a field between Rauray and Granville-sur-Odon. See *Supplementary Report of the SHAEF Court of Inquiry re Shooting of Allied Prisoners of War by 12 SS Panzer Division (Hitler-Jugend) in Normandy, France, 7–21 June 1944*, part 3, p. 11, ibid., vol. 10427, file 205S1.023 (D 9).

6 As of late evening on 7 June, the Panzer Lehr still had not made an appearance in the Bayeux sector. See the testimony of Meyer, Meyer Trial, 579. The first unit of the Panzer Lehr to arrive the next morning was the 902nd Panzer Grenadier Regiment. See the secret report by SHAEF (G-2), 7 July 1944, p. 2, NA, RG 24, vol. 10717, file 215C1.98 (D 399). Even on the morning of 9 June, many of the formations of the Panzer Lehr were still south and west of the front of the 12th SS, around Thury-Harcourt. See the enclosure to the war diary (High Command of the German 7th Army), entry for 8 June 1944, NARA, RG 242, T-312, roll 1565, frame 900.

7 In a postwar interrogation, SS General Josef 'Sepp' Dietrich, the commander of 1st SS Panzer Corps, referred to the 'desperate' situation on the German left flank, where on 7 June 'only a screen of light armoured cars offered protection.' See the interrogation of SS General Josef 'Sepp' Dietrich, p. 2, NA, RG 24, vol. 10474, file 212C1.3009 (D 60).

8 H.W. Koch, *The Hitler Youth: Origins and Development, 1922–1945* (New York, 1975), 244. The names of the battalion's company commanders are listed in Craig W.H. Luther, *Blood and Honor: The History of the 12th SS Panzer Division 'Hitler Youth,' 1943–1945* (San José, CA, 1987), 250. According to Kurt Bergmann, the battalion adjutant, the three company commanders were the only Wehrmacht officers in the 3rd Battalion. See the testimony of SS First Lieutenant Kurt Bergmann, Meyer Trial, 467.

9 File on Georg-Walter Stahl, NARA, RG 242 BDC A 3433, SS Officer Dossier, roll 148B, frames 42–5

10 Hubert Meyer, *Kriegsgeschichte der 12.SS-Panzerdivision 'Hitlerjugend'* (Osnabrück, 1982), 1:18–19

11 His combat experience would be shortlived. The young officer was killed in action on 8 June. See the file on Stahl, NARA, RG 242 BDC A 3433, SS Officer Dossier, roll 148B, frame 42.

12 Information on Milius's career was gleaned from the file on Karl-Heinz Milius, ibid., roll 319A, frames 391–476.

13 Record of the further evidence of SS Brigadier General Kurt Meyer, undated, SHAEF Report, *12 SS*, exhibit no. 9, pp. 12–13. A contemporary evaluation of Milius's performance in Normandy criticized him for his lack of 'drive.' See the assessment of SS Lieutenant Colonel Karl-Heinz Milius, 12 November 1944, file on Milius, NARA, RG 242 BDC A 3433, SS Officer Dossier, roll 319A, frame 409.

14  Assessment, 8 October 1940, file on Milius, NARA, RG 242 BDC A 3433, SS Officer Dossier, roll 319A, frame 431

15  Milius's height is mentioned in his SS personnel file, ibid., frame 391. The height requirement for membership in the 12th SS is cited in the memorandum from Berger to Himmler, 18 February 1943, NA, RG 24, vol. 20531, file 981SSPzD12.(D 1), folder 1.

16  On the occasion of his entry into a battalion commander's school in April 1943, the receiving officer noted in Milius's preliminary evaluation that his command deportment needed work. See the assessment, 3 April 1943, file on Milius, NARA, RG 242 BDC A 3433, SS Officer Dossier, roll 319A, frame 419. An evaluation prepared after the Normandy campaign criticized Milius for his lack of sympathy in dealing with the young recruits under his command. See the assessment, 12 November 1944, ibid., frame 409.

17  Named after Jeb Stuart, the legendary Confederate cavalry officer of the American Civil War, this tank was really a lightly armoured reconnaissance vehicle on which a 37mm gun had been mounted. With a top speed of forty miles per hour, it was the swiftest tank on the Normandy battlefield. See Major L.F. Ellis, *Victory in the West*, vol. 1, *The Battle of Normandy* (London, 1962), 548–9.

18  War diary (North Nova Scotia Highlanders), entry for 6 June 1944, NA, RG 24, vol. 15122, file June 1944

19  War diary (Headquarters of the 3rd Canadian Infantry Division), entry for 7 June 1944, and war diary (Headquarters of the 7th Canadian Infantry Brigade), entry for 7 June 1944, ibid., vol. 13766, file June 1944, and reel T-12014, frame 1548

20  War diary (Headquarters of the 8th Canadian Infantry Brigade), entry for 7 June 1944, NA, reel T-12158, frames 776–7. The radar station was not captured until 17 June. See intelligence summary no. 10, 17 June 1944, war diary (Headquarters of the 3rd Canadian Infantry Division), appendix 1, p. 46, NA, RG 24, vol. 13766, folder 17, file June 1944, and Will R. Bird, *North Shore (New Brunswick) Regiment* (Fredericton, 1963), 234–6?

21  War diary (North Nova Scotia Highlanders), entry for 7 June 1944, NA, RG 24, vol. 15122, file June 1944

22  Ibid., entries for 6 and 7 June 1944; appendix 8 to the war diary (Cameron Highlanders of Ottawa), entry for 7 June 1944, ibid., vol. 15026, file June 1944; affidavit of Major J.D. Learment, Meyer Trial, 135; and Lieutenant Colonel Richard M. Ross, *The History of the 1st Battalion Cameron Highlanders of Ottawa (MG)* (Ottawa, 1946), 42

23  Affidavit of Learment, Meyer Trial, 135. Reference is made to Fraser's nickname in Will R. Bird, *No Retreating Footsteps: The Story of the North Nova Scotia Highlanders* (Kentville, NS, n.d.), 89.

24  War diary (Headquarters of the 9th Canadian Infantry Brigade), entry for 7 June

1944; war diary (North Nova Scotia Highlanders), entry for 7 June 1944; and war diary (27th Canadian Armoured Regiment), entry for 7 June 1944, NA, RG 24, vols. 14152, 15122, file June 1944, and reel T-12758, frame 763

25 The 88 is generally considered to have been the most deadly gun in the German arsenal. Originally designed as an anti-aircraft gun, the 88 was used to great effect against tanks and infantry by Rommel's forces during the campaign in North Africa. In Normandy, the Germans employed a refined version of the gun, which could knock out any Allied tank at a range of up to two thousand yards and wreaked havoc among Allied infantry when it fired fused shells to create airbursts. See Carlo d'Este, *Decision in Normandy: The Unwritten Story of Montgomery and the Allied Campaign* (London, 1983), 155–6.

26 War diary (North Nova Scotia Highlanders), entry for 7 June 1944, and war diary (27th Canadian Armoured Regiment), entry for 7 June 1944, NA, RG 24, vol. 15122, file June 1944, and reel T-12758, frame 763

27 War diary (27th Canadian Armoured Regiment), entry for 7 June 1944, NA, RG 24, vol. 15122, file June 1944, and reel T-12758, frame 763; summary of events of A Squadron, 27th Canadian Armoured Regiment, ibid., frame 962; and summary of events of C Squadron, 27th Canadian Armoured Regiment, ibid., frame 965; war diary (Headquarters of the 9th Canadian Infantry Brigade), entry for 7 June 1944, NA, RG 24, vol. 14152, file June 1944; and testimony of Constance Raymond Guilbert, Meyer Trial, 102

28 Testimony of Sergeant Stanley Dudka, Meyer Trial, 141, and appendix 8 to the war diary (Cameron Highlanders of Ottawa), entry for 7 June 1944, NA, RG 24, vol. 15026, file June 1944

29 At 1:40 PM, the North Novas reported that they were being held up by mortar and gun fire. See the intelligence log, entries for 7 June 1944, sheet 2, war diary (Highland Light Infantry of Canada), NA, RG 24, vol. 15076, folder 7, file June 1944. See also the war diary (North Nova Scotia Highlanders), entry for 7 June 1944, ibid., vol. 15122, file June 1944, and Bird, *Footsteps*, 80.

30 Appendix 8 to the war diary (Cameron Highlanders of Ottawa, C Company), entry for 7 June 1944, NA, RG 24, vol. 15026, file June 1944, and Ross, *Cameron Highlanders*, 42

31 Kurt Meyer, *Grenadiere* (Munich, 1957), 216, and Samuel W. Mitcham, *Hitler's Legions: The German Army Order of Battle in World War II* (London, 1985), 314, 376

32 War diary (North Nova Scotia Highlanders), entry for 7 June 1944; war diary (14th Canadian Field Artillery Regiment), entries for 6 and 7 June 1944; and summary of events of C Squadron, 27th Canadian Armoured Regiment, NA, RG 24, vols. 15122, 14471, file June 1944; and reel T-12758, frame 890. See also Stacey, *Victory Campaign*, 128.

33  Summary of events of A and B Squadrons, 27th Canadian Armoured Regiment, NA, reel T-12758, frames 962 and 889, and war diary (North Nova Scotia Highlanders), entry for 7 June 1944, NA, RG 24, vol. 15122, file June 1944

34  Bird, *Footsteps*, 82

35  At 1:50 PM, Fraser reported that enemy armour had been sighted some five hundred yards east of Authie. Ten minutes later, he reported that his company and elements of the 27th Canadian Armoured Regiment were engaging eight or nine German Panthers. See the intelligence log, entries for 7 June 1944, sheets 2–3, war diary (Highland Light Infantry of Canada), NA, RG 24, vol. 15076, folder 7, file June 1944. See also the war diary (North Nova Scotia Highlanders), entry for 7 June 1944, ibid., vol. 15122, file June 1944.

36  War diary (27th Canadian Armoured Regiment), entry for 7 June 1944, NA, reel T-12758, frame 764

37  Meyer, *Grenadiere*, 215–16

38  The imposing Scappini was a veteran of the French and Russian campaigns and a holder of the Iron Cross First and Second Class. He was killed in action later the same day, during his battalion's attack on St Contest. See the file on Hans Scappini, NARA, RG 242 BDC A 3433, SS Officer Dossier, roll 63B, frames 901–20.

39  Testimony of Meyer, Meyer Trial, 566

40  Ibid., 565–7

41  Ibid., 567; Meyer, *Grenadiere*, 216; and Meyer, *Kriegsgeschichte*, 78

42  Messages received regarding operations along the invasion front (High Command of the German 7th Army), 7 June 1944 (1200 hrs), NARA, RG 242, T-312, roll 1568, frame 955, and testimony of Meyer, Meyer Trial, 568–9

43  One of the Leibstandarte officers to be transferred into the 12th SS, the twenty-six-year-old Siegel was a decorated veteran of the fighting on the eastern front. See the file on Hans-Siegfried Siegel, NARA, RG 242 BDC A 3433, SS Officer Dossier, roll 135B, frames 906–20.

44  Conversation with Hans Siegel, cited in John A. English, *The Canadian Army and the Normandy Campaign: A Study of Failure in High Command* (New York and London, 1991), 233n. 15

45  Meyer, *Grenadiere*, 216–17

46  On the change in the battle plan, see recommendation no. 2 for the award of the Oak Leaves with Swords to the Knight's Cross of the Iron Cross, 15 August 1944, NARA, RG 242 BDC A 3433, SS Officer Dossier, roll 313A, frame 1350; Meyer, *Grenadiere*, 217; Meyer, *Kriegsgeschichte*, 81; and the testimony of Meyer, Meyer Trial, 569, 571.

47  War diary (27th Canadian Armoured Regiment), entry for 7 June 1944, and summary of events of B Squadron, 27th Canadian Armoured Regiment, NA, reel T-12758, frames 764 and 890

48  War diary (Headquarters of the 2nd Canadian Armoured Brigade), entry for 7 June 1944, NA, reel T-10651, frame 110

49  War diary (27th Canadian Armoured Regiment), entry for 7 June 1944, and summary of events of A Squadron, 27th Canadian Armoured Regiment, NA, reel T-12758, frames 764 and 963

50  Summary of events of A Squadron, 27th Canadian Armoured Regiment, ibid., frame 963; will-say of Lieutenant Colonel R.A.H. McKeen, undated, 'Abstract of Evidence in the Case of SS Brigadier General Kurt Meyer,' p. 17, NA, RG 24, vol. 12839, file 67/Kurt Meyer Case/1 (392/51); and the questionnaire filled out by Captain K.Y. Dick (27th Canadian Armoured Regiment), 27 July 1944, PRU, file 04-76311 (Thomas Windsor), p. 20

51  Statement given by Sergeant Lewis H. Wilson, 19 November 1945, NA, RG 24, vol. 12840, file 67/Kurt Meyer/5 (392/55), p. 9

52  Summary of events of B Squadron, 27th Canadian Armoured Regiment, NA, reel T-12758, frames 890–1

53  War diary (North Nova Scotia Highlanders), entry for 7 June 1944, NA, RG 24, vol. 15122, file June 1944

54  In his report on the fighting of 7 June, Sergeant T.C. Reid of No. 2 troop of the Sherbrooke regiment's B Squadron described having been fired on by German anti-tank guns around Buron. Summary of events of No. 2 troop, B Squadron, 27th Canadian Armoured Regiment, NA, reel T-12758, frame 886. This suggests that elements of the 25th Panzer Grenadier Regiment's anti-tank battalion, whose standard armament was a 75mm anti-tank gun mounted on a Mark IV chassis, had made it to the front in time to take part in the regiment's attack on 7 June. According to Kurt Meyer, only two of the 12th SS's four companies of 75mm anti-tank guns mounted on Mark IV chassis, totalling twenty-two anti-tank guns, were available to the division on D-Day. See the interrogation of Meyer, p. 2, NA, RG 24, vol. 10474, file 212C1.3009 (D 60). The anti-tank battalion was under the command of thirty-three-year-old SS Major Jakob Hans Hanreich. See the file on Jakob Hans Hanreich, NARA, RG 242 BDC A 3433, SS Officer Dossier, roll 61A, frames 749–57. The Viennese-born Hanreich was a veteran of the Leibstandarte's campaigns in France, the Balkans, and Russia. He was transferred from the Leibstandarte to the Hitler Youth Division near the end of 1943.

55  War diary (Headquarters of the 9th Canadian Infantry Brigade), entry for 7 June 1944, NA, RG 24, vol. 14152, file June 1944

56  Testimony of Meyer, Meyer Trial, 571; war diary (North Nova Scotia Highlanders), entry for 7 June 1944, NA, RG 24, vol. 15122, file June 1944; and Stacey, *Victory Campaign*, 131

57  Only C Company's 15 Platoon managed to withdraw relatively intact. See the testimony of Dudka, Meyer Trial, 142.

58 War diary (North Nova Scotia Highlanders), entry for 7 June 1944, NA, RG 24, vol. 15122, file June 1944

59 Bird, *Footsteps*, 86. The Sherman tank that was the bulwark of Canadian armoured forces at Normandy had a 75mm gun that was inferior to the guns on either of the two main German battle tanks, the Mark IV and the Mark V Panther. However, experiments to mount a seventeen-pound gun – more powerful than anything in the Germans' arsenal except for the Mark VI Tiger – on the Sherman proved successful, and a rush conversion program meant that by D-Day roughly one in four had been rearmed. On the evolution of the Sherman, see John Keegan, *Six Armies in Normandy* (New York, 1982), 197–8, and Ellis, *Victory*, 548–9.

60 Testimony of Meyer, Meyer Trial, 571, and war diary (Headquarters of the 9th Canadian Infantry Brigade), entry for 7 June 1944, NA, RG 24, vol. 14152, file June 1944

61 Intelligence log, entries for 7 June 1944, sheets 2–3, war diary (Highland Light Infantry of Canada), NA, RG 24, vol. 15076, folder 7, file June 1944, and Bird, *Footsteps*, 84

62 We owe much of our knowledge of what transpired at Authie on 7 June 1944 to C Company's Lieutenant Jack M. Veness, commander of 13 Platoon, and five of his men, all of whom escaped from the orchard just before the Germans surrounded the position. On Veness, see Will R. Bird, *The Two Jacks: The Amazing Adventures of Major Jack M. Veness and Major Jack L. Fairweather* (Toronto, [1955?]), passim, and Bird, *Footsteps*, 89–90. Though taken prisoner shortly thereafter, Veness survived the ordeal of captivity in the hands of the Hitler Youth Division. See the list of officers missing and dead 7–9 June 1944 now reported safe, undated, NA, RG 24, vol. 12839, file 67/Kurt Meyer Case/1, p. 28. Along with Major Learment and another officer, Veness escaped from the train taking them to a POW camp in Germany, joined a unit of the French resistance, and eventually succeeded in getting to England and rejoining the Canadian army. On Veness's odyssey, see Stacey, *Victory Campaign*, 132n. Another survivor of the battle of Authie was Lieutenant Sutherland, commander of A Company's 7 Platoon, who narrowly escaped with one other member of the platoon when his position along the Authie-Cussy road was overrun. Miraculously, Sutherland made it all the way back to battalion headquarters. On Sutherland, see Bird, *Footsteps*, 91–2.

63 Ellis, *Victory*, 548–9

64 Bird, *Footsteps*, 84. The Cameron Highlanders were equipped with a four-ton carrier known as the 'Lloyd,' which mounted a Vickers 42 machine gun. Compared with the slower Bren gun, the Vickers had a maximum rate of fire of twelve hundred rounds per minute. See Jack F. Bartlett, *1st Battalion The Highland Light Infantry of Canada* (Galt, ON, n.d.), 24; Ellis, *Victory*, 543; and English, *Canadian Army*, 233n. 17.

65 Bird, *Two Jacks*, 10

66 Bird, *Footsteps*, 85
67 Bird, *Two Jacks*, 10–11
68 Bird, *Footsteps*, 85, and Ross, *Cameron Highlanders*, 42. According to the Camerons' war diary, Baulne and Goodall were brought back critically wounded to C Company's headquarters. See appendix 8 to the war diary (Cameron Highlanders of Ottawa, C Company), entry for 7 June 1944, NA, RG 24, vol. 15026, file June 1944.
69 Recollections of SS Private Karl Vasold (9th Company), quoted in Meyer, *Kriegsgeschichte*, 79
70 Bird, *Footsteps*, 85
71 Ibid., 85, and record of the evidence of Lieutenant Colonel Charles Petch, undated, *Report of the Supreme Headquarters Allied Expeditionary Force Court of Inquiry re Shooting of Allied Prisoners of War by the German Armed Forces in the Vicinity of Le Mesnil-Patry, Les Saullets and Authie, Calvados, Normandy, 7–11 June 1944*, exhibit no. 29, p. 2, DHist, vol. 90/168
72 Bird, *Footsteps*, 89
73 On Captain Fraser's last stand in the orchard, see Bird, *Two Jacks*, 13, and the record of the evidence of Lieutenant Colonel Charles Petch, undated, SHAEF Report, *Authie*, exhibit no. 29, pp. 2–3. At 4:00 PM, the 9th Brigade reported that the enemy tanks were being 'withdrawn' from Authie. See the intelligence log, entries for 7 June 1944, sheet 3, war diary (Highland Light Infantry of Canada), NA, RG 24, vol. 15076, folder 7, file June 1944.
74 War diary (North Nova Scotia Highlanders), entry for 7 June 1944; war diary (Stormont, Dundas and Glengarry Highlanders), entry for 7 June 1944 (2145 hours); war diary (Headquarters of the 9th Canadian Infantry Brigade), entry for 7 June 1944; and war diary (27th Canadian Armoured Regiment), entry for 7 June 1944, NA, RG 24, vols. 15122, 15270, 14152, file June 1944, and reel T-12758, frame 764
75 On casualties, see the figures cited in the war diary (Headquarters of the 9th Canadian Infantry Brigade), entry for 7 June 1944; the war diary (27th Canadian Armoured Regiment), entry for 7 June 1944; and the war diary (Headquarters of the 2nd Canadian Armoured Brigade), entry for 8 June 1944, ibid., vol. 14152, file June 1944; reel T-12758, frame 764; and reel T-10651, frame 110. There is a discrepancy between Canadian and German sources regarding the number of Canadian tanks that had been put out of action on 7 June. According to the headquarters of the 9th Canadian Brigade, twenty-five tanks had been lost. See the war diary (Headquarters of the 9th Canadian Infantry Brigade), entry for 7 June 1944, NA, RG 24, vol. 14152, file June 1944. According to a report filed by the 27th Canadian Armoured Regiment during the early morning hours of 8 June, 'they had ... 21 tanks knocked out, and ... in turn [had] knocked out 31 enemy tanks, 4 enemy SP [self-propelled] guns and 18 a tk [anti-tank] guns.' See the war diary (Headquarters of the 2nd Canadian Armoured Brigade), entry for 8 June 1944, NA, reel T-10651, frame 110. On the other hand, in

recommending SS Major Karl-Heinz Prinz for the Knight's Cross of the Iron Cross for his conduct during the battles of the Normandy bridgehead, SS Lieutenant Colonel Wünsche credited Prinz's 2nd Battalion with having knocked out thirty Shermans and Stuarts on 7 June. See recommendations' list no. 1 for the award of the Knight's Cross of the Iron Cross, 20 June 1944, file on Karl-Heinz Prinz, NARA, RG 242 BDC A 3433, SS Officer Dossier, roll 394A, frame 361.

### 5: The Milius Murders

1 At its northernmost point, the front of the 25th Panzer Grenadier Regiment ran through St Contest, more than six miles from the coast. See the war diary (1st Battalion of the 25th Panzer Grenadier Regiment), entry for 7 June 1944 (1615 hrs), NARA, RG 242, T-354, roll 156, frame 3799974.

2 Colonel C.P. Stacey, *The Victory Campaign: The Operations in North-West Europe, 1944–1945* (Ottawa, 1966), 3:133

3 See the statement given by Private C.B. MacPherson, 21 November 1945, NA, RG 24, vol. 12840, file 67/Kurt Meyer/5 (392/55), p. 6, and the testimony of Corporal Walter Terence McLeod, Meyer Trial, 219, DHist, vol. 159.95023 (D 7).

4 Statement given by Private J.M. MacDonald, undated, NA, RG 24, vol. 12842, file 67/Treatment/1/2 (393/56), pp. 179–80

5 Affidavit of Major John Donald Learment, Meyer Trial, 132

6 Major Learment and Sergeant Stanley Dudka were among the prisoners about to be executed. See ibid., 134, and the testimony of Sergeant Stanley Dudka, ibid., 144.

7 These figures refer only to casualties suffered by Milius's troops. Along the front of Meyer's 25th Panzer Grenadier Regiment, the 2nd Battalion lost 21 killed, 38 wounded, and 5 missing, while the 1st Battalion lost 15 dead, 87 wounded, and 10 missing. In addition, the 2nd Battalion of the 12th SS Panzer Regiment lost 22 killed, 21 wounded, and at least 30 tanks put out of action. Thus, the total number of casualties incurred by the Germans on 7 June were 331 (88 killed, 216 wounded, 27 missing). For the various German casualty figures, see Hubert Meyer, *Kriegsgeschichte der 12.SS-Panzerdivision 'Hitlerjugend'* (Osnabrück, 1982), 1:84–5; war diary (1st Battalion of the 25th Panzer Grenadier Regiment), entry for 7 June 1944 (1615 hrs), NARA, RG 242, T-354, roll 156, frame 3799974; war diary (Headquarters of the 9th Canadian Infantry Brigade), entry for 7 June 1944, NA, RG 24, vol. 14152, file June 1944; and war diary (27th Canadian Armoured Regiment), entry for 7 June 1944, NA, reel T-12758, frame 764.

8 In this regard, the Hitler Youth troops were experiencing the same kind of battlefield shock that had overcome the Leibstandarte's 2nd Battalion near Wormhoudt four years earlier. Like its predecessor, Milius's battalion would respond to its baptism of

fire in murderous fashion. See Ian Sayer and Douglas Botting, *Hitler's Last General: The Case against Wilhelm Mohnke* (London and New York, 1989), 56, 63, 133–4.

9  In the context of the battle for Authie, the term 'berserk state' is not merely a descriptive one. Rather, it has been recognized and accorded scientific validity by Dr Jonathan Shay, a clinical psychiatrist who treated numerous Vietnam veterans. According to Shay, any number of battlefield situations can trigger the 'berserk state,' but the most common tend to be feelings of vengeance, unexpected deliverance, real or perceived humiliation, and the bodies of dead comrades. In such a state, the affected soldier or soldiers are likely to manifest feelings of omnipotence, a loss of all restraint, and, most importantly for the case with which we are concerned here, inhuman behaviour. For more on this very real and frightening by-product of war, see Jonathan Shay, *Achilles in Vietnam: Combat Trauma and the Undoing of Character* (New York, 1994), 77–99.

10  On the fate of Mackay's outpost, see the testimony of Sergeant W.L. Mackay, Meyer Trial, 188; *Report of the Supreme Headquarters Allied Expeditionary Force Court of Inquiry re Shooting of Allied Prisoners of War by the German Armed Forces in the Vicinity of Le Mesnil-Patry, Les Saullets and Authie, Calvados, Normandy, 7–11 June 1944*, p. 15, DHist, vol. 90/168; and Will R. Bird, *No Retreating Footsteps: The Story of the North Nova Scotia Highlanders* (Kentville, NS, n.d.), 93.

11  After the war, another Canadian witness came forward to state that Brown had been killed with his own knife. See the statement given by Corporal J.R.B. Campbell, undated, NA, RG 24, vol. 12837, file 67/Canada/1 (391/50), pp. 83–4. This led to speculation that Brown had struggled with his captor and had been killed as a consequence. In the face of the evidence that Brown was already wounded by this time, the witness's testimony was dismissed as implausible. See SHAEF Report, *Authie*, 15–16. In this regard, the forensic evidence was inconclusive. According to a Canadian army pathologist, while Brown died of eight stab wounds in the chest and abdomen, it was not clear whether these had been inflicted by a knife or a bayonet. See the record of the evidence of Lieutenant Colonel Dr Robert A.H. MacKeen, 11 October 1944, ibid., part 3, exhibit no. 53, p. 4, and the testimony of Lieutenant Colonel Dr MacKeen, Meyer Trial, 409.

12  SHAEF Report, *Authie*, pp. 15–16, and testimony of Sergeant W.L. Mackay, Meyer Trial, 188–9

13  Testimony of Constance Raymond Guilbert, Meyer Trial, 102

14  Ibid.

15  Record of the evidence of MacKeen, 11 October 1944, SHAEF Report, *Authie*, part 3, exhibit no. 53, p. 1, and testimony of MacKeen, Meyer Trial, 407

16  Testimony of Guilbert, Meyer Trial, 106–8, 113–15

17  Testimony of Mackay, ibid., 188

18  The men were identified by Sergeant Stanley Dudka, who served with them in the

North Novas' 15 Platoon, C Company. See the testimony of Dudka, ibid., 147. Biographical data on the four men can be found in NA, PRU, files 05-55978 (Thomas Roy Davidson), 41-01175 (John Bernard Murray), 39-38804 (Anthony Julian), and 43-14056 (James Stanley Webster).

19  Testimony of Mackay, Meyer Trial, 190–2

20  Ibid., 192

21  SHAEF Report, *Authie*, p. 19

22  Testimony of Guilbert, Meyer Trial, 111

23  Testimony of Dudka, ibid., 148

24  SHAEF Report, *Authie*, p. 19

25  Born at Belle Isle, Newfoundland, Metcalfe was twenty-five years old at the time of his murder. See NA, PRU, file 40-74180 (John Metcalfe).

26  The killing of Private Metcalfe is recounted in the affidavit of Major John Donald Learment and the testimonies of Dudka and Private Gordon Percy Talbot, Meyer Trial, 130–1, 141–4, and 164–6. See also the statement given by Sergeant Major James Alexander McKay, 18 June 1945, NA, RG 24, file 67/Atrocity Statements/1 (391/32), p. 1.

27  Affidavit of Learment, Meyer Trial, 130

28  According to the two witnesses, all of the troops had been issued such emergency packets, which they tended to carry in either their jacket or pants pockets. See the testimonies of Sergeant Stanley Dudka and Private Gordon Percy Talbot, ibid., 145 and 164.

29  Arsenault was a resident of Summerside, Prince Edward Island. For more biographical information on him, see NA, PRU, file 04-28112 (Joseph Ralph Arsenault).

30  The killing of Arsenault is recounted in the statement given by Private J.M. MacDonald, undated, NA, RG 24, vol. 12842, file 67/Treatment/1/2 (393/56), pp. 179–80, and the statement given by Private Ralph Richards, undated, ibid., vol. 12837, file 67/Canada/1 (391/50), p. 58.

31  Intermittent throughout 7 June, the shelling became concerted at about 6.30 PM. For the next two hours, HMS Rodney and HMS Warspite fired hundreds of shells from their respective sixteen- and six-inch guns. See Craig W.H. Luther, *Blood and Honor: The History of the 12th SS Panzer Division 'Hitler Youth,' 1943–1945* (San José, CA, 1987), 145n. 53.

32  The twenty-four-year-old Hargreaves was a resident of Upper Sackville, Nova Scotia. See NA, PRU, file 06-82897 (Jeffrey Douglas Hargreaves).

33  Testimony of Dudka, Meyer Trial, 145

34  Taylor was from River Herbert, Nova Scotia, while McKinnon was from St Peters, Prince Edward Island. They were twenty-four and twenty-three years old respectively. See NA, PRU, files 42-69335 (James Albert Taylor) and 40-39191 (William Lewis McKinnon).

35 The killing of McKinnon and Taylor is recounted in the testimonies of Captain Joseph Austin Trainor, Sergeant W.L. McKay, Private Ralph J. Richards, and Corporal John Robert Bell Campbell, Meyer Trial, 187, 193–6, 237–40, and 248–9. See also the statement given by Private J.M. MacDonald, undated, NA, RG 24, 12842, file 67/Treatment/1/2 (393/56), pp. 179–80.

36 The incident took place in the home of Mme Godet, who was an eyewitness. See SHAEF Report, *Authie*, p. 19.

37 Ibid., 16

38 It was first thought that the medic had been the stretcher bearer sent by Captain Fraser into Authie along with Lieutenants Veness and Graves. According to Veness, however, that man was a Private Conrad, who survived 7 June and who was eventually repatriated from POW captivity. See Will R. Bird, *The Two Jacks: The Amazing Adventures of Major Jack M. Veness and Major Jack L. Fairweather* (Toronto, [1955?]), 10.

39 Testimony of Talbot, Meyer Trial, 167–8

40 Bird, *Footsteps*, 97

41 This incident was recounted in the testimonies of Corporal Walter Terrence McLeod and Private J.A. Conrad, Meyer Trial, 217–19 and 225–8. See also SHAEF Report, *Authie*, pp. 17–18. For biographical information on Orford and Arsenault, see NA, PRU, files 41-20841 (Douglas Sumner Orford) and 04-28090 (Joseph Francis Arsenault).

42 The incident was recounted in the statement given by Private J.M. MacDonald, undated, NA, RG 24, vol. 12842, file 67/Treatment/1/2 (393/56), pp. 179–80, and statements given by: Private Thomas Bird, 18 October 1945, ibid., vol. 12840, file 67/Kurt Meyer/5 (392/55), pp. 19–20; Private Ralph Richards, undated, ibid., vol. 12837, file 67/Canada/1 (391/50), p. 58; Sergeant Major James Alexander McKay, 18 June 1945, ibid., file 67/Atrocity Statements/1 (391/32), p. 1. Biographical data on the two men can be found in PRU, files 40-50059 (Roderick Roman MacRae) and 42-81148 (Douglas Vincent Tobin).

43 Statement given by Sergeant Stanley Dudka, 16 August 1944, NA, RG 24, vol. 12837, file 67/Atrocity Statements/1 (391/32), p. 31

44 SHAEF Report, *Authie*, p. 18

45 For biographical data on Brown, see PRU, file 03-98868 (Walter Leslie Brown).

46 War diary (27th Canadian Armoured Regiment), entry for 8 June 1944 (1700 hrs), NA, reel T-12758, frame 765

47 Record of the evidence of Lieutenant W.F. Grainger, 29 October 1945, NA, RG 24, vol. 12838, file 67/Galmanche/1 (392/3)

48 Letter by Lieutenant Colonel F.T. Jennings, 22 February 1945, ibid., p. 4

49 Record of the evidence of MacKeen, undated, ibid., pp. 18–20

50 Major Learment expressed it best when he offered the opinion after the war that

'nobody seemed to be actually in charge of this group.' Quoted from the affidavit of Learment, Meyer Trial, 132

51 *Supplementary Report of the SHAEF Court of Inquiry re Shooting of Allied Prisoners of War by 12 SS Panzer Division (Hitler-Jugend) in Normandy, France, 7–21 June 1944*, part 3, p. 14 and part 5, p. 32, NA, RG 24, vol. 10427, file 205S1.023 (D 9)

52 Charges against SS Brigadier General Kurt Meyer forwarded to the UNWCC in June 1945, ibid., vol. 12837, file 67/CNO/12 SS/1 (392/5)

53 Memorandum from Lieutenant Colonel B.J.S. Macdonald to the Deputy Adjutant General, 12 January 1946, p. 2, NA, RG 25, vol. 5782, file 213(s), part 1

**6: The Meyer Murders**

1 Testimony of SS Brigadier General Kurt Meyer, Meyer Trial, 575, DHist, vol. 159.95023 (D 7), and affidavit of Kurt Meyer in 'Petition of Kurt Meyer and Memorandum by Counsel Re Trial, Conviction and Sentence,' 12 December 1950, pp. 10–11, NA, RG 2, vol. 209, file W-41, part 1. For biographical information on Doldi, see the wanted report, undated, NA, RG 24, vol. 12837, file 67/CROWCASS/1 (392/7), pp. 125–verso.

2 See 'Instructions for the divisional intelligence officer regarding the treatment and interrogation of prisoners of war' issued by the 86th (German) Army Corps, 24 June 1944, NARA, RG 242, T-314, roll 1607, frames 804–9.

3 Affidavit of Kurt Meyer in 'Petition of Kurt Meyer,' p. 10, NA, RG 2, vol. 209, file W-41, part 1. The order of battle of the 12th SS included one motorized Feldgendarmerie company, which comprised five platoons. Sections from each platoon were assigned to various of the division's subunits. See the memorandum by SS Lieutenant General Jüttner, 30 October 1943, NA, RG 24, vol. 20531, file 981SSPzD12. (D 1), folder 3. The duties of the Feldgendarmerie are described in the testimony of SS Corporal (Feldgendarmerie) Ewald Wetzel, Meyer Trial, 502, and the order issued by the Commander of the 12th SS Division, 30 March 1944, NARA, RG 242, T-354, roll 154, frame 3797985.

4 On 7 June, the 3rd Battalion's headquarters were located about a thousand yards southwest of the Abbaye d'Ardenne, astride the Caen-Bayeux road. It was not until the next day that the battalion would set up headquarters at Cussy. See the testimony of Meyer, Meyer Trial, 600.

5 Testimony of Sergeant Stanley Dudka, ibid., 149, 155–6

6 Testimony of Meyer, ibid., 576. See also the affidavit of Kurt Meyer in 'Petition of Kurt Meyer,' p. 9, NA, RG 2, vol. 209, file W-41, part 1.

7 According to Meyer, the physicians and medical orderlies who were treating the Canadians 'saw no uniforms.' Quoted from Kurt Meyer, *Grenadiere* (Munich, 1957),

221. At his trial, Meyer testified that the wounded were being bandaged in the north entrance of the abbey. See the testimony of Meyer, Meyer Trial, 596.

8  Testimony of Dudka, ibid., 156, 159

9  This incident is described in B.J.S. Macdonald, *The Trial of Kurt Meyer* (Toronto, 1954), 124.

10  Testimony of Dudka, Meyer Trial, 158

11  Determining the identities of the ten prisoners is no easy task. Still, the evidence is almost incontrovertible that at least seven of the men named were among the ten. The selection of Private Moss was witnessed by two other prisoners. See the testimony of Corporal John Robert Bell Campbell, and the testimony of Sergeant Stanley Dudka, ibid., 251 and 150, and the statement given by Sergeant Stanley Dudka, 16 August 1944, NA, RG 24, vol. 12837, file 67/Atrocity Statement/1 (391/32), p. 31. Doucette's and MacIntyre's selection can be deduced from the fact that their paybooks were found among the personal items returned to the surviving Canadian prisoners the following morning. See Ian J. Campbell, *Murder at the Abbaye: The Story of Twenty Canadian Soldiers Murdered at the Abbaye d'Ardenne* (Ottawa, 1996), 109. The presence of Windsor, Bolt, Lockhead, and Philip at the abbey on the night of 7 June is confirmed by the account of Trooper Marcel Dagenais, the fifth member of Windsor's crew. See the testimony of Trooper Marcel Dagenais, Meyer Trial, 451. As for Troopers Gill and Henry of the Sherbrooke regiment, the evidence that they were at the abbey on the night of 7 June, while circumstantial, is still persuasive. Having been involved in the big tank battle between Authie and Buron earlier in the afternoon, they, like Windsor's crew, probably were captured after their Sherman was knocked out of action. Perhaps more compelling is the fact that autopsies determined that they had suffered the same kind of blunt-force trauma injuries that had been meted out by the Germans to many of the ten. See the will-say of Lieutenant Colonel Dr R.A.H. MacKeen, undated, 'Abstract of Evidence in the Case of SS Brigadier General Kurt Meyer,' NA, RG 24, vol. 12839, file 67/Kurt Meyer Case/1 (392/51), pp. 18–19. So did Private Crowe, who apparently was captured along with other members of C Company. See ibid., p. 18, and Campbell, *Murder*, 70. For biographical information on the prisoners, see PRU, files 04-76311 (James Elgin Bolt), 05-44719 (Ivan Lee Crowe), 05-79336 (Charles Doucette), 06-47462 (George Vincent Gill), 06-96145 (Thomas Haliburton Henry), 40-33110 (Joseph Francis MacIntyre), 40-95286 (James Alvin Moss), 40-05027 (Roger Lockhead), 41-45569 (Harold George Philip), and 43-31063 (Thomas Alfred Lee Windsor).

12  See the affidavit of Kurt Meyer in 'Petition of Kurt Meyer,' p. 9, NA, RG 2, vol. 209, file W-41, part 1. The time was confirmed by Dudka and by Daniel Lachèvre, a fourteen-year-old whose family was living at the abbey at the time. See the testimonies of Sergeant Stanley Dudka and Daniel Lachèvre, Meyer Trial, 158 and 472.

13  According to Daniel Lachèvre, the Germans who guarded the prisoners were wearing the camouflage jackets of the 12th SS and were carrying machine pistols, which were standard issue for SS NCOs. See the testimony of Lachèvre, Meyer Trial, 472–3. On the small arms with which the division was equipped, see Craig W.H. Luther, *Blood and Honor: The History of the 12th SS Panzer Division 'Hitler Youth,' 1943–1945* (San José, CA, 1987), 141n. 45.

14  According to Sergeant Dudka, he did not see the Feldgendarmerie until the prisoners arrived at a schoolhouse in Bretteville-sur-Odon. Dudka correctly pointed out that the military police were easily distinguished from rank-and-file infantrymen by the metal breastplate they wore bearing the inscription 'Feldgendarmerie.' Testimony of Dudka, Meyer Trial, 161. For corroboration of Dudka's testimony, see the testimony of Campbell, ibid., 252.

15  Meyer himself had selected Venoix as the site of the divisional headquarters during his ride to the front on 6 June. The 12th SS would set up a more permanent headquarters at Verson, which was just east of Caen, on the Caen-Villers road, but, by Meyer's own admission, the move was not made until 8 June. See the record of the evidence of SS Brigadier General Kurt Meyer, undated, *Supplementary Report of the SHAEF Court of Inquiry re Shooting of Allied Prisoners of War by 12 SS Panzer Division (Hitler-Jugend) in Normandy, France, 7–21 June 1944*, exhibit no. 8, p. 23, NA, RG 24, vol. 10427, file 205S1.023 (D 9).

16  Testimony of Wetzel, Meyer Trial, 502

17  Testimony of Lachèvre, ibid., 473

18  The details of the interrogations and subsequent murders are based on the examination of the bodies by a Canadian military pathologist, the testimony of a member of the Feldgendarmerie, and a summary of the evidence introduced at the trial of Kurt Meyer. See the will-say of MacKeen, undated, 'Abstract of Evidence,' NA, RG 24, vol. 12839, file 67/Kurt Meyer Case/1 (392/51), pp. 17–19; the testimony of Wetzel, Meyer Trial, 497–500; and Macdonald, *Trial*, 122, 135.

19  According to the owner of the chateau, three clubs were found in the shed that opened into the courtyard adjoining the garden. See the will-say of Jean Marie Vico, undated, 'Abstract of Evidence,' p. 12, NA, RG 24, vol. 12839, file 67/Kurt Meyer Case/1 (392/51).

20  Significantly, one of the three clubs that were found in the courtyard shed was covered with congealed blood. See ibid. and the will-say of MacKeen, undated, ibid., pp. 18–19.

21  See the will-say of MacKeen, undated, ibid., p. 17.

22  McKeil had received shrapnel wounds to the chest and ankle on the morning of 7 June. Though he was having some difficulty breathing, his condition apparently had been stabilized by a medic. See the questionnaire regarding the missing Private H.T. McKeil, 19 December 1944; the statement given by Lance Corporal R. Phillips,

undated; and Major L.S. Appleford's letter, undated, PRU, file 40-35496 (Hollis Leslie McKeil), pp. 21–3.

23  Charges against SS Brigadier General Kurt Meyer forwarded to the United Nations War Crimes Commission in June 1945, NA, RG 24, vol. 12837, file 67/CNO/12 SS/1 (392/5)

24  See the general order of 21 January 1944, undated, NARA, RG 242, T-354, roll 604, frame 203, and the testimony of Wetzel, Meyer Trial, 502. In his appeal for clemency, Meyer admitted that it was within his authority to arrest either Doldi or members of the Feldgendarmerie for 'derelictions of duty' of which he had knowledge and which he could have prevented. See the affidavit of Kurt Meyer in 'Petition of Kurt Meyer,' 12 December 1950, p. 10, NA, RG 2, vol. 209, file W-41, part 1.

25  At Meyer's trial, Feldgendarmerie NCO Ewald Wetzel ventured that the order to shoot a prisoner at a regimental headquarters could only come from the regimental commander or one of his staff officers. See the testimony of Wetzel, Meyer Trial, 504.

26  The second and third admissions can be found in the affidavit of Kurt Meyer in 'Petition of Kurt Meyer,' 12 December 1950, pp. 8–9, 11, NA, RG 2, vol. 209, file W-41, part 1.

27  According to the witness Daniel Lachèvre, the marching off of the mass of Canadian prisoners coincided with the entry into the chateau of the smaller group of POWs. See the testimony of Lachèvre, Meyer Trial, 473.

28  Memorandum from Lieutenant Colonel B.J.S. Macdonald to the Deputy Adjutant General, 12 January 1946, p. 4, NA, RG 25, vol. 5782, file 213(s), part 1

29  Affidavit of Kurt Meyer in 'Petition of Kurt Meyer,' 12 December 1950, p. 11, NA, RG 2, vol. 209, file W-41, part 1.

30  On the locations of Mohnke's regiment and the Panzer Lehr Division, see Luther, Blood and Honor, 162, and the testimony of Meyer, Meyer Trial, 579.

31  Affidavit of Kurt Meyer in 'Petition of Kurt Meyer,' 12 December 1950, p. 11, NA, RG 2, vol. 209, file W-41, part 1

32  Hubert Meyer, Kriegsgeschichte der 12.SS-Panzerdivision 'Hitlerjugend' (Osnabrück, 1982), 1:83–4

33  Waldmüller was another of the many Leibstandarte officers transferred to the Hitler Youth Division in the summer of 1943. A veteran of the fighting on the eastern front, Waldmüller held all of Germany's high war decorations, including the Knight's Cross of the Iron Cross, which he was awarded for his heroics during the fighting in Normandy. Two weeks after receiving this award, he was killed in action. See the file on SS Major Johann Waldmüller, NARA, RG 242 BDC A 3433, SS Officer Dossier, roll 218B, frames 582–666.

34  Testimony of Meyer, Meyer Trial, 586–7

35 War diary (Regina Rifles), entry for 7 June 1944 (1200 hrs), NA, RG 24, vol. 15198, file June 1944

36 Testimony of Meyer, Meyer Trial, 579

37 The account of these murders is based on the testimony of SS Private Jan Jesionek, ibid., 299–309, 330, 359.

38 Testimony of Meyer, ibid., 579

39 The determination of the identities of the seven prisoners was made mainly by the process of elimination. Nonetheless, there is evidence that Doherty and Mont, at least, had been captured too late to have been taken to the abbey on the night of 7 June. According to a report filed by his unit, Doherty had been seen at his position as late as 6 PM. See the questionnaire on the missing Private W.M. Doherty, 22 June 1944, PRU, file 05-75858 (Walter Michael Doherty), p. 7. As for Mont, after sustaining an injury to his arm in a mortar attack early in the afternoon on 7 June, he was last seen at the northern end of Buron. With the situation there very confused, it seems likely that Mont was not taken prisoner until much later in the day. On Mont's whereabouts prior to his capture, see Lieutenant Colonel D.F. Forbes to the officer in charge (Canadian Section GHQ, 21 Army Group), 9 September 1944; the questionnaire on the missing Private T.E. Mont, 5 December 1944; and the statement given by Corporal C.O. Gourley, 28 May 1945, PRU, file 40-85673 (Thomas Edward Mont), pp. 21, 31–verso, and 49. See also Campbell, *Murder*, 67–8. For biographical information on the seven men who were brought to the abbey on 8 June, see PRU, files 05-75858 (Walter Michael Doherty), 39-42975 (Reginald Keeping), 40-23087 (Hugh Allan MacDonald), 40-46646 (George Richard McNaughton), 40-77567 (George Edward Millar), 40-85673 (Thomas Edward Mont), 40-87968 (Raymond Moore).

40 Since Meyer admitted having lunched with SS Lieutenant Colonel Max Wünsche, the commander of the 12th Panzer Regiment, it is possible that Wünsche was one of the officers standing with him. On Meyer's movements on the morning and early afternoon of 8 June, see his affidavit in 'Petition of Kurt Meyer,' 12 December 1950, p. 12, NA, RG 2, vol. 209, file W-41, part 1.

41 The quoted passages are from the testimony of Jesionek, Meyer Trial, 301.

42 SHAEF Report, *12 SS*, part 1, p. 4

## 7: The Battle of Putot-en-Bessin

1 The 12th Reconnaissance Battalion consisted of five companies, two of which were motorized and two of which were armoured. See Craig W.H. Luther, *Blood and Honor: The History of the 12th SS Panzer Division 'Hitler Youth,' 1943–1945* (San José, CA, 1987), 251. SS personnel files were found on four of the five company commanders. Of the four, all had previous combat experience on the eastern front,

and all held high war decorations. See the files on Willi-Peter Hansmann, Walter Hauck, Günther Keue, and Gert von Reitzenstein, NARA, RG 242 BDC A 3433, SS Officer Dossier, roll 62A, frames 924–8; roll 69A, frames 1093–5; roll 166A, frames 670–1; and roll 23B, frames 194–205. Only Keue, incidentally, had previously served with the Leibstandarte.

2 Hubert Meyer, *Kriegsgeschichte der 12.SS-Panzerdivision 'Hitlerjugend'* (Osnabrück, 1982), 1:88, and recommendation no. 1 for the award of the German Cross in Gold, undated, file on Gerhard Bremer, NARA, RG 242 BDC A 3433, SS Officer Dossier, roll 104, frame 648

3 The information in this paragraph was gleaned from Bremer's SS personnel file NARA, RG 242 BDC A 3433, SS Officer Dossier, roll 104, frames 632–57.

4 According to Allied intelligence, the 26th Regiment's march to the front had been more or less continuous, with only one delay occurring as the result of air attack. Except for the last two or three miles, main roads were used throughout. See the secret report by SHAEF (G-2), 8 July 1944, p. 1, NA, RG 24, vol. 10717, file 215C1.98 (D 399). In view of its relatively uneventful march, it is not clear why Mohnke's troops took so long in getting to the front. By contrast, Meyer's regiment, which had to travel about the same distance, arrived at the invasion front in roughly one-third of the time.

5 The deployment of the 26th Panzer Grenadier Regiment's three battalions on 7 June is described in Meyer, *Kriegsgeschichte*, 88, 92, 95. For the glittering service records of the three battalion commanders, see the files on Bernhard Krause, Bernhard Siebken, and Erich Olboeter, NARA, RG 242 BDC A 3433, SS Officer Dossier, rolls 208A, frames 982–1102; roll 135B, frames 662–711; and roll 357A, frames 133–51.

6 Record of the evidence of SS Brigadier General Kurt Meyer, undated, *Supplementary Report of the SHAEF Court of Inquiry re Shooting of Allied Prisoners of War by 12 SS Panzer Division (Hitler-Jugend) in Normandy, France, 7–21 June 1944*, exhibit no. 8, p. 27, NA, RG 24, vol. 10427, file 205S1.023 (D 9)

7 B.J.S. Macdonald, *The Trial of Kurt Meyer* (Toronto, 1954), 29–30

8 The information on Mohnke was gleaned from the file on Wilhelm Mohnke, NARA, RG 242 BDC A 3433, SS Officer Dossier, roll 323A, frames 76–160, and Ian Sayer and Douglas Botting, *Hitler's Last General: The Case against Wilhelm Mohnke* (London and New York, 1989), 55–6, 62–3, 141. The circumstances surrounding the drunken brawl are recounted in Reinhard Heydrich to Sepp Dietrich, 23 August 1939, NARA, RG 242 BDC A 3433, SS Officer Dossier, roll 323A, frames 121–2.

9 The deployment of the Canadian forces facing Mohnke's regiment is described in Luther, *Blood and Honor*, 160; the war diary (Headquarters of the 7th Canadian Infantry Brigade), entry for 7 June 1944, NA, reel T-12014, frame 1548; the questionnaire, undated, PRU, file 42-41067 (George Richard Smith), p. 12; the statement

given by Lieutenant Colonel J.M. Meldram, undated, *Report of the SHAEF Court of Inquiry regarding the Shooting of Prisoners of War by German Armed Forces at Château d'Audrieu on 8 June 1944*, part 3, exhibit no. 28, p. 1, NA, RG 24, vol. 10429, file 205S1.023 (D 18); the war diary (Royal Winnipeg Rifles), entries for 6 June (1800 hrs) and 7 June 1944 (2100 hrs), ibid., vol. 15233, file June 1944, pp. 4F4, 4F6; and the war diary (Regina Rifles), entry for 7 June 1944 (1200 hrs), ibid., vol. 15198, file June 1944.

10 The deployment of the forces supporting the Winnipegs and the Reginas is described in the war diary (3rd Canadian Anti-Tank Regiment, RCA), entry for 8 June 1944, NA, RG 24, vol. 14562, file June 1944, p. 3; appendix 9 to the war diary (D Company, Cameron Highlanders of Ottawa), entry for 6 June 1944, p. 2, ibid., vol. 15026, file June 1944; appendix 6 to the war diary (A Company, Cameron Highlanders of Ottawa), entry for 7 June 1944 (1200 hrs), p. 1, ibid.; the statement given by Lieutenant Colonel J.M. Meldram, undated, SHAEF Report, *Château d'Audrieu*, part 3, exhibit no. 28, p. 1; and the war diary (Royal Winnipeg Rifles), entry for 7 June 1944 (1600 hrs), NA, RG 24, vol. 15233, file June 1944, p. 4F5.

11 Enclosure to the war diary (High Command of the German 7th Army), 8 June 1944, NARA, RG 242, T-312, roll 1565, frame 895

12 War diary (Headquarters of the 7th Canadian Infantry Brigade), entry for 7 June 1944, NA, reel T-12014, frame 1548; war diary (Royal Winnipeg Rifles), entry for 7 June 1944 (2100 hrs), NA, RG 24, vol. 15233, file June 1944, p. 4F6; and war diary (Regina Rifles), entry for 8 June 1944, ibid., vol. 15198, file June 1944.

13 The incident is recounted in the report by Major T.R. Murphy, 17 June 1944, p. 2, appendix 3 of the war diary (6th Field Company, Royal Canadian Engineers), NA, RG 24, vol. 14696, file June 1944; the extract from the war diary (C Company, Royal Winnipeg Rifles), entry for 7 June 1944, *Report of the No. 1 Canadian War Crimes Investigation Unit regarding the Shooting of Canadian Prisoners of War by German Armed Forces at Haut du Bosq on 11 June 1944*, exhibit no. 17, NA, RG 25, vol. 2609, #172 in box; the statements given by Corporal H.L. Chartrand and Corporal H.A. Roque, undated, PRU, file 41-23862 (Allan Ralph Owens), p. 14. See also the statement given by Private David C. Pattison, 14 August 1945, NA, RG 24, vol. 12837, file 67/Canada/1 (391/50), p. 82. SS Privates Withold Stangenberg and Heinz Schmidt witnessed the arrival of the three Canadian prisoners at Mohnke's regimental headquarters at between 4:30 and 5:00 PM on 11 June. See the record of the evidence of Withold Stangenberg, 28 June 1945, pp. 5–7, DHist, file 1325–1, and the record of the evidence of Heinz Schmidt, undated, CWCIU Report, *Haut du Bosq*, exhibit no. 8, pp. 7, 9.

14 The progress of the attack of the 1st Battalion can be followed in Meyer, *Kriegsgeschichte*, 92; the war diary (Canadian Scottish Regiment), entry for 8 June 1944 (0145 hrs), p. 8, NA, RG 24, vol. 15036, file June 1944; the war diary (Regina

Rifles), entry for 8 June 1944 (0850, 1220, and 1700 hrs), ibid., vol. 15198, file June 1944; and the message sent by the 3rd Canadian Infantry Division, 8 June 1944 (1540 hrs), recorded on 'Log and Summary of Events' in the appendix to the war diary of the Headquarters of the (British) 1st Corps, sheet 4, NA, reel T-2451.

15 Military historian John English has suggested that the Winnipegs were wrong in assuming that they were under attack by German armour at Putot, and that the vehicles they saw likely were the tanks of the 24th Lancers, a British armoured regiment, which counterattacked eastward down the Bayeux-Caen highway. See John A. English, *The Canadian Army and the Normandy Campaign: A Study of Failure in High Command* (New York and London, 1991), 208. This conclusion fails to take into account two important facts. First, the Winnipegs began reporting the presence of German 'tanks' to the west of their position as early as 5:30 on the morning of 8 June. See the battle log (Headquarters of the 7th Canadian Infantry Brigade), 8 June 1944, entries for 0530 and 0605 hrs in the war diary (Headquarters of the 7th Canadian Infantry Brigade), NA, reel T-12015, frame 15. Second, the attack of the 24th Lancers did not begin until 7:00 AM. See Luther, *Blood and Honor*, 160n. 36. Thus, the vehicles that the Winnipegs saw on the morning of 8 June could not have been the tanks of the 24th Lancers. Indeed, they were not tanks at all. Rather, they had to have been the armoured personnel carriers of the 3rd Battalion of the 26th Panzer Grenadier regiment. Unlike the other five battalions in the 12th SS's Panzer Grenadier regiments, the 26th Regiment's 3rd Battalion was equipped with armoured personnel carriers, and so was the only one to be designated as 'armoured.' See ibid., 250n. 4. According to the Winnipegs' war diary, anti-tank fire knocked out one armoured vehicle and the Mark III tank during the early stages of the battle of Putot-en-Bessin. See the war diary (Royal Winnipeg Rifles), entry for 8 June 1944, NA, RG 24, vol. 15233, file June 1944, p. 4F7.

16 The 2nd Battalion's initial lack of success is described in Meyer, *Kriegsgeschichte*, 93; the battle log, 8 June 1944, entry for 0520 hrs, in the war diary (Headquarters of the 7th Canadian Infantry Brigade), NA, reel T-12015, frame 15; the statement given by Lieutenant Colonel J.M. Meldram, undated, SHAEF Report, *Château d'Audrieu*, part 3, exhibit no. 28, p. 1; and the battle log, 8 June 1944, entry for 0635 hrs, in the war diary (Headquarters of the 7th Canadian Infantry Brigade), NA, reel T-12015, frame 15.

17 The progress of the 2nd Battalion's attack can be followed in Meyer, *Kriegsgeschichte*, 93; the war diary (Headquarters of the 3rd Canadian Infantry Division), entry for 8 June 1944 (0800 hrs), NA, RG 24, vol. 13766, folder 17, file June 1944, p. 3; Luther, *Blood and Honor*, 157n. 23; the intelligence log, entry for 8 June 1944, in the war diary (Headquarters of the 9th Canadian Infantry Brigade), NA, RG 24, vol. 14152, file June 1944; the war diary (Royal Winnipeg Rifles), entry for 8 June 1944, ibid., vol. 15233, file June 1944, p. 4F7; the battle log, 8 June 1944, entries for

1200 and 1310 hrs, in the war diary (Headquarters of the 7th Canadian Infantry Brigade), NA, reel T-12015, frame 21; and the statement given by Lieutenant Colonel J.M. Meldram, undated, SHAEF Report, *Château d'Audrieu*, part 3, exhibit no. 28, p. 1.

18 The setback at Putot is described in Bruce Tascona, *Little Black Devils: A History of the Royal Winnipeg Rifles* (Winnipeg, 1983), 152–3; the statement given by Lieutenant Colonel J.M. Meldram, undated, SHAEF Report, *Château d'Audrieu*, part 3, exhibit no. 28, p. 1; the war diary (Royal Winnipeg Rifles), entry for 8 June 1944, NA, RG 24, vol. 15233, file June 1944, p. 4F7; appendix 9 to the war diary (D Company, Cameron Highlanders of Ottawa), entry for 8 June 1944, p. 2, ibid., vol. 15026, file June 1944; appendix 6 to the war diary (A Company, Cameron Highlanders of Ottawa), entry for 8 June 1944, p. 2, ibid.; and Lieutenant Colonel Richard M. Ross, *The History of the 1st Battalion Cameron Highlanders of Ottawa (MG)* (Ottawa, 1946), 44.

19 The attack of the 3rd Battalion of Mohnke's regiment is described in Meyer, *Kriegsgeschichte*, 95.

20 The honour of retaking Putot fell to the Canadian Scottish Regiment. In the vicious fighting that followed the 8:00 PM attack, the Canadian Scottish suffered 125 casualties, including 45 killed. By 9:30 PM Putot was back in Canadian hands. See the war diary (Canadian Scottish Regiment), entry for 8 June, NA, RG 24, vol. 15036, file June 1944, p. 8, and Colonel C.P. Stacey, *The Victory Campaign: The Operations in North-West Europe, 1944–1945* (Ottawa, 1966), 3:136.

21 Stacey, *Victory Campaign*; battle log, 8 June 1944, entry for 1615 hrs, in the war diary (Headquarters of the 7th Canadian Infantry Brigade), NA, reel T-12015, frame 25; intelligence log, 8 June 1944, entry for 1723 hrs, in the war diary (Headquarters of the 9th Canadian Infantry Brigade), NA, RG 24, vol. 14152, file June 1944; and war diary (Royal Winnipeg Rifles), entry for 9 June 1944, ibid., vol. 15233, file June 1944, p. 4F8

22 The capture of the various units of Winnipegs is described in the record of the evidence of August Henne, 11 October 1945, *Report of the No. 1 Canadian War Crimes Investigation Unit regarding the Shooting of Canadian Prisoners of War by the German Armed Forces near Fontenay-le-Pesnel on 8 June 1944*, exhibit no. 15, p. 15, NA, RG 25, F-3, vol. 2609, #171 in box; the statement given by Lieutenant R.S. Moglove, undated, SHAEF Report, *Château d'Audrieu*, part 3, exhibit no. 29, p. 1; and SHAEF Report, *12 SS*, part 5, p. 30. See also the battle log, 8 June 1944, entry for 1600 hrs, in the war diary (Headquarters of the 7th Canadian Infantry Brigade), NA, reel T-12015, frame 24; Canmilitary to Defensor, 22 July 1944, NA, RG 24, vol. 12842, file 67/Treatment/1 (393/53), pp. 210–verso; Captain J. Allen to the officer in charge (Canadian Section, 21st Army Group), 31 July 1944, and the report by F. Stephaniuk, 4 August 1944, PRU, files 04-67578 (Hillard John Henry Birston), p. 10, and 06-13313 (Roger Joseph Firman), p. 10.

23 Record of the evidence of August Henne, 11 October 1945, CWCIU Report, *Fontenay-le-Pesnel*, exhibit no. 15, p. 16

24 Record of the evidence of Heinz Schmidt, undated, CWCIU Report, *Haut du Bosq*, exhibit no. 8, p. 8

25 UNWCC Charge Sheet against Wilhelm Mohnke, undated, NA, RG 24, vol. 12837, file 67/Canadian National Office/1 (392/4), p. 3, and CWCIU Report, *Fontenay-le-Pesnel*, statement of facts, pp. 1, 4

## 8: The Bremer Murders

1 The twenty-five-year-old Hodge was a reservist who enlisted a few days after the evacuation of the BEF from Dunkirk. For more biographical information on him, see PRU, file 39-03884 (Frederick Edward Hodge). The thirteen men from 9 Platoon included Corporal George Edward Meakin, Lance Corporal Frank Vernon Meakin, Riflemen William Charles Adams, Emmanuel Bishoff, Lawrence Chartrand, Sidney James Cresswell, Anthony Fagnan, Robert James Harper, Hervé Alfred Labrecque, John Lewis Lychowich, Robert Mutch, Henry Rodgers, and Steve Slywchuk. For biographical information on them, see PRU, files 40-70314, 40-70312, 04-13809, 04-67709, 05-09689, 04-50661, 06-05705, 06-83815, 39-62208, 40-12530, 41-02048, 41-89124, and 42-35393. The rest of the men from A Company included Lance Corporals Austin Ralph Fuller and William Poho, Riflemen David Sidney Gold, James Donald McIntosh, William David Thomas, Louis Chartrand, Kenneth Samuel Lawrence, and Frank Ostir. For biographical information on them, see PRU, files 06-29596, 41-51255, 06-53798, 40-32416, 42-75900, 05-09706, 39-83569, and 41-21932. The reinforcements from the Queen's Own were Privates Francis David Harrison and Frederick Smith. For biographical information on them, see PRU, files 06-85334 and 42-38215.

2 Statement given by Lieutenant R.S. Moglove, undated, in the *Report of the SHAEF Court of Inquiry regarding the Shooting of Prisoners of War by German Armed Forces at Château d'Audrieu on 8 June 1944*, part 3, exhibit no. 29, p. 1, NA, RG 24, vol. 10429, file 205S1.023 (D 18).

3 Three weeks later, a unit of the (British) 50th Northumbrian Division found the personal effects of a number of the prisoners at the junction, suggesting that they had been searched and divested of these items at this spot. See ibid., part 2, p. 10.

4 Ibid., pp. 4, 8, 10. See also the statements given by Raymond Marcel Lanoue and Monique Level, 3 July 1944, NA, RG 24, vol. 10513, file 215A21.009 (D 125), pp. 10, 6.

5 Carlo d'Este, *Decision in Normandy: The Unwritten Story of Montgomery and the Allied Campaign* (London, 1983), 507n. 1

6 Statement given by Level, 3 July 1944, NA, RG 24, vol. 10513, file 215A21.009

(D 125), p. 7, and SHAEF Report, *Château d'Audrieu*, part 2, p. 3

7  See the file on Gerhard Bremer, NARA, RG 242 BDC A 3433, SS Officer Dossier, roll 104, frame 632.

8  Statement given by Level, 3 July 1944, NA, RG 24, vol. 10513, file 215A21.009 (D 125), p. 7

9  For more on this incident, see PRU, file 39-03884 (Frederick Edward Hodge).

10 Captain J. Allen to the Canadian Section (21st Army Group), 31 July 1944, PRU, file 04-67578 (Hilliard John Henry Birston), p. 10

11 Statements given by Lanoue, Beatrice Marie Delafon, and Level, 3 July 1944, NA, RG 24, vol. 10513, file 215A21.009 (D 125), pp. 7, 9–10

12 Even among the cynical, battle-hardened veterans of Nazi Germany's dirty war on the eastern front, Stun had acquired a reputation as a homicidal thug. See the testimony of SS Second Lieutenant Becker, *Supplementary Report of the SHAEF Court of Inquiry re Shooting of Allied Prisoners of War by 12 SS Panzer Division (Hitler-Jugend) in Normandy, France, 7–21 June 1944*, part 4, p. 21, NA, RG 24, vol. 10427, file 205S1.023 (D 9).

13 This was deduced from the fact that both Fuller's and Smith's bodies bore close-range wounds to the chest, while Smith had also been hit in the armpit. See SHAEF Report, *Château d'Audrieu*, part 2, pp. 3–4.

14 Ibid., p. 1

15 Statements given by Delafon and Level, 3 July 1944, NA, RG 24, vol. 10513, file 215A21.009 (D 125), pp. 6–7, 9

16 SHAEF Report, *Château d'Audrieu*, part 2, pp. 1, 6, and record of the evidence of Reverend A. Inglis, 11 July 1944, ibid., part 3, exhibit no. 7, p. 1

17 Statement given by Delafon, 3 July 1944, NA, RG 24, vol. 10513, file 215A21.009 (D 125), p. 9

18 Craig W.H. Luther, *Blood and Honor: The History of the 12th SS Panzer Division 'Hitler Youth,' 1943–1945* (San José, CA, 1987), 160

19 Ibid., 160–1

20 SHAEF Report, *Château d'Audrieu*, part 2, p. 7

21 Record of the evidence of Eugene André Leopold Buchart, 14 July 1944, ibid., part 3, exhibit no. 21, p. 2

22 Record of the evidence of Captain (Chaplain) Herbert Samuel Griffiths Thomas, 12 July 1944, ibid., exhibit no. 9, p. 2

23 Ibid., part 2, pp. 7–8

24 The circumstances of the 12th SS Reconnaissance Battalion's withdrawal from Audrieu are recounted in SHAEF Report, *12 SS*, part 4, p. 21; Hubert Meyer, *Kriegsgeschichte der 12.SS-Panzerdivision 'Hitlerjugend'* (Osnabrück, 1982), 1:98; and the statement given by Level, 3 July 1944, NA, RG 24, vol. 10513, file 215A21.009 (D 125), p. 5.

25 SHAEF Report, *Château d'Audrieu*, part 2, pp. 8–10
26 See PRU, file 06-85334 (Francis David Harrison)
27 SHAEF Report, *Château d'Audrieu*, part 2, p. 9
28 SHAEF Report, *12 SS*, part 4, p. 21
29 Record of the evidence of Monique Level, 12 July 1944, SHAEF Report, *Château d'Audrieu*, part 3, exhibit no. 12, p. 4

## 9: The Mohnke Murders

1 Personal information can be found on thirty-five of the forty prisoners. See PRU, files 06-10340 (William Stewart Ferguson), 41-72960 (James Allen Reid), 03-96484 (George Andrew Brown), 06-13313 (Roger Joseph Firman), 39-49743 (Clare Davidson Kines), 39-60907 (James Ferris Kyle), 42-17350 (Robert Scott), 04-46074 (Stewart Culleton), 39-00635 (John William Hill), 04-78490 (Walter James Booth), 03-85937 (Ernest William Bradley), 05-53433 (Walter Daniels), 06-12524 (Robert Munro Findlay), 06-27336 (Lant Freeman), 06-70915 (Lawrence Roderick Guiboche), 39-10531 (Charles Allan Horton), 39-36421 (Henry Charles Jones), 39-91114 (Elmer Joseph Lefort), 40-00080 (Gordon James Lewis), 40-42884 (Angus Murdo MacLeod), 40-64639 (Frederick Marych), 40-93928 (Wesley Kenneth Morrison), 41-28851 (Percy Parisian), 41-42837 (Alfred Martin Peterson), 42-02048 (Frank Ryckman), 42-28907 (Kjartan Sigurdson), 42-37716 (Edward Smith), 42-77067 (John Allen Thompson), 42-41067 (Richard George Smith), 04-40918 (Reginald Donald Barker), 04-60020 (William Beresford), 04-67578 (Hilliard John Henry Birston), 06-62111 (Thomas John Douglas Grant), 06-83039 (Alvin John James Harkness), and 04-06032 (Donald James Burnett).
2 Thus, I am disagreeing with the chronology postulated in Ian Sayer and Douglas Botting, *Hitler's Last General: The Case against Wilhelm Mohnke* (London and New York, 1989), 231–2. In their otherwise excellent analysis of the events of 8 June, Sayer and Botting contend that Mohnke called Siebken to complain about having received a shipment of forty prisoners. This ignores the evidence, adduced in chapter 7, that more than a hundred Canadian prisoners had arrived at Mohnke's HQ earlier in the afternoon.
3 Record of the evidence of Bernard [*sic*] Siebken, 15/16 March and 20 March 1946, pp. 27 and 7–8, MA, Macdonald Papers, War Crimes box 5, file I-2/17. Siebken's claim that he had disputed Mohnke's order was confirmed by the man who was in charge of the telephone exchange in the sector of the 26th Panzer Grenadier Regiment and who had overheard their conversation. See the testimony of the witness Steinmann, cited in Sayer and Botting, *Hitler's Last General*, 206.
4 Sergeant William Beresford of the 3rd Canadian Anti-Tank Regiment and Corporal James Kyle of the Royal Winnipeg Rifles, both of whom had sustained serious leg

wounds in battle, had to be carried to Mohnke's headquarters on stretchers. See the statement given by W.R. Glasspoole, 23 April 1945; the interrogation of S.W. Lawrence, 28 May 1945, PRU, file 06-83039 (Alvin John Harkness), pp. 12, 23; and the statement given by Rifleman James Ferris, 15 June 1945, *Report of the No. 1 Canadian War Crimes Investigation Unit regarding the Shooting of Canadian Prisoners of War by the German Armed Forces near Fontenay-le-Pesnel on 8 June 1944*, exhibit no. 7, p. 4, NA, RG 25, F-3, vol. 2609, #171 in box.

5  Deposition of Dietrich Schnabel, 18 June 1948, quoted in Sayer and Botting, *Hitler's Last General*, 187–8

6  UNWCC Charge Sheet against Wilhelm Mohnke, undated, NA, RG 24, vol. 12837, file 67/Canadian National Office/1 (392/4), p. 3, and CWCIU Report, *Fontenay-le-Pesnel*, statement of facts, p. 1

7  Statement given by Hector Clement McLean, 16 June 1945, NA, RG 24, vol. 12837, file 67/Atrocity Statements/1 (391/32), p. 3; statement given by John MacDougall, 18 June 1945, ibid., file 67/Canada/1 (391/50), p. 43; and statement given by Gunner W.F. Clark, undated, CWCIU Report, *Fontenay-le-Pesnel*, exhibit no. 4, p. 1

8  Record of the evidence of Private G.J. Ferris, 15 June 1945; statement given by Gunner W.F. Clark, 16 June 1945; and statement given by Corporal H.C. McLean, 15 June 1945, CWCIU Report, *Fontenay-le-Pesnel*, exhibit no. 7, p. 18; exhibit no. 5, p. 7; and exhibit no. 2, p. 9

9  Ibid., statement of facts, pp. 1–2

10  Record of the evidence of Ferris, 15 June 1945, ibid., exhibit no. 7, p. 18

11  Once safely in German POW custody, McLean recounted to two of his fellow prisoners what Barker had told him. See the record of the evidence of Clark, 16 June 1945, ibid., exhibit no. 5, p. 12, and the interrogation of S.W. Lawrence, 28 May 1945, PRU, file 04-60020 (William Beresford), p. 38.

12  CWCIU Report, *Fontenay-le-Pesnel*, statement of facts, p. 2

13  UNWCC Charge Sheet against Wilhelm Mohnke, undated, NA, RG 24, vol. 12837, file 67/Canadian National Office/1 (392/4), p. 3

14  CWCIU Report, *Fontenay-le-Pesnel*, statement of facts, p. 2

15  Statement given by McLean, 15 June 1945, ibid., exhibit no. 2, p. 9

16  Statement given by McLean, 16 June 1945, NA, RG 24, file 67/Atrocity Statements/1 (391/32), p. 3, and CWCIU Report, *Fontenay-le-Pesnel*, statement of facts, p. 2

17  Barker's last words were quoted in the record of the evidence of H.C. McLean, 15 June 1945, CWCIU Report, *Fontenay-le-Pesnel*, exhibit no. 2, p. 10.

18  Private Ferris related the taunt to fellow Royal Winnipeg Rifleman Private David Pattison during their POW captivity. See the statement given by Private David C. Pattison, 12 September 1944, NA, RG 24, vol. 12842, file 67/Treatment/1/2 (393/56), p. 184.

19  The various escapes are described in the statement given by Gunner W.F. Clark,

14 June 1945, PRU, file 04-67578 (Hilliard John Henry Birston), p. 36; the statement given by Gunner W.F. Clark, undated, CWCIU Report, *Fontenay-le-Pesnel*, exhibit no. 4, p. 2; *Supplementary Report of the SHAEF Court of Inquiry re Shooting of Allied Prisoners of War by 12 SS Panzer Division (Hitler-Jugend) in Normandy, France, 7–21 June 1944*, part 5, p. 30, NA, RG 24, vol. 10427, file 205S1.023 (D 9); and the statement given by MacDougall, 18 June 1945, NA, RG 24, vol. 12837, file 67/Canada/1 (391/50), p. 43.

20 Statement given by Arthur Desjarlais, 16 June 1945, NA, RG 24, vol. 12837, file 67/Canada/1 (390/50), p. 51

21 Interestingly, two other Canadian prisoners, Lieutenant D.A. James and Private W.R. Lebar, both of the Royal Winnipeg Rifles, appear to have witnessed the massacre from a distance. Both were in the custody of other German units that happened to be passing through the area when the killings took place. See SHAEF Report, *12 SS*, part 5, p. 29, and the statement given by Lieutenant D.A. James, 15 August 1944, PRU, file 41-72960 (James Allen Reid), p. 11.

22 On the investigative dead end reached in the case of the Fontenay-le-Pesnel massacre, see *Report of the No. 1 Canadian War Crimes Investigation Unit on Miscellaneous War Crimes against Members of the Canadian Armed Forces in the European Theatre of Operations, 9 September 1939 to 8 May 1945*, part II, p. 9, NA, RG 25, vol. 1001 (F-3), numbered 174 in the box, and B.J.S. Macdonald, *The Trial of Kurt Meyer* (Toronto, 1954), 22.

23 Lieutenant Colonel Bruce Macdonald, Canada's chief war crimes prosecutor at the end of the Second World War, first linked the two massacres in his 1954 book on the Kurt Meyer trial. See Macdonald, *Trial*, p. 22. The Malmedy theme was picked up by authors Ian Sayer and Douglas Botting in their book on Wilhelm Mohnke. See Sayer and Botting, *Hitler's Last General*, 164–5.

24 Though he did not see the officer's face clearly, McLean described him as 5'8" and about forty years of age, wearing a grey topcoat adorned on the shoulders with gold braid. See the statement given by McLean, 15 June 1945, CWCIU Report, *Fontenay-le-Pesnel*, exhibit no. 2, p. 8. McLean's estimate of the officer's height is a bit lower than Mohnke's actual height (see the file on Wilhelm Mohnke, NARA, RG 242 BDC A 3433, SS Officer Dossier, roll 323A, frame 76), but several wartime photographs do show Mohnke wearing the kind of coat described by the Winnipegs' corporal. Incidentally, Gunner Clark of the 3rd Anti-Tank Regiment corroborated the presence of gold braid on the shoulders of the officer's coat. See the statement given by Clark, 31 July 1945, CWCIU Report, *Fontenay-le-Pesnel*, exhibit no. 6, p. 11. As for the disparity between Mohnke's real age at the time (thirty-three) and McLean's estimate, two points ought to be noted. First, Mohnke's receding hairline and his generally harsh and austere appearance made him look older than he really was. Secondly, two members of the headquarters company of Mohnke's regiment who were in fre-

quent contact with him during the fighting in Normandy also described their commander as having been an older-looking man. See the record of the evidence of SS Private Withold Stangenberg, 28 June 1945, p. 12, DHist, file 1325-1, and the record of the evidence of SS Private Heinz Schmidt, 23 October 1945, *Report of the No. 1 Canadian War Crimes Investigation Unit regarding the Shooting of Canadian Prisoners of War by German Armed Forces at Haut du Bosq on 11 June 1944*, exhibit no. 8, p. 18, NA, RG 25, vol. 2609, #172 in box.

25  This version of the events surrounding the incident is recounted in both Hubert Meyer, *Kriegsgeschichte der 12.SS-Panzerdivision 'Hitlerjugend'* (Osnabrück, 1982), 1:96–7, and Kurt Meyer, *Grenadiere* (Munich, 1957), 230.

26  According to Helmut Ritgen's *Die Geschichte der Panzer-Lehr-Division im Westen, 1944–1945* (Stuttgart, 1979), 109, Major Zeissler, at least, survived his encounter with the Inns of Court Regiment, for he was mentioned in dispatches several months after his alleged murder.

27  Deposition of Dietrich Schnabel, 21 July 1948, quoted in Sayer and Botting, *Hitler's Last General*, 189

28  Ibid., 205

29  The discovery of the three men is recounted in ibid., 196–7. The battle injuries of the three men were described by the pathologist who examined their bodies in *Report of the Supreme Headquarters Allied Expeditionary Force Court of Inquiry re Shooting of Allied Prisoners of War by the German Armed Forces in the Vicinity of Le Mesnil-Patry, Les Saullets and Authie, Calvados, Normandy, 7–11 June 1944*, part 2, pp. 5–6, DHist, vol. 90/168.

30  SHAEF Report, *Authie*, part 2, p. 6. For biographical information on the three men, see PRU, files 04-23376 (Harold Sendford Angel), 39-07452 (Frederick William George Holness), and 04-44672 (Ernest Charles Baskerville).

31  See the report on Private H.S. Angel, 22 June 1944, PRU, file 04-23376 (Harold Sendford Angel), no page number.

32  Testimony of Michael Wimplinger, quoted in Sayer and Botting, *Hitler's Last General*, 197

33  Testimony of Bernhard Siebken, cited in ibid., 205

34  Testimonies of Klöden and Siebken, cited in ibid., 205–6

35  Testimony of Hubert Meyer, quoted in ibid., 206

36  Ibid., 206–7

37  Testimonies of Henne, Siebken, and Klöden, cited in ibid., 208

38  Ibid.

39  Testimonies of Michael Wimplinger and Mme St Martin, quoted in ibid., 197–8

40  Affidavit of Dietrich Schnabel, 9 November 1948, quoted in ibid., 214

41  Testimony of Michael Wimplinger, quoted in ibid., 199

42  Macdonald, *Trial*, 23, and testimonies of St Martin and Fritz Bundschuh, quoted in

Sayer and Botting, *Hitler's Last General*, 200–1

43  For example, see Meyer, *Kriegsgeschichte*, 97.

44  A description of the headquarters area can be found in the record of the evidence of Captain Isaac Tucker Burr, 15 August 1945, CWCIU Report, *Haut du Bosq*, exhibit no. 6, pp. 2–3.

45  Record of the evidence of Heinz Schmidt, 23 October 1945, ibid., exhibit no. 8, p. 7

46  Records of the evidence of Withold Stangenberg and Heinz Schmidt, 28 June 1945 and 23 October 1945, ibid., exhibit no. 4, p. 9 and exhibit no. 8, pp. 9–10

47  Ibid.

48  Report on the interrogation of Stangenberg, 10 July 1944, ibid., exhibit no. 1, p. 1

49  Records of the evidence of Schmidt and Stangenberg, 23 October 1945 and 9 August 1945, ibid., exhibit no. 8, p. 10 and exhibit no. 5, p. 11. See also the UNWCC Charge Sheet against Wilhelm Mohnke, undated, NA, RG 24, vol. 12837, file 67/Canadian National Office/1, 392/4, p. 9

50  The proceedings were witnessed by two troopers attached to the headquarters of the 26th Panzer Grenadier Regiment. See the records of the evidence of Schmidt and Stangenberg, 23 October 1945 and 9 August 1945, CWCIU Report, *Haut du Bosq*, exhibit no. 8, pp. 11–13, and exhibit no. 5, pp. 12–15.

## 10: The Murders at Bretteville and Norrey

1  Messages received regarding operations along the invasion front (High Command of the German 7th Army), 8 June 1944 (1740 hrs), NARA, RG 242, T-312, roll 1568, frame 955

2  On preparations for the attack, see the testimonies of SS Private Jan Jesionek and SS Brigadier General Kurt Meyer, Meyer Trial, 340 and 594, DHist, vol. 159.95023 (D 7). See also Hubert Meyer, *Kriegsgeschichte der 12.SS-Panzerdivision 'Hitlerjugend'* (Osnabrück, 1982), 1:100, and Kurt Meyer, *Grenadiere* (Munich, 1957), 223–4.

3  The advance on Rots and the crossing of the Mue are described in Meyer, *Grenadiere*, 224, and Meyer, *Kriegsgeschichte*, 100.

4  Testimony of Meyer, Meyer Trial, 594

5  Battle log, 8 June 1944, entry for 2156 hrs, in the war diary (Headquarters of the 7th Canadian Infantry Brigade), NA, reel T-12015, frame 33

6  On these last-minute deployments, see the deposition of Sergeant Edward A. Smith, 21 November 1945, NA, RG 24, vol. 12840, file 67/Kurt Meyer/5 (392/55), p. 60, and appendix 6 to the war diary (Cameron Highlanders of Ottawa, A Company), entry for 9 June 1944, p. 2, ibid., vol. 15026, file June 1944.

7  On the initial skirmish, see the testimony of Meyer, Meyer Trial, 594–5, and Meyer, *Grenadiere*, 227–8.

8  The Reginas reported that tanks had broken into Bretteville at 10:30 PM. See the war diary (Regina Rifles), entry for 8 June 1944 (2230 hrs), and the account by Lieutenant Colonel F.M. Matheson, 24 June 1944, p. 3, NA, RG 24, vol. 15198, file June 1944. On the escape of members of the forward section of the support company's carrier platoon, see the depositions of Smith, 21 November 1945, and Private James P. Boyer, 14 December 1945, ibid., vol. 12840, file 67/Kurt Meyer/5 (392/55), pp. 53 and 60.

9  The battle is described in stirring detail in the war diary (Regina Rifles), entry for 9 June 1944 (0030, 0200, 0315, 0423, 0445, and 0745 hrs), ibid., vol. 15198, file June 1944; the account by Matheson, 24 June 1944, p. 3, ibid.; and appendix 6 to the war diary (Cameron Highlanders of Ottawa, A Company), entry for 9 June 1944, p. 2, ibid., vol. 15026, file June 1944. See also the war diary (Headquarters of the 3rd Canadian Infantry Division), entry for 9 June 1944 (0800 hrs), p. 3, ibid., vol. 13766, folder 17, file June 1944; the war diary (Headquarters of the 7th Canadian Infantry Brigade), entry for 8 June 1944, NA, reel T-12014, frame 1548; and the battle log, 8 June 1944, entry for 2335 hrs, in the war diary (Headquarters of the 7th Canadian Infantry Brigade), NA, reel T-12015, frame 34.

10  War diary (Headquarters of the 3rd Canadian Infantry Division), entry for 9 June 1944, p. 3, NA, RG 24, vol. 13766, folder 17, file June 1944

11  Depositions of Smith, 21 November 1945, and Boyer, 14 December 1945, ibid., vol. 12840, file 67/Kurt Meyer/5 (392/55), pp. 59 and 52. Biographical information on the four men can be found in PRU, files 40-84714 (David Thomas Moloney), 04-79191 (Cecil Murray Borne), 40-91327 (Norman Joseph Morin), and 42-11134 (John Sawatzky).

12  Deposition of Boyer, 14 December 1945, NA, RG 24, vol. 12840, file 67/Kurt Meyer/5 (392/55), p. 52. Biographical information on the two men can be found in PRU, files 04-50979 (Charles Wesley Bebee) and 06-72398 (Robert Joseph Gurney).

13  Depositions of Boyer, 14 December 1945, and Smith, 21 November 1945, NA, RG 24, vol. 12840, file 67/Kurt Meyer/5 (392/55), pp. 51–2 and 58–9. Biographical information on Vickery and Povol can be found in PRU, files 42-99526 (Nelson Joseph Vickery) and 41-56488 (Ervin Povol). No military personnel file for Private Anderson was retrieved.

14  Jesionek was wounded during the attack. See the testimony of Jesionek, Meyer Trial, 310.

15  In its final report, the No. 1 Canadian War Crimes Investigation Unit left open a case of five Regina Rifles who allegedly were murdered near the headquarters of Bernhard Siebken's 2nd Battalion, 26th Panzer Grenadier Regiment, on the morning of 9 June 1944 – that is, on the same morning as and in the same location where Angel, Holness, and Baskerville were shot. See *Report of the No. 1 Canadian War Crimes Investigation Unit on Miscellaneous War Crimes Against Members of the Canadian*

*Armed Forces in the European Theatre of Operations, 9 September 1939 to 8 May 1945*, part 2, p. 13, NA, RG 25, vol. 1001 (F-3), numbered 174 in the box. This crime has never been verified.

16 At 7:45 AM on 9 June, the Reginas reported that the Germans were withdrawing from Bretteville. See the war diary (Regina Rifles), entry for 9 June 1944 (0745 hrs), NA, RG 24, vol. 15198, file 1944. According to Meyer, his forces regrouped at Rots. See the testimony of Meyer, Meyer Trial, 595.

17 The historian of the 12th SS Division has speculated that the always aggressive Meyer revised his own battle plan. See Craig W.H. Luther, *Blood and Honor: The History of the 12th SS Panzer Division 'Hitler Youth,' 1943–1945* (San José, CA, 1987), 171. Though plausible, there is nothing in Meyer's postwar testimony or memoirs that supports such a conclusion. On the other hand, under questioning by Canadian investigators, Wünsche implied that he was the author of the revised plan. See CWCIU Report, *Miscellaneous War Crimes*, part 2, p. 5.

18 After the war, Meyer attributed the failure of the attack on Bretteville to the Canadians' firm hold on Norrey. See the testimony of Meyer, Meyer Trial, 595. See also Colonel C.P. Stacey, *The Victory Campaign: The Operations in North-West Europe, 1944–1945* (Ottawa, 1966), 3:137.

19 Meyer, *Kriegsgeschichte*, 101–2, 106–7

20 CWCIU Report, *Miscellaneous War Crimes*, part 2, p. 5

21 On the battle for Norrey and the decimation of German armour there, see the war diary (Headquarters of the 7th Canadian Infantry Brigade), entry for 9 June 1944, NA, reel T-12014, frame 1548, and the battle log, 9 June 1944, entries for 1225, 1235, 1315, 1345, and 1411 hrs, in NA, reel T-12015, frames 41–5.

22 Wünsche's reaction is quoted in Meyer, *Kriegsgeschichte*, 107.

23 *Supplementary Report of the SHAEF Court of Inquiry re Shooting of Allied Prisoners of War by 12 SS Panzer Division (Hitler-Jugend) in Normandy, France, 7–21 June 1944*, part 5, p. 31, NA, RG 24, vol. 10427, file 205S1.023 (D 9). Biographical information on Gilbank can be found in PRU, file 06-46473 (Ernest Nelson Gilbank). Lee's personnel file was not retrieved.

24 Affidavit of Thomas Victor Wood, 24 November 1945, NA, RG 24, vol. 12840, file 67/Kurt Meyer/5 (392/55), p. 63

25 Luther, *Blood and Honor*, 175

26 Affidavit of Wood, 24 November 1945, NA, RG 24, vol. 12840, file 67/Kurt Meyer/5 (392/55), pp. 62–63

27 SHAEF Report, *12 SS*, part 5, p. 31

28 Ibid., and the affidavit of Wood, 24 November 1945, NA, RG 24, vol. 12840, file 67/Kurt Meyer/5 (392/55), pp. 61–2

29 SHAEF Report, *12 SS*, part 3, p. 14, and part 5, p. 31

30 CWCIU Report, *Miscellaneous War Crimes*, part 2, p. 5

31  Berlin had served in several of the notorious Death's Head formations before joining
the Leibstandarte in 1942. Ribbentrop also was a Leibstandarte veteran. See the files
on Anton Berlin and Rudolf von Ribbentrop, NARA, RG 242 BDC A 3433, SS
Officer Dossier, roll 61, frames 838–92, and roll 23B, frames 1050–78.

32  Luther, *Blood and Honor*, 172, and Meyer, *Kriegsgeschichte*, 106

## 11: The Murders at Le Mesnil-Patry

1  The British plan is outlined in Major L.F. Ellis, *Victory in the West*, vol. 1, *The Battle
of Normandy* (London, 1962), 247, 250, 252–3; Colonel C.P. Stacey, *The Victory
Campaign: The Operations in North-West Europe, 1944–1945* (Ottawa, 1966),
3:142; and the battle log, 11 June 1944, entry for 1200 hrs, appended to the war diary
(Headquarters of I [British] Corps), entry for 11 June 1944, NA, reel T-2451, sheet
22.

2  War diary (Headquarters of the 2nd Canadian Armoured Brigade), entry for 10 June
1944, and war diary (6th Canadian Armoured Regiment), entry for 10 June 1944,
NA, reel T-10651, frame 110, and reel T-12657, frame 135

3  The starting time for the attack is recorded in the war diary (6th Canadian Armoured
Regiment), entry for 10 June 1944, NA, reel T-12657, frame 136.

4  On the initial phase of the Canadian attack, see ibid.; the war diary (Queen's Own
Rifles of Canada), entry for 11 June 1944, NA, RG 24, vol. 15168, file June 1944;
the war diary (Headquarters of the 2nd Canadian Armoured Brigade), entry for 11
June 1944, NA, reel T-10651, frame 110; Hubert Meyer, *Kriegsgeschichte der 12.SS-
Panzerdivision 'Hitlerjugend'* (Osnabrück, 1982), 1:121; and the battle log, 11 June
1944, entry for 3:50 PM, in the war diary (Headquarters of the 7th Canadian Infantry
Brigade), NA, reel T-12015, frame 67. Captured German records credit SS First
Lieutenant Bruno Asmus, who only the day before had replaced (Wehrmacht) First
Lieutenant Otto Toll as commander of the engineering battalion's 1st Company, with
the early detection of the Canadian attack. See the notice issued by SS Major and
Battalion Commander Müller, 1 August 1944, NARA, RG 242, T-354, roll 154,
frame 3798049. For biographical information on Asmus, see his SS personnel file,
ibid., BDC A 3433, SS Officer Dossier, roll 18, 2 frames, not numbered (near end of
reel).

5  In fact, only one infantry party, consisting of Lieutenant H.G. Bean, Sergeant Sam
Scrutton, and seven other members of D Company of the Queen's Own Rifles, actually made it into Le Mesnil-Patry on 11 June. For their heroism, Lieutenant Bean and
Sergeant Scrutton were awarded the Military Cross and the Military Medal respectively. See the war diary (Queen's Own Rifles of Canada), 11 June 1944, NA, RG 24,
vol. 15168, file June 1944, and W.T. Barnard, *The Queen's Own Rifles of Canada,
1860–1960: One Hundred Years of Canada* (Don Mills, ON, 1960), 202.

6　War diary (Headquarters of the 2nd Canadian Armoured Brigade), entry for 11 June 1944, and war diary (6th Canadian Armoured Regiment), entry for 11 June 1944, NA, reel T-10651, frame 110, and reel T-12657, frames 136–7

7　In his book on the battle of Caen, Alexander McKee erroneously attributes the bombardment to the (British) 50th Division. See Alexander McKee, *Caen: Anvil of Victory* (London, 1964), 91.

8　Citing the proximity to the front of Prinz's armour, Canadian sources have suggested that the attack on Le Mesnil-Patry may have broken up a major attack by the 12th SS. See the war diary (6th Canadian Armoured Regiment), entry for 11 June 1944, NA, reel T-12657, frame 138. See also Barnard, *Queen's Own*, 203, and the reminiscences of Sergeant Leo Gariepy of the 1st Hussars B Squadron, cited in McKee, *Caen*, 91. Yet captured German records give no indication that the Hitler Youth Division was preparing for an attack on 11 June. On the contrary, the evidence seems to point in the other direction – the Germans had been caught by surprise, and improvised a successful defence and counterattack. For example, see the enclosure to the war diary (High Command of the 7th German Army), entries for 10–11 June 1944, NARA, RG 242, T-312, roll 1565, frames 925, 954, 957. See also recommendations' list no. 1 for the award of the Knight's Cross of the Iron Cross, 20 June 1944, file on Karl-Heinz Prinz, ibid., BDC A 3433, SS Officer Dossier, roll 394A, frame 361, and recommendation no. 1 for the award of the Knight's Cross of the Iron Cross, 21 June 1944, file on Wilhelm Mohnke, ibid., roll 323A, frame 153. As a matter of overall Normandy strategy, on 11 June Field Marshal Rommel ordered the battered German armoured formations to be pulled back and redeployed as mobile reserves. Their place in the line was to be taken by fresh infantry divisions. See the estimate of the situation on 11 June 1944 prepared by Field Marshal Erwin Rommel, 12 June 1944, NA, RG 24, vol. 20433, file 981.013 (D 46), p. 15. This was hardly indicative of any burning desire on the part of the Germans to undertake offensive operations.

9　This was the conclusion drawn by 2nd Canadian Armoured Brigade commander Brigadier R.A. Wyman, who lamented the shortage of Shermans refitted with seventeen-pound guns. See the war diary (Headquarters of the 2nd Canadian Armoured Brigade), entry for 12 June 1944, NA, reel T-10651, frame 111.

10　On the number of Canadian tanks destroyed on 11 June, see recommendation no. 1 for the award of the Knight's Cross of the Iron Cross, 21 June 1944, file on Wilhelm Mohnke, NARA, RG 242, BDC A 3433, SS Officer Dossier, roll 323A, frame 153; Craig W.H. Luther, *Blood and Honor: The History of the 12th SS Panzer Division 'Hitler Youth,' 1943–1945* (San José, CA, 1987), 201n. 23; and the war diary (Headquarters of the 2nd Canadian Armoured Brigade), entry for 11 June 1944, NA, reel T-10651, frames 110–111.

11　These casualty figures are cited in Stacey, *Victory Campaign*, 140, and Barnard, *Queen's Own*, 202.

12  The division reported 150 casualties in the fighting on 11 June. See Meyer, *Kriegsge-schichte*, 123. In terms of armour, German sources claim that Prinz's battalion lost only four tanks, while Canadian sources put the figure at a more impressive fourteen. For the German view, see ibid. For Canadian estimates, see the war diary (6th Canadian Armoured Regiment), entry for 11 June 1944, NA, reel T-12657, frame 137, and the battle log, 11 June 1944, entry for 2030 hrs, in the war diary (Headquarters of the 7th Canadian Infantry Brigade), NA, reel T-12015, frame 70.

13  Wartime critics included the British newspaper that labelled the attack 'a modern version of the Charge of the Light Brigade.' One of the participants was more biting, describing the operational plan as having been 'conceived in sin and born in iniquity.' Quoted in Barnard, *Queen's Own*, 202–3. Postwar critics of the attack have been less lyrical, but no less cutting. The military historian John English described the attack as a 'disgraceful affair' and took to task Brigadier R.A. Wyman, the commander of the 2nd Canadian Armoured Brigade, for having sent the Canadian task force out with the infantry riding on tanks. See John A. English, *The Canadian Army and the Normandy Campaign: A Study of Failure in High Command* (New York and London, 1991), 214. Historians Terry Copp and Robert Vogel made similar accusations, claiming that Wyman 'was breaking every rule of ... battle doctrine' by having sent out a vanguard of infantry riding on tanks. See Terry Copp and Robert Vogel, *Maple Leaf Route: Caen* (Alma, ON, 1983), 84. By contrast, the official Canadian and British military histories, noting that the time of the attack had been moved up unexpectedly, have attributed its failure to the lack of adequate preparation. See Stacey, *Victory Campaign*, 139, and Ellis, *Victory*, 253.

14  More than any other factor, the debacle at Le Mesnil-Patry was caused by the delay by (British) 2nd Army in informing Canadian forces that the time of the attack had been advanced. Initially scheduled for 12 June, the attack was moved up a day in order to better coordinate it with British operations. Inexplicably, it was not until 7:30 on the morning of 11 June, more than fourteen hours after the decision had been made, that the 2nd Canadian Armoured Brigade learned of the change in plan. Indeed, as late as 4:00 AM on the day before the attack, Wyman's squadron commanders were told that they had twenty-four hours to prepare. By the time that Wyman held his 'orders group' (10:30–11:00 AM) on 11 June, it was too late to adequately brief them. Accordingly, there was insufficient time to prepare artillery support or to carry out reconnaissance. Nonetheless, had Wyman reviewed divisional intelligence reports, he would have learned that French civilians had been observing the concentration of Müller's engineers and Prinz's tanks just south of Le Mesnil-Patry. On the change in plan, the failure to inform the Canadians, and the inadequate preparation that resulted, see Stacey, Victory Campaign, 139; the war diary (Headquarters of the 2nd Canadian Armoured Brigade), entry for 11 June 1944, NA, reel T-10651, frame 110; the war diary (6th Canadian Armoured Regiment), entry for

11 June 1944, NA, reel T-12657, frame 136; and intelligence summary no. 4, 11 June 1944, in the war diary (Headquarters of the 3rd Canadian Infantry Division), NA, RG 24, vol. 13766, folder 17, file June 1944, appendix no. 1, p. 65. During the attack itself, Canadian forces committed a major blunder by sending out a vanguard of infantry riding on tanks. In the level grainfields south of Norrey, these advance elements made excellent targets, and probably accounted for the inordinately high number of casualties suffered by D Company of the Queen's Own Rifles. Another costly error was made when brigade headquarters mistakenly informed Lieutenant Colonel Colwell that the tanks firing on him were not German, but British. Finally, B Squadron might not have been so thoroughly decimated had it not been for Sergeant Leo Gariepy, who, while riding in the lead Sherman, had turned off his wireless set so as to spare himself the endless radio chatter, and thus did not hear Colwell's order to withdraw. On these and other battlefield errors, see English, *Canadian Army*, 214; McKee, *Caen*, 90; and Barnard, *Queen's Own*, 202.

15　War diary (6th Canadian Armoured Regiment), entry for 11 June 1944, NA, reel T-12657, frame 138. Simmons's confrontation with the Panther was not the first time that he distinguished himself by his heroism on 11 June. Only minutes earlier, after his tank had first been hit, Simmons had ordered his crew to bail out, then had extinguished the fire. See the statement given by Major J.W. Rowell, undated, and E.S. Payne to Captain A. Gordon, 26 April 1945, PRU, file 42-30392 (William Ernest Simmons), pp. 26 and 30.

16　British War Crimes Investigative Unit (Canadian Team) to Canadian Military Headquarters in London, 9 January 1947, NA, RG 24, vol. 12843, file 67/War Crimes IU/ 1 (393/67), p. 131. Biographical information on Simmons can be found in PRU, file 42-30392 (William Ernest Simmons).

17　The killing of Preston and the wounding of Payne is recounted in *Report of the Supreme Headquarters Allied Expeditionary Force Court of Inquiry re Shooting of Allied Prisoners of War by the German Armed Forces in the Vicinity of Le Mesnil-Patry, Les Saullets and Authie, Calvados, Normandy, 7–11 June 1944*, part 2, p. 9, DHist, vol. 90/168, and *Report of the No. 1 Canadian War Crimes Investigation Unit on Miscellaneous War Crimes against Members of the Canadian Armed Forces in the European Theatre of Operations, 9 September 1939 to 8 May 1945*, part 2, p. 15, NA, RG 25, vol. 1001 (F-3), numbered 174 in the box. Biographical information on Preston can be found in PRU, file 41-58504 (Lee Irwin Preston). The military personnel files of Payne and McClean were not retrieved.

18　Account of personal experiences in action on 11 June 1944 by Trooper A.O. Dodds, undated, NA, reel T-12657, frame 170

19　Ibid.

20　The circumstances surrounding the murder of Smuck, Charron, Hancock, and Leclaire are recounted in CWCIU Report, *Miscellaneous War Crimes*, part 2, p. 16, and B.J.S. Macdonald, *The Trial of Kurt Meyer* (Toronto, 1954), 27. Biographical information on the four victims can be found in PRU, files 42-42661 (Harry Lee Smuck), 05-09065 (Albert Alexander Charron), 06-79658 (Arthur Richard Hugh Hancock), and 39-88177 (Joseph André Marcel Leclaire).

21 Eyewitnesses to the capture and murder of Silverberg and Loucks were themselves taken prisoner in the area and brought to the headquarters of the engineering battalion. There they were interrogated by an officer fitting the description of SS Major Siegfried Müller, the battalion commander. See the deposition of Anthony J. Hundt, 3 December 1945, and the statutory declaration of Robert B. Munro, 14 November 1945, NA, RG 24, vol. 12837, file 67/Atrocity Statements/1 (391/32), pp. 44–6 and 47.

22 Ibid., p. 48, and account of personal experiences in action on 11 June 1944 by Trooper A.O. Dodds, undated, NA, reel T-12657, frame 170. Biographical information on Loucks and Silverberg can be found in PRU, files 40-08235 (William David Clinton Loucks) and 42-29257 (Frank Silverberg).

23 The capture of Cybulsky's tank crew and the murder of Dumont and Sutton are described in the statements given by Leslie W. Soroke, 19 December 1945, and by Corporal James J. Floyd, 5 December 1945, NA, RG 24, vol. 12840, file 67/Kurt Meyer/5 (392/55), pp. 38–9 and 30. Biographical information on the murdered men can be found in PRU, files 05-88618 (John Donald Dumont) and 42-62959 (Lawrence Francis Sutton). The personnel files of Cybulsky and Soroke were not retrieved.

24 The circumstances surrounding the murders of Bowes, Scriven, and Forbes are outlined in SHAEF Report, *Authie*, part 2, pp. 2, 6–7; *Supplementary Report of the SHAEF Court of Inquiry re Shooting of Allied Prisoners of War by 12 SS Panzer Division (Hitler-Jugend) in Normandy, France, 7–21 June 1944*, part 3, p. 14 and part 4, pp. 24–5, NA, RG 24, vol. 10427, file 205S1.023 (D 9); CWCIU Report, *Miscellaneous War Crimes*, part 2, p. 12; and Macdonald, *Trial*, 25–6. Biographical information on the murdered men can be found in PRU, files 04-86152 (Arnold David Bowes), 42-17996 (Gilbert Harold Scriven), and 06-18587 (J. Forbes). The personnel file of Trooper K.O. Pedlar was not retrieved.

25 UNWCC Charge Sheet against Wilhelm Mohnke, undated, NA, RG 24, vol. 12837, file 67/Canadian National Office/1, 392/4, p. 6

**12: An End to the Killing?**

1 As of mid-June, the Americans were hung up north of St Lo, while the British and Canadians were bogged down to the north and west of Caen. Hitler seized the opportunity afforded by the stalemate to split the Allied front in the centre. On 20 June, the Führer ordered the dispatch of the 1st, 9th, and 10th SS Panzer Divisions to the St Lo–Caumont sector. There they were to join with the 2nd Panzer and Panzer Lehr

Divisions in a major armoured offensive scheduled for early July. See *Kriegstage-buch des Oberkommandos der Wehrmacht (Wehrmachtsführungsstab)*, ed. Percy Ernst Schramm, vol. IV/7, 317–8. Alerted to these new developments, General Montgomery saw the pending enemy offensive as the opportunity to draw German mobile reserves toward Caen and away from the American front, thereby facilitating the capture of the port of Cherbourg by the U.S. 1st Army. Accordingly, on 18 June he issued orders to (British) 2nd Army for the conduct of operations aimed at increasing the pressure on the flanks of Caen. These were to culminate in Operation Epsom, whose objective was the envelopment of the city from the west. See Chester Wilmot, *The Struggle for Europe* (London, 1952), 320, and Colonel C.P. Stacey, *The Victory Campaign: The Operations in North-West Europe, 1944–1945* (Ottawa, 1966) 3:145.

2 War diary (Headquarters of the 3rd Canadian Infantry Division), entry for 14 June 1944, NA, RG 24, vol. 13766, folder 17, file June 1944, p. 5

3 See B.J.S. Macdonald, *The Trial of Kurt Meyer* (Toronto, 1954), 16–17, and Craig W.H. Luther, *Blood and Honor: The History of the 12th SS Panzer Division 'Hitler Youth,' 1943–1945* (San José, CA, 1987), 183n. 4.

4 Patrol programme, 16 June 1944, and patrol report, 17 June 1944, in the war diary (Stormont, Dundas and Glengarry Highlanders), NA, RG 24, vol. 15270, file June 1944, appendix 3. Though only twenty-two years old, Williams was described by his superiors as having been of 'excellent character' and possessed of the 'energy and imagination' and leadership abilities required to be an officer. See PRU, file 43-25536 (Fred Williams).

5 On the patrol's miscue, see the patrol programme, 16 June 1944, and the patrol report, 17 June 1944, in the war diary (Stormont, Dundas and Glengarry Highlanders), NA, RG 24, vol. 15270, file June 1944, appendix 3. See also the testimony of SS Second Lieutenant Kurt Bergmann, Meyer Trial, 486, 488, DHist, vol. 159.95023 (D 7).

6 Patrol report, 17 June 1944, in the war diary (Stormont, Dundas and Glengarry Highlanders), NA, RG 24, vol. 15270, file June 1944, appendix 3; war diary (Stormont, Dundas and Glengarry Highlanders), entry for 17 June 1944 (0220 hrs), ibid.; Major F.W. Lander to Mr Pollard, 25 June 1944, and statement given by Private W.M. Wood, 17 June 1944, PRU, file 41-52763 (George Gerald Pollard)

7 War diary (Stormont, Dundas and Glengarry Highlanders), entry for 17 June 1944 (0330 and 0425 hrs), NA, RG 24, vol. 15270, file June 1944; statement given by Private J.L. Labonte, undated, Meyer Trial, exhibit no. T-63; statement given by Private J.L. Klentz, 17 June 1944; statement given by Wood, 17 June 1944; and statement given by Private J.L. Labonte, 10 April 1945, PRU, file 41-52763 (George Gerald Pollard)

8 War diary (Stormont, Dundas and Glengarry Highlanders), entry for 17 June (0740

and 1200 hrs), NA, RG 24, vol. 15270, file June 1944, and Lander to Pollard, 25 June 1944, PRU, file 41-52763 (George Gerald Pollard)

9 See the telegrams in PRU, files 41-52763 (George Gerald Pollard) and 43-25536 (Fred Williams).

10 On the capture of the abbey and the discovery of Lieutenant Williams's body, see Stacey, *Victory Campaign*, 161; *Report of the No. 1 Canadian War Crimes Investigation Unit on Miscellaneous War Crimes against Members of the Canadian Armed Forces in the European Theatre of Operations, 9 September 1939 to 8 May 1945*, p. 2, NA, RG 25, vol. 1001 (F-3), numbered 174 in the box; and the testimony of Captain M. Bluteau, Meyer Trial, 479.

11 See the testimonies of SS Second Lieutenant Kurt Bergmann, SS (Feldgendarmerie) Corporal Ewald Wetzel, and SS Private Hermann Sue, Meyer Trial, 487, 500, and 491–3. See also CWCIU Report, *Miscellaneous War Crimes*, p. 2.

12 Testimony of Bergmann, Meyer Trial, 486–7

13 On the personnel changes and their timing, see the testimonies of SS First Lieutenant Bernhard Meitzel and Bergmann, ibid., 467 and 481–2. See also CWCIU Report, *Miscellaneous War Crimes*, p. 2.

14 *Supplementary Report of the SHAEF Court of Inquiry re Shooting of Allied Prisoners of War by 12 SS Panzer Division (Hitler-Jugend) in Normandy, France, 7–21 June 1944*, part 4, p. 26, NA, RG 24, vol. 10427, file 205S1.023 (D 9). For biographical information on the seven men, see PRU, files 41-41443 (Clayton George Perry), 40-40435 (Thomas Charles McLaughlin), 05-29368 (Etsel John Cook), 04-93390 (John Ramage Campbell), 43-24890 (Gerald Leslie Willett), 05-4084 (Ernest William Cranfield), and 04-03718 (Paul Bullock).

15 McLaughlin and his men had gone missing on 11 June, during the Le Mesnil-Patry operation. See the war diary (Queen's Own Rifles of Canada), entry for 11 June 1944 (1300 hrs), NA, RG 24, vol. 15168, file June 1944. Perry, a tankman who had also gone missing on 11 June, had somehow hooked up with them. See the telegram, 19 June 1944, PRU, file 41-41443 (Clayton George Perry).

16 *Supplementary Report of No. 1 Canadian War Crimes Investigation Unit Re Shooting of Canadian Prisoners of War by the German Armed Forces at Mouen, Normandy, France, 17 June 1944*, statement of facts by SHAEF, pp. 1–2, NA, RG 25, F-3, vol. 2609, #173 in box, and CWCIU Report, *Miscellaneous War Crimes*, p. 17. The official version of the Mouen killings is contradicted by the recollections of Charles Martin, a former member of the Queen's Own Rifles of Canada. According to Martin, while on patrol on 12 June he discovered the bodies of McLaughlin and his men in Le Mesnil-Patry. All had been shot in the head. See Charles C. Martin, *Battle Diary: From D-Day and Normandy to the Zuider Zee and VE* (Toronto and Oxford, 1994), 22–3. If Martin is correct, then the German witnesses must have been mixed up as to the dates.

17 CWCIU Report, *Mouen*, additional evidence, p. 1. Bischoff's Waffen-SS career path certainly rendered him a possible suspect. Prior to joining the 12th SS, Bischoff had participated in the murder of Nazi Stormtroopers by the SS in July 1934. He later spent six years as a member of one of the Death's Head battalions before being transferred into the Leibstandarte in March 1941. Unfortunately for Canadian war crimes investigators, Bischoff was killed in action on 3 September 1944. On his career, see the file on Herbert Bischoff, NARA, RG 242 BDC A 3433, SS Officer Dossier, roll 73, frames 344–5.

18 Müller had named Kuret his 'tactical second-in-command' just prior to the Normandy invasion. See order no. 47/44, 25 May 1944, NARA, RG 242, T-354, roll 153, frame 3796920. If Müller did not interrogate the prisoners, Kuret may have.

19 SHAEF Report, *12 SS*, part 4, p. 26

20 CWCIU Report, *Miscellaneous War Crimes*, p. 17

21 On the five days of Epsom, see the battle report, 26 June 1944, NARA, RG 242, T-354, reel 154, frames 3797709-14; Kurt Meyer, *Grenadiere* (Munich, 1957), 248; Major L.F. Ellis, *Victory in the West*, vol. 1, *The Battle of Normandy* (London, 1962), 280–4; and Hubert Meyer, *Kriegsgeschichte der 12.SS-Panzerdivision 'Hitlerjugend'* (Osnabrück, 1982), 1:216–27. The code name for the operation came from one of its planners, who was confident that British forces would go through the Germans 'like a dose of salts.' Lieutenant General Crocker, quoted in Tony Foster, *Meeting of Generals* (Toronto and New York, 1986), 330.

22 Stacey, *Victory Campaign*, 147

23 Most rank and file of the 12th SS wore camouflage jackets over their field grey uniforms. However, at least one battalion of Mohnke's regiment, the 3rd, was outfitted with complete camouflage uniforms. See Luther, *Blood and Honor*, 130n. 13.

24 Record of the evidence of Private Bogdan-Andricj Ziolek, 25 July 1945, NA, RG 24, vol. 12838, file 67/Falaise/1 (392/22), pp. 8–11

25 On the dead end reached by Canadian investigators, see Captain F.W. Kemp to the commander of the No. 1 Canadian War Crimes Investigation Unit, 28 August 1945; the memorandum to file by Lieutenant Colonel C.S. Campbell, 11 October 1945; and the status sheet on the 'Falaise Case,' undated, ibid., pp. 18, 20, 28.

26 Samuel W. Mitcham, *Hitler's Legions: The German Army Order of Battle in World War II* (London, 1985), 434, and Stacey, *Victory Campaign*, 160–1

27 Stacey, *Victory Campaign*, 158–61; Meyer, *Kriegsgeschichte*, 253; and Meyer, *Grenadiere*, 268–9

28 See the war diary (1st Battalion of the 25th Panzer Grenadier Regiment), entry for 10 June 1944, NARA, RG 242, T-354, roll 156, frame 3799979, and sketch 11 in Stacey, *Victory Campaign*, 159.

29 Woersdörfer's statement is summarized in CWCIU Report, *Miscellaneous War Crimes*, p. 7.

30 Five days after the alleged incident, forward elements of the Régiment de la Chaudière entered Cambes. Based on their account, it appears that the town was so full of unburied Allied and German dead that it would have been all but impossible to determine which of them, if any, had been the victims of a war crime. See the war diary (Régiment de la Chaudière), entry for 13 July 1944 (0600 hrs), NA, RG 24, vol. 15180, file July 1944, pp. 384–5.

31 Stacey, *Victory Campaign*, 140

32 The number was arrived at by subtracting the 340 fatal casualties suffered by Canadian forces on D-Day from the total number of fatal casualties – 1,017 – inflicted on them during the period 6–11 June.

33 This happened despite the best efforts of Canada's senior military commanders to prevent it. In a message to his troops, Lieutenant General H.D.G. Crerar, the commander of the 1st Canadian Army, admonished that 'the universal and natural determination of Canadian soldiers to avenge the death of our comrades must NOT under any circumstances take the form of retaliation in kind.' Instead, Crerar declared, 'Canadian anger must be converted into a steel-hard determination to destroy the enemy in battle, to hit harder, to advance faster and above all never to stop fighting and fighting hard, while life remains.' Quoted from Lieutenant General Crerar to all commanders and commanding officers, 1 August 1944, NA, MG 30 E 157 (Crerar Papers), file 6-3, p. 16.

34 War diary (Headquarters of the 7th Canadian Infantry Brigade), entry for 8 July 1944, NA, reel T-12015, frame 488

35 Memorandum by Brigadier Walford, 8 July 1944, NA, RG 24, vol. 10513, file 215A21.009 (D 125), p. 18

**13: Indictment**

1 Statement given by Monique Level, 3 July 1944, NA, RG 24, vol. 10513, file 215A21.009 (D 125), p. 5, and Craig W. H. Luther, *Blood and Honor: The History of the 12th SS Panzer Division 'Hitler Youth,' 1943–1945* (San José, CA, 1987), 162

2 Report from Captain J. Neil to the 231st Infantry Brigade, 14 June 1944, NA, RG 24, vol. 12842, file 67/Treatment/1 (393/53), p. 132

3 Bruce Tascona, *Little Black Devils: A History of the Royal Winnipeg Rifles* (Winnipeg, 1983), 153

4 Statement given by Beatrice Marie Delafon, 3 July 1944, NA, RG 24, vol. 10513, file 215A21.009 (D 125), pp. 8–9

5 Report from Captain J. Neil to the 231st Infantry Brigade, 14 June 1944, forwarded to the headquarters of 21st Army Group, 22 June 1944, ibid., vol. 12842, file 67/Treatment/1 (393/53), p. 132

6 *Report of the SHAEF Court of Inquiry regarding the Shooting of Prisoners of War by*

*German Armed Forces at Château d'Audrieu on 8 June 1944*, part 2, pp. 4, 8–10, NA, RG 24, vol. 10429, file 205S1.023 (D 18); Major D.F. Cameron to the AAG, 8 March 1945, ibid., vol. 12838, file 67/Galmanche/1 (392/3), containing SHAEF secret file on 'Cussy Case,' p. 3; and *Report of the Supreme Headquarters Allied Expeditionary Force Court of Inquiry re Shooting of Allied Prisoners of War by the German Armed Forces in the Vicinity of Le Mesnil-Patry, Les Saullets and Authie, Calvados, Normandy, 7–11 June 1944*, part 2, pp. 2, 5–6, DHist, vol. 90/168

7  *Supplementary Report of No. 1 Canadian War Crimes Investigation Unit re Shooting of Canadian Prisoners of War by the German Armed Forces at Mouen, Normandy, France, 17 June 1944*, NA, RG 25, F-3, vol. 2609, #173 in box, facts disclosed by SHAEF, p. 1, and exhibit 'O,' Meyer Trial, DHist, vol. 159.95.023 (D7)

8  In the Canadian army, this function was carried out by the Judge Advocate General's section, which was part of the Personnel Services division of the Adjutant General's branch of Canadian Military Headquarters in London. See Colonel C.P. Stacey, *Six Years of War: The Army in Canada, Britain and the Pacific* (Ottawa, 1957), 1:199–201.

9  Memorandum from Lieutenant Colonel B.J.S. Macdonald to Colonel W.A.I. Anglin, 28 April 1945, NA, RG 24, vol. 12842, file 67/Treatment/1/2 (393/56), p. 255

10  Appendix to the war diary (Canadian Section, Headquarters 1st Echelon, 21st Army Group), ibid., vol. 10513, file 215A21.009 (D 125), p. 17

11  Crerar letter, undated, and summary of the conference held at CMHQ on 4 July 1944, undated, ibid., pp. 12 and 14

12  Charles Ashman and Robert J. Wagman, *The Nazi Hunters* (New York, 1988), 68

13  Brigadier Lloyd to the headquarters of 1st Canadian Army, 7 July 1944, NA, RG 24, vol. 10513, file 215A21.009 (D 125), p. 29

14  War diary (Lieutenant General H.D.C. Crerar), entry for 8 July 1944, NA, MG 30 E 157 (Crerar Papers), vol. 15, file 958C.009 (D 265), vol. July 1944; interim report issued by the court of inquiry, 15 July 1944, NA, RG 24, vol. 12842, file 67/Treatment/1 (393/53), pp. 188–9; *Report of the No. 1 Canadian War Crimes Investigation Unit on Miscellaneous War Crimes against Members of the Canadian Armed Forces in the European Theatre of Operations, 9 September 1939 to 8 May 1945*, part 2, pp. 8, 17, NA, RG 25, vol. 1001 (F-3), numbered 174 in the box; and SHAEF Report, *Château d'Audrieu*, part 2, pp. 3–10

15  SHAEF to the headquarters of 21st Army Group and other subordinate agencies, 14 December 1944, NA, RG 24, vol. 12842, file 67/Treatment/1/2 (393/56), p. 150

16  Ibid.

17  Orders issued by SHAEF, 17 October 1944, ibid., p. 3

18  The procedures to be followed by the SHAEF standing court were retrospectively outlined in the memorandum from Macdonald to Anglin, 28 April 1945, ibid., p. 254

19  Ibid.

20 On Boraston, see Ian Sayer and Douglas Botting, *Hitler's Last General: The Case against Wilhelm Mohnke* (London and New York, 1989), 171.

21 Believing that he had been treated unfairly by Brigadier Hugh Young, the commander of the 6th Canadian Infantry Brigade, of which his regiment was a part, Macdonald lodged a protest with 2nd Canadian Corps, to which the brigade was subordinated. It was while he was awaiting a decision from 2nd Corps that he received the appointment to SHAEF. For biographical information on Macdonald, see Tony Foster, *Meeting of Generals* (Toronto and New York, 1986), 348–9, and Patrick Brode, 'Bruce Macdonald and the Drafting of Canada's War Crimes Regulations, 1945,' *Gazette of the Law Society of Upper Canada* 29 (1995): 275–6. On the circumstances surrounding Macdonald's ouster as commander of the Essex Scottish Regiment and his subsequent protest, see the documentation in NA, MG 30 E 480 (Macdonald Papers), file on the Verrières Ridge action, July–August 1944.

22 On Colonel Page, see his telephone interview with the author, 23 November 1996. See also the memorandum from Macdonald to Anglin, 28 April 1945, NA, RG 24, vol. 12842, file 67/Treatment/1/2 (393/56), p. 254.

23 Memorandum from Macdonald to Anglin, 28 April 1945, NA, RG 24, vol. 12842, file 67/Treatment/1/2 (393/56), p. 253

24 Lieutenant Colonel J.H. Boraston to the headquarters of (British) 2nd Army, 10 September 1944, ibid., vol. 10836, file 229C2.(D 27); memorandum from Macdonald to Anglin, 28 April 1945, ibid., vol. 12842, file 67/Treatment/1/2 (393/56), p. 253; and *Supplementary Report of the SHAEF Court of Inquiry re Shooting of Allied Prisoners of War by 12 SS Panzer Division (Hitler-Jugend) in Normandy, France, 7–21 June 1944*, part 1, p. 2, and part 3, p. 14, ibid., vol. 10427, file 205S1.023 (D 9)

25 The report's conclusions can be found in *Trial of the Major War Criminals before the International Military Tribunal*, vol. 31, document no. PS-2997 (Exhibit USA-472), 451–61.

26 Quoted from SHAEF Report, *12 SS*, part 1, p. 1

27 Ibid., pp. 2–3. Included among these thirty victims were Privates Tobin, MacRae, and Metcalfe of the North Nova Scotia Highlanders, as well as Captain Brown. Though all four men had died on 7 June at the hands of Milius's battalion, their bodies had not been interred in the mass grave near Authie that contained the remains of nearly three dozen of their martyred comrades. Accordingly, SHAEF considered their murders as separate cases.

28 This is the figure cited in the memorandum from Macdonald to Anglin, 28 April 1945, NA, RG 24, vol. 12842, file 67/Treatment/1/2 (393/56), p. 253.

29 The court certainly was aware of these killings. See ibid., p. 252.

30 SHAEF Report, *12 SS*, part 3, p. 16

31 Macdonald to Barker, 7 April 1945, NA, RG 24, vol. 12842, file 67/Treatment/1/2 (393/56), p. 219

32  On Jesionek's surrender and initial interrogation, see the testimony of SS Private Jan
Jesionek, Meyer Trial, 310; the statement given by Jan Jesionek, 22 April 1945,
NA, RG 24, vol. 12837, file 67/CNO/12 SS/1 (392/5), no page numbers; and B.J.S.
Macdonald, *The Trial of Kurt Meyer* (Toronto, 1954), 59–65.
33  Memorandum from Macdonald to Brigadier Bruce Matthews, 8 May 1945; Briga-
dier Macklin to the DAG, 23 February 1945; Colonel H.H. Newman to the headquar-
ters of 21st Army Group, 8 March 1945; and Macdonald to Barker, 7 April 1945,
NA, RG 24, vol. 12842, file 67/Treatment/1/2 (393/56), pp. 261, 197A, 213, and 218

## 14: The Twisted Road to Justice

1  Long before the SHAEF standing court released its final report on the criminal activities of the 12th SS Division, Canadians had been subjected to a steady diet of atrocity stories. As early as 21 June 1944, a major newspaper had reported some of the Le
Mesnil-Patry killings under the headline 'German Guard Shoots Captured Men in
Back.' See *Globe and Mail*, 21 June 1944, 2. The next day, the *Globe* ran British
reports on the discovery of the bodies of murdered Canadian POWs at the Château
d'Audrieu. See ibid., 22 June 1944, 1. Soon other stories followed, with each being
more sensational and inaccurate than the one before. For example, stories about the
Château d'Audrieu incident had the number of victims multiplying exponentially.
See the story under the headline '30 Canadian Soldiers Said Slain by Gestapo,' ibid.,
17 July 1944, 1, and the story cited in Secretary of State for External Affairs to the
High Commissioner in London, 13 July 1944, NA, reel C-7053 (King Papers), frame
317090, which had referred to '48 Canadian soldiers found shot in an inn yard.'
Eventually, even atrocity stories where the victims had not been Canadian began to
appear. For example, see the story entitled 'Army Padre Murdered Seeking to Aid
Troops' about the murder on D-Day of George E. Parry, the padre of the (British)
6th Airborne Division, *Globe and Mail*, 1 July 1944, 11, and Defensor to Canmilitary,
1 July 1944, NA, MG 30 E 157 (Crerar Papers), vol. 5, file 6–3, p. 2. Anxious that
such unrestrained reporting might compromise SHAEF's investigations, Ottawa first
tried to have all atrocity stories censored. See Lieutenant General H.D.G. Crerar to
CMHQ, 10 July 1944, NA, RG 24, vol. 10513, file 215A21.009 (D 125), p. 22 verso;
minutes of the cabinet war committee, p. 3, 12 July 1944, NA, reel C-4876; and Secretary of State for External Affairs to the High Commissioner, 13 July 1944, NA,
MG 26 J (King Papers), reel C-7053, frame 317090. When this initiative was rejected
by SHAEF's public relations section, the government suddenly shifted gears and tried
to milk the stories for maximum propaganda value. See Canmilitary to Crerar, 1
August 1944, NA, MG 30 E 157 (Crerar Papers), file 6–3, p. 23, and the story written
under the headline 'Murder of Soldiers Stirs Canada's Hatred,' *Globe and Mail*, 3
August 1944, 1. The army also saw some utility in giving the story publicity. Besides

the impact on fighting spirit that the story was bound to have, there was also the very real concern of making the troops aware that surrendering to the Germans had become a somewhat risky business. See Canmilitary to Defensor, 19 July 1944, NA, MG 30 E 157 (Crerar Papers), vol. 5, file 6–3, p. 6. Accordingly, on 1 August 1944, General Crerar issued a statement to the army in which he denounced the killings in the strongest possible terms. See Crerar to all commanders and commanding officers, 1 August 1944, ibid., p. 16.

2 In commenting on a proposal to establish an international commission to investigate German war crimes, the secretary of state for dominion affairs, for example, noted that the undertaking of a commitment to hunt down and try German war criminals 'might prove embarrassing.' It would be safer, in the secretary's view, to leave the Germans 'to the vengeance of their neighbours.' Quoted from the Secretary of State for Dominion Affairs to the Secretary of State for External Affairs, 13 October 1941, Canada, NA, RG 25, reel T-2204, vol. 821, file 696, p. 2. A similar view was expressed by an aide to Prime Minister King, who presented a draft declaration on war crimes policy to his boss with the recommendation that it be approved because it kept 'carefully free of any embarrassing commitment to take specific action.' Quoted from the memorandum for the Prime Minister, 16 October 1941, ibid., p. 6.

3 The Germans claimed that they did so in retaliation for British violations in this regard. To follow the progress of the shackling incident and the diplomatic furore it caused, see Massey to External Affairs, 3 September and 8–9, 12, and 22 October 1942, NA, RG 24, vol. 12842, file 67/Treatment/1 (393/53), pp. 1–2, 4, 12, 24, and 35; the memorandum for N.A. Robertson, 17 November 1942, NA, RG 25, reel T-2207, vol. 825, file 722, frame 137; the minutes of meetings of the cabinet war committee, 21 and 27 January and 7 April 1943, NA, RG 2, 7c, vol. 12, reel C-4875, frames 2–6; and the entries for 12 December 1942 and 17 May 1943, in *The Goebbels Diaries*, ed. and trans. Louis Lochner (New York, 1948), 239–40 and 382.

4 Secretary of State for External Affairs to the Secretary of State for Dominion Affairs, 30 October 1942, NA, RG 2, 18, vol. 12, file W-41

5 On the war crimes advisory panel, see the memorandum from the High Commissioner to the Chief of Staff at CMHQ, 18 April 1945, NA, RG 24, vol. 12842, file 67/Treatment/1/2 (393/56), pp. 229B–verso; the announcement by the Prime Minister, 13 September 1945, ibid., vol. 12839, file 67/Kurt Meyer Case/1, page between pp. 47 and 48; and the interim report from Arthur G. Slaght to the Honourable W.L. Mackenzie King, 15 March 1944, NA, RG 2, 18, vol. 12, file W–41.

6 Memorandum from the High Commissioner to the Chief of Staff at CMHQ, 18 April 1945, NA, RG 24, vol. 12842, file 67/Treatment/1/2 (393/56), p. 229C

7 On the composition of the panel, see the interim report from Arthur G. Slaght to the Honourable W.L. Mackenzie King, 15 March 1944, NA, RG 2, 18, vol. 12, file W-41, and the announcement by the Prime Minister in the House of Commons,

13 September 1945, NA, RG 24, vol. 12839, file 67/Kurt Meyer Case/1, page between pp. 47 and 48.

 8 On the relationship between the high commissioner and CMHQ, see C.P. Stacey, *Arms, Men, and Governments: The War Policies of Canada, 1939–1945* (Ottawa, 1970), 206–7.

 9 Major General E.G. Weeks to the commander of the Canadian Section (21st Army Group), 27 February 1945, NA, RG 24, vol. 12842, file 67/Treatment/1/2 (393/56), p. 198. Two days earlier, Weeks had opined that 'a British/Cdn show would be preferable to an independent Cdn investigating team.' Quoted from Weeks to the Deputy Adjutant General, 25 February 1945, ibid., p. 197.

10 Major General E.L.M. Burns to CMHQ, 7 March 1945, ibid., p. 207

11 Lieutenant-Colonel B.J.S. Macdonald to Major General R.W. Barker, 7 April 1945, ibid., pp. 217–19. For the path that Macdonald's letter took up CMHQ's chain of command, see Colonel H.H. Newman to CHMQ, 14 April 1945, and Brigadier W.H.S. Macklin to the Deputy Adjutant General, 18 April 1945, ibid.

12 Summary of the meeting held in the office of the High Commissioner on 24 April 1945, 28 April 1945, ibid., pp. 233–4

13 Memorandum from Macdonald to Brigadier B. Matthews, 8 May 1945, ibid., p. 261

14 Memorandum from Macdonald to Colonel W.A.I. Anglin, 28 April 1945, ibid., p. 249

15 Memorandum from Macdonald to Matthews, 8 May 1945, ibid., p. 261

16 Canmilitary to Defensor, 17 May 1945, ibid., p. 245

17 War diary (No. 1 CWCIU), entry for 4 June 1945, ibid., vol. 16408, file June 1944 (vol. 1), and memorandum from Macdonald to Matthews, 8 May 1945, ibid., vol. 12842, file 67/Treatment/1/2 (393/56), p. 258

18 Order issued by Matthews for the Chief of Staff at CMHQ, 5 July 1945, ibid., vol. 12840, file 67/Office/1, p. 34; Canmilitary to Defensor, 17 May 1945, ibid., vol. 12842, file 67/Treatment/1/2 (393/56), p. 245; and the nominal roll of the No. 1 Canadian War Crimes Investigation Unit, undated, appended to the memorandum from Capt. G.K.M. Johnston to CMHQ, 30 June 1945, ibid., vol. 12840, file 67/Office/1, p. 12

19 On Macdonald's appointment as Canada's chief war crimes prosecutor, see the announcement by the Prime Minister, 13 September 1945, appended to the letter from Macdonald to the Deputy Judge Advocate General, 31 October 1945, ibid., vol. 12839, file 67/Kurt Meyer Case/1, between pp. 48 and 47, and Brigadier R. Younger to CMHQ, 19 September 1945, ibid., vol. 12840, file 67/Office/1, p. 151. On Campbell's appointment, see B.J.S. Macdonald, *The Trial of Kurt Meyer* (Toronto, 1954), 13.

20 On the consideration given to invoking the British royal warrant, see the memorandum from Macdonald to Matthews, 8 June 1945, NA, RG 24, vol. 12842, file

67/Treatment/1/2 (393/56), p. 293, and Macdonald, *Trial*, 54–5. For the wording of the royal warrant, see the draft 'Regulations for the Trial of War Criminals' appended to the memorandum from Andrew Bell to Macdonald, 14 June 1945, and 'Regulations for the Trial of War Criminals,' 18 June 1945, MA, Macdonald Papers, War Crimes box 1, file I-1/2 and box 7, file I-4/3.

21  Minutes of the extraordinary meeting of the war crimes advisory panel held on 20 June 1945, undated, MA, Macdonald Papers, War Crimes box 1, file I-1/2, and Macdonald, *Trial*, 55

22  This was the opinion of the lawyers at the Department of Justice. See the memorandum from the Department of Justice to the Acting Secretary of State for External Affairs, 9 November 1945, DHist, vol. 159.95 (D 1), tab 1-1-2.

23  Between 1945 and 1948, British military courts were extremely busy. Just over 1,700 persons were tried under the Royal Warrant, of whom just over 1,400 were convicted. Of those convicted, 372 received the death sentence. The figures on British war crimes prosecutions are cited in Patrick Brode, 'Bruce Macdonald and the Drafting of Canada's War Crimes Regulations, 1945,' *Gazette of the Law Society of Upper Canada* 29 (1995): 277.

24  Macdonald, *Trial*, 51. In a speech given years later, Macdonald decried those 'pedantic legalists' who criticized the changes made to the rules of evidence. See the address given by Macdonald, undated, p. 10, MA, Macdonald Papers, War Crimes box 7, file I-3/14.

25  So many witnesses were lost because of demobilization and repatriation that the government had reinstate many of them on the active duty list in order to be able to subpoena them. On this problem, see the summary of a conference held at National Defence Headquarters in Ottawa on 28 August 1945, NA, RG 24, vol. 12839, file 67/Kurt Meyer Case/1, p. 9; the memorandum from Macdonald to the Deputy Adjutant General, 4 September 1945, ibid., vol. 12843, file 67/War Crimes IU/1 (393/67), p. 5; and Canmilitary to Defensor, 10 November 1945, ibid., vol. 12839, file 67/Kurt Meyer/2/2, p. 170.

26  Macdonald had warned of this in the weeks following the closure of the SHAEF standing court. See Macdonald to Barker, 7 April 1945, ibid., vol. 12842, file 67/Treatment/1/2 (393/56), p. 218.

27  Macdonald, *Trial*, 55–6

28  Ibid., 55.

29  This problem caused considerable consternation among the bureaucrats in Ottawa. After much toing and froing, counsel for the Departments of Justice, External Affairs, and National Defence finally decided that the maximum penalty prescribed by the War Measures Act could not restrict a military court from imposing the (harsher) penalties prescribed by international law. See the memorandum [from the Department of Justice] to the Acting Secretary of State for External Affairs,

9 November 1945, and the draft report from L.S. St Laurent to the Governor General in Council, November 1945, DHist, vol. 159.95 (D 1), tabs 1-1-2 and 1-1-1. See also Group Captain C.M.A. Strathy to F.P. Varcoe, 17 November 1945; Strathy to Brigadier R.J. Orde, 17 November 1945; Orde to Lieutenant Colonel W.B. Bredin, 17 November 1945; and Varcoe to Strathy, 19 November 1945, ibid., accordion volume, file 29/War Crimes/1.

30  This was admitted by government lawyers during subsequent hearings on legislation proposed to enshrine the 1945 war crimes regulations in statute law. See the minutes of evidence given before the Standing Committee on External Affairs, 30 May and 7 June 1946, ibid.

31  The tortuous and frustrating drafting process is described in considerable detail in the memorandum from Macdonald to the Deputy Adjutant General, 4 September 1945, NA, RG 24, vol. 12843, file 67/War Crimes IU/1 (393/67), pp. 3–4.

32  Ibid., p. 4; minutes of the cabinet meeting, 29 August 1945, NA, reel T-2364, frame 604; and announcement by the Prime Minister, 13 September 1945, appended to the letter from Macdonald to the Judge Advocate General, 31 October 1945, NA, RG 24, vol. 12839, file 67/Kurt Meyer Case/1, between pp. 47 and 48.

33  See the War Crimes Regulations (Canada), 30 August 1945, in *Canadian War Orders and Regulations*, vol. 3, no. 10, NA, RG 24, vol. 12841, file 67/Procedure 1 (393/9), p. 193(3).

34  Ibid., p. 193(4)

35  For example, section 443 of the *Manual of Military Law*, to which Canada adhered during the Second World War, stipulated that 'members of the armed forces who commit such violations of the recognized rules of warfare as are ordered by their Government, or by their commander, are not war criminals and cannot be punished by the enemy.' The manual allowed that the aggrieved party 'may punish the officials or commanders responsible for such orders if they fall into his hands, but otherwise he may only resort to ... other means of obtaining redress.' *Manual of Military Law*, quoted in Macdonald, *Trial*, 43. Interestingly, Canada's war crimes regulations backed away a little from the manual's implied sanction of a defence based on superior orders. After the fashion of the Nuremberg tribunal, section 15 of the regulations stipulated that 'the fact that an accused acted pursuant to the order of a superior or of his government shall not constitute an absolute defence to any charge.' It could, however, be considered 'either as a defence or in mitigation of punishment.' Quotes from the War Crimes Regulations (Canada), 30 August 1945, in *Canadian War Orders and Regulations*, vol. 3, no. 10, NA, RG 24, vol. 12841, file 67/Procedure 1 (393/9), p. 193(6).

36  War Crimes Regulations (Canada), 30 August 1945, in *Canadian War Orders and Regulations*, vol. 3, no. 10, NA, RG 24, vol. 12841, file 67/Procedure 1 (393/9), pp. 193(4)–3(5)

37  On this last point, Macdonald all but conceded as much in a letter to the Judge Advo-

cate General written on the day that Prime Minister King announced the regulations in the House of Commons. See Macdonald to the Judge Advocate General, 13 September 1945, ibid., vol. 12839, file 67/Kurt Meyer Case/1, p. 7.

38  On the safeguards written into the regulations, see Brigadier R. Younger to CMHQ, 19 September 1945, ibid., vol. 12840, file 67/Office/1, p. 151, and subsections 7(1) and 7(7), along with sections 12 and 14 of the War Crimes Regulations (Canada), 30 August 1945, in *Canadian War Orders and Regulations*, vol. 3, no. 10, ibid., vol. 12841, file 67/Procedure 1 (393/9), pp. 193(3) and 193(5)–3(6).

39  This condemnation of Canada's war crimes regulations is from Tony Foster, *Meeting of Generals* (Toronto and New York, 1986), 453.

## 15: The Case against Kurt Meyer

1  Craig W.H. Luther, *Blood and Honor: The History of the 12th SS Panzer Division 'Hitler Youth,' 1943–1945* (San José, CA, 1987), 225–6, and Kurt Meyer, *Grenadiere* (Munich, 1957), 271–3

2  Affidavit of Kurt Meyer in 'Petition of Kurt Meyer and Memorandum by Counsel Re Trial, Conviction and Sentence,' 12 December 1950, p. 14, NA, RG 2, vol. 209, file W-41, part 1

3  On the 12th SS's hair-raising escape from the Falaise pocket, see Meyer, *Grenadiere*, 302–10.

4  Meyer's promotion to the rank of Brigadier General was effective 1 September 1944. See the file on Kurt Meyer, NARA, RG 242 BDC A 3433, SS Officer Dossier, roll 313A, frame 1335.

5  For an account of the events surrounding Meyer's capture, see Meyer, *Grenadiere*, 313–21; the record of the evidence of SS Brigadier General K. Meyer, undated, *Supplementary Report of the SHAEF Court of Inquiry re Shooting of Allied Prisoners of War by 12 SS Panzer Division (Hitler-Jugend) in Normandy, France, 7–21 June 1944*, exhibit no. 8, pp. 8–9, NA, RG 24, vol. 10427, file 205S1.023 (D 9); and the affidavit of Kurt Meyer in 'Petition of Kurt Meyer,' 12 December 1950, pp. 14–15, NA, RG 2, vol. 209, file W-41, part 1.

6  Tony Foster, *Meeting of Generals* (Toronto and New York, 1986), 402, 407–8

7  Affidavit of Kurt Meyer in 'Petition of Kurt Meyer,' 12 December 1950, p. 15, NA, RG 2, vol. 209, file W-41, part 1

8  Foster, *Generals*, 416–17

9  Affidavit of Kurt Meyer in 'Petition of Kurt Meyer,' 12 December 1950, p. 15, NA, RG 2, vol. 209, file W-41, part 1

10  On Scotland and his London Cage staff, see Patrick Brode, *Casual Slaughters and Accidental Judgments: Canadian War Crimes Prosecutions, 1944–1948* (Toronto, 1997), 22–3; Ian Sayer and Douglas Botting, *Hitler's Last General: The Case against Wilhelm Mohnke* (London and New York, 1989), 87–91; B.J.S.

Macdonald, *The Trial of Kurt Meyer* (Toronto, 1954), 65; and Foster, *Generals*, 421, 430.

11 Record of the evidence of Meyer, undated, SHAEF Report, *12 SS*, exhibit no. 8, p. 41, and interrogation of SS Brigadier General Kurt Meyer, pp. 1–2, NA, RG 24, vol. 10474, file 212C1.3009 (D 60). Meyer's ability to thwart Allied war crimes investigators was confirmed recently by Colonel John Page, whose stint with the SHAEF courts of inquiry provided him with the opportunity to attend one of Meyer's interrogations. Conceding that Meyer 'was a pretty clever guy,' Page attributed the Nazi's success in stymieing Allied war crimes investigators to the fact that he viewed the interrogations as an opportunity to continue the war by other means. As the retired colonel put it, Meyer was bent on 'showing that he was superior to all of them.' Telephone interview with the author, 23 November 1996

12 Affidavit of Kurt Meyer in 'Petition of Kurt Meyer,' 12 December 1950, p. 15, NA, RG 2, vol. 209, file W-41, part 1

13 Record of the evidence of Meyer, undated, SHAEF Report, *12 SS*, exhibit no. 8, pp. 46–7 and exhibit 9, p. 32; Macdonald, *Trial*, 65–6; and Lieutenant Colonel B.J.S. Macdonald to Major General R.W. Barker, 7 April 1945, NA, RG 24, vol. 12842, file 67/Treatment/1/2 (393/56), p. 219

14 Will-say of SS Private Friedrich Torbanisch, undated, 'Abstract of Evidence in the Case of SS Brigadier General Kurt Meyer,' pp. 1–2, NA, RG 24, vol. 12839, file 67/Kurt Meyer Case/1 (392/51)

15 Record of the evidence of F. Torbanisch, undated, SHAEF Report, *12 SS*, exhibit no. 5, pp. 1–4

16 According to Meyer, Hagetorn had been killed during the 12th SS's attack on Bretteville during the night of 8–9 June. See the record of the evidence of Meyer, undated, ibid., exhibit no. 8, p. 21. This was contradicted by SS Private Jan Jesionek, who claimed to have seen Hagetorn alive on 10 June. See the will-say of SS Private Jan Jesionek, undated, 'Abstract of Evidence,' p. 7, NA, RG 24, vol. 12839, file 67/Kurt Meyer Case/1 (392/51).

17 Macdonald to Barker, 7 April 1945, ibid., vol. 12842, file 67/Treatment/1/2 (393/56), pp. 217–9

18 Will-say of Jesionek, undated, 'Abstract of Evidence,' pp. 6–7, ibid., vol. 12839, file 67/Kurt Meyer Case/1 (392/51)

19 For the progress of the American advance in the Brilon-Paderborn sector, see the briefings on the military situation summarized in the entries for 30–1 March 1945, *Final Entries, 1945: The Diaries of Joseph Goebbels*, ed. Hugh Trevor-Roper, trans. Richard Barry (New York, 1978), 294, 297.

20 Testimony of Jesionek, Meyer Trial, 310, DHist, vol. 159.95023 (D 7)

21 Ibid.

22 For an example of the way this kind of information sharing was supposed to work,

see Captain T. Klocek (Polish Ministry of National Defence) to the British Security Service, 20 November 1944, and Colonel Miniewski (Polish General Headquarters) to CMHQ, 21 July 1945, NA, RG 24, vol. 12838, file 67/Falaise/1 (392/22), pp. 1 and 5.

23 Testimony of Jesionek, Meyer Trial, 310
24 See the statement given by Jan Jesionek, 22 April 1945, NA, RG 24, vol. 12837, file 67/CNO/12 SS/1 (392/5), no page numbers, and the testimony of Sigmund Stern, Meyer Trial, 269–82.
25 Testimony of Jesionek, Meyer Trial, 312
26 Macdonald, Trial, 61
27 Ibid.
28 Ibid., 60–1, and testimony of Jesionek, Meyer Trial, 312–13
29 Will-say of Jesionek, undated, 'Abstract of Evidence,' p. 8, NA, RG 24, vol. 12839, file 67/Kurt Meyer Case/1 (392/51)
30 Testimony of Jesionek, Meyer Trial, 310
31 Macdonald, Trial, 61–4, and memorandum from Macdonald to Brigadier Matthews, 8 June 1945, NA, RG 24, vol. 12842, file 67/Treatment/1/2 (393/56), p. 293
32 Charge sheet, undated, appended to the letter from Macdonald to the UNWCC, 19 June 1945, NA, RG 24, vol. 12837, file 67/CNO/12 SS/1 (392/5), no page number
33 Macdonald admitted as much to the judge advocate general. See the memorandum from Macdonald to Brigadier R.J. Orde, 21 October 1945, pp. 2–3, 5, MA, Macdonald Papers, War Crimes box 1, file I-1/3.
34 Note for the Prime Minister, p. 1, appended to memorandum from J.E. Read to L.S. St Laurent (minister of justice), 12 June 1945, NA, MG 26 L (St Laurent Papers), vol. 4, file 27–27, and war diary (No. 1 CWCIU), entry for 20 June 1945, NA, RG 24, vol. 16408, file June 1945 (part 1)
35 War diary (No. 1 CWCIU), entry for 24 June 1945, NA, RG 24, vol. 16408, file June 1945 (part 1)
36 The figures are reported in the memorandum from Macdonald to the DAG, 4 September 1945, pp. 1, 7, ibid., vol. 12843, file 67/War Crimes IU/1 (393/67). For the chief prosecutor's recollections of the trip, see Macdonald, Trial, 48.
37 The meagre results obtained from the interviews of the German witnesses were summarized in the list of witnesses from the 25th Panzer Grenadier Regiment 'with reference to their knowledge of orders concerning treatment of Allied PW or any atrocities,' undated, MA, Macdonald Papers, War Crimes box 7, file I-3/14.
38 Macdonald, Trial, 47–8
39 As a former reconnaissance commander, Meyer felt a special attachment to the 15th Company. During training at Beverloo, Belgium, he had promised to lead the company's youthful recruits on their first mission. See the testimony of SS Brigadier General Kurt Meyer, Meyer Trial, 555–6.

40  Memorandum from Macdonald to the DAG, 4 September 1945, p. 1, NA, RG 24, vol. 12843, file 67/War Crimes IU/1 (393/67), and will-say of SS Private Alfred Helzel, undated, 'Abstract of Evidence,' pp. 4–5, ibid., vol. 12839, file 67/Kurt Meyer Case/1 (392/51)

41  Memorandum from Macdonald to the DAG, 4 September 1945, pp. 3, 5, ibid., vol. 12843, file 67/War Crimes IU/1 (393/67)

42  War diary (No. 1 CWCIU), entries for 12 and 18 September, 2–3 and 17 October 1945, ibid., vol. 16408, files September and October 1945, and testimonies of SS Private Hermann Sue, SS First Lieutenant Bernhard Meitzel, SS Second Lieutenant Kurt Bergmann, and SS Private Horst Heyer, Meyer Trial, 493, 467–9, and 84

43  War diary (No. 1 CWCIU), entries for 31 August, 8 and 11 September 1945, NA, RG 24, vol. 16408, files August and September 1945, and testimony of SS Corporal (Feldgendarmerie) Ewald Wetzel, Meyer Trial, 502, 504

44  As late as 25 October, the Canadian Army still had not appointed defence counsel for Meyer. See the war diary (No. 1 CWCIU), entry for 25 October 1945, NA, RG 24, vol. 16408, file October 1945. Ten days earlier, Macdonald had visited Meyer and informed him that application would be made to try him as a war criminal. To Macdonald's query as to his wishes regarding legal representation, Meyer responded that his preference would be for a British or German civilian barrister assisted by a qualified Canadian officer, but that he would accept two qualified Canadian officers. See ibid., entry for 15 October 1945, and the memoranda from Macdonald to the ADAG, 10 and 18 October 1945, ibid., vol. 12839, file 67/Kurt Meyer Case/1, pp. 16–17 and 27. Macdonald tried to persuade the judge advocate general to approve Meyer's request for a civilian, but this was rejected on the rather spurious grounds of cost. See the memorandum from Colonel L.R. McDonald to the AAG, 19 October 1945; Orde to Brigadier W.A.I Anglin, 24 October 1945; and Defensor to Canmilitary, 27 October 1945, ibid., pp. 30, between pp. 45 and 46, and 43. With the civilian option foreclosed, Macdonald then sought out qualified military counsel. His first choice, Colonel Peter Wright, felt that the verdict was a foregone conclusion and begged off. Macdonald's second choice, Lieutenant Colonel Maurice W. Andrew, was similarly reluctant, although in his case the main concern seemed to be how the public in Canada would regard anyone who defended Meyer. After receiving assurances that his appointment would be under orders, Andrew agreed to take the case. See the memorandum from McDonald to the AAG, 19 October 1945; Canmilitary to HQ CFN, 20 October 1945; the memorandum from Lieutenant Colonel C.S. Campbell to the DAG, 22 October 1945; the memorandum from Lieutenant Colonel M.J. Griffin, AAG, to ADAG, 25 October 1945; Canmilitary to HQ CFN, 30 October 1945; Canmilitary to HQ CFN, 31 October 1945; HQ CFN to Canmilitary, 1 November 1945; Canmilitary to the headquarters of the 3rd Canadian Infantry Division, CAOF, 2 November 1945; HQ CFN to Canmilitary, 2 November 1945,

ibid., pp. 30, between pp. 30 and 31, 45, 49, 50, 52, and 53. See also Macdonald, *Trial*, 83–4.

45 Captured on 23 December 1944, von der Heydte took it upon himself to advise fellow prisoners of their rights should their captors accuse them of having perpetrated violations of international law. See the extracts from his 3 April 1945 lecture entitled 'The Legal Aspects of War Crimes,' MA, Macdonald Papers, War Crimes box 1, file I-1/2.

46 Memorandum from Campbell to file, 26 October 1945, NA, RG 24, vol. 12839, file 67/Kurt Meyer Case/1, between pp. 39 and 38; Macdonald, *Trial*, 66; record of the evidence of Kurt Meyer, 26 October 1945, pp. 1–2, MA, Macdonald Papers, War Crimes box 5, file I-3/4, and war diary (No. 1 CWCIU), entry for 26 October 1945, NA, RG 24, vol. 16408, file October 1945.

47 War diary (No. 1 CWCIU), entries for 21 and 27 October 1945, NA, RG 24, vol. 16408, file October 1945, and Macdonald, *Trial*, 66

48 War diary (No. 1 CWCIU), entry for 28 October 1945, NA, RG 24, vol. 16408, file October 1945, and Macdonald, *Trial*, 66–7

49 Record of the evidence of Meyer, 28 October 1945, pp. 8–9, MA, Macdonald Papers, War Crimes box 5, file I-3/4

50 Macdonald, *Trial*, 68

51 Abstract of the evidence of Daniel Lachèvre, undated, 'Abstract of the Evidence to be Adduced at the Trial of Brigadeführer Kurt Meyer,' undated, pp. 39–40, MA, Macdonald Papers, War Crimes box 6, file I-3/5

52 War diary (No. 1 CWCIU), entry for 31 October 1945, NA, RG 24, vol. 16408, file October 1945, and Foster, *Generals*, 456–7

53 War diary (No. 1 CWCIU), entry for 31 October 1945, NA, RG 24, vol. 16408, file October 1945; Major General C. Vokes's order, 31 October 1945, DHist, vol. 159.95 (D 1), tab 1-2-1

54 As late as mid-October, Macdonald was contemplating the laying of nine separate charges against Meyer. See the charge sheet, undated, NA, RG 24, vol. 12839, file 67/Kurt Meyer Case/1 (392/51), between pp. 24 and 23.

55 With the exception of the sixth count, the charges read by Lieutenant Colonel Clark were identical to those read out in court. See the charge sheet signed by Major General C. Vokes, 4 December 1945, DHist, vol. 159.95 (D 1), tab 1-2-3, pp. 3–4. See also Macdonald, *Trial*, 89–90.

56 Foster, *Generals*, 457

57 See Major General C. Vokes's orders, 4 December 1945, p. 1, Meyer Trial.

**16: Reckoning: The Trial of Kurt Meyer**

1 Tony Foster, *Meeting of Generals* (Toronto and New York, 1986), xvii–xviii

2 At the time of their appointments to the court, Foster commanded the 4th Canadian Armoured Division, Roberts the 8th Canadian Infantry Brigade, Sparling the 3rd Canadian Infantry Division's Royal Canadian Artillery units, Johnston the 5th Canadian Armoured Division, and Bell-Irving the 10th Canadian Infantry Brigade. Bredin was serving with the Judge Advocate General's section. See Major General C. Vokes's orders, 4 December 1945, p. 1, Meyer Trial, DHist, vol. 159.95.023 (D 7).

3 Subsection 7(7) called for the appointment to a court, preferably as president, of at least one officer possessing legal qualifications. If the prospective president was not so qualified, then it was recommended that a judge advocate be appointed. See the War Crimes Regulations (Canada), 30 August 1945, in Canadian War Orders and Regulations, vol. 3, no. 10, NA, RG 24, vol. 12841, file 67/Procedure 1 (393/9), p. 193(3).

4 Foster, Generals, xix

5 See subsections 7(1) and 7(2) of the War Crimes Regulations (Canada), 30 August 1945, in Canadian War Orders and Regulations, vol. 3, no. 10, NA, RG 24, vol. 12841, file 67/Procedure 1 (393/9), p. 193(3).

6 Major General Chris Vokes, My Story (Ottawa, 1985), 204

7 Foster, Generals, xix

8 Globe and Mail, 11 December 1945, 7

9 The quoted passages are from the opening address by the prosecution, Meyer Trial, 10.

10 Globe and Mail, 11 December 1945, 7

11 Quoted from the opening address by the prosecution, Meyer Trial, 21

12 See the testimony of Major J.J. Stonborough, ibid., 175–80.

13 For Macdonald's attempt to wriggle out of his predicament, see ibid., 32–47.

14 The culprit was subsection 10(1) of the regulations. For an analysis, see chapter 14. Though dressed up to look like official German correspondence, the alleged orders did not fool the initiated. That any court, even a military one, could be compelled to admit such a document, bordered on a travesty of justice. Copies of the alleged orders, both in German and in Flemish and English translation, are registered as exhibit no. T-3, ibid.

15 It is not known whether the Torbanisch incident worked against the prosecution in the long run. What is clear is that Court President Foster had not been swayed by what he regarded as Macdonald's excessive emphasis on the alleged POW orders. See Foster, Generals, 463–4.

16 The quoted passage is from B.J.S. Macdonald, The Trial of Kurt Meyer (Toronto, 1954), 95.

17 For an example, see the testimony of SS Private Alfred Helzel, Meyer Trial, 52.

18 Quoted from Macdonald, Trial, 95–6

19 See the War Crimes Regulations (Canada), 30 August 1945, in Canadian War Orders

*and Regulations*, vol. 3, no. 10, NA, RG 24, vol. 12841, file 67/Procedure 1 (393/9), p. 193(4).

20 Testimony of SS Private Alfred Helzel, Meyer Trial, 55, 58, 62

21 Macdonald, *Trial*, 95–6

22 Testimony of SS Private Horst Heyer, Meyer Trial, 83–4, 87

23 The materials that were read into evidence were all excerpts from *Report of the Supreme Headquarters Allied Expeditionary Force Court of Inquiry re Shooting of Allied Prisoners of War by the German Armed Forces in the Vicinity of Le Mesnil-Patry, Les Saullets and Authie, Calvados, Normandy, 7–11 June 1944*, quoted in Meyer Trial, 89–100.

24 Testimony of Constance Raymond Guilbert, Meyer Trial, 101–15

25 See the extracts from SHAEF Report, *Authie*, cited in ibid., 116–35.

26 See the testimonies of Major John D. Learment, Sergeant Stanley Dudka, Private Gordon P. Talbot, Captain Joseph A. Trainor, Sergeant W.L. McKay, Corporal Walter T. McLeod, Private J.A. Conrod, and Private Ralph J. Richards, Meyer Trial, 129–240.

27 Though revolted by the gross misconduct of the SS troops, General Foster, at least, did not appear to have been convinced that Meyer had been responsible. See Foster, *Generals*, 465.

28 Testimony of Corporal John R.B. Campbell, Meyer Trial, 248–51

29 On the uniform episode, see the testimony of SS Private Jan Jesionek, ibid., 289–90.

30 Ibid., 290–307

31 Andrew's valiant but futile cross-examination can be found in ibid., 316–54.

32 For General Foster's impressions, see Foster, *Generals*, 467.

33 See Meyer Trial, 375–523

34 See the testimonies of SS First Lieutenant Bernhard Meitzel, SS Second Lieutenant Kurt Bergmann, SS Private Hermann Sue, and SS Corporal (Feldgendarmerie) Ewald Wetzel, ibid., 466–7, 467–89, 490–5, and 497–504.

35 Andrew's steadfast refusal to make an opening statement, even in the face of the court's prodding, can be found in ibid., 550. There is no indication in the trial transcript as to his motivation in this regard. Perhaps he thought Meyer's own testimony would be more compelling than anything he might say in Meyer's defence.

36 For examples of this, see the testimony of SS Brigadier General Kurt Meyer, ibid., 562–7, 569–71.

37 For example, see ibid., 577, 594.

38 That, at least, was the impression of the court president. See Foster, *Generals*, 472.

39 During an interview with Colonel John Page, I asked him what might have prompted Macdonald's apparent personal enmity towards Meyer. Page, who knew Macdonald well, said that the chief prosecutor had 'a chip on his shoulder' as a result of his sacking for the Verrières Ridge debacle, and speculated that he therefore may have

been 'out to redeem himself' in the eyes of his superiors. Telephone interview with the author, 23 November 1996

40  The cross-examination can be found in the testimony of Meyer, Meyer Trial, 607ff. For press reports of the encounter, see *Globe and Mail*, 20 December 1945, 2, and 21 December 1945, 1–2.

41  Testimony of Meyer, Meyer Trial, 693–4

42  Quoted from Macdonald, *Trial*, 145

43  Testimony of Meyer, Meyer Trial, 696–7

44  Quoted from Macdonald, *Trial*, 145–6

45  On Meyer's various miscues, see the testimony of Meyer, Meyer Trial, 608–10, 614 (answer no. 2817), 615–16.

46  See the testimony of Daniel Lachèvre, ibid., 773.

47  Macdonald, *Trial*, 153

48  Foster, *Generals*, 478–80

49  Summing up by the Judge Advocate (Lieutenant Colonel W.B. Bredin), 28 December 1945, pp. 5, 7–8, NA, RG 25, vol. 5782, file 213(s), part 1; Memorandum from Lieutenant Colonel B.J.S. Macdonald to the DAG, 12 January 1946, pp. 2, 4–5, ibid.; and Foster, *Generals*, 480–1

50  Quoted from Foster, *Generals*, 481. Another court member, Brigadier Roberts, held a similar view. See J.A. Roberts, *The Canadian Summer: The Memoirs of James Alan Roberts* (Toronto, 1981), 165.

51  According to press reports, 'Meyer began to flush as the impact of the words sank home. His face was beet-red at the end of the statement but his hands were clutched firmly at his sides and he bowed deeply at the end.' See *Globe and Mail*, 29 December 1945, pp. 1–2.

52  Statement to the court by SS Brigadier General Kurt Meyer, Meyer Trial, 856

53  Sentencing, ibid., 857

54  On Meyer's appeal and its initial rejection by Vokes, see the petition from Major General Kurt Meyer to Major General C. Vokes, 31 December 1945, DHist, vol. 159.95 (D 1), binder, tab 1-2-7; Vokes, *My Story*, 205; and Macdonald to the UNWCC, 7 January 1946, NA, RG 24, CMHQ, vol. 12839, file 67/Kurt Meyer Case/1, p. 177.

55  On the process that led to the commutation of Meyer's sentence, see the note to file from Vokes, 6 January 1945, DHist, vol. 159.95 (D 1), tab 1-2-6; Vokes to CMHQ, 5 January 1946, NA, RG 24, vol. 12839, file 67/Kurt Meyer Case/1, pp. 181–2; the memorandum regarding the conference held at 1030 hours on 9 January 1946, ibid., p. 192; and Vokes to Canmilitary, 14 January 1946, ibid., p. 187.

56  See Vokes to the commanding officer of the Royal Winnipeg Rifles, undated, DHist, vol. 159.95 (D 1), tab 1-2-8. Almost a decade later, Meyer wrote to Vokes thanking him for the commutation. In his awkward English, Meyer sent his greetings and

thanked his benefactor 'that through your impulsion [*sic*], the death sentence which
was passed on me, wasn't carried out.' In addition, Meyer tried to reassure Vokes:
'No doubt the resolution was a difficult one for you, however you have nothing to
regret – I fought as a soldier.' The quotes are in Meyer to Vokes, 4 October 1955,
RMC, Vokes Papers.

57 On public reaction to the commutation of Meyer's sentence, see Foster, *Generals*,
490.

58 On 1 April 1946, John Diefenbaker, then the member from Lake Centre,
Saskatchewan, submitted a motion in the House of Commons in which he requested
that the government produce 'all letters, papers, memos of telephone conversations
and other documents which passed between Lieutenant General [*sic*] Chris Vokes
and any officer or officers of the trial, tribunal, and/or any senior staff officers of the
Canadian Army, and/or legal officers of the Department of Justice and the Department of External Affairs, touching on the commutation of the sentence passed on
S.S. General Kurt Meyer.' As was to be expected, Minister of Defence Douglas C.
Abbott declined on the grounds that 'communications between junior officers and
senior officers or between departmental officials are privileged.' See *Official Report
of Debates: House of Commons* (2nd Session, 20th Parliament), vol. 1, 1946, 432.

59 Vokes to CMHQ, 5 January 1946, NA, RG 24, vol. 12839, file 67/Kurt Meyer
Case/1, p. 181, and memorandum regarding the conference held at 1030 hours on
9 January 1946, ibid., p. 192

60 See Vokes to the Chief of Staff (30th Corps), 13 January 1946, ibid., p. 211; the article entitled 'Silence Changes Nothing' *Globe and Mail*, 18 January 1946, NA, RG
25, vol. 5782, file 213(s), part 1; and Canmilitary to CANCOF Germany, 21 January
1946, NA, RG 24, vol. 12839, file 67/Kurt Meyer Case/1, p. 217. Under pressure
from the government, Vokes quickly backtracked, stating for the record that he and
he alone had made the decision to commute. The old warhorse would stick to that
story until the end of his life. See the minutes of the cabinet meeting, 16 January
1946, NA, reel T-2364, frame 919; the public relations release, undated [approved by
cabinet on 16 January 1946], NA, RG 2, 18, vol. 120, file W-41; the Secretary to the
Cabinet to the Chief of the Air Staff, 18 January 1946, NA, RG 24, E 1, vol. 5203,
file C-15-24-47A, part 2; CANCOF to Canmilitary, 21 January 1946, ibid., vol.
12839, file 67/Kurt Meyer Case/1, p. 222; the remarks by the confirming officer,
appended to Vokes to Lieutenant General Murchie, 21 January 1946, ibid., p. 232;
and Canmilitary to the Adjutant General, 22 January 1946, NA, RG 25, vol. 5782,
file 213(s), part 1. See also Vokes, *My Story*, 205–6, 208.

61 See Robertson to Massey, 19 January 1946; Prime Minister King's retyped note,
20 January 1946; and the retyped note from the Prime Minister's Office, 22 January
1946, NA, RG 25, vol. 5782, file 213(s), part 1.

## 17: The Ones Who Got Away

1 Note for the prime minister, p. 1, appended to the memorandum from J.E. Read to L.S. St Laurent (minister of justice), 12 June 1945, NA, MG 26 L (St Laurent Papers), vol. 4, file 27–27

2 Macklin to Andrew Bell, 15 December 1945, NA, RG 24, vol. 12843, file 67/War Crimes IU/1 (393/67), p. 55, and Lieutenant Colonel B.J.S. MacDonald to the ADAG, 3 December 1945, ibid., vol. 12841, file 67/Office/1, p. 215

3 The quoted passages are from Macklin to Bell, 15 December 1945, ibid., vol. 12843, file 67/War Crimes IU/1 (393/67), pp. 55–6.

4 Bell to Macklin, 17 December 1945; draft from Massey to External Affairs, 17 December 1945; and Canmilitary to Defensor, 17 December 1945, ibid., pp. 58, 57, and 60–verso.

5 Ibid., p. 60

6 Colonel C.P. Stacey, *The Victory Campaign: The Operations in North-West Europe, 1944–1945* (Ottawa, 1966), 3:622; Macdonald to the DAG, 28 March 1946, NA, RG 24, vol. 12843, file 67/War Crimes IU/1 (393/67), p. 78b; Macdonald to Colonel H.M. Cathcart, 23 October 1946, ibid., vol. 2887, file H.Q.S. 8959-9, part 12, no page number; Major General A.E. Walford to the heads of branches and all directorates, appended to the letter from Walford to CMHQ, 15 November 1945, ibid., vol. 12840, file 67/Office/1, p. 235; and memorandum from Cathcart to the Adjutant General, 23 January 1947, ibid., vol. 8018, file TOK-1-2-5, part 2, no page number. All in all, it appears that Canada was more vigorous in its attempts to prosecute Japanese atrocities against Canadian servicemen than German ones. See Jonathan F. Vance, *Objects of Concern: Canadian Prisoners of War through the Twentieth Century* (Vancouver, 1994), 226. On the Canadian trials of Japanese war criminals, see Patrick Brode, *Casual Slaughters and Accidental Judgments: Canadian War Crimes Prosecutions, 1944–1948* (Toronto, 1997), chaps. 9 and 10.

7 On Macklin's lobbying for the closure of CWCIU and the response by National Defence Headquarters, see Massey to Lieutenant General J.C. Murchie, 3 January 1946; Defensor to Canmilitary, 22 December 1945; Massey to Murchie, 3 January 1946; Canmilitary to Defensor, 7 January 1946; and Defensor to Canmilitary, 17 January 1946, NA, RG 24, vol. 12843, file 67/War Crimes IU/1 (393/67), pp. 65, 61, 66, and 71.

8 On the sea change in Macdonald's thinking, compare the memorandum from Macdonald to Brigadier Matthews, 8 June 1945, ibid., vol. 12842, file 67/Treatment/1/2 (393/56), p. 293, and Macdonald to the DAG, 17 January 1946, ibid., vol. 12843, file 67/War Crimes IU/1 (393/67), pp. 69–70.

9 See *Record of Proceedings of the Trial by Canadian Military Court of Wilhelm Jung and Johann Georg Schumacher held at Aurich, Germany, 15–25 March 1946*, 2

vols.; *Record of Proceedings of the Trial by Canadian Military Court of Robert Hoe-lzer, Walter Weigel, and Wilhelm Ossenbach held at Aurich, Germany, 25 March–6 April 1946*, 2 vols.; and *Record of Proceedings of the Trial by Canadian Military Court of Johann Neitz held at Aurich, Germany, 15–20 March 1946*, NA, RG 25, vol. 2606, nos. 169 and 170 in box, and vol. 2608. A total of six defendants were tried in these cases. Three were sentenced to death, one to life imprisonment, and the other two to ten and fifteen years' imprisonment.

10  On the process whereby CWCIU was shut down, see H.R. Horne, 'Transfer of War Crimes Administration,' undated [May 1946], NA, RG 25, vol. 2109, file AR 405/4/12, no page number, and the minutes of the cabinet meeting, 6 May 1946, NA, reel T-2364, frames 1191–2. The quote is from the war diary (No. 1 CWCIU), entry for 31 May 1946, NA, RG 24, vol. 16408, file May 1946.

11  See Macdonald to the DAG, 28 March 1946, NA, RG 24, vol. 12843, file 67/War Crimes IU/1 (393/67), p. 78b, and H.T. Goodeve to Director of Administration, 20 January 1947, ibid., vol. 2887, file H.Q.S. 8959-9, pt. 12, no page number. An interesting piece of war crimes trivia is the fact that a Canadian RCAF officer, Wing Commander Thompson, served on the prosecution side during the trial of the German doctors at Nuremberg. See the war diary (Canadian Military Mission in Berlin), entries for 6 and 31 December 1946 and 17 March 1947, ibid., vol. 13585, folder 1X, vols. 14 (December 1946) and 17 (March 1947).

12  For the official view of this unwelcome by-product of the closure of CWCIU, see the minutes of the cabinet meeting, 24 May 1946, NA, reel T-2364, frame 1244; Murchie to the (British) Judge Advocate General, 5 April 1946; the memorandum from the Secretary of State for External Affairs to the High Commissioner, 8 May 1946; Massey to External Affairs, 20 May 1946; and Frederic Hudd to Murchie, 4 June 1946, NA, RG 24, vol. 12843, file 67/War Crimes IU/1 (393/67), pp. 82, 90, 92, and 95.

13  Commission of Inquiry on War Criminals, *Report,* part 1 (Ottawa, 1986), 31

14  The number of 171 active cases was arrived at by counting the extant investigative files in NA, RG 24, vols. 12837–43 and RG 25, vol. 2109. Of the extant files, the vast majority involved atrocities allegedly perpetrated against Canadian airmen. There were also a significant number of cases of crimes alleged to have been committed against Canadian inmates of German POW camps. The remainder, of course, were the 12th SS files. The particulars of six of the Canadian trials held before British military courts are reported in correspondence from the British Ministry of Defence to the Deschenes Commission. The seventh trial was that of Bernhard Siebken, Dietrich Schnabel, Heinrich Albers, and Fritz Bundschuh of the 2nd Battalion of the 26th Panzer Grenadier Regiment of the 12th SS Division for the murder on 9 June 1944 of Privates Angel, Holness, and Baskerville. The verdict in this trial is reported in Ian Sayer and Douglas Botting, *Hitler's Last General: The Case against*

*Wilhelm Mohnke* (London and New York, 1989), 217.

15 The quote is from the memorandum from Air Marshal Robert Leckie (chief of the air staff) to the Minister of National Defence, 15 February 1946, NA, RG 24, E 1, vol. 5203, file C-15-24-47A, part 2, no page number.

16 UNWCC Charge Sheet against Wilhelm Mohnke, undated, ibid., vol. 12837, file 67/ Canadian National Office/1 (392/4), p. 8

17 Report on the interrogation of SS Private Withold Stangenberg, 10 July 1944, *Report of the No. 1 Canadian War Crimes Investigation Unit regarding the Shooting of Canadian Prisoners of War by German Armed Forces at Haut du Bosq on 11 June 1944*, exhibit no. 1, p. 1, NA, RG 25, vol. 2609, #172 in box

18 *Supplementary Report of the SHAEF Court of Inquiry re Shooting of Allied Prisoners of War by 12 SS Panzer Division (Hitler-Jugend) in Normandy, France, 7–21 June 1944*, part 5, p. 33, and part 3, pp. 14 and 16, NA, RG 24, vol. 10427, file 205S1.023 (D 9)

19 War diary (No. 1 CWCIU), entry for 28 June 1945, NA, RG 24, vol. 16408, file June 1945; record of the evidence of SS Private Withold Stangenberg, 28 June 1945, appended to the memorandum from P.A.C. Chaplin to the Directorate of History, 4 June 1976, DHist, file 1325-1; record of the evidence of Captain Isaac T. Burr, 15 August 1945; record of the evidence of Lieutenant Roger Cloutier, 9 October 1945; and autopsy report by Captain B.B. Wagman, 7 August 1945, CWCIU Report, *Haut du Bosq*, exhibit no. 6, pp. 2–3; exhibit no. 7, p. 3; and exhibit no. 10

20 War diary (No. 1 CWCIU), entries for 12 and 18 September and 11, 12, and 23 October 1945, NA, RG 24, vol. 16408, files September and October 1945, and record of the evidence of SS Private Heinz Schmidt, 23 October 1945, CWCIU Report, *Haut du Bosq*, exhibit no. 8, pp. 7–15

21 This was the view set forth in Macdonald to the Adjutant General, 10 November 1945, NA, RG 24, vol. 12840, file 67/Office/1, p. 219.

22 On Mohnke's capture, see Uwe Bahnsen and James P. O'Donnell, *Les Hommes du Bunker*, trans. Frank Sirnich (Paris, 1976), 284–96.

23 Note of acknowledgment from the UNWCC, 5 November 1945; memorandum from Major W.D.S. Morden to CMHQ, 8 November 1945; minutes of the meeting of Committee 1 of the UNWCC, 16 November 1945; and Macdonald to the war crimes advisory panel, 17 November 1945, NA, RG 24, vol. 12837, file 67/Cdn National Office/1 (392/4), between pp. 193 and 200, 201, and 205–6

24 On Canadian attempts to effect the extradition of Mohnke, see B.J.S. Macdonald, *The Trial of Kurt Meyer* (Toronto, 1954), 29; the war diary (No. 1 CWCIU), entries for 15 September and 8 October 1945, NA, RG 24, vol. 16408, files September and October 1945; Macdonald to the DAG, 15 February 1946, ibid., vol. 12843, file 67/ Wilhelm Mohnke/1 (393/73), no page number; and Macdonald to the DAG, 19 February 1946, ibid., file 67/War Crimes IU/1 (393/67), p. 73 verso.

25  On the Soviets' use of Mohnke during the early stages of the Cold War, see William
    Stevenson, *The Bormann Brotherhood* (London, 1973), 165–6.
26  Macdonald to the DAG, 15 February 1946, NA, RG 24, vol. 12843, file 67/Wilhelm
    Mohnke/1 (393/73), no page number
27  The quoted passages are from Macdonald to the DAAG, 27 February 1946, ibid.,
    vol. 12839, file 67/Kurt Meyer/2/2, p. 455.
28  Major A.F.A.I. Terry to Macdonald, 28 February 1946, ibid., p. 456
29  On the collapse of diplomatic efforts to obtain Mohnke, see Massey to Murchie, 12
    March 1946, and the memorandum to file by H.R. Horne, 16 March 1946, NA, RG
    25, A-12, vol. 2109, file AR 405/4/12, no page numbers.
30  The transfer of files is reported in Murchie to the Department of National Defence,
    19 July 1946, NA, RG 24, vol. 12843, file 67/War Crimes IU/1 (393/67), p. 99.
31  Memorandum from Cathcart to the JAG, 15 August 1946; memorandum from Briga-
    dier R.J. Orde to the Directorate of Administration, 16 August 1946; Brigadier J.A.F.
    Lister to the Directorate of Administration, 27 September 1946; memorandum from
    Orde to the Adjutant General, 1 October 1946; memorandum from Orde to the
    Directorate of Administration, 16 August 1946; and memorandum from Orde to the
    AG, 1 October 1946, ibid., vol. 2887, file H.Q.S. 8959-9, part 12, pp. 17, 18, 22, and
    23
32  Memorandum from the (British) JAG to the War Office, 28 October 1947; Canmili-
    tary to Macklin, 11 December 1947; Major J.R. Fishbourne to Canadian Army HQ,
    26 November 1947, ibid., file H.Q.S. 8959-9-B, pp. 2, 34, and 6
33  On the discovery that the records were missing and the initial search for them, see
    the note by Lieutenant Colonel J.A. Hutchins handwritten at the bottom of Fish-
    bourne to Canadian Army HQ, 26 November 1947; the note to file by Hutchins, 26
    November 1947; the memorandum from Hutchins to Macklin, 27 November 1947;
    Defensor to Canmilitary, 15 December 1947; and Canmilitary to Brigadier W.H.S.
    Macklin, 16 December 1947, ibid., pp. 6, 7, 9, 35, and 38.
34  See the correspondence, which spans November 1947 to February 1948, in ibid
35  Macklin to Macdonald, 1 December 1947; Macdonald to Macklin, 9 December
    1947; and Macklin to the adjutant general, 15 December 1947, ibid., pp. 22, 32, 36
36  Major R.A. Briggs to the VAG, 30 January 1948, ibid., no page numbers
37  Canmilitary to the Directorate of Administration, 11 February 1948, ibid., no page
    numbers
38  On the termination of the British war crimes prosecution effort and its impact on the
    Reitzenstein investigation, see the telegram from the Commonwealth Relations
    Office to the governments of Canada, Australia, New Zealand, South Africa, India,
    Pakistan, and Ceylon, 13 July 1948, Deschenes Commission exhibit P-100, and the
    detention card for Gerd Freiherr von Reitzenstein, Public Records Office – London,
    WO354, appended to the letter from J.J. Harding (Army Historical Branch, UK Min-

istry of Defence) to the author, 8 January 1996.

39 The controversy over the trial was revisited recently in Sayer and Botting, *Hitler's Last General*, 194–236.

## Epilogue

1 Craig W.H. Luther, *Blood and Honor: The History of the 12th SS Panzer Division 'Hitler Youth,' 1943–1945* (San José, CA, 1987), 240

2 See Defensor to Canmilitary, 13 April 1946, and the order issued by Lieutenant General J.C. Murchie, 16 April 1946, NA, RG 24, vol. 12839, file 67/Kurt Meyer Case/1, pp. 287, 289. Meyer arrived at and was processed into Dorchester Penitentiary at 3:00 AM on 1 May 1946. See Deputy Minister of National Defence to the Deputy Minister of Justice, 6 May 1946, DHist, vol. 159.95 (D 1), tab 1-2-12, p. 5. He was assigned Dorchester prisoner number 2265. See 'Newcomers Questions' Form for Kurt Meyer, 1 May 1946, NA, RG 73, acc. 85/86/162, vol. 9, file 2265, part 4.

3 During one of his monthly sessions with the Canadian army chaplain, Meyer bemoaned the 'animal existence' of his internment. See Major James R. Millar (Protestant chaplain) to Lieutenant Colonel C.G.F. Stone (principal chaplain), 3 December 1948, NA, RG 73, acc. 85/86/162, vol. 9, file 2265, part 4.

4 Memorandum from Warden Goad to the Assistant Deputy Warden, 7 May 1946; proceedings of a board of classification at Dorchester Penitentiary, 28 October 1946; report on prisoner number 2265 (Kurt Meyer) by R.G. Rowcliffe (classification officer, Dorchester Penitentiary), 19 October 1951; and Commissioner R.B. Gibson to the Deputy Minister of National Defence, 8 November 1951, ibid., parts 9, 4, and 2

5 Dr J.E. Milligan (penitentiary physician) to the warden, 8 July 1950; Milligan to the warden, 14 August 1950; Dorchester Penitentiary special medical treatment form, appended to Dr L.P. Gendreau to the warden, 21 August 1950; memorandum from Dr R.S. Grant (penitentiary physician) to the warden, 29 March 1950; Warden G.T. Goad letter, 1 April 1950; Lieutenant Colonel J. Andrew (Toronto Military Hospital) to army headquarters in Ottawa, 8 May 1950; Commissioner R.B. Gibson to Major General W.H.S. Macklin, 18 May 1950; and Dr Grant to the warden, 3 February 1947, 30 August 1949, 23 September 1949, and 2 February 1950, ibid., parts 2–5, and 7

6 See the minutes of the cabinet meetings, 16 January 1946; 21 February 1946; and 22 May 1946, NA, reel T-2364, frames 919–20, 1013–14, 1239–40. See also the memorandum from N.A. Robertson to the Secretary of State for External Affairs, 21 February 1946, NA, RG 25, vol. 5782, file 213(s), part 1, and the memorandum from R.B. Gibson to the Deputy Minister of Justice, 20 November 1946, NA, RG 73, acc. 85–86/162, vol. 9, file 2265, part 7.

7  In Canada, pressure for Meyer's release came from a small but vociferous and committed group of supporters organized by Fritz and Ina Lichtenberg of Moncton, New Brunswick. A general contractor of German extraction, Lichtenberg had arrived in Canada in 1913 and had been naturalized in 1930. During the 1930s, he maintained ties to the various home-grown fascist movements in Canada, finally joining Adrien Arcand's National Unity Party in August 1939. In addition to his pro-Nazi activities in Canada, Lichtenberg also spied on German Canadians and sent reports back to Berlin. After the war, Lichtenberg took up Meyer's cause, visiting him monthly in prison, writing letters on his behalf, and eventually enlisting the aid of two prominent attorneys. On Lichtenberg's activities, see Tony Foster, *Meeting of Generals* (Toronto and New York, 1986), 501, 505; Inspector J. Leopold (RCMP Special Section) to RCMP Headquarters, 16 August 1946; the letter by Deputy Minister of Justice F.P. Varcoe, 1 March 1949; Warden Goad to the Commissioner of Penitentiaries, 5 May 1949; Inspector J. Leopold (RCMP Special Section) to RCMP Headquarters, 16 August 1950, NA, RG 73, acc. 85–86/162, vol. 9, file 2265, parts 7 and 3. In December 1950, Halifax lawyers H.P. MacKeen and R.A. Ritchie submitted a legal brief to the government in which they labelled the trial of their client a perversion of justice and castigated the war crimes regulations on which it had been based. See the 'Petition of Kurt Meyer and Memorandum by Counsel Re Trial, Conviction and Sentence,' 12 December 1950, NA, RG 2, vol. 209, file W-41, part 1. Some of their criticisms were valid and have been summarized in chapter 14 of this book. For examples of people in Germany who lobbied various authorities on Meyer's behalf, see Gisellier Reutsche to Kurt Meyer, 10 March 1947; Dr Schapp to Meyer, 16 June 1947; Schapp to Meyer, 1 September 1948; and Schapp to General Vokes, 1 September 1948, NA, RG 73, acc. 85–86/162, vol. 9, file 2265, parts 1, 3, and 4.

8  On the German government's intervention in Meyer's case, see the note from the Consul General of the Federal Republic of Germany to the Department of External Affairs, 20 July 1951, NA, RG 73, acc. 85–86/162, vol. 9, file 2265, part 2; the cabinet conclusion, 18 October 1951, p. 3, NA, RG 2, vol. 2649, file 13/10/51-29/12/51, and K.J. Burbridge to the Canadian ambassador in Bonn, 15 January 1952, ibid., vol. 241, file W-20-3-G, no page number.

9  The evolution of Canadian policy with respect to Meyer can be followed in the minutes of the cabinet meetings, 16 March 1950; 7 February 1951; 12 September 1951; and 21 September 1951, NA, reel T-2366, frame 1356, and reel T-2367, frames 606–7, 1488–9, and 1501. See also the High Commissioner to the Secretary of State for External Affairs, 14 March 1951, NA, RG 25, vol. 3729, file 5908-D-40, part 1; the cross reference sheet, 11 September 1951, NA, RG 2, 18, vol. 209, file W-41, part 1; and the cabinet conclusion, 17 October 1951, p. 7, ibid., vol. 2649, file 13/10/51–29/12/51.

10  The logistics of Meyer's transfer are reported in Warden Goad to the Commissioner

of Penitentiaries, 18 October 1951, NA, RG 73, acc. 85–86/162, vol. 9, file 2265, part 8; Minister of National Defence Brooke Claxton to Werl Prison, 18 October 1951, and Lieutenant Colonel J.R. Stewart (provost marshal) to the Directorate of Administration, undated, DHist, vol. 159.95 (D 1), tabs 3-1-2 and 3-1-4.

11 Stewart to the Directorate of Administration, undated, DHist, vol. 159.95 (D 1), tab 3-1-4.

12 On the German government's linkage of the war crimes and European defence issues, see T.C. Davis to the Undersecretary of State for External Affairs, 11 September 1950, and the Head of the Canadian Mission in Bonn to the Secretary of State for External Affairs, 23 December 1950, NA, MG 32 B 5 (Brooke Claxton Papers), vol. 123, file 'Re-Arming of Germany.' See also A.D.P. Heeney to L.B. Pearson, 24 November 1952, NA, MG 26 N (L.B. Pearson Papers), vol. 5, file A.D.P. Heeney; Frank M. Buscher, *The U.S. War Crimes Trial Program in Germany, 1946–1955* (New York and Westport, CT, 1989), 56–7, 70–82; and Buscher, 'The U.S. High Commission and German Nationalism, 1949–1952,' *Central European History* (March 1990): 68. For the specific actions taken by Bonn to obtain Kurt Meyer's release, see the memorandum from Heeney to the Prime Minister, 16 October 1951, NA, RG 25, vol. 3729, file 5908-D-40, part 1; the press release issued by External Affairs, 27 March 1953; the memorandum by C.S.A. Ritchie for the European Division of External Affairs, 18 April 1953; the notes on the Canadian–German conversations held at Ottawa on 18 April 1953, appended to memorandum by Ritchie for the European Division of External Affairs, 20 April 1953, ibid., vol. 6570, file 10935-B-40, part 2.1. See also the memorandum by Legal Division for the Undersecretary of State for External Affairs, 9 July 1953, and the Canadian Ambassador in Bonn to the Secretary of State for External Affairs, 17 July 1953, ibid., vol. 4229, file 5908-D-40, part 4.

13 On the trend towards leniency in American policy regarding German war criminals, see Buscher, *War Crimes*, 63–4. On the same trend in British policy, see the Secretary of State for Commonwealth Relations to the High Commissioner for the United Kingdom, 22 December 1951, NA, RG 24, vol. 2887, file 8959-9, part 13.

14 On Davis's prolonged and prominent role in the release of Meyer, see the Secretary of State for External Affairs to the Canadian ambassador in Bonn, 9 April 1952; the Canadian ambassador in Bonn to the Secretary of State for External Affairs, 16 July 1952; the note for the Heads of Divisions' meeting, 2 September 1952; the Canadian ambassador in Bonn to the Secretary of State for External Affairs, 4 September 1952; the Secretary of State for External Affairs to the Canadian ambassador in Bonn, 14 August 1953; the memorandum from the Secretary of State for External Affairs to the Canadian ambassador in Bonn, 8 October 1953; the Canadian ambassador in Bonn to the Secretary of State for External Affairs, 12 November 1953, NA, RG 25, vol. 4229, file 5908-D-40, parts 3, 4, and 5. See also the Canadian ambassador Fed-

eral Republic of Germany to the Secretary of State for External Affairs, 31 March 1953, ibid., vol. 6570, file 10935-B-40, part 2.1; Claxton to T.C. Davis, 8 September 1952, NA, RG 24, vol. 2887, file 8959-9, part 13; the Canadian ambassador in Bonn to the Secretary of State for External Affairs, 17 September 1952, ibid.; and T.C. Davis to Pearson, 6 October 1953, NA, MG 26 N (L.B. Pearson Papers), vol. 3, file T.C. Davis.

15 For the movement of the government towards clemency in Meyer's case, see the cabinet conclusions, 23 January 1952, p. 12, NA, RG 2, vol. 2649, file 09/01/52–29/02/52; 11 March 1952, p. 14, ibid., vol, 2650, file 03/03/52–02/05/52; 21 May 1952, p. 6, ibid., file 06/05/52–30/06/52; 13 August 1953, p. 6, ibid., vol. 2653, file 05/05/53–07/10/53; 21 October 1953, p. 11, ibid. See also the Minister of National Defence to the Governor in Council, 23 January 1952, ibid., vol. 241, file W-20-3-G, no page number; the memorandum from the Minister of National Defence to cabinet, 25 January 1952, ibid., vol. 212, file C-20-5, cabinet document 37–52; the memorandum to Robertson, 30 January 1952, ibid., vol. 241, file W-20-3-G; the High Commissioner to the Secretary of State for External Affairs, 30 January 1952; the memorandum from the Office of the Judge Advocate General to the Minister of National Defence, 13 February 1952; the memorandum from the Office of the Judge Advocate General to the Minister of National Defence, 17 April 1952; the High Commissioner to the Secretary of State for External Affairs, 23 April 1952; the report from Sherwood Lett to the Minister of National Defence, 6 January 1954; the minutes of a meeting of the Committee of the Privy Council, 15 January 1954, DHist, vol. 159.95 (D 1), tabs 4-1-4, 4-1-6, 4-1-7, 4-1-8, 4-2-1, and 4-3-4; and Heeney to the Minister of National Defence, 23 April 1952, NA, MG 26 N (L.B. Pearson Papers), vol. 5, file A.D.P. Heeney.

16 Canadian ambassador to the Federal Republic of Germany to the Secretary of State for External Affairs, 7 September 1954, DHist, vol. 159.95 (D 1), tab 4-12-5

17 Meyer's welcome is reported in the dispatch from C.S.A Ritchie to the Under-Secretary of State for External Affairs, 10 September 1954, NA, RG 25, vol. 4293, file 10934-F-40, part 1.

18 See the minutes of the cabinet meeting, 13 July 1954, pp. 2–3, NA, RG 2, vol. 2655.

19 Ian J. Campbell, *Murder at the Abbaye: The Story of Twenty Canadian Soldiers Murdered at the Abbaye d'Ardenne* (Ottawa, 1996), 171

20 Meyer's last years are recounted in Foster, *Generals*, 499–515

21 Ian Sayer and Douglas Botting, *Hitler's Last General: The Case against Wilhelm Mohnke* (London and New York, 1989), 321

22 Aitken's early work on the Mohnke case is described in his letter to the Commissioner of the RCMP, 5 March 1976, DHist, file 1325-1.

23 Aitken's contact with Ludwigsburg is described in ibid.

24 The Lübeck prosecutor's reply is reported in ibid.

25  The quoted passages are from ibid.
26  Inspector J.J.E. Poirier to the Department of National Defence, 24 March 1976;
    memorandum from the Office of the Judge Advocate General to the Directorate of
    History, 20 April 1976; and W.A.B. Douglas to the Reverend L.R. Aitken, 17 May
    1976, ibid., file 1325-500/A
27  For a summary of the results of the Directorate's research, see the memorandum
    from Senior Research Officer P.A.C. Chaplin to the Director of the Directorate of
    History, 4 June 1976, ibid., file 1325-1.
28  On the government's tepid reaction to the new evidence, see C.R. Nixon to Under-
    secretary of State for External Affairs H.B. Robinson, 8 July 1976; Colonel R.F.
    Barnes to the Deputy Minister, 2 July 1976; and the Undersecretary of State for
    External Affairs to the Canadian embassy in Bonn, 17 August 1976, ibid. See also
    W.A.B. Douglas to the Reverend L.R. Aitken, 16 September 1976, ibid., file 1325-
    500/A.
29  Quoted from the entry for 3 March 1943, *The Goebbels Diaries*, ed. and trans. Louis
    Lochner (New York, 1948), 270.

# Selected List of Primary Sources

**Canada**

*Directorate of History and Heritage, Department of National Defence*

Dossier on the Kurt Meyer Case [159.95 (D 1)]
Records of the Proceedings against Kurt Meyer [159.95023 (D 7)]
*Report of the Supreme Headquarters Allied Expeditionary Force Court of Inquiry re Shooting of Allied Prisoners of War by the German Armed Forces in the Vicinity of Le Mesnil-Patry, Les Saullets and Authie, Calvados, Normandy, 7–11 June 1944* [90/168]

*Municipal Archives – Windsor Public Library*

B.J.S Macdonald Papers [acc. 1988/24]

*National Archives of Canada*

Canadian Security and Intelligence Service Records [RG 146]
B. Claxton Papers [MG 32 B 5]
H.D.G. Crerar Papers [MG 30 E 157]
Department of External Affairs Records [RG 25]
Department of National Defence Records [RG 24]
Department of the Solicitor General Records [RG 73]
W.L.M. King Papers [MG 26 J]
B.J.S. Macdonald Papers [MG 30 E 480]
L.B. Pearson Papers [MG 26 N]
Personnel Records, Army

Privy Council Office Records [RG 2]
J.E. Read Papers [MG 30 E 148]
E.M. Reid Papers [MG 31 E 46]
L.S. St Laurent Papers [MG 26 L]

*Royal Military College Library*

Major General C. Vokes file and notebook

**United States**

*National Archives and Records Administration*

Foreign Military Studies, 1945–1959, Historical Division, Headquarters United States Army, Europe [RG 338, ETHINT]
Records of German Field Commands: Armies [RG 242, T-312]
Records of German Field Commands: Corps [RG 242, T-314]
Records of German Field Commands: Divisions [RG 242, T-315]
Records of the Reich Leader of the SS and Chief of the German Police [RG 242, T-175]
Records of the Waffen-SS [RG 242, T-354]
Schumacher Collection [RG 242, T-611]
SS Officer Dossiers [RG 242, BDC A 3433]

**Interview**

Colonel (ret.) John Page, 23 November 1996

# Picture Credits

# Index